AF679089

LINUX CRASH COURSE

```
USEFILE("readme.txt");
USERES("experts.res");
USEFORM("filters.cpp",
FilterDlg);
USEFORM("dlg.cpp", DlgEx-
pert);
USEFORM("app.cpp", AppEx-
pert);
USERC("exptbmps.rc");
```

```
#include <ShareMem.hpp>
#include <Forms.hpp>
#include <Windows.hpp>
#include <ExptIntf.hpp>
#include <ToolIntf.hpp>
#include <VirtIntf.hpp>
#include <SysUtils.hpp>
```

```
public:
    String __stdcall GetName(void);
    String __stdcall GetCom-
ment(void);
    HICON __stdcall GetGlyph(void);
    TExpertStyle __stdcall Get-
Style(void);
    TExpertState __stdcall Get-
State(void);
    String __stdcall GetID
```

```
{
   int P;

  Description->Text =
"";
  Extension->Text = "";
  if (Value > "")
  {
    P = Value.Pos("|");
    if (!P) P = 256;
   Description->Text =
Value.SubString(1, P -
1);
```

```
  NETERM   X
 drwxr-wr-x   2 root  root   3.0k Feb
20  03:00
-rwx-r- -r- - 3 root root  2.0k Feb
20  00:16
drwxr-wr-x  16root  root   10.0k Feb
01 18:27
root@skynet  / >ethernet &
gcc -g  -L/usr/local/lib/usr/
X11R6/lib  basicunix
actionslert.o areas.o
atoms.oboders.ognome.ohandlers.o
iclass.ofocus.1retrogress.okde.1setti
```

```
if
(Definition.Contains(daBtn
sV))
  {
    DrawBitmap->Handle =
LoadBitmap(instance,
"BTNSV");
    X = 75;
    Y = 22;
```

```
NETERM   X   drwxr-wr-x  roroot@skynet   / >ethernet &gcc -g  -L/usr/local/lib/usr/
```

```
spriteRect.Top = 0;
    spriteRect.Left =
0;
    spriteRect.Right =
spriteImage-
>Picture>Width;
    spriteRect.Bottom
= spriteImage-
>Picture->Height;
```

```
#include <vcl.h>
#pragma hdrstop
USEFORM("EP.cpp", Form1);
USERES("Png.res");
//-------------------------------
-------------------------------
---------------

WINAPI WinMain(HINSTANCE,
HINSTANCE, LPSTR, int)
{
```

```
       {
            Application-
>Initialize();
            Application-
>CreateForm(__classid(TForm1),
&Form1);
            Application>Run;
```

KnowledgeWorks

Linux Crash Course

```
&:::!::!!!!!!!!*=!!:::::::;;==
&:;&%&%%jjj3333333333$$$j=*
&:;8&&%j33$SSS44UAR##@HHHN~=*
&:=4jj33$$SS84UARR#@@HHNNM~*&
&:=Uj3$$SS844AAR##@HHHNMMM~&%
&;*A3$SP844UARR#@HHHNMMMMM~&%
&;&A$SP84UARR#@HHHNNMMMMMM!&%
&;*US84UAAR##@HHHNMMMMMMMM!&&
&;*U44UARR#@HHHNMMMMMMMMMM!&&
&:*SRRR#@@HHHHHHNNNNNHHHHH!&%
&:::::::::::;;;====*&&&&%&%%%
   `%3jj3$333$3S$SS$$%$3
       &MMMMMMMMMMM
=j33j&~;:!!!:::!::::&&&&&&%%%j3$$8j
=jjj&;~~~!~~!!!!::::=#RA&=*=&==:jSj
;jjj&&j$88S88888888S%::;===*&&%&j$$
:%%%***&&&=&&%jj*jjjj33j$3$$$SS$S$$
;jjj&&j$88S88888888S%::;===*&&%&j$$
:%%%***&&&=&&%jj*jjjj33j$3$$$SS$S$$
  33;&*&jS3333$33j&=%==*;%&:;;&jjRR&%%;:;
 $$33jjjjj%&%&%j%&%%&%%%j%%&44S==!~~!!~:&4
$jjjxxxxxxxx$$$@@@@%%%%%%%%&&&SP*8&&&&*::!!!
```


ISBN: 0-9703083-1-0

KnowledgeWorks, Inc.
P.O. Box 2701
Gainesville, GA 30503

Table Of Contents

Table Of Contents

Chapter 1

Linux Tutorial

1.1 Introduction.

If you're new to UNIX and Linux, you may be a bit intimidated by the size and apparent complexity of the system before you. This chapter does not go into great detail or cover advanced topics. Instead, we want you to hit the ground running.

We assume very little here about your background, except perhaps that you have some familiarity with personal computer systems, and MS-DOS. However, even if you're not an MS-DOS user, you should be able to understand everything here. At first glance, Linux looks a lot like MS-DOS—after all, parts of MS-DOS were modeled on the CP/M operating system, which in turn was modeled on UNIX. However, only the most superficial features of Linux resemble MS-DOS. Even if you're completely new to the PC world, this tutorial should help.

And, before we begin: *Don't be afraid to experiment.* The system won't bite you. You can't destroy anything by working on the system. Linux has built-in security features to prevent "normal" users from damaging files that are essential to the system. Even so, the worst thing that can happen is that you may delete some or all of your files and you'll have to re-install the system. So, at this point, you have nothing to lose.

1.2 Basic Linux concepts.

Linux is a multitasking, multiuser operating system, which means that many people can run many different applications on one computer at the same time. This differs from MS-DOS, where only one person can use the system at any one time. Under Linux, to identify yourself to the system, you must **log in**, which entails entering your **login name** (the name the system uses to identify you), and entering your **password**, which is your personal key for logging in to your account. Because only you know your password, no one else can log in to the system under your user name.

On traditional UNIX systems, the system administrator assigns you a user name and an initial password when you are given an account on the system. However, because in Linux

tt you are the system administrator, you must set up your own account before you can log in. For the following discussions, we'll use the imaginary user name, "larry."
In addition, each system has a **host name** assigned to it. It is this host name that gives your machine a name, gives it character and charm. The host name is used to identify individual machines on a network, but even if your machine isn't networked, it should have a host name. For our examples below, the system's host name is "mousehouse".

1.2.1 Creating an account.

Before you can use a newly installed Linux system, you must set up a user account for yourself. It's usually not a good idea to use the root account for normal use; you should reserve the root account for running privileged commands and for maintaining the system as discussed below.
In order to create an account for yourself, log in as root and use the useradd or adduser command. See Section 4.6 for information on this procedure.

1.2.2 Logging in.

At login time, you'll see a prompt resembling the following:

```
mousehouse login:
```

Enter your user name and press the Enter key. Our hero, larry, would type:

```
mousehouse login: larry

Password:
```

Next, enter your password. The characters you enter won't be echoed to the screen, so type carefully. If you mistype your password, you'll see the message:

```
Login incorrect.
```

and you'll have to try again.
Once you have correctly entered the user name and password, you are officially logged in to the system, and are free to roam.

1.2.3 Virtual consoles.

The system's **console** is the monitor and keyboard connected directly to the system. (Because Linux is a multiuser operating system, you may have other terminals connected to serial ports on your system, but these would not be the console.) Linux, like some other versions of UNIX, provides access to **virtual consoles** (or VCs), that let you have more than one login session on the console at one time.

To demonstrate this, log in to your system. Next, press Alt-F2 . You should see the login: prompt again. You're looking at the second virtual console. To switch back to the first VC, press Alt-F1 . *Voila!* You're back to your first login session.

A newly-installed Linux system probably lets you to access only the first half-dozen or so VCs, by pressing Alt-F1 through Alt-F4 , or however many VCs are configured on your system. It is possible to enable up to 12 VCs—one for each function key on your keyboard. As you can see, use of VCs can be very powerful because you can work in several different sessions at the same time.

While the use of VCs is somewhat limiting (after all, you can look at only one VC at a time), it should give you a feel for the multiuser capabilities of Linux. While you're working on the first VC, you can switch over to the second VC and work on something else.

1.2.4 Shells and commands.

For most of your explorations in the world of Linux, you'll be talking to the system through a **shell**, a program that takes the commands you type and translates them into instructions to the operating system. This can be compared to the COMMAND.COM program under MS-DOS, which does essentially the same thing. A shell is just one interface to Linux. There are many possible interfaces—like the X Window System, which lets you run commands by using the mouse and keyboard.

As soon as you log in, the system starts the shell, and you can begin entering commands. Here's a quick example. Larry logs in and is waiting at the shell **prompt**:

```
mousehouse login:     larry

Password:          larry's password.

Welcome to Mousehouse!

/home/larry#
```

The last line of this text is the shell's prompt, indicating that it's ready to take commands. (More on what the prompt itself means later.) Let's try telling the system to do something interesting:

```
/home/larry#    make love

make:        * * * No way to make target 'love'. Stop.

/home/larry#
```

Well, as it turns out, make is the name of an actual program on the system, and the shell executed this program when given the command. (Unfortunately, the system was being unfriendly.)

This brings us to the burning question: What is a command? What happens when you type "make love"? The first word on the command line, "make", is the name of the command to be executed. Everything else on the command line is taken as arguments to this command. Example:

```
/home/larry# cp foo bar
```

The name of this command is "cp", and the arguments are "foo"and"bar".

When you enter a command, the shell does several things. First, it checks the command to see if it is internal to the shell. (That is, a command which the shell knows how to execute itself. There are a number of these commands, and we'll go into them later.) The shell also checks to see if the command is an alias, or substitute name, for another command. If neither of these conditions apply, the shell looks for a program, on disk, having the specified name. If successful, the shell runs the program, sending the arguments specified on the command line.

In our example, the shell looks for a program called make, and runs it with the argument love. Make is a program often used to compile large programs, and takes as arguments the name of a "target" to compile. In the case of "make love", we instructed make to compile the target love. Because make can't find a target by this name, it fails with a humorous error message, and returns us to the shell prompt.

What happens if we type a command to a shell and the shell can't find a program having the specified name? Well, we can try the following:

```
/home/larry# eat dirt.

eat: command not found

/home/larry#
```

Quite simply, if the shell can't find a program having the name given on the command line (here, "eat"), it prints an error message. You'll often see this error message if you mistype a command (for example, if you had typed "mkae love" instead of "make love").

1.2.5 Logging out.

Before we delve much further, we should tell you how to log out of the system. At the shell prompt, use the command:

```
/home/larry# exit
```

to log out. There are other ways of logging out, but this is the most foolproof one.

1.2.6 Changing your password.

You should also know how to change your password. The command passwd prompts you for your old password, and a new password. It also asks you to reenter the new password for validation. Be careful not to forget your password—if you do, you will have to ask the system administrator to reset it for you. (If you are the system administrator, read on.)

1.2.7 Files and directories.

Under most operating systems (including Linux), there is the concept of a **file**, which is just a bundle of information given a name (called a **filename**). Examples of files might be your history term paper, an e-mail message, or an actual program that can be executed. Essentially, anything saved on disk is saved in an individual file.

Files are identified by their file names. For example, the file containing your history paper might be saved with the file name history-paper. These names usually identify the file and its contents in some form that is meaningful to you. There is no standard format for file names as there is under MS-DOS and some other operating systems; in general, a file name can contain any character (except the / character—see the discussion of path names, below) and is limited to 256 characters in length.

With the concept of files comes the concept of directories. A **directory** is a collection of files. It can be thought of as a "folder" that contains many different files. Directories are given names, with which you can identify them. Furthermore, directories are maintained in a tree-like structure; that is, directories may contain other directories.

Consequently, you can refer to a file by its **path name**, which is made up of the filename, preceded by the name of the directory containing the file. For example, let's say that Larry has a directory called papers, which contains three files: history-final, english-lit,andmasters-thesis. Each of these three files contains information for three of Larry's ongoing projects. To refer to the english-lit file, Larry can specify the file's pathname, as in:

papers/english-lit

As you can see, the directory and filename are separated by a single slash (/). For this reason, filenames themselves cannot contain the / character. MS-DOS users will find this convention familiar, although in the MS-DOS world the backslash (\) is used instead.

As mentioned, directories can be nested within each other as well. For example, let's say that there is another directory within papers, called notes.Thenotes di-rectory contains the files math-notes and cheat-sheet. The pathname of the file cheat-sheet would be:

papers/notes/cheat-sheet

Therefore, a path name is really like a path to the file. The directory that contains a given subdirectory is known as the **parent directory**. Here, the directory papers is the parent of the notes directory.

1.2.8 The directory tree.

Most Linux systems use a standard layout for files so that system resources and programs can be easily located. This layout forms a directory tree, which starts at the "/" directory, also known as the "root directory". Directly underneath / are important subdirectories: /bin, /etc, /dev,and/usr, among others. These directories in turn contain other directories which contain system configuration files, programs, and so on.

In particular, each user has a **home directory,** which is the directory set aside for that user to store his or her files. In the examples above, all of Larry's files (like cheat-sheet and history-final) are contained in Larry's home directory. Usually, user home directories are contained under /home, and are named for the user owning that directory.
Larry's home directory is /home/larry.
This diagram on the next page shows a sample directory tree, which should give you an idea of how the directory tree on your system is organized:

```
/-------------bin
        |-----dev
        |-----etc
        |-----home-------larry
        |                  |__sam
        |
        |___lib
        |___proc
        |___tmp
        |___usr-------------X11R6
                        |__bin
                        |__emacs
                          |__etc
                        |__g++include
                        |__include
                        |__lib
                        |__local_____bin
                        |             |___emacs
                        |             |___etc
                        |             |___lib
                       |__man
                        |__spool
                        |__src-----------linux
                        |__tmp
```

Figure 1.1: A typical (abridged) Linux directory tree.

1.2.9 The current working directory.

At any moment, commands that you enter are assumed to be relative to your **current working directory**. You can think of your working directory as the directory in which you are currently "located". When you first log in, your working directory is set to your home directory—/home/larry, in our case. Whenever you refer to a file, you may refer to it in relationship to your current working directory, rather than specifying the full pathname of the file.

Here's an example. Larry has the directory papers,andpapers contains the file history-final. If Larry wants to look at this file, he can use the command:

```
/home/larry# more /home/larry/papers/history-final
```

The more command simply displays a file, one screen at a time. However, because Larry's current working directory is /home/larry, he can instead refer to the file *relative* to his.

current location by using the command:

/home/larry# more papers/history-final

If you begin a filename (like papers/final) with a character other than /, you're referring to the file in terms relative to your current working directory. This is known as a **relative path name.**

On the other hand, if you begin a file name with a /, the system interprets this as a full path name—that is, a path name that includes the entire path to the file, starting from the root directory, /. This is known as an **absolute path name.**

1.2.10 Referring to home directories.

Under both tcsh and bash(1) you can specify your home directory with the tilde character (˜). For example, the command:

/home/larry# more ˜/papers/history-final

is equivalent to:

/home/larry# more /home/larry/papers/history-final

The shell replaces the ~ character with the name of your home directory.

You can also specify other user's home directories with the tilde character. The pathname ˜karl/letters translates to /home/karl/letters by the shell (if /home/karl is karl's home directory). Using a tilde is simply a shortcut; there is no directory named ˜—it's just syntactic sugar provided by the shell.

(1) **tcsh** and **bash** are two *shells* that run under Linux. The shell is a program that reads user commands and executes them; most Linux systems enable either **tcsh** or **bash** for new user accounts.

1.3 First steps into Linux.

Before we begin, it is important to know that all file and command names on a Linux system are case-sensitive (unlike operating systems such as MS-DOS). For example, the command make is very different from Make or MAKE. The same is true for file and directory names.

1.3.1 Moving around.

Now that you can log in, and you know how to refer to files using pathnames, how can you change your current working directory, to make life easier?

The command for moving around in the directory structure is cd, which is short for "change directory". Many often-used Linux commands are two or three letters. The usage of the cd command is:

```
cd directory
```

where directory is the name of the directory which you wish to become the current working directory.

As mentioned earlier, when you log in, you begin in your home directory. If Larry wanted to switch to the papers subdirectory, he'd use the command:

```
/home/larry# cd papers

/home/larry/papers#
```

As you can see, Larry's prompt changes to reflect his current working directory (so he knows where he is). Now that he's in the papers directory, he can look at his history final with the command:

```
/home/larry/papers# more history-final
```

Now, Larry is stuck in the papers subdirectory. To move back up to the next higher (or parent) directory, use the command:

```
/home/larry/papers# cd ..

/home/larry#
```

(Note the space between the "cd" and the "..".) Every directory has an entry named ".." which refers to the parent directory. Similarly, every directory has an entry named "." which refers to itself. Therefore, the command:

```
/home/larry/papers# cd .
```

get's us nowhere.

You can also use absolute pathnames with the cd command. To cd into Karl's home directory, we can use the command:

```
/home/larry/papers# cd /home/karl

/home/karl#
```

Also, using cd with no argument will return you to your own home directory.

```
/home/karl# cd

/home/larry#
```

1.3.2 Looking at the contents of directories.

Now that you know how to move around directories, you might think, "So what?" Moving around directories is fairly useless by itself, so let's introduce a new command, ls.The ls command displays a listing of files and directories, by default from your current directory. For example:

```
/home/larry# ls

Mail

letters

papers

/home/larry#
```

Here we can see that Larry has three entries in his current directory: Mail, letters, and papers. This doesn't tell us much—are these directories or files? We can use the -F option of the ls command to get more detailed information:

```
/home/larry# ls --F

Mail/

letters/

papers/

/home/larry#
```

From the / appended to each filename, we know that these three entries are in fact subdirectories.

Using ls -F may also append "*" to the end of a filename in the resulting list which would indicate that the file is an **executable**, or a program which can be run. If nothing is appended to the filename using ls -F, the file is a "plain old file", that is, it's neither a directory nor an executable.

In general, each UNIX command may take a number of options in addition to other arguments. These options usually begin with a "-", as demonstrated above with the -F option. The -F option tells ls to give more information about the type of the files involved—in this case, printing a / after each directory name.

If you give ls a directory name, the system will print the contents of that directory.

```
/home/larry# ls --F papers

english-lit

history-final

masters-thesis

notes/

/home/larry#
```

Or, for a more interesting listing, let's see what's in the system's /etc directory:

```
/home/larry# ls /etc

Images      ftpusers     lpc         rc.new     shells
adm         getty        magic       rc0.d      startcons
bcheckrc    gettydefs    motd        rc1.d      swapoff
brc         group        mount       rc2.d      swapon
brc~        inet         mtab        rc3.d      syslog.conf
csh.cshrc   init         mtools      rc4.d      syslog.pid
csh.login   init.d       pac         rc5.d      syslogd.
default     initrunlvl   passwd      rmt        termcap
disktab     inittab      printcap    rpc        umount
fdprm       inittab.old  profile     rpcinfo    update
fstab       issue        psdatabase  securetty  utmp
ftpaccess   lilo         rc          services   wtmp
/home/larry#
```

If you're a MS-DOS user, you may notice that the filenames can be longer than 8 characters, and can contain periods in any position. You can even use more than one period in a filename.

Let's move to the top of the directory tree, and then down to another directory with the commands:

```
/home/larry# cd ..

/home# cd ..

/# cd usr

/usr# cd bin

/usr/bin#
```

You can also move into directories in one step, as in cd /usr/bin.

Try moving around various directories, using ls and cd. In some cases, you may run into the foreboding "Permission denied" error message. This is simply UNIX security kicking in: in order to use the ls or cd commands, you must have permission to do so.

1.3.3 Creating new directories.

It's time to learn how to create directories. This involves the use of the mkdir command. Try the following:

```
/home/larry# mkdir foo

/home/larry# ls -F

Mail/

foo/

letters/

papers/

/home/larry# cd foo

/home/larry/foo# ls

/home/larry/foo#
```

Congratulations! You made a new directory and moved into it. Since there aren't any files in this new directory, let's learn how to copy files from one place to another.

1.3.4 Copying files.

To copy files, use the command cp, as shown here:

```
/home/larry/foo# cp /etc/termcap .
/home/larry/foo# cp /etc/shells .
/home/larry/foo# ls --F
shells termcap

/home/larry/foo# cp shells bells
/home/larry/foo# ls --F
bells shells termcap
/home/larry/foo#
```

The cp command copies the files listed on the command line to the file or directory given as the last argument. Notice that we use "." to refer to the current directory.

1.3.5 Moving files.

The mv command moves files, rather than copying them. The syntax is very straight-forward:

```
/home/larry/foo# mv termcap sells
/home/larry/foo# ls -F
bells sells shells
/home/larry/foo#
```

Notice that the termcap file has been renamed sells. You can also use the mv command to move a file to a completely new directory.

- **Note:** mv and cp will overwrite a destination file having the same name without asking 3 you. Be careful when you move a file into another directory. There may already be a file having the same name in that directory, which you'll overwrite!

1.3.6 Deleting files and directories.

You now have an ugly rhyme developing with the use of the ls command. To delete a file, use the rm command, which stands for "remove", as shown here:

```
/home/larry/foo# rm bells sells

/home/larry/foo# ls -F

shells

/home/larry/foo#
```

We're left with nothing but shells, but we won't complain. Note that rm by default won't prompt you before deleting a file—so be careful.

A related command to rm is rmdir. This command deletes a directory, but only if the directory is empty. If the directory contains any files or subdirectories, rmdir will complain.

1.3.7 Looking at files.

The commands more and cat are used for viewing the contents of files. more displays a file, one screenful at a time, while cat displays the whole file at once.

To look at the file shells, use the command:

```
/home/larry/foo# more shells.
```

In case you're interested what shells contains, it's a list of valid shell programs on your system. On most systems, this includes /bin/sh, /bin/bash,and/bin/csh. We'll talk about these different types of shells later.

While using more,press Space to display the next page of text, and b to display the previous page. There are other commands available in more as well, these are just the basics. Pressing q will quit more.

Quit more and try cat /etc/termcap. The text will probably fly by too quickly for you to read it all. The name "cat" actually stands for "concatenate", which is the real use of the program. The cat command can be used to concatenate the contents of several files and save the result to another file. You will see this again in section 3.14.1.

1.3.8 Getting online help.

Almost every UNIX system, including Linux, provides a facility known as **manual pages.** These manual pages contain online documentation for system commands, resources, configuration files and so on.

The command used to access manual pages is man. If you're interested in learning about other options of the ls command, you can type:

```
/home/larry# man ls
```

and the manual page for ls will be displayed.

Unfortunately, most manual pages are written for those who already have some idea of what the command or resource does. For this reason, manual pages usually contain only the technical details of the command, without much explanation. However, manual pages can be an invaluable resource for jogging your memory if you forget the syntax of a command. Manual pages will also tell you about commands that we don't cover in this book.

I suggest that you try man for the commands that we've already gone over and whenever I introduce a new command. Some of these commands won't have manual pages, for several reasons. First, the manual pages may not have been written yet. (The Linux Documentation Project is responsible for manual pages under Linux as well. We are gradually accumulating most of the manual pages available for the system.) Second, the the command might be an internal shell command, or an alias which would not have a manual page of its own. One example is cd, which is an internal shell command. The shell itself actually processes the cd—there is no separate program that implements this command.

1.4 Accessing MS-DOS files.

If, for some twisted and bizarre reason, you want to access files from MS-DOS, it's easily done under Linux.

The usual way to access MS-DOS files is to mount an MS-DOS partition or floppy under Linux, allowing you to access the files directly through the file system. For example, if you have an MS-DOS floppy in /dev/fd0, the command:

```
# mount -t msdos /dev/fd0 /mnt
```

will mount it under /mnt. See Section 4.8.4 for more information on mounting floppies.

You can also mount an MS-DOS partition of your hard drive for access under Linux. If you have an MS-DOS partition on /dev/hda1, the command:

```
# mount -t msdos /dev/hda1 /mnt
```

mounts it. Be sure to umount the partition when you're done using it. You can have a MS-DOS partition automatically mounted at boot time if you include the entry in

/etc/fstab. See Section 4.4 for details. The following line in /etc/fstab will mount an MS-DOS partition on /dev/hda1 on the directory /dos:

```
/dev/hda1        /dos        msdos        defaults
```

You can also mount the VFAT file systems that are used by Windows 95:

```
# mount -t vfat /dev/hda1 /mnt
```

This allows access to the long filenames of Windows 95. This only applies to partitions that actually have the long filenames stored. You can't mount a normal FAT16 file system and use this to get long filenames.

The Mtools software may also be used to access MS-DOS files. The commands mcd, mdir,andmcopy all behave like their MS-DOS counterparts. If you install Mtools, there should be manual pages available for these commands.

Accessing MS-DOS files is one thing; running MS-DOS programs is another. There is an MS-DOS Emulator under development for Linux; it is widely available, and included in most distributions. It can also be retrieved from a number of locations, including the various Linux FTP sites listed in Appendix B. The MS-DOS Emulator is reportedly powerful enough to run a number of applications, including WordPerfect, from Linux. However, Linux and MS-DOS are vastly different operating systems. The power of any MS-DOS emulator under UNIX is limited. In addition, a Microsoft Windows emulator that runs under X Windows is under development.

1.5 Summary of basic UNIX commands.

This section introduces some of the most useful basic commands of a UNIX system, including those that are covered in the previous section.

Note that options usually begin with "-", and in most cases you can specify more than one option with a single "-". For example, rather than use the command ls -l -F, you can use ls -lF.

Rather than listing every option for each command, we only present useful or important commands at this time. In fact, most of these commands have many options that you'll never use. You can use man to see the manual pages for each command, which list all of the available options.

Also note that many of these commands take as arguments a list of files or directories, denoted in this table by " file1 ... fileN". For example, the cp command takes as arguments a list of files to copy, followed by the destination file or directory. When copying more than one file, the destination must be a directory.

cd Change the current working directory.
Syntax: cd directory
Where directory is the directory which you want to change to. ("." refers to the current directory, ".." the parent directory. If no directory is specified it defaults you your home directory.)

Example: cd ../foo sets the current directory up one level, then back down to foo.

ls Displays information about the named files and directories.
Syntax: ls files
Where files consists of the the filenames or directories to list. The most commonly used options are -F (to display the file type), and -l (to give a "long" listing including file size, owner, permissions, and so on).

Example: ls -lF /home/larry displays the contents of the directory /home/larry.

cp Copies one or more file to another file or directory.
Syntax: cp files destination
Where files lists the files to copy, and destination is the destination file or directory.

Example: cp ../frog joe copies the file ../frog to the file or. directory joe

mv Moves one or more file to another file or directory. This command does the equivalent of a copy followed by the deletion of the original file. You can use this to rename files, like in the MS-DOS command RENAME.
Syntax: mv files destination
Where files lists the files to move, and destination is the destination file or directory.

Example: mv ../frog joe moves the file ../frog to the file or directory joe.

rm Deletes files. Note that when you delete a file under UNIX, they are unrecoverable (unlike MS-DOS, where you can usually "undelete" the file).
Syntax: rm files
Where files describes the filenames to delete.

The -i option prompts for confirmation before deleting the file.

Example: rm -i /home/larry/joe /home/larry/frog
deletes the files joe and frog in /home/larry.

mkdir Creates new directories.
Syntax: mkdir dirs
Where dirs are the directories to create.

Example: mkdir /home/larry/test creates the directory test
in /home/larry.

rmdir Deletes empty directories. When using rmdir, the current working di-rectory must not be within the directory to be deleted.
Syntax: rmdir dirs
Where dirs defines the directories to delete.

Example: rmdir /home/larry/papers deletes the directory
/home/larry/papers, if empty.

man Displays the manual page for the given command or resource (that is, any system utility that isn't a command, such as a library function.)
Syntax: man command
Where command is the name of the command or resource to get help on.

Example: man ls gives help on the ls command.

more Displays the contents of the named files, one screenful at a time.

Syntax: more files
Where files lists the files to display.

Example: more papers/history-final displays the file
papers/history-final.

cat Officially used to concatenate files, cat is also used to display the con-tents of a file on screen.
Syntax: cat files
Where files lists the files to display.

Example: cat letters/from-mdw displays the file
letters/from-mdw.

echo Displays the given arguments on the screen.
Syntax: echo args
Where args lists arguments to echo.

Example: echo "Hello world" displays the string "Hello world".

grep Display every line in one or more files that match the given pattern.
Syntax: grep pattern files
Where pattern is a regular expression pattern, and files lists the files to search.

Example: grep loomer /etc/hosts displays every line in the file /etc/hosts that contains the pattern "loomer".

1.6 Exploring the file system.

A **file system** is the collection of files and the hierarchy of directories on a system. The time has now come to escort you around the file system.

You now have the skills and the knowledge to understand the Linux file system, and you have a roadmap.

First, change to the root directory (cd /), and then enter ls -F to display a listing of its contents. You'll probably see the following directories:

bin, dev, etc, home,
install, lib, mnt, proc, root, tmp, user, usr,and var.

Note:
You may see others, and you might not see all of them. Every release of Linux differs in some respects.

Now, let's take a look at each of these directories.

/bin /bin is short for "binaries", or executables, where many essential system programs reside. Use ls -F /bin to list the files here. If you look down the list you may see a few commands that you recognize, such as cp, ls,andmv. These are the actual programs for these commands. When you use the cp command, for example, you're running the program /bin/cp.

Using ls -F, you'll see that most (if not all) of the files in /bin have an asterisk ("*") appended to their filenames. This indicates that the files are executables.

/dev The "files"in/dev are **device files**—they access system devices and resources like disk drives, modems, and memory. Just as your system can read data from a file, it can also read input from the mouse by accessing /dev/mouse.

Filenames that begin with fd are floppy disk devices. fd0 is the first floppy disk drive, and fd1 is the second. You may have noticed that there are more floppy disk devices than the two listed above: these represent specific types of floppy disks. For example, fd1H1440 accesses high-density, 3.5" diskettes in drive 1.

The following is a list of some of the most commonly used device files. Even though you may not have some of the physical devices listed below, chances are that you'll have drivers in /dev for them anyway.

- /dev/console refers to the system's console—that is, the monitor connected directly to your system.
- The various /dev/ttyS and /dev/cua devices are used for accessing serial ports. /dev/ttyS0 refers to "COM1" under MS-DOS. The /dev/cua devices are "callout" devices, and used with a modem.
- Device names beginning with hd access hard drives. /dev/hda refers to the *whole* first hard disk, while /dev/hda1 refers to the first *partition* on /dev/hda.
- Device names that begin with sd are SCSI drives. If you have a SCSI hard drive, instead of accessing it through /dev/hda, you would access /dev/sda. SCSI tapes are accessed via st devices, and SCSI CD-ROM via sr devices.
- Device names that begin with lp access parallel ports. /dev/lp0 is the same as "LPT1" in the MS-DOS world.

/dev/null is used as a "black hole"—data sent to this device is gone forever.

Why is this useful? Well, if you wanted to suppress the output of a command appearing on your screen, you could send that output to /dev/null. We'll talk more about this later.

- Devices whose names are /dev/tty followed by a number refer to the "virtual consoles" on your system (accessed by pressing Alt-F1 , Alt-F2 , and so on). /dev/tty1 refers to the first VC, /dev/tty2 refers to the second, and so on.
- Device names beginning with /dev/pty are **pseudo-terminals,** which are used to provide a "terminal" to remote login sessions. For example, if your machine is on a network, incoming telnet logins would use one of the /dev/pty devices.

/etc /etc contains a number of miscellaneous system configuration files. These include /etc/passwd (the user database), /etc/rc (the system initialization script), and so on.

/sbin /sbin contains essential system binaries that are used for system administration.

/home /home contains user's home directories. For example, /home/larry is the home directory for the user "larry". On a newly installed system, there may not be any users in this directory.

/lib /lib contains **shared library images**, which are files that contain code which many programs share in common. Rather than each program using its own copy of these shared routines, they are all stored in one common place, in /lib. This makes executable files smaller, and saves space on your system.

/proc /proc supports a "virtual file system", where the files are stored in memory, not on disk. These "files" refer to the various **processes** running on the system, and let you get information about the programs and processes that are running at any given time.

/tmp Many programs store temporary information and in a file that is deleted when the program has finished executing. The standard location for these files is in /tmp.

/usr /usr is a very important directory which contains subdirectories that contain some of the most important and useful programs and configuration files used on the system.

The various directories described above are essential for the system to operate, but most of the items found in /usr are optional. However, it is these optional items that make the system useful and interesting. Without /usr, you'd have a boring system that supports only programs like cp and ls. /usr contains most of the larger software packages and the configuration files that accompany them.

/usr/X11R6 /usr/X11R6 contains The X Window System, if you installed it. The X Window System is a large, powerful graphical environment that provides a large number of graphical utilities and programs, displayed in "windows" on your screen. If you're at all familiar with the Microsoft Windows or Macintosh environments, X Windows will look familiar. The /usr/X11R6 directory contains all of the X Windows executables, configuration files, and support files. This is covered in more detail in Chapter **??**.

/usr/bin /usr/bin is the real warehouse for software on any Linux system, containing most of the executables for programs not found in other places, like /bin.

/usr/etc Just as /etc contains essential miscellaneous system programs and configuration files, /usr/etc contains miscellaneous utilities and files, that in general, are not essential to the system.

/usr/include
/usr/include contains **include files** for the C compiler. These files (most of which end in .h, for "header") declare data structure names, subroutines, and constants used when writing programs in C. Files in. /usr/include/sys are generally used when programming on the UNIX system level. If you are familiar with the C programming language, here you'll find header files like stdio.h, which declare func-tions like printf().

/usr/g++-include
/usr/g++-include contains include files for the C++ compiler (much like /usr/include).

/usr/lib /usr/lib contains the "stub" and "static" library equivalents for the files found in /lib. When compiling a program, the program is "linked" with the libraries found in /usr/lib, which then directs the program to look in /lib when it needs the actual code in the library. In addition, various other programs store configuration files in /usr/lib.

/usr/local /usr/local is much like /usr—it contains various programs and files not essential to the system, but which make the system fun and exciting. In general, programs in /usr/local are specialized for your system—consequently, /usr/local differs greatly between Linux systems.

/usr/man This directory contains manual pages. There are two subdirectories in it for every manual page "section" (use the command man man for details). For example, /usr/man/man1 contains the source (that is, the unformatted original) for manual pages in section 1, and /usr/man/cat1 contains the formatted manual pages for section 1.

/usr/src /usr/src contains the source code (the uncompiled instructions) for various programs on your system. The most important directory here is /usr/src/linux, which contains the source code for the Linux kernel.

/var /var holds directories that often change in size or tend to grow. Many of those directories used to reside in /usr, but since those who sup-port Linux are trying to keep it relatively unchangeable, the directories that change often have been moved to /var. Some Linux distributions maintain their software package databases in directories under /var.

/var/log /var/log contains various files of interest to the system administrator, specifically system logs, which record errors or problems with the system. Other files record logins to the system as well as failed login attempts. This will be covered in Chapter 4.

/var/spool /var/spool contains files which are "spooled" to another program. For example, if your machine is connected to a network, incoming mail is stored in /var/spool/mail until you read or delete it. Outgoing or incoming news articles are in /var/spool/news, and so on.

1.7 Types of shells.

As mentioned before, Linux is a multitasking, multiuser operating system. Multitasking is *very* useful, and once you understand it, you'll use it all of the time. Before long, you'll run programs in the background, switch between tasks, and pipeline programs together to achieve complicated results with a single command.

Many of the features we'll cover in this section are features provided by the shell itself. Be careful not to confuse Linux (the actual operating system) with a shell—a shell is just an interface to the underlying system. The shell provides functionality inaddition to Linux itself.

A shell is not only an interpreter for the interactive commands you type at the prompt, but also a powerful programming language. It lets you to write **shell scripts**, to "batch" several shell commands together in a file. If you know MS-DOS you'll recognize the similarity to "batch files". Shell scripts are a very powerful tool, that will let you automate and expand your use of Linux.

There are several types of shells in the Linux world. The two major types are the "Bourne shell" and the "C shell". The Bourne shell uses a command syntax like the original shell on early UNIX systems, like System III. The name of the Bourne shell on most Linux systems is /bin/sh (where sh stands for "shell"). The C shell (not to be confused with sea shell) uses a different syntax, somewhat like the programming language C, and on most Linux systems is named /bin/csh.

Under Linux, several variations of these shells are available. The two most commonly used are the Bourne Again Shell, or "Bash" (/bin/bash), and "Tcsh" (/bin/tcsh). bash is a form of the Bourne shell that includes many of the advanced features found in the C shell. Because bash supports a superset of the Bourne shell syntax, shell scripts written in the standard Bourne shell should work with bash. If you prefer to use the C shell syntax, Linux supports tcsh, which is an expanded version of the original C shell.

The type of shell you decide to use is mostly a religious issue. Some folks prefer the Bourne shell syntax with the advanced features of bash, and some prefer the more structured C shell syntax. As far as normal commands such as cp and ls are concerned, the shell you use doesn't matter—the syntax is the same. Only when you start to write shell scripts or use advanced features of a shell do the differences between shell types begin to matter.

As we discuss the features of the various shells, we'll note differences between Bourne and C shells. However, for the purposes of this manual most of those differences are minimal. (If you're really curious at this point, read the man pages for bash and tcsh).

1.8 Wildcards.

A key feature of most Linux shells is the ability to refer to more than one file by name using special characters. These **wildcards** let you refer to, say, all file names that contain the character "n".

The wildcard "*" specifies any character or string of characters in a file name. When you use the character "*" in a file name, the shell replaces it with all possible substitutions from file names in the directory you're referencing.

Here's a quick example. Suppose that Larry has the files frog, joe,and stuff in his current directory:

```
/home/larry# ls

frog joe stuff

/home/larry#
```

To specify all files containing the letter "o" in the filename, use the command:

```
/home/larry# ls *o*

frog joe

/home/larry#
```

As you can see, each instance of "*" is replaced with all substitutions that match the wild-card from filenames in the current directory.

The use of "*" by itself simply matches all filenames, because all characters match the wildcard.

```
/home/larry# ls *
frog joe stuff
/home/larry#
```

Here are a few more examples:

```
/home/larry# ls f*
frog
/home/larry# ls *ff
stuff
/home/larry# ls *f*
frog stuff
/home/larry# ls s*f
stuff
/home/larry#
```

The process of changing a "*" into a series of filenames is called **wildcard expansion** and is done by the shell. This is important: an individual command, such as ls, *never* sees the "*" in its list of parameters. The shell expands the wildcard to include all filenames that match. So, the command:

```
/home/larry# ls *o*
```

is expanded by the shell to:

```
/home/larry# ls frog joe
```

One important note about the "*" wildcard: it does *not* match file names that begin with a single period ("."). These files are treated as **hidden** files—while they are not really hidden, they don't show up on normal ls listings and aren't touched by the use of the "*" wildcard.

Here's an example. We mentioned earlier that each directory contains two special entries: "." refers to the current directory, and ".." refers to the parent directory. However, when you use ls, these two entries don't show up:

```
/home/larry# ls

frog joe stuff

/home/larry#
```

If you use the -a switch with ls, however, you can display filenames that begin with ".". Observe:

```
/home/larry#    ls    -a
.       ..       .bash profile       .bashrc     frog     joe

stuff

/home/larry#
```

The listing contains the two special entries, "."and"..", as well as two other "hidden" files—.bash profile and .bashrc. These two files are startup files used by bash when larry logs in.

Note that when you use the "*" wildcard, none of the filenames beginning with "."are displayed.

```
/home/larry# ls *

frog joe stuff

/home/larry#
```

This is a safety feature: if the "*" wildcard matched filenames beginning with ".", it would also match the directory names "."and"..". This can be dangerous when using certain commands.
Another wildcard is "?". The "?" wildcard expands to only a single character. Thus, "ls ?" displays all one-character filenames. And "ls termca?" would display:

"termcap"but*not* "termcap.backup". Here's another example:

```
/home/larry# ls j?e

joe

/home/larry# ls f??g

frog

/home/larry# ls ????f

stuff

/home/larry#
```

As you can see, wildcards lets you specify many files at one time. cp and mv commands actually can copy or move more than one file at a time. For example:

```
/home/larry# cp /etc/s* /home/larry
```

copies all filenames in /etc beginning with "s" to the directory /home/larry.The format of the cp command is really:

```
cp    files    destination
```

where files lists the filenames to copy, and destination is the destination file or directory. mv has an identical syntax.

If you are copying or moving more than one file, the destination must be a directory. You can only copy or move a single file to another file.

1.9 Linux plumbing.

1.9.1 Standard input and standard output.

Many Linux commands get input from what is called **standard input** and send their output to **standard output** (often abbreviated as stdin and stdout). Your shell sets things up so that standard input is your keyboard, and standard output is the screen. Here's an example using the cat command. Normally, cat reads data from all of the files specified by the command line, and sends this data directly to stdout. Therefore, using the command:

```
/home/larry/papers# cat history-final masters-thesis
```

displays the contents of the file history-final followed by masters-thesis.

However, if you don't specify a filename, cat reads data from stdin and sends it back to stdout. Here's an example:

```
/home/larry/papers# cat

Hello there.

Hello there.

Bye.

Bye.

Ctrl-D

/home/larry/papers#
```

Each line that you type is immediately echoed back by cat. When reading from standard input, you indicate the input is "finished" by sending an EOT (end-of-text) signal, in general, generated by pressing Ctrl-D .

Here's another example. The sort command reads lines of text (again, from stdin, unless you specify one or more filenames) and sends the sorted output to stdout. Try the following:

```
/home/larry/papers# sort

bananas

carrots

apples

Ctrl-D

apples

bananas

carrots

/home/larry/papers#
```

Now we can alphabetize our shopping list... isn't Linux useful?

1.9.2 Redirecting input and output.

Now, let's say that you want to send the output of sort to a file, to save our shopping list on disk. The shell lets you **redirect** standard output to a filename, by using the ">" symbol. Here's how it works:

```
/home/larry/papers#   sort   >  > shopping - list

bananas

carrots

apples

Ctrl-D

/home/larry/papers#
```

As you can see, the result of the sort command isn't displayed, but is saved to the file named shopping-list. Let's look at this file:

```
/home/larry/papers#  cat  shopping - list

apples

bananas

carrots

/home/larry/papers#
```

Now you can sort your shopping list, and save it, too! But let's suppose that you are storing the unsorted, original shopping list in the file items. One way of sorting the information and saving it to a file would be to give sort the name of the file to read, in lieu of standard input, and redirect standard output as we did above, as follows:

```
/home/larry/papers#      sort items     >      shopping  -  list

/home/larry/papers# cat shopping - list

apples

bananas

carrots
```

```
/home/larry/papers#
```

However, there's another way to do this. Not only can you redirect standard output, you can redirect standard *input* as well, using the "<" symbol:

```
/home/larry/papers#  <  sort < items

apples

bananas

carrots

/home/larry/papers#
```

Technically, sort < items is equivalent to sort items, but lets you demonstrate the following point: sort < items behaves as if the data in the file items was typed to standard input. The shell handles the redirection. sort wasn't given the name of the file (items) to read; as far as sort is concerned, it still reads from standard input as if you had typed the data from your keyboard.

This introduces the concept of a **filter**. A filter is a program that reads data from standard input, processes it in some way, and sends the processed data to standard output. Using redirection, standard input and standard output can be referenced from files. As mentioned above, stdin and stdout default to the keyboard and screen respectively. sort is a simple filter. It sorts the incoming data and sends the result to standard output. cat is even simpler. It doesn't do anything with the incoming data, it simply outputs whatever is given to it.

1.9.3 Using pipes.

We already demonstrated how to use sort as a filter. However, these examples assume that you have data stored in a file somewhere or are willing to type the data from the standard input yourself. What if the data that you wanted to sort came from the output of another command, like ls?

The -r option to sort sorts the data in reverse-alphabetical order. If you want to list the files in your current directory in reverse order, one way to do it is follows:

/home/larry/papers# ls

english-list

history-final

masters-thesis

notes

Now redirect the output of the ls command into a file called file-list:

/home/larry/papers# ls > > file - list

/home/larry/papers# sort -r file - list.

notes

masters-thesis

history-final

english-list

home/larry/papers#

Here, you save the output of ls in a file, and then run sort -r on that file. But this is unwieldy and uses a temporary file to save the data from ls.

The solution is **pipelining.** This is a shell feature that connects a string of commands via a "pipe." The stdout of the first command is sent to the stdin of the second command. In this case, we want to send the stdout of ls to the stdin of sort. Use the "|" symbol to create a pipe, as follows:

/home/larry/papers# ls | j sort - r

notes

masters-thesis

history-final

english-list

/home/larry/papers#

This command is shorter and easier to type.

Here's another useful example, the command:

/ home / larry / papers#   ls   /usr /bin

displays a long list of files, most of which fly past the screen too quickly for you to read. So, let's use more to display the list of files in /usr/bin.

/home/larry/papers#   ls   /usr/ bin j more

Now you can page down the list of files at your leisure.

But the fun doesn't stop here! You can pipe more than two commands together. The command head is a filter that displays the first lines from an input stream (in this case, input from a pipe). If you want to display the last filename in alphabetical order in the current directory, use commands like the following:

/home/larry/papers# ls | j sort -r | j head -1

notes

/home/larry/papers#

where head -1 displays the first line of input that it receives (in this case, the stream of reverse-sorted data from ls).

1.9.4 Non - destructive redirection of output.

Using ">" to redirect output to a file is destructive: in other words, the command:

/ home / larry / papers# ls > >   file-list

overwrites the contents of the file file-list. If instead, you redirect with the symbol ">>", the output is appended to (added to the end of) the named file instead of overwriting it. For example:

/home/larry/papers# ls   > > >> file - list

appends the output of the ls command to file-list.

Keep in mind that redirection and pipes are features of the shell—which supports the use of ">", ">>"and"|". It has nothing to do with the commands themselves.

1.10 File permissions.

1.10.1 Concepts of file permissions.

Because there is typically more than one user on a Linux system, Linux provides a mechanism known as **file permissions**, which protect user files from tampering by other users. This mechanism lets files and directories be "owned" by a particular user. For example, because Larry created the files in his home directory, Larry owns those files and has access to them.

Linux also lets files be shared between users and groups of users. If Larry desired, he could cut off access to his files so that no other user could access them. However, on most systems the default is to allow other users to read your files but not modify or delete them in any way.

Every file is owned by a particular user. However, files are also owned by a particular **group**, which is a defined group of users of the system. Every user is placed into at least one group when that user's account is created. However, the system administrator may grant the user access to more than one group.

Groups are usually defined by the type of users who access the machine. For example, on a university Linux system users may be placed into the groups student, staff, faculty or guest. There are also a few system-defined groups (like bin and admin) which are used by the system itself to control access to resources—very rarely do actual users belong to these system groups.

Permissions fall into three main divisions: read, write, and execute. These permissions may be granted to three classes of users: the owner of the file, the group to which the file belongs, and to all users, regardless of group.

Read permission lets a user read the contents of the file, or in the case of directories, list the contents of the directory (using ls). Write permission lets the user write to and modify the file. For directories, write permission lets the user create new files or delete files within that directory. Finally, execute permission lets the user run the file as a program or shell script (if the file is a program or shell script). For directories, having execute permission lets the user cd into the directory in question.

1.10.2 Interpreting file permissions.

Let's look at an example that demonstrates file permissions. Using the ls command with the -l option displays a "long" listing of the file, including file permissions.

```
/home   /larry / foo #   ls  - l   stuff

-rw-r--r--        1 larry      users        505   Mar  13   19:05  stuff

/home  /  larry  / foo#
```

The first field in the listing represents the file permissions. The third field is the owner of the file (larry) and the fourth field is the group to which the file belongs (users). Obviously, the last field is the name of the file (stuff). We'll cover the other fields later.

This file is owned by larry, and belongs to the group users. The string -rw-r--r-- lists, in order, the permissions granted to the file's owner, the file's group, and everybody else.

The first character of the permissions string ("-") represents the type of file. A "-" means that this is a regular file (as opposed to a directory or device driver). The next three characters ("rw-") represent the permissions granted to the file's owner, larry.The "r" stands for "read" and the "w" stands for "write". Thus, larry has read and write permission to the file stuff.

As mentioned, besides read and write permission, there is also "execute" permission—represented by an "x". However, a "-" is listed here in place of an "x", so Larry doesn't have execute permission on this file. This is fine, as the file stuff isn't a program of any kind. Of course, because Larry owns the file, he may grant himself execute permission for the file if he so desires. (This will be covered shortly).

The next three characters, ("r--"), represent the group's permissions on the file. The group that owns this file is users. Because only an "r" appears here, any user who belongs to the group users may read this file.
The last three characters, also ("r--"), represent the permissions granted to every other user on the system (other than the owner of the file and those in the group users). Again, because only an "r" is present, other users may read the file, but not write to it or execute it.

Here are some other examples of permissions:

-rwxr-xr-x — The owner of the file may read, write, and execute the file. Users in the file's group, and all other users, may read and execute the file.

-rw------- — The owner of the file may read and write the file. No other user can access the file.

-rwxrwxrwx — All users may read, write, and execute the file.

1.10.3 Permissions Dependencies.

The permissions granted to a file also depend on the permissions of the directory in which the file is located. For example, even if a file is set to -rwxrwxrwx, other users cannot access the file unless they have read and execute access to the directory in which the file is located. For example, if Larry wanted to restrict access to all of his files, he could set the permissions to his home directory /home/larry to -rwx------. In this way, no other user has access to his directory, and all files and directories within it. Larry doesn't need to worry about the individual permissions on each of his files.

In other words, to access a file at all, you must have execute access to all directories along the file's pathname, and read (or execute) access to the file itself.

Typically, users on a Linux system are very open with their files. The usual set of permissions given to files is -rw-r--r--, which lets other users read the file but not change it in any way. The usual set of permissions given to directories is -rwxr-xr-x, which lets other users look through your directories, but not create or delete files within them.

However, many users wish to keep other users out of their files. Setting the permissions of a file to -rw------- will prevent any other user from accessing the file. Likewise, setting the permissions of a directory to -rwx------ keeps other users out of the directory in question.

1.10.4 Changing permissions.

The command chmod is used to set the permissions on a file. Only the owner of a file may change the permissions on that file. The syntax of chmod is:

chmod {a,u,g,ogo} {+,-} {r, w, x } xg filenames

Briefly, you supply one or more of all, user, group, or other. Then you specify whether you are adding rights (+) or taking them away (-). Finally, you specify one or more of read, write, and execute. Some examples of legal commands are:

chmod a+r stuff

Gives all users read access to the file.

chmod +r stuff

Same as above—if none of a, u, g,or o is specified, a is assumed.

chmod og-x stuff

Remove execute permission from users other than the owner.

chmod u+rwx stuff

Let the owner of the file read, write, and execute the file.

chmod o-rwx stuff

Remove read, write, and execute permission from users other than the owner and users in the file's group.

1.11 Managing file links.

Links let you give a single file more than one name. Files are actually identified by the system by their **inode number**, which is just the unique file system identifier for the file. A directory is actually a listing of inode numbers with their corresponding filenames. Each filename in a directory is a **link** to a particular inode.

1.11.1 Hard links.

The ln command is used to create multiple links for one file. For example, let's say that you have a file called foo in a directory. Using ls -i, you can look at the inode number for this file:

```
/home/larry # ls -i foo
22192 foo
/home/larry #
```

Here, foo has an inode number of 22192 in the file system. You can create another link to foo, named bar, as follows:

```
/home/larry # ln foo bar
```

With ls -i, you see that the two files have the same inode:

```
/home/larry # ls -i foo bar
22192 bar    22192 foo
/ home / larry #
```

Now, specifying either foo or bar will access the same file. If you make changes to foo, those changes appear in bar as well. For all purposes, foo and bar are the same file.

These links are known as **hard links** because they create a direct link to an inode. Note that you can hard-link files only when they're on the same file system; symbolic links (see below) don't have this restriction.

When you delete a file with rm, you are actually only deleting one link to a file. If you use the command:

```
/ home / larry # rm foo
```

then only the link named foo is deleted, bar will still exist. A file is only truly deleted on the system when it has no links to it. Usually, files have only one link, so using the rm command deletes the file. However, if a file has multiple links to it, using rm will delete only a single link; in order to delete the file, you must delete all links to the file.

The command ls -l displays the number of links to a file (among other information).

```
/ home / larry #   ls   - l   foo  bar
-rw-r--r--    2 root    root         12 Aug    5  16 : 51   bar
-rw-r--r--    2 root    root         12 Aug    5  16 : 50   foo
/ home / larry #
```

The second column in the listing, "2", specifies the number of links to the file.

As it turns out, a directory is actually just a file containing information about link-to-inode associations. Also, every directory contains at least two hard links: "." (a link pointing to itself), and ".." (a link pointing to the parent directory). The root directory (/)".." link just points back to /. (In other words, the parent of the root directory is the root directory itself.).

1.11.2 Symbolic links.

Symbolic links, or **symlinks**, are another type of link, which are different from hard links. A symbolic link lets you give a file another name, but doesn't link the file by inode.

The command ln -s creates a symbolic link to a file. For example, if you use the command:

```
/ home / larry #   ln  - s   foo   bar
```

you will create a symbolic link named bar that points to the file foo. If you use ls -i, you'll see that the two files have different inodes, indeed.

```
/home/larry#    ls  - i  foo bar
22195 bar       22192    foo
/ home / larry #
```

However, using ls -l, we see that the file bar is a symlink pointing to foo:

```
/home/larry #  ls -l  foo  bar
lrwxrwxrwx    1 root    root     3 Aug   5 16:51 bar  ->  foo
-rw-r--r--    1root     root    12 Aug   5 16:50  foo
/ home / larry #
```

The file permissions on a symbolic link are not used (they always appear as rwxrwxrwx). Instead, the permissions on the symbolic link are determined by the permissions on the target of the symbolic link (in our example, the file foo).

Functionally, hard links and symbolic links are similar, but there are differences. For one thing, you can create a symbolic link to a file that doesn't exist; the same is not true for hard links. Symbolic links are processed by the kernel differently than are hard links, which is just a technical difference but sometimes an important one. Symbolic links are helpful because they identify the file they point to; with hard links, there is no easy way to determine which files are linked to the same inode.

Links are used in many places on the Linux system. Symbolic links are especially important to the shared library images in /lib.

1.12 Job control.

1.12.1 Jobs and processes.

Job control is a feature provided by many shells (including bash and tcsh) that. let you control multiple running commands, or **jobs**, at once. Before we can delve much further, we need to talk about **processes.**

Every time you run a program, you start what is called a process. The command ps displays a list of currently running processes, as shown here:

```
/ home / larry #   ps
PID  TT   STAT    TIME   COMMAND
 24   3    S      0:03    (bash)
161   3    R      0:00     ps
/ home / larry #
```

The PID listed in the first column is the **process ID**, a unique number given to every running process. The last column, COMMAND, is the name of the running command. Here, we're looking only at the processes which Larry himself is currently running. (There are many other processes running on the system as well—"ps -aux" lists them all.) These are bash (Larry's shell), and the ps command itself. As you can see, bash is running concurrently with the ps command. bash executed ps when Larry typed the command. After ps has finished running (after the table of processes is displayed), control is returned to the bash process, which displays the prompt, ready for another command.

A running process is also called a *job*. The terms *process* and *job* are interchangeable. However, a process is usually referred to as a "job" when used in conjunction with **job control**—a feature of the shell that lets you switch between several independent jobs.

In most cases users run only a single job at a time—whatever command they last typed to the shell. However, using job control, you can run several jobs at once, and switch between them as needed.

How might this be useful? Let's say you are editing a text file and want to interrupt your editing and do something else. With job control, you can temporarily suspend the editor, go back to the shell prompt and start to work on something else. When you're done, you can switch back to the editor and be back where you started, as if you didn't leave the editor. There are many other practical uses of job control.

1.12.2 Foreground and background.

Jobs can either be in the **foreground** or in the **background.** There can only be one job in the foreground at a time. The foreground job is the job with which you interact—it receives input from the keyboard and sends output to your screen, unless, of course, you. have redirected input or output). On the other hand,
jobs in the background do not receive input from the terminal—in general, they run along quietly without the need for interaction.

Some jobs take a long time to finish and don't do anything interesting while they are running. Compiling programs is one such job, as is compressing a large file. There's no reason why you should sit around being bored while these jobs complete their tasks; just run them in the background. While jobs run in the background, you are free to run other programs.

Jobs may also be **suspended.** A suspended job is a job that is temporarily stopped. After you suspend a job, you can tell the job to continue in the foreground or the background as needed. Resuming a suspended job does not change the state of the job in any way—the job continues to run where it left off.

Suspending a job is not equal to interrupting a job. When you **interrupt** a running process (by pressing the interrupt key, which is usually Ctrl-C), the process is killed, for good. Once the job is killed, there's no hope of resuming it. You'll must run the command again. Also, some programs trap the interrupt, so that pressing Ctrl-C won't immediately kill the job. This is to let the program perform any necessary cleanup operations before exiting. In fact, some programs don't let you kill them with an interrupt at all.

1.12.3 Backgrounding and killing jobs.

Let's begin with a simple example. The command yes is a seemingly useless command that sends an endless stream of y's to standard output. (This is actually useful. If you piped the output of yes to another command which asked a series of yes and no questions, the stream of y's would confirm all of the questions.)

Try it out:

```
/home/larry# yes
y
y
y
y
y
```

The y's will continue *ad infinitum*. You can kill the process by pressing the interrupt key, which is usually Ctrl-C . So that we don't have to put up with the annoying stream of (3) y's, let's redirect the standard output of yes to /dev/null. As you may remember, /dev/null acts as a "black hole" for data. Any data sent to it disappears. This is a very effective method of quieting an otherwise verbose program.

```
/home/larry#   yes   >     > /dev/null
```

Ah, much better. Nothing is printed, but the shell prompt doesn't come back. This is because yes is still running, and is sending those inane y's to /dev/null. Again, to kill the job, press the interrupt key.

(3)You can set the interrupt key with the stty command.

Let's suppose that you want the yes command to continue to run but wanted to get the shell prompt back so that you can work on other things. You can put yes into the background, allowing it to run, without need for interaction.

One way to put a process in the background is to append an "&" character to the end of the command:

```
/home/larry# yes    >    > /dev/null &

[1]      164

/ home / larry #
```

As you can see, the shell prompt has returned. But what is this "[1] 164"? And is the yes command really running?

The "[1]" represents the **job number** for the yes process. The shell assigns a job number to every running job. Because yes is the one and only job we're running, it is assigned job number 1.The"164" is the process ID, or PID, number given by the system to the job. You can use either number to refer to the job, as you'll see later.
You now have the yes process running in the background, continuously sending a stream of y's to /dev/null. To check on the status of this process, use the internal shell command jobs.

```
/home/larry#   jobs

[1]+ Running                 yes    >  / dev / null      &

/ home / larry #
```

Sure enough, there it is. You could also use the ps command as demonstrated above to check on the status of the job.

To terminate the job, use the kill command. This command takes either a job number or a process ID number as an argument. This was job number 1, so using the command:

```
/ home /  larry #    kill     %1
```

kills the job. When identifying the job with the job number, you must prefix the number with a percent ("%") character.

Now that you've killed the job, use jobs again to check on it:

```
/home/larry#     jobs

[1]+       Terminated           yes  > / dev / null

/ home / larry #
```

The job is in fact dead, and if you use the jobs command again nothing should be printed. You can also kill the job using the process ID (PID) number, displayed along with the job ID when you start the job. In our example, the process ID is 164, so the command:

```
/home/larry# kill      164
```

is equivalent to:

```
/home/larry# kill      %1
```

You don't need to use the "%" when referring to a job by its process ID.

1.12.4 Stopping and restarting jobs.

There is another way to put a job into the background. You can start the job normally (in the foreground), **stop** the job, and then restart it in the background.

First, start the yes process in the foreground, as you did before:

```
/ home / larry #    >    yes > / dev / null
```

Again, because yes is running in the foreground, you shouldn't get the shell prompt back. Now, rather than interrupt the job with Ctrl-C , **suspend** the job. Suspending a job doesn't kill it: it only temporarily stops the job until you restart it. To do this, press the suspend key, which is usually Ctrl-Z .

```
/ home / larry #  yes    >  > / dev / null

ctrl-Z

[1] +       Stopped yes        >  / dev / null

/ home / larry #
```

While the job is suspended, it's simply not running. No CPU time is used for the job. However, you can restart the job, which causes the job to run again as if nothing ever happened. It will continue to run where it left off.

To restart the job in the foreground, use the fg command (for "foreground").

```
/home/larry#  fg

yes   > /  dev / null
```

The shell displays the name of the command again so you're aware of which job you just put into the foreground. Stop the job again with Ctrl-Z . This time, use the bg command to put the job into the background. This causes the command to run just as if you started the command with "&" as in the last section.

```
/ home / larry #    bg

[1]    +      yes >   / dev / null    &

/ home / larry #
```

And you have your prompt back. Jobs should report that yes is indeed running, and you can kill the job with kill as we did before.

How can you stop the job again? Using Ctrl-Z won't work, because the job is in the background. The answer is to put the job in the foreground with fg, and then stop it. As it turns out, you can use fg on either stopped jobs or jobs in the background.

There is a big difference between a job in the background and a job that is stopped. A stopped job is not running—it's not using any CPU time, and it's not doing any work (the job still occupies system memory, although it may have been swapped out to disk). A job in the background is running and using memory, as well as completing some task while you do other work.

However, a job in the background may try to display text on your terminal, which can be annoying if you're trying to work on something else. For example, if you used the command:

```
/ home / larry #      yes    &
```

without redirecting stdout to /dev/null, a stream of y's would be displayed on your screen, without any way for you to interrupt it. (You can't use Ctrl-C to interrupt jobs in the background.) In order to stop the endless y's, use the fg command to bring the job to the foreground, and then use Ctrl-C to kill it.

Another note. The fg and bg commands normally affect the job that was last stopped (indicated by a "+" next to the job number when you use the jobs command). If you are running multiple jobs at once, you can put jobs in the foreground or background by giving the job ID as an argument to fg or bg,as in:

```
/ home / larry #    fg    %2
```

(to put job number 2 into the foreground), or.

```
/ home / larry #  bg    %3
```

(to put job number 3 into the background). You can't use process ID numbers with fg or bg.

Furthermore, using the job number alone, as in:

```
/ home / larry #   %2
```

is equivalent to:

```
/ home / larry #   fg    %2
```

Just remember that using job control is a feature of the shell. The fg, bg and jobs commands are internal to the shell. If for some reason you use a shell that doesn't support job control, don't expect to find these commands available.

In addition, there are some aspects of job control that differ between bash and tcsh.

In fact, some shells don't provide job control at all—however, most shells available for Linux do.

1.13 Using the vi editor.

A **text editor** is a program used to edit files that are composed of text: a letter, C program, or a system configuration file. While there are many such editors available for Linux, the only editor that you are guaranteed to find on any UNIX or Linux system is vi— the "visual editor." vi is not the easiest editor to use, nor is it very self-explanatory. However, because vi is so common in the UNIX/Linux world, and sometimes necessary, it deserves discussion here.

Your choice of an editor is mostly a question of personal taste and style. Many users prefer the baroque, self-explanatory and powerful emacs—an editor with more features than any other single program in the UNIX world. For example, Emacs has its own built-in dialect of the LISP programming language, and has many extensions (one of which is an Eliza-like artificial intelligence program). However, because Emacs and its support files are relatively large, it may not be installed on some systems. vi, on the other hand, is small and powerful but more difficult to use. However, once you know your way around vi, it's actually very easy.

This section presents an introduction to vi—we won't discuss all of its features, only the ones you need to know to get started. You can refer to the man page for vi if you're interested in learning more about this editor's features. Alternatively, you can read the book. *Learning the vi Editor* from O'Reilly and Associates, or the *VI Tutorial* from Specialized Systems Consultants (SSC) Inc.

1.13.1 Concepts.

While using vi, at any one time you are in one of three modes of operation. These modes are called *command mode*, *insert mode*,and*last line mode*.

When you start up vi, you are in *command mode*. This mode lets you use commands to edit files or change to other modes. For example, typing "x" while in command mode deletes the character underneath the cursor. The arrow keys move the cursor around the file you're editing. Generally, the commands used in command mode are one or two characters long.

You actually insert or edit text within *insert mode*. When using vi, you'll probably spend most of your time in this mode. You start insert mode by using a command such as "i" (for "insert") from command mode. While in insert mode, you can insert text into the document at the current cursor location. To end insert mode and return to command mode, press Esc .

Last line mode is a special mode used to give certain extended commands to vi. While typing these commands, they appear on the last line of the screen (hence the name). For example, when you type ":" in command mode, you jump into last line mode and can use commands like "wq" (to write the file and quit vi), or "q!" (to quit vi without saving changes). Last line mode is generally used for vi commands that are longer than one character. In last line mode, you enter a single-line command and press Enter to execute it.

1.13.2 Starting vi.

The best way to understand these concepts is to fire up vi and edit a file. The example "screens" below show only a few lines of text, as if the screen were only six lines high instead of twenty-four.

The syntax for vi is:

```
vi  filename
```

where filename is the name of the file to edit.

Start up vi by typing:

```
/ home / larry #   vi   test
```

to edit the file test. You should see something like:

```
~
~
~
~
~
~
"test" [New file]
```

This column of "~" characters indicates you are at the end of the file. The represents the cursor.

1.13.3 Inserting text.

The vi program is now in command mode. Insert text into the file by pressing i , which places the editor into insert mode, and begin typing:

```
Now is the time for all good men to come to the aid
of the party.
~
~
~
~
~
```

Type as many lines as you want (pressing Enter after each). You may correct mistakes with the Backspace key.

To end insert mode and return to command mode, press Esc .
In command mode you can use the arrow keys to move around in the file. (If you have only one line of text, trying to use the up- or down-arrow keys will probably cause vi to beep at you.)

There are several ways to insert text other than the i command. The a command inserts text beginning after the current cursor position, instead of at the current cursor position. For example, use the left arrow key to move the cursor between the words "good" and "men.".

```
Now is the time for all good men to come to the aid
of the party.
~
~
~
~
~
```

Press a to start insert mode, type "wo", and then press Esc to return to command mode:

```
Now is the time for all good women to come to the aid
of the party.
~
~
~
~
~
```

To begin inserting text at the next line, use the o command. Press o and enter another line or two:

```
Now is the time for all good humans to come to the
aid of the party.
Afterwards, we'll go out for pizza and beer.
~
~
~
~
```

1.13.4 Deleting text.

From command mode, the x command deletes the character under the cursor. If you press x five times, you'll end up with:

```
Now is the time for all good humans to come to the
aid of the party.
Afterwards, we'll go out for pizza and
~
~
~
~.
```

Now press a and insert some text, followed by esc :

```
Now is the time for all good humans to come to the
aid of the party.
Afterwards, we'll go out for pizza and Diet Coke.
~
~
~
~
```

You can delete entire lines using the command dd (that is, press d twice in a row). If the cursor is on the second line and you type dd, you'll see:

```
Now is the time for all good humans to come to the
aid of the party.
~
~
~
~
~
```

To delete the word that the cursor is on, use the dw command. Place the cursor on the word "good", and type dw:

```
Now is the time for all humans to come to the aid of
the party.
~
~
~
~
~
```

1.13.5 Changing text.

You can replace sections of text using the R command. Place the cursor on the first letter in "party", press R , and type the word "hungry".

```
Now is the time for all humans to come to the aid of
the hungry.
~
~
~
~
~
```

Using R to edit text is like the i and a commands, but R overwrites, rather than inserts, text.

The r command replaces the single character under the cursor. For example, move the cursor to the beginning of the word "Now", and press r followed by C, you'll see:

```
Cow is the time for all humans to come to the aid of
the hungry.
~
~
~
~
~
```

The "~" command changes the case of the letter under the cursor from upper- to lowercase, and back. For example, if you place the cursor on the "o" in "Cow" above and repeatedly press ~ , you'll end up with:

```
COW IS THE TIME FOR ALL WOMEN TO COME TO THE AID OF
THE HUNGRY.
```

```
~
~
~
~
~
```

1.13.6 Commands for moving the cursor.

You already know how to use the arrow keys to move around the document. In addition, you can use the h, j, k,andl commands to move the cursor left, down, up, and right, respectively. This comes in handy when (for some reason) your arrow keys aren't working correctly.

The w command moves the cursor to the beginning of the next word; the b command moves it to the beginning of the previous word.

The 0 command (that's the zero key) moves the cursor to the beginning of the current line, and the $ command moves it to the end of the line.

When editing large files, you'll want to move forwards or backwards through the file a screenful at a time. Pressing Ctrl-F moves the cursor one screenful forward, and Ctrl-B moves it a screenful back.

To move the cursor to the end of the file, press G. You can also move to an arbitrary line; for example, typing the command 10G would move the cursor to line 10 in the file. To move to the beginning of the file, use 1G.

You can couple moving commands with other commands, such as those for deleting text. For example, the d$ command deletes everything from the cursor to the end of the line; dG deletes everything from the cursor to the end of the file, and so on.

1.13.7 Saving files and quitting vi.

To quit vi without making changes to the file, use the command :q!. When you press the ":", the cursor moves to the last line on the screen and you'll be in last line mode:

```
COW IS THE TIME FOR ALL WOMEN TO COME TO THE AID OF
THE HUNGRY.
~
~
~
~
~

:_
```

In last line mode, certain extended commands are available. One of them is q!, which quits vi without saving. The command :wq saves the file and then exits vi. The command ZZ (from command mode, without the ":") is equivalent to :wq. If the file has not been changed since the last save, it merely exits, preserving the modification time of the last change. Remember that you must press Enter after a command entered in last line mode.

To save the file without quitting vi, use : w.

1.13.8 Editing another file.

To edit another file, use the :e command. For example, to stop editing test and edit the file foo instead, use the command:

```
COW IS THE TIME FOR ALL WOMEN TO COME TO THE AID OF
THE HUNGRY.
~
~
~
~
~
:e foo_
```

If you use :e without saving the file first, you'll get the error message:

No write since last change (": edit! " overrides)

which means that vi doesn't want to edit another file until you save the first one. At this point, you can use :w to save the original file, and then use :e, or you can use the command:

```
COW IS THE TIME FOR ALL WOMEN TO COME TO THE AID OF
THE HUNGRY.
~
~
~
~
~
:e!     foo_
```

The "!" tells vi that you really mean it—edit the new file without saving changes to the first.

1.13.9 Including other files.

If you use the :r command, you can include the contents of another file in the current file. For example, the command:

```
:r  foo . txt
```

inserts the contents of the file foo.txt in the text at the location of the cursor.

1.13.10 Running shell commands.

You can also run shell commands within vi.The:r! command works like :r,but rather than read a file, it inserts the output of the given command into the buffer at the current cursor location. For example, if you use the command:

```
: r !   ls  -F
```

you'll end up with:

```
COW IS THE TIME FOR ALL WOMEN TO COME TO THE AID OF
THE HUNGRY.
letters/
misc/
papers/_
~
~
```

You can also "shell out" of vi, in other words, run a command from within vi,and return to the editor when you're done. For example, if you use the command:

```
: !   ls   -F
```

the ls -F command will be executed and the results displayed on the screen, but not inserted into the file you're editing. If you use the command:

```
: shell
```

vi starts an instance of the shell, letting you temporarily put vi "on hold" while you execute other commands. Just log out of the shell (using the exit command) to return to vi.

1.13.11 Getting vi help.

vi doesn't provide much in the way of interactive help (most Linux programs don't), but you can always read the man page for vi. vi is a visual front-end to the ex editor; which handles many of the last-line mode commands in vi. So, in addition to reading the man page for vi,see ex as well.

1.14 Customizing your environment.

A shell provides many mechanisms to customize your work environment. As mentioned above, a shell is more than a command interpreter—it is also a powerful programming language. Although writing shell scripts is an extensive subject, we'd like to introduce you to some of the ways that you can simplify your work on a Linux system by using these advanced features of the shell.

As mentioned before, different shells use different syntaxes when executing shell scripts. For example, Tcsh uses a C-like syntax, while Bourne shells use another type. of syntax. In this section, we won't be encountering many differences between the two, but we will assume that shell scripts are executed using the Bourne shell syntax.

1.14.1 Shell scripts.

Let's say that you use a series of commands often and would like to save time by grouping all of them together into a single "command". For example, the three commands:

```
/ home / larry #  cat  chapter1  chapter2  chapter3    >    book

/ home/larry# wc    -l   book

/ home/larry#   lp   book
```

concatenates the files chapter 1, chapter 2,and chapter 3 and places the result in the file book. The second command displays a count of the number of lines in book,and the third command lp book prints book.

Rather than type all these commands, you can group them into a **shell script.** The shell script used to run all these commands might look like this:

```
#! / bin / sh

# A shell script to create and print the book

cat chapter1 chapter2 chapter3   >  book

wc  -l   book

lp    book
```

Shell scripts are just plain text files; you can create them with an editor such as emacs or vi.

Let's look at this shell script. The first line, "# ! /bin/sh", identifies the file as a shell script and tells the shell how to execute the script. It instructs the shell to pass the script to /bin/sh for execution, where /bin/sh is the shell program itself. Why is this important? On most Linux systems, /bin/sh is a Bourne-type shell, like bash.By forcing the shell script to run using /bin/sh, you ensure that the script will run under a Bourne-syntax shell (rather than a C shell). This will cause your script to run using the Bourne syntax even if you use tcsh (or another C shell) as your login shell.

The second line is a **comment.** Comments begin with the character "#" and continue to the end of the line. Comments are ignored by the shell—they are commonly used to identify the shell script to the programmer and make the script easier to understand.

The rest of the lines in the script are just commands, as you would type them to the shell directly. In effect, the shell reads each line of the script and runs that line as if you had typed it at the shell prompt.

Permissions are important for shell scripts. If you create a shell script, make sure that you have execute permission on the script in order to run it. When you create text files, the default permissions usually don't include execute permission, and you must set them explicitly.Briefly, if this script were saved in the file called makebook, you could use the command:

```
/home/larry# chmod u+x makebook
```

to give yourself execute permission for the shell script makebook.
You can use the command:

```
/home/larry# makebook
```

to run all the commands in the script.

1.14.2 Shell variables and the environment.

A shell lets you define **variables**, as do most programming languages. A variable is just a piece of data that is given a name.

tcsh, as well as other C-type shells, use a different mechanism for setting variables 3 than is described here. This discussion assumes the use of a Bourne shell like bash.See the tcsh manual page for details.

When you assign a value to a variable (using the "=" operator), you can access the variable by prepending a "$" to the variable name, as demonstrated below:

```
/home/larry# foo="hello there"
```

The variable foo is given the value hello there. You can then refer to this value by the variable name prefixed with a "$" character. For example, the command:

```
/home/larry# echo $foo
hello there
/home/larry#
```

produces the same results as:

```
/home/larry# echo "hello there"
hello there
/home/larry#
```

These variables are internal to the shell, which means that only the shell can access them. This can be useful in shell scripts; if you need to keep track of a filename, for example, you can store it in a variable, as above. Using the set command displays a list of all defined shell variables.

However, the shell lets you **export** variables to the **environment.** The environment is the set of variables that are accessible by all commands that you execute. Once you define a variable inside the shell, exporting it makes the variable part of the environment as well. Use the export command to export a variable to the environment.

• Again, here we differ between bash and tcsh. If you use tcsh, another syntax is 3 used for setting environment variables (the setenv command is used). See the tcsh manual page for more information.

The environment is very important to the UNIX system. It lets you configure certain commands just by setting variables which the commands know about.

Here's a quick example. The environment variable PAGER is used by the man command and it specifies the command to use to display manual pages one screenful at a time. If you set PAGER to the name of a command, it uses that command to display the man pages, instead of more (which is the default).

Set PAGER to "cat". This causes output from man to be displayed to the screen all at once, without pausing between pages.

```
/home/larry# PAGER=cat
```

Now, export PAGER to the environment.

```
/home/larry# export PAGER
```

Try the command man ls. The man page should fly past your screen without pausing for you.

Now, if we set PAGER to "more", the more command is used to display the man page:

```
/home/larry# PAGER=more
```

Note that we don't have to use the export command after we change the value of PAGER. We only need to export a variable once; any changes made to it thereafter will automatically be propagated to the environment.

It is often necessary to quote strings in order to prevent the shell from treating various characters as special. For example, you need to quote a string in order to prevent the shell from interpreting the special meaning of characters such as "*", "?" or a space. There are many other characters that may need to be protected from interpretation. A detailed explanation and desription of quoting is described in SSC's *Bourne Shell Tutorial*.

The manual pages for a particular command tell you if the command uses any environment variables. For example, the man man page explains that PAGER is used to specify the pager command.

Some commands share environment variables. For example, many commands use the EDITOR environment variable to specify the default editor to use when one is needed. The environment is also used to keep track of important information about your login session. An example is the HOME environment variable, which contains the name of your home directory:

```
/home/larry/papers# echo $HOME

/home/larry
```

Another interesting environment variable is PS1, which defines the main shell prompt. For example:

```
/home/larry# PS1="Your command, please: "
Your command, please:
```

To set the prompt back (which contains the current working directory followed by a "#" symbol):

Your command, please: PS1="\ w # "

/home/larry#

The bash manual page describes the syntax used for setting the prompt.
The PATH **environment variable.** When you use the ls command, how does the shell find the ls executable itself? In fact, ls is in /bin on most systems. The shell uses the environment variable PATH to locate executable files for commands you type.

For example, your PATH variable may be set to:

/bin:/usr/bin:/usr/local/bin:.

This is a list of directories for the shell to search, each directory separated by a ":". When you use the command ls, the shell first looks for /bin/ls, then /usr/bin/ls,and so on.

Note that the PATH has nothing to do with finding regular files. For example, if you use the command:

/home/larry# cp foo bar

the shell does not use PATH to locate the files foo and bar—those filenames are assumed to be complete. The shell only uses PATH to locate the cp executable.

This saves you time, and means that you don't have to remember where all the command executables are stored. On many systems, executables are scattered about in many places, such as /usr/bin, /bin,or/usr/local/bin. Rather than give the command's full pathname (such as /usr/bin/cp), you can set PATH to the list of directories that you want the shell to automatically search.

Notice that PATH contains ".", which is the current working directory. This lets you create a shell script or program and run it as a command from your current directory without having to specify it directly (as in ./makebook). If a directory isn't in your PATH, then the shell will not search it for commands to run; this also includes the current directory.

1.14.3 Shell initialization scripts.

In addition to the shell scripts that you create, there are a number of scripts that the shell itself uses for certain purposes. The most important of these are **initialization scripts**, which are scripts executed by the shell when you log in.

The initialization scripts themselves are simply shell scripts. However, they initialize your environment by executing commands automatically when you log in. If you always use the mail command to check your mail when you log in, you place the command in the initialization script so it will execute automatically.

Both bash and tcsh distinguish between a **login shell** and other invocations of the shell. A login shell is a shell invoked when you log in. Usually, it's the only shell you'll use. However, if you "shell out" of another program like vi, you start another instance of the shell, which isn't your login shell. In addition, whenever you run a shell script, you automatically start another instance of the shell to execute the script.

The initialization files used by bash are: /etc/profile (set up by the system administrator and executed by all bash users at login time), $HOME/.bash profile (executed by a login bash session), and $HOME/.bashrc (executed by all non-login instances of bash). If .bash profile is not present, .profile is used in-stead.
tcsh uses the following initialization scripts: /etc/csh.login (executed by all tcsh users at login time), $HOME/.tcshrc (executed at login time and by all new instances of tcsh), and $HOME/.login (executed at login time, following .tcshrc).
If .tcshrc is not present, .cshrc is used instead.

A complete guide to shell programming would be beyond the scope of this book. See the manual pages for bash or tcsh to learn more about customizing the Linux environment.

1.15 So you want to strike out on your own ?

This chapter should give you enough information for basic Linux use. The manual pages are indispensable tools for learning about Linux. They may appear confusing at first, but if you dig beneath the surface, there is a wealth of information.
We also suggest that you read a general Linux reference book. Linux has more features than first meet the eye. Unfortunately, many of them are beyond the scope of this book. Other recommended Linux books are listed in Appendix A..

Chapter 2

System Administration

This chapter covers the most important things that you need to know about system administration under Linux in sufficient detail to start using the system comfortably. In order to keep the chapter manageable, it covers just the basics and omits many important details. The *Linux System Administrator's Guide*, by Lars Wirzenius (see Appendix A) provides considerably more detail on system administration topics. It will help you understand better how things work and hang together. At least, skim through the SAG so that you know what it contains and what kind of help you can expect from it.

2.1 The **root** account.

Linux differentiates between different users. What they can do to each other and the system is regulated. File permissions are arranged so that normal users can't delete or modify files in directories like /bin and /usr/bin. Most users protect their own files with the appropriate permissions so that other users can't access or modify them. (One wouldn't want anybody to be able to read one's love letters.) Each user is given an **account** that includes a user name and home directory. In addition, there are special, system defined accounts which have special privileges. The most important of these is the **root account**, which is used by the system administrator. By convention, the system administrator is the user, root.

There are no restrictions on root. He or she can read, modify, or delete any file on the system, change permissions and ownerships on any file, and run special programs like those which partition a hard drive or create file systems. The basic idea is that a person who cares for the system logs in as root to perform tasks that cannot be executed as a normal user. Because root can do anything, it is easy to make mistakes that have catastrophic consequences.

If a normal user tries inadvertently to delete all of the files in /etc, the system will not permit him or her to do so. However, if root tries to do the same thing, the system doesn't complain at all. It is very easy to trash a Linux system when using root. The best way to prevent accidents is:

- Sit on your hands before you press Enter for any command that is non-reversible. If you're about to clean out a directory, re-read the entire command to make sure that it is correct.

- Use a different prompt for the root account. root's .bashrc or .login file should set the shell prompt to something different than the standard user prompt. Many people reserve the character "#" in prompts for root and use the prompt character "$" for everyone else.
- Log in as root only when absolutely necessary. When you have finished your work as root, log out. The less you use the root account, the less likely you are to damage the system. You are less likely to confuse the privileges of root with those of a normal user.

Picture the root account as a special, magic hat that gives you lots of power, with which you can, by waving your hands, destroy entire cities. It is a good idea to be a bit careful about what you do with your hands. Because it is easy to wave your hands in a destructive manner, it is not a good idea to wear the magic hat when it is not needed, despite the wonderful feeling.

2.2 Booting the system.

Some people boot Linux with a floppy diskette that contains a copy of the Linux kernel. This kernel has the Linux root partition coded into it, so it knows where to look for the root file system. This is the type of floppy created by Slackware during installation, for example.

To create your own boot floppy, locate the kernel image on your hard disk. It should be in the file /vmlinuz,or/vmlinux. In some installations, /vmlinuz is a soft link to the actual kernel, so you may need to track down the kernel by following the links.

Once you know where the kernel is, set the root device of the kernel image to the name of your Linux root partition with the rdev command. The format of the command is:

```
rdev    kernel-name    root-device
```

where kernel-name is the name of the kernel image, and root-device is the name of the Linux root partition. For example, to set the root device in the kernel /vmlinuz to /dev/hda2, use the command:

```
# rdev /vmlinuz /dev/hda2
```

rdev can set other options in the kernel, like the default SVGA mode to use at boot time. The command:

```
# rdev    -h
```

prints a help message on the screen. After setting the root device, simply copy the kernel image to the floppy. Before copying data to any floppy, however, it's a good idea to use the MS-DOS FORMAT.COM or the Linux fdformat program to format the diskette. This lays down the sector and track information that is appropriate to the floppy's capacity.

Device driver files, as mentioned earlier, reside in the /dev directory. To copy the kernel in the file /etc/Image to the floppy in /dev/fd0, use the command:

```
# cp /vmlinuz /dev/fd0
```

This floppy should now boot Linux.

2.2.1 Using LILO.

LILO is a separate boot loader which resides on your hard disk. It is executed when the system boots from the hard drive and can automatically boot Linux from a kernel image stored there.

LILO can also be used as a first-stage boot loader for several operating systems, which allows you to select the operating system you to boot, like Linux or MS-DOS. With LILO, the default operating system is booted unless you press Shift during the boot-up sequence, or if the prompt directive is given in the lilo.conf file. In either case, you will be provided with a boot prompt, where you type the name of the operating system to boot (such as "linux"or"msdos"). If you press Tab at the boot prompt, a list of operating systems that the system knows about will be provided.

The easy way to install LILO is to edit the configuration file, /etc/lilo.conf.The command:

```
# /sbin / lilo
```

rewrites the modified lilo.conf configuration to the boot sector of the hard disk, and must be run every time you modify lilo.conf.

The LILO configuration file contains a "stanza" for each operating system that you want to boot. The best way to demonstrate this is with an example. The lilo.conf file below is for a system which has a Linux root partition on /dev/hda1 and a MS-DOS partition on /dev/hda2 :

```
# Tell LILO to modify the boot record on /dev/hda (the first
# non-SCSI hard drive). If you boot from a drive other than
# /dev/hda, change the following line.
boot = /dev/hda

# Set a sane videomode
vga = normal

# Set the delay in milli-seconds. This is the time you have to
# press the 'SHIFT' key to bring up the LILO: prompt if you
```

```
# haven't specified the 'prompt' directive.
delay = 60

# Name of the boot loader. No reason to modify this unless you're
# doing some serious hacking on LILO.
install = /boot/boot.b

# This forces LILO to prompt you for the OS you want to boot.
# A 'TAB' key at the LILO: prompt will display a list of the OSs
# available to boot according to the names given in the 'label='
# directives below.
prompt

# Have LILO perform some optimization.
compact

# Stanza for Linux root partition on /dev/hda1.
image = /vmlinuz # Location of kernel

label = linux # Name of OS (for the LILO boot menu)
root = /dev/hda1 # Location of root partition
read-only # Mount read only

# Stanza for MSDOS partition on /dev/hda2.
other = /dev/hda2 # Location of partition
table = /dev/hda # Location of partition table for /dev/hda2
label = msdos # Name of OS (for boot menu)
```

The first operating system stanza is the default operating system for LILO to boot. Also note that if you use the "root =" line, above, there's no reason to use rdev to set the root partition in the kernel image. LILO sets it at boot time.

The Microsoft Windows '95 installer will overwrite the LILO boot manager. If you are going to install Windows '95 on your system after installing LILO, make sure to create a boot disk first (see Section 4.2). With the boot disk, you can boot Linux and re-install LILO after the Windows '95 installation is completed. This is done simply by typing, as root, the command /sbin/lilo, as in the step above. Partitions with Windows '95 can be configured to boot with LILO using the same lilo.conf entries that are used to boot the MS-DOS partition.

The *Linux FAQ* (see Appendix A) provides more information on LILO, including how to use LILO to boot with the OS/2 Boot Manager.

2.3 Shutting down.

Shutting down a Linux system can be tricky. You should never simply turn off the power or press the reset switch. The kernel keeps track of the disk read/write data in memory buffers. If you reboot the system without giving the kernel a chance to write its buffers to disk, you can corrupt the file systems.

Other precautions are taken during shutdown as well. All processes are sent a signal that allows them to die gracefully (by first writing and closing all files, for example). File systems are unmounted for safety. If you wish, the system can also alert users that the system is going down and give them a chance to log off.

The easiest way to shut down is with the shutdown command. The format of the command is:

```
shutdown     time     warning-message
```

The time argument is the time to shut down the system (in the format *hh:mm:ss*), and warning-message is a message displayed on all user's terminals before shutdown. Alternately,you can specify the time as "now", to shut down immediately. The -r option may be given to shutdown to reboot the system after shutting down.

For example, to shut down and reboot the system at 8:00 pm, use the command:

```
# shutdown    -r    20:00
```

The command halt may be used to force an immediate shutdown without any warning messages or grace period. halt is useful if you're the only one using the system and want to shut down and turn off the machine.

Don't turn off the power or reboot the system until you see the message:

```
The    system    is    halted
```

It is very important that you shut down the system, "cleanly," using the shutdown or halt command. On some systems, pressing Ctrl - Alt - Del will be trapped and cause a shutdown. On other systems, using the "Vulcan nerve pinch" will reboot the system immediately and cause disaster.

2.3.1 The / etc / inittab file.

Immediately after Linux boots and the kernel mounts the root file system, the first program that the system executes is init. This program is responsible for starting the system startup scripts, and modifies the system operatiing from its initial boot-up state to its standard, multiuser state. init also spawns the login: shells for all of the tty devices on the system, and specifies other startup and shutdown procedures.

After startup, init remains quietly in the background, monitoring and if necessary altering the running state of the system. There are many details that the init program must see to. These tasks are defined in the /etc/inittab file. A sample /etc/inittab file is shown below.

Modifying the /etc/inittab file incorrectly can prevent you from logging in to 3 your system. At the very least, when changing the /etc/inittab file, keep on hand a copy of the original, correct file, and a boot/root emergency floppy in case you make a mistake :

```
#
# inittab
This file describes how the INIT process should set up
# the system in a certain run-level.
#
# Version: @(#)inittab 2.04 17/05/93 MvS
# 2.10 02/10/95 PV
#
# Author:
Miquel van Smoorenburg, <miquels@drinkel.nl.mugnet.org>
# Modified by: Patrick J. Volkerding, <volkerdi@ftp.cdrom.com>
# Minor modifications by:
# Robert Kiesling, <kiesling@terracom.net>
#
# Default runlevel.
id:3:initdefault:

# System initialization (runs when system boots).
si:S:sysinit:/etc/rc.d/rc.S

# Script to run when going single user (runlevel 1).
su:1S:wait:/etc/rc.d/rc.K

# Script to run when going multi user.
rc:23456:wait:/etc/rc.d/rc.M

# What to do at Ctrl-Alt-Del
ca::ctrlaltdel:/sbin/shutdown -t5 -rfn now

# Runlevel 0 halts the system.
l0:0:wait:/etc/rc.d/rc.0

# Runlevel 6 reboots the system.
l6:6:wait:/etc/rc.d/rc.6
```

```
# What to do when power fails (shutdown to single user).
pf::powerfail:/sbin/shutdown -f +5 "THE POWER IS FAILING"

# If power is back before shutdown, cancel the running shutdown.
pg:0123456:powerokwait:/sbin/shutdown -c "THE POWER IS BACK"

# If power comes back in single user mode, return to multi user mode.
ps:S:powerokwait:/sbin/init 5

# The getties in multi user mode on consoles an serial lines.
#
# NOTE NOTE NOTE adjust this to your getty or you will not be
# able to login !!
#
# Note: for 'agetty' you use linespeed, line.
# for 'getty_ps' you use line, linespeed and also use 'gettydefs'
c1:1235:respawn:/sbin/agetty 38400 tty1 linux
c2:1235:respawn:/sbin/agetty 38400 tty2 linux
c3:1235:respawn:/sbin/agetty 38400 tty3 linux
c4:1235:respawn:/sbin/agetty 38400 tty4 linux
c5:1235:respawn:/sbin/agetty 38400 tty5 linux
c6:12345:respawn:/sbin/agetty 38400 tty6 linux

# Serial lines
# s1:12345:respawn:/sbin/agetty -L 9600 ttyS0 vt100
s2:12345:respawn:/sbin/agetty -L 9600 ttyS1 vt100

# Dialup lines
d1:12345:respawn:/sbin/agetty -mt60 38400,19200,9600,2400,1200 ttyS0 vt100
#d2:12345:respawn:/sbin/agetty -mt60 38400,19200,9600,2400,1200 ttyS1 vt100

# Runlevel 4 used to be for an X-window only system, until we discovered
# that it throws init into a loop that keeps your load avg at least 1 all
# the time. Thus, there is now one getty opened on tty6. Hopefully no one
# will notice. ;^)
# It might not be bad to have one text console anyway, in case something
# happens to X.
x1:4:wait:/etc/rc.d/rc.4

# End of /etc/inittab
```

At startup, this /etc/inittab starts six virtual consoles, a login: prompt on the modem attached to /dev/ttyS0,andalogin: prompt on a character terminal connected via a RS-232 serial line to /dev/ttyS1.

Briefly, init steps through a series of **run levels,** which correspond to various operational states of the system. Run level 1 is entered immediately after the system boots,

run levels 2 and 3 are the normal, multiuser operation modes of the system, run level 4 starts the X Window System via the X display manager xdm, and run level 6 reboots the system. The run level(s) associated with each command are the second item in each line of the /etc/inittab file.

For example, the line:

```
s2:12345:respawn:/sbin/agetty -L 9600 ttyS1 vt100
```

will maintain a login prompt on a serial terminal for runlevels 1–5. The "s2" before the first colon is a symbolic identifier used internally by init. respawn is an init keyword that is often used in conjunction with serial terminals. If, after a certain period of time, the agetty program, which spawns the terminal's login: prompt, does not receive input at the terminal, the program times out and terminates execution. "respawn" tells init to re-execute agetty, ensuring that there is always a login: prompt at the terminal, regardless of whether someone has logged in. The remaining parameters are passed directly to agetty and instruct it to spawn the login shell, the data rate of the serial line, the serial device, and the terminal type, as defined in /etc/termcap or /etc/terminfo.

The /sbin/agetty program handles many details related to terminal I/O on the system. There are several different versions that are commonly in use on Linux systems.

They include mgetty, psgetty, or simply, getty.
In the case of the /etc/inittab line:

```
d1:12345:respawn:/sbin/agetty -mt60
38400,19200,9600,2400,1200 ttyS0 vt100
```

which allows users to log in via a modem connected to serial line /dev/ttyS0, the /sbin/agetty parameters "-mt60" allow the system to step through all of the modem speeds that a caller dialing into the system might use, and to shut down /sbin/agetty if there is no connection after 60 seconds. This is called **negotiating** a connection. The supported modem speeds are enumerated on the command line also, as well as the serial line to use, and the terminal type. Of course, both of the modems must support the data rate which is finally negotiated by both machines.

Many important details have been glossed over in this section. The tasks that /etc/inittab maintains would comprise a book of their own. For further information, the manual pages of the init and agetty programs, and the Linux Documentation Project's Serial HOWTO, available from the sources listed in Appendix A, are starting points.

2.4 Managing file systems.

Another task of the system administrator is caring for file systems. Most of this job entails periodically checking the file systems for damage or corrupted files. Many Linux systems also automatically check the file systems at boot time.

2.4.1 Mounting file systems.

Before a file system is accessible to the system, it must be **mounted** on a directory. For example, if you have a file system on a floppy, you must mount it under a directory like /mnt in order to access the files on the floppy. After mounting the file system, all of the files in the file system appear in that directory. After unmounting the file system, the directory (in this case, /mnt) will be empty.

The same is true of file systems on the hard drive. The system automatically mounts file systems on your hard drive at bootup time. The so-called "root file system" is mounted on the directory /. If you have a separate file system for /usr, it is mounted on /usr. If you only have a root file system, all files (including those in /usr) exist on that file system. mount and umount (not *unmount*) are used to mount and unmount file systems. The command:

```
mount   -av
```

is executed automatically by the file /etc/rc at boot time, or by the file /etc/rc.d/boot on some Linux systems. The file /etc/fstab provides information on file systems and mount points. An example /etc/fstab file is:

```
# device      directory    type    options
/dev / hda2   /            ext2    defaults
/dev/hda3     /usr         ext2    defaults
/dev / hda4   none         swap    sw
/proc         /proc        proc    none
```

The first field, device, is the name of the partition to mount. The second field is the mount point. The third field is the file system type, like ext2 (for ext2fs) or minix (for Minix file systems). Table 4.1 lists the various file system types that are mountable under Linux.

Not all of these file system types may be available on your system, because the kernel must have support for them compiled in.

This table is current as of kernel version 2.0.33.

File system	Type name	Comment
Second Extended File system	ext2	Most common Linux file system.
Extended File system	ext	Superseded by ext2.
Minix File system	minix	Original Minix file system; rarely used.
Xia File system	xia	Like ext2, but rarely used.
UMSDOS File system	umsdos	Used to install Linux on an MS-DOS partition.
MS-DOS File system	msdos	Used to access MS-DOS files.
/proc File system	proc	Provides process information for ps,etc.
ISO 9660 File system	iso9660	Format used by most CD-ROMs.
Xenix File system	xenix	Used to access files from Xenix.
System V File system	sysv	Used to access files from System V variants for the x86.
Coherent File system	coherent	Used to access files from Coherent.
HPFS File system	hpfs	Read-only access for HPFS partitions (DoubleS

Table 2.1: Linux File system Types

The last field of the fstab file are the mount options. This is normally set to defaults.

Swap partitions are included in the /etc/fstab file. They have a mount directory of none, and type swap.Theswapon -a command, which is executed from /etc/rc or /etc/init.d/boot, is used to enable swapping on all of the swap devices that are listed in /etc/fstab.

The /etc/fstab file contains one special entry for the /proc file system. The /proc file system is used to store information about system processes, available memory, and so on. If /proc is not mounted, commands like ps will not work.

- The mount command may be used only by root. This ensures security on the system. 3 You wouldn't want regular users mounting and unmounting file systems on a whim. Several software packages are available which allow non-root users to mount and unmount file systems, especially floppies, without compromising system security.

The mount -av command actually mounts all of the file systems other than the root file system (in the table above, /dev/hda2). The root file system is automatically mounted at boot time by the kernel.

Instead of using mount -av, you can mount a file system by hand. The command:

```
# mount -t ext2 /dev/hda3 /usr
```

is equivalent to mounting the file system with the entry for /dev/hda3 in the example

/etc/fstab file, above.

2.4.2 Device driver names.

In addition to the partition names listed in the /etc/fstab file, Linux recognizes a number of fixed and removable media devices. They are classified by type, interface, and the order they are installed. For example, the first hard drive on your system, if it is an IDE or older MFM hard drive, is controlled by the device driver pointed to by /dev/hda.The first partition on the hard drive is /dev/hda1, the second partition is /dev/hda2, the third partition is /dev/hda3, and so on. The first partition of the second IDE drive is often /dev/hdb1, the second partition /dev/hdb2, and so on. The naming scheme for the most commonly installed IDE drives for Intel-architecture, ISA and PCI bus machines, is given in Table 4.2.

Device driver	Drive
/dev/hda	Master IDE drive, primary IDE bus.
/dev/hdb	Slave IDE drive, primary IDE bus.
/dev/hdc	Master IDE drive, secondary IDE bus.
/dev/hdd	Slave IDE drive, secondary IDE bus.

Table 2.2: IDE device driver names

CD-ROM and tape drives which use the extended IDE/ATAPI drive interface also use these device names.

Many machines, however, including high-end personal computer workstations, and machines based on Digital Equipment Corporation's Alpha processor, use the Small Computer System Interface (SCSI). The naming conventions for SCSI devices are somewhat different than that given above, due the greater flexibility of SCSI addressing. The first SCSI hard drive on a system is /dev/sda, the second SCSI drive is /dev/sdb, and so on. A list of common SCSI devices is given in Table 4.3.

Note that SCSI CD-ROM and tape drives are named differently than SCSI hard drives. Removable SCSI media, like the Iomega Zip drive, follow naming conventions for non-removable SCSI drives :

Device driver	Drive
/dev/sda	First SCSI hard drive.
/dev/sdb	Second SCSI hard drive.
/dev/st0	First SCSI tape drive.
/dev/st1	Second SCSI tape drive.
/dev/scd0	First SCSI CD-ROM drive.
/dev/scd1	Second SCSI CD-ROM drive.

Table 2.3: SCSI device drivers

Floppy disk drives use still another naming scheme, outlined elsewhere in this book.

2. 4. 3 Checking file systems.

It is usually a good idea to check your file systems for damaged or corrupted files every now and then. Some systems automatically check their file systems at boot time (with the appropriate commands in /etc/rc or /etc/init.d/boot).

The command used to check a file system depends on the type of the file system. For ext2fs file systems (the most commonly used type), this command is e2fsck. For example, the command:

```
# e2fsck  -av /  dev /  hda 2
```

checks the ext2fs file system on /dev/hda2 and automatically corrects any errors.

It is usually a good idea to unmount a file system before checking it, and necessary, if e2fsck is to perform any repairs on the file system. The command:

```
# umount /dev/hda2
```

unmounts the file system on /dev/hda2. The one exception is that you cannot unmount the root file system. In order to check the root file system when it's unmounted, you should use a maintenance boot/root diskette. You also cannot unmount a file system if any of the files which it contains are "busy"—that is, in use by a running process. For example, you cannot unmount a file system if any user's current working directory is on that file system. You will instead receive a "Device busy" error message.

Other file system types use different forms of the e2fsck command, like efsck and xfsck. On some systems, you can simply use the command fsck, which automatically determines the file system type and executes the appropriate command.

If e2fsck reports that it performed repairs on a mounted file system, you *must* reboot 3 the system immediately. You should give the command shutdown -r to perform the reboot. This allows the system to re-synchronize the information about the file system after e2fsck modifies it.

The /proc file system never needs to be checked in this manner. /proc is a memory file system and is managed directly by the kernel.

2 . 5 Using a swap file.

Instead of reserving a separate partition for swap space, you can use a swap file. However, you need to install Linux and get everything running before you create the swap file.

With Linux installed, you can use the following commands to create a swap file. The command below creates a swap file of size 8208 blocks (about 8 Mb) :

```
# dd if=/dev/zero of=/swap bs=1024 count=8208
```

This command creates the swap file, /swap.The"count=" parameter is the size of the swap file in blocks :

```
# mkswap /swap 8208
```

This command initializes the swap file. Again, replace the name and size of the swapfile with the appropriate values :

```
# sync

# swapon /swap
```

Now the system is swapping on the file /swap.Thesync command ensures that the file has been written to disk.

One major drawback to using a swap file is that all access to the swap file is done through the file system. This means the blocks which make up the swap file may not be contiguous. Performance may not be as good as a swap partition, where the blocks are always contiguous and I/O requests are made directly to the device.

Another drawback of large swap files is the greater chance that the file system will be corrupted if something goes wrong. Keeping the regular file systems and swap partitions separate prevents this from happening.

Swap files can be useful if you need to use more swap space temporarily. If you're compiling a large program and would like to speed things up somewhat, you can create a temporary swap file and use it in addition to the regular swap space.

To remove a swap file, first use swapoff, as in:

```
# swapoff / swap
```

Then the file can be deleted:

```
# rm / swap
```

Each swap file or partition may be as large as 128 megabytes, but you may use up to 8 swap files or partitions on your system.

2.6 Managing users.

Even if you're the only user on your system, it's important to understand the aspects of user management under Linux. You should at least have an account for yourself (other than root) to do most of your work.

Each user should have his or her own account. It is seldom a good idea to have several people share the same account. Security an issue, and accounts uniquely identify users to the system. You must be able to keep track of who is doing what.

2.6.1 User management concepts.

The system keeps track of the following information about each user:
user name This identifier is unique for every user. Example user names are larry, karl,andmdw. Letters and digits may be used, as well as " "and"." (period). User names are usually limited to 8 characters in length.

user ID This number, abbreviated UID, is unique for every user. The system generally keeps track of users by UID, not user name.

group ID This number, abbreviated GID, is the user's default group. In Section 3.10, we discuss group permissions. Each user belongs to one or more groups as defined by the system administrator.

password This is the user's encrypted password. The passwd command is used to set and change user passwords.

full name The user's "real name," or "full name," is stored along with the user name. For example, the user schmoj may be "Joe Schmo" in real life.

home directory
This is the directory the user is initially placed in at login, and where his or her personal files are stored. Every user is given a home directory, which is commonly located under /home.

login shell The shell that is started for the user at login. Examples are /bin/bash and /bin/tcsh.

This information is stored in the file /etc/passwd. Each line in the file has the format:

user name:encrypted password:UID:GID:full name:home

directory:login shell

An example might be:

kiwi:Xv8Q981g71oKK:102:100:Laura

Poole:/home/kiwi:/bin/bash

In this example, the first field, "kiwi," is the user name.

The next field, "Xv8Q981g71oKK", is the encrypted password. Passwords are not stored on the system in human-readable format. The password is encrypted using itself as the secret key. In other words, one must know the password in order to decrypt it. This form of encryption is reasonably secure.

Some systems use "shadow passwords," in which password information is stored in the file /etc/shadow. Because /etc/passwd is world-readable, /etc/shadow provides some degree of extra security because its access permissions are much more restricted.

Shadow passwords also provide other features, like password expiration.

The third field, "102", is the UID. This must be unique for each user. The fourth field, "100", is the GID. This user belongs to the group numbered 100. Group information is stored in the file /etc/group. See Section 4.6.5 for more information.

The fifth field is the user's full name, "Laura Poole". The last two fields are the user's home directory (/home/kiwi), and login shell (/bin/bash), respectively. It is not required that the user's home directory be given the same name as the user name. It simply helps identify the directory.

2.6.2 Adding users.

When adding users, several steps must be taken. First, the user is given an entry in /etc/passwd, with a unique user name and UID. The GID, full name, and other information must be specified. The user's home directory must be created, and the permissions on the directory set so that the user owns the directory. Shell initialization files must be installed in the home directory, and other files must be configured system-wide (for example, a spool for the user's incoming e-mail).

It is not difficult to add users by hand, but when you are running a system with many users, it is easy to forget something. The easiest way to add users is to use an interactive program which updates all of the system files automatically. The name of this program is useradd or adduser, depending on what software is installed.

The adduser command takes its information from the file /etc/adduser.conf, which defines a standard, default configuration for all new users.

A typical /etc/adduser.conf file is shown below:

```
# /etc/adduser.conf: 'adduser' configuration.
# See adduser(8) and adduser.conf(5) for full documentation.

# The DSHELL variable specifies the default login shell on your
# system.
DSHELL=/bin/bash

# The DHOME variable specifies the directory containing users' home
# directories.
DHOME=/home

# If GROUPHOMES is "yes", then the home directories will be created as
# /home/groupname/user.
GROUPHOMES=no

# If LETTERHOMES is "yes", then the created home directories will have
# an extra directory - the first letter of the user name. For example:
# /home/u/user.
LETTERHOMES=no

# The SKEL variable specifies the directory containing "skeletal" user
# files; in other words, files such as a sample .profile that will be
# copied to the new user's home directory when it is created.
SKEL=/etc/skel

# FIRST_SYSTEM_UID to LAST_SYSTEM_UID inclusive is the range for UIDs
# for dynamically allocated administrative and system accounts.
FIRST_SYSTEM_UID=100
LAST_SYSTEM_UID=999

# FIRST_UID to LAST_UID inclusive is the range of UIDs of dynamically
# allocated user accounts.
FIRST_UID=1000
LAST_UID=29999

# The USERGROUPS variable can be either "yes" or "no". If "yes" each
# created user will be given their own group to use as a default, and
# their home directories will be g+s. If "no", each created user will
# be placed in the group whose gid is USERS_GID (see below).
USERGROUPS=yes
```

```
# If USERGROUPS is "no", then USERS_GID should be the GID of the group
# 'users' (or the equivalent group) on your system.
USERS_GID=100

# If QUOTAUSER is set, a default quota will be set from that user with
# 'edquota -p QUOTAUSER newuser'
QUOTAUSER=""
```

In addition to defining preset variables that the *adduser* command uses, /etc/adduser.conf also specifies where default system configuration files for each user are located. In this example, they are located in the directory /etc/skel, as defined by the SKEL= line, above. Files which are placed in this directory, like a system-wide, default .profile, .tcshrc,or.bashrc file, will be automatically installed in a new user's home directory by the adduser command.

2.6.3 Deleting users.

Deleting users can be accomplished with the commands userdel or deluser,depending on the software installed on the system.

If you'd like to temporarily "disable" a user from logging in to the system without deleting his or her account, simply prepend an asterisk ("*") to the password field in /etc/passwd. For example, changing kiwi's : /etc/passwd entry to :

kiwi:*Xv8Q981g71oKK:102:100:Laura

Poole : / home /kiwi : / bin / bash

prevents kiwi from logging in.

2.6.4 Setting user attributes.

After you have created a user, you may need to change attributes for that user, like the home directory or password. The easiest way to do this is to change the values directly in /etc/passwd. To set a user's password, use *passwd.* The command :

```
# passwd larry
```

will change larry's password. Only root may change other users' passwords in this manner. Users can change their own passwords, however.

On some systems, the commands chfn and chsh allow users to set their own full name and login shell attributes. If not, the system administrator must change these attributes for them.

2.6.5 Groups.

As mentioned above, each user belongs to one or more groups. The only real importance of group relationships pertains to file permissions. As you'll recall from Section 3.10, each file has a "group ownership" and a set of group permissions which defines how users in that group may access the file.

There are several system-defined groups, like bin, mail,and sys. Users should not belong to any of these groups; they are used for system file permissions. Instead, users should belong to an individual group like users. You can also maintain several groups for users, like student, staff,and faculty.

The file /etc/group contains information about groups. The format of each line is:

group name : password : GID : other members

Some example groups might be:

root : * : 0 :
users : * : 100 : mdw , larry
guest : * : 200:
other : * : 250:kiwi

The first group, *root*, is a special system group reserved for the *root* account. The next group, *users*, is for regular users. It has a GID of 100. The users *mdw* and *larry* are given access to this group. Remember that in */etc/passwd* each user was given. a default GID. However, users may belong to more than one group, by adding their user names to other group lines in */etc/group.*The *groups* command lists what groups you are given access to.

The third group, *guest,* is for guest users, and *other* is for "other" users. The user kiwi is given access to this group as well.

The "password" field of */etc/group* is sometimes used to set a password on group access. This is seldom necessary. To protect users from changing into privileged groups (with the *newgroup* command), set the password field to "*" .

The commands *addgroup* or *groupadd* may be used to add groups to your system. Usually, it's easier just to add entries in */etc/group* yourself, as no other configuration needs to be done to add a group. To delete a group, simply delete its entry in */etc/group.*

2.6.6 System administration responsibilities.

Because the system administrator has so much power and responsibility, when some users have their first opportunity to login as *root.* either on a Linux system or elsewhere, the tendency is to abuse *root's* privileges. I have known so-called "system administrators" who read other users' mail, delete users' files without warning, and generally behave like children when given such a powerful "toy".

Because the administrator has such power on the system, it takes a certain amount of maturity and self-control to use the *root* account as it was intended—to run the system. There is an unspoken code of honor which exists between the system administrator and the users on the system. How would you feel if your system administrator was reading your e-mail or looking over your files? There is still no strong legal precedent for electronic privacy on time-sharing computer systems. On UNIX systems, the *root* user has the ability to forego all security and privacy mechanisms on the system. It is important that the system administrator develop a trusting relationship with his or her users. I can't stress that enough.

2.6.7 Coping with users.

System administrators can take two stances when dealing with abusive users: they can be either paranoid or trusting. The paranoid system administrator usually causes more harm than he or she prevents. One of my favorite sayings is, "Never attribute to malice anything which can be attributed to stupidity." Put another way, most users don't have the ability or knowledge to do real harm on the system. Ninety percent of the time, when a user is. causing trouble on the system (for instance, by filling up the user partition with large files, or running multiple instances of a large program), the user is simply unaware that he or she is creation a problem. I have come down on users who were causing a great deal of trouble, but they were simply acting out of ignorance—not malice.

When you deal with users who cause potential trouble, don't be accusatory. The burden of proof is on you; that is, the rule of "innocent until proven guilty" still holds. It is best to simply talk to the user and question him or her about the trouble instead of being confrontational. The last thing you want is to be on the user's bad side. This will raise a lot of suspicion about you—the system administrator—running the system correctly. If a user believes that you distrust or dislike them, they might accuse you of deleting files or breaching privacy on the system. This is certainly not the kind of position you want to be in.

If you find that a user is attempting to "crack," or otherwise intentionally do harm to the system, don't return the malicious behavior with malice of your own. Instead, provide a warning, but be flexible. In many cases, you may catch a user "in the act" of doing harm to the system. Give them a warning. Tell them not to let it happen again. However, if you *do* catch them causing harm again, be absolutely sure that it is intentional. I can't even begin to describe the number of cases where it appeared as though a user was causing trouble, when in fact it was either an accident or a fault of my own.

2.6.8 Setting the rules.

The best way to run a system is not with an iron fist. That may be how you run the military, but Linux is not designed for such discipline. It makes sense to lay down a few simple and flexible guidelines. The fewer rules you have, the less chance there is of breaking them. Even if your rules are perfectly reasonable and clear, users will still at times break them without intending to. This is especially true of new users learning the ropes of the system. It is not patently obvious that you shouldn't download a gigabyte of files and mail them to everyone on the system. Users need help to understand the rules and why they are there.

If you do specify usage guidelines for your system, make sure also that the rationale for a particular guideline is clear. If you don't, users will find all sorts of creative ways to get around the rule, and not know that they are breaking it.

2.6.9 What it all means.

We don't tell you how to run your system down to the last detail. That depends on how you're using the system. If you have many users, things are much different than if you have. only a few users, or if you're the only user on the system. However, it's always a good idea—in any situation—to understand what being the system administrator *really* means.

Being the system administrator doesn't make a Linux wizard. There are many administrators who know very little about Linux. Likewise, many "normal" users know more about Linux than any system administrator. Also, being the system administrator does not allow one to use malice against users. Just because the system gives administrators the ability to mess with user files does not mean that he or she has a right to do so.

Being the system administrator is not a big deal. It doesn't matter if your system is a tiny 386 or a Cray supercomputer. Running the system is the same, regardless. Knowing the root password isn't going to earn you money or fame. It will allow you to maintain the system and keep it running. That's it.

2.7 Archiving and compressing files.

Before we can talk about backups, we need to introduce the tools used to archive files on UNIX systems.

2.7.1 Using tar.

The tar command is most often used to archive files. Its command syntax is :

tar options files

where options is the list of commands and options for tar,andfiles is the list of files to add or extract from the archive.

For example, the command:

```
# tar cvf backup.tar /etc
```

packs all of the files in */etc* into the tar archive *backup.tar.* The first argument to *tar,"cvf",* is the *tar* "command." *c* tells *tar* to create a new archive file. *v* forces *tar* to use verbose mode, printing each file name as it is archived. The *"f"* option tells *tar* that the next argument, *backup.tar,* is the name of the archive to create. The rest of the arguments to tar are the file and directory names to add to the archive.

The command :

```
# tar xvf backup.tar.
```

will extract the tar file *backup.tar* in the current directory.

• Old files with the same name are overwritten when extracting files into an existing 3 directory.

Before extracting tar files it is important to know where the files should be un-packed. Let's say that you archive the following files: /etc/hosts, /etc/group, and /etc/passwd. If you use the command :

```
# tar cvf backup.tar /etc/hosts /etc/group /etc/passwd
```

the directory name /etc/ is added to the beginning of each file name. In order to extract the files to the correct location, use :

```
#cd /

# tar xvf backup.tar
```

because files are extracted with the path name saved in the archive file.

However, if you archive the files with the command:

```
# cd /etc

# tar cvf hosts group passwd
```

the directory name is not saved in the archive file. Therefore, you need to *"cd /etc"* before extracting the files. As you can see, how the tar file is created makes a large difference in where you extract it. The command :

```
# tar tvf backup.tar
```

can be used to display a listing of the archive's files without extracting them. You can see what directory the files in the archive are stored relative to, and extract the archive in the correct location.

2.7.2 gzip and compress.

Unlike archiving programs for MS-DOS, tar does not automatically compress files as it archives them. If you are archiving two, 1-megabyte files, the resulting tar file is two megabytes in size. The gzip command compresses a file (it need not be a tar file). The command :

```
# gzip -9 backup.tar
```

compresses backup.tar and leaves you with backup.tar.gz, a compressed version of the file. The -9 switch tells gzip to use the highest compression factor.
The gunzip command may be used to uncompress a gzipped file. Equivalently, you may use "gzip -d".

gzip is a relatively new tool in the UNIX community. For many years, the *compress* command was used instead. However, because of several factors, including a software patent dispute against the *compress* data compression algorithm, and the fact that gzip is much more efficient, *compress is* being phased out.

Files that are output by *compress* end in ".Z." backup.tar.Z is the compressed version of *backup.tar*, while *backup.tar.gz is* the gzipped version
2
.The *uncompress* command is used to expand a compressed file. It is equivalent to *"compress -d." gunzip* knows how to handle compressed files as well.

2.7.3 Putting them together.

To archive a group of files and compress the result, use the commands :

```
# tar cvf backup.tar /etc

# gzip -9 backup.tar
```

The result is *backup.tar.gz.* To unpack this file, use the reverse commands :

```
# gunzip backup.tar.gz

# tar xvf backup.tar
```

Always make sure that you are in the correct directory before unpacking a tar file. You can use some Linux cleverness to do this on one command line :

```
# tar cvf - /etc j gzip -9c > backup.tar.gz
```

Here, we send the tar file to "-", which stands for tar's standard output. This is piped to gzip, which compresses the incoming tar file. The result is saved in backup.tar.gz. The -c option tells gzip to send its output to standard output, which is redirected to backup.tar.gz.

A single command to unpack this archive would be :

```
# gunzip -c backup.tar.gz j tar xvf -
```

Again, gunzip uncompresses the contents of backup.tar.gz and sends the resulting tar file to standard output. This is piped to tar, which reads "-", this time referring to tar's standard input.

Note:
For some time, the extension .z (lowercase "z") was used for gzipped files. The conventional gzip extension is now .gz..

Happily, the tar command also includes the z option to automatically compress/ uncompress files on the fly, using the gzip compression algorithm.

The command :

```
# tar cvfz backup.tar.gz /etc
```

is equivalent to :

```
# tar cvf backup.tar /etc

# gzip backup.tar
```

Just as the command :

```
# tar xvfz backup.tar.Z
```

may be used instead of :

```
# uncompress backup.tar.Z
```

```
# tar xvf backup.tar
```

Refer to the *tar* and *gzip* manual pages for more information.

2.8 Using floppies and making backups.

Floppies are often used as backup media. If you don't have a tape drive connected to your system, floppy disks can be used (although they are slower and somewhat less reliable).

As mentioned earlier, floppy diskettes must be formatted with the MS-DOS

FORMAT.COM or the Linux fdformat program. This lays down the sector and track information that is appropriate to the floppy's capacity.

A few of the device names and formats of floppy disks which are accessible by Linux are given in Table 2.4.

Devices which begin with fd0 are the first floppy diskette drive, which is named the A: drive under MS-DOS. The driver file names of second floppy device begin with fd1. Generally, the Linux kernel can detect the format of a diskette that has already been formatted—you can simply use /dev/fd0 and let the system detect the format. But when you first use completely new, unformatted floppy disks, you may need to use the driver specification if the system can't detect the diskette's type.

A complete list of Linux devices and their device driver names is given in *Linux Allocated Devices,* by H. Peter Anvin (see Appendix A).

Floppy device driver	Format
/dev/fd0d360	Double density, 360 Kb, 5.25 inch.
/dev/fd0h1200	High density, 1.2 MB, 5.25 inch.
/dev/fd0h1440	High density, 1.44 MB, 3.5 inch.

Table 2.4: Linux floppy disk formats.

You can also use floppies to hold individual file systems and mount the floppy to access the data on it. See section 2.8.4.

2.8.1 Using floppies for backups.

The easiest way to make a backup using floppies is with *tar.* The command :

```
# tar cvfzM /dev/fd0 /
```

will make a complete backup of your system using the floppy drive */dev / fd0*. The"M" option to *tar* allows the backup to span multiple volumes; that is, when one floppy is full, *tar* will prompt for the next. The command :

```
# tar xvfzM /dev/fd0
```

restores the complete backup. This method can also be used with a tape drive connected to your system. See section 4.8.3.

Several other programs exist for making multiple-volume backups; the backflops program found on *tsx-11.mit.edu* may come in handy.

Making a complete backup of the system with floppies can be time and resource consuming. Many system administrators use an **incremental backup** policy. Every month, a complete backup is made, and every week only those files which have been modified in the last week are backed up. In this case, if you trash your system in the middle of the month, you can simply restore the last full monthly backup, and then restore the last weekly backups as needed.

The *find* command is useful for locating files which were modified after a certain date. Several scripts for managing incremental backups can be found on *sunsite.unc.edu.*

2.8.2 Backups with a Zip drive.

Making backups to a Zip drive is similar to making floppy backups, but because Zip disks commonly have a capacity of 98 Kb, it is feasible to use a single, mounted Zip disk for a single backup archive.

Zip drives are available with three different hardware interfaces: a SCSI interface, an IDE interface and a parallel port PPA interface. Zip drive support is not included as a pre-compiled Linux option, but it can be specified when building a custom kernel for your system.

The SCSI and PPA interface Zip drives use the SCSI interface and follow the naming conventions for other SCSI devices.

Zip disks are commonly pre-formatted with a MS-DOS file system. You can either use the existing MS-DOS filesystem, which must be supported by your Linux kernel, or use mke2fs or a similar program to write a Linux file system to the disk.

A Zip disk, when mounted as the first SCSI device, is /dev/sda4 :

```
# mount /dev/sda4 /mnt
```

It is often convenient to provide a separate mount point for Zip file systems; for example, /zip. The following steps, which must be executed as root, would create the mount point:

```
# mkdir /zip

# chmod 0755 /zip
```

Then you can use /zip for mounting the Zip file system.

Writing archives to Zip disks is similar to archiving to floppies. To archive and compress the /etc directory to a mounted Zip drive, the command used would be:

```
# tar zcvf /zip/etc.tgz /etc
```

This command could be executed from any directory because it specifies absolute path names. The archive name *etc.tgz* is necessary if the Zip drive contains a MS-DOS file system, because any files written to the disk must have names which conform to MS-DOS 8+3 naming conventions; otherwise, the file names will be truncated.

Similarly, extracting this archive requires the commands:

```
#cd /

# tar zxvf /zip/etc.tgz
```

To create, for example, an ext2 file system on a Zip drive, you would give the command (for an *unmounted* Zip disk) :

```
# mke2fs /dev/sda4
```

With a Zip drive mounted in this manner, with an ext2 file system, it is possible to back up entire file systems with a single command :

```
# tar zcvf /zip/local.tar.gz /usr/local
```

Note that backing up with tar is still preferable in many cases to simply making an archival copy with the cp -a command, because tar preserves the original files' modification times.

2.8.3 Making backups to tape devices.

Archiving to a streaming tape drive is similar to making a backup to a floppy file system, only to a different device driver. Tapes are also formatted and handled differently that floppy diskettes. Some representative tape device drivers for Linux systems are listed in Table 2.5:

Tape device driver	Format
/dev/rft0	QIC-117 tape, rewind on close.
/dev/nrft0	QIC-117 tape, no rewind on close.
/dev/tpqic11	QIC-11 tape, rewind on close.
/dev/ntpqic11	QIC-11 tape, no rewind on close.
/dev/qft0	Floppy tape drive, rewind on close.
/dev/nqft0	Floppy tape drive, no rewind on close.

Table 2.5: Tape device drivers.

Floppy tape drives use the floppy drive controller interface and are controlled by the ftape device driver, which is covered below. Installation of the ftape device driver module is described on page 221. SCSI tape devices are listed in Table 2.3.

To archive the /etc directory a tape device with tar, use the command:

```
# tar cvf /dev/qft0 /etc
```

Similarly, to extract the files from the tape, use the commands:

```
#cd /
# tar xvf /dev/qft0
```

These tapes, like diskettes, must be formatted before they can be used. The ftape driver can format tapes under Linux. To format a QIC-40 format tape, use the command:

```
# ftformat --format-parameter qic40-205ft --mode-auto

--omit-erase --discard-header
```

Other tape drives have their own formatting software. Check the hardware documentation for the tape drive or the documentation of the Linux device driver associated with it.

Before tapes can be removed from the drive, they must be rewound and the I/O buffers written to the tape. This is analogous to unmounting a floppy before ejecting it, because the tape driver also caches data in memory. The standard UNIX command to control tape drive operations is mt. Your system may not provide this command, depending on whether it has tape drive facilities. The ftape driver has a similar command, ftmt, which is used to control tape operations.

To rewind a tape before removing it, use the command:

```
# ftmt -f /dev/qft0 rewoffl
```

Of course, substitute the correct tape device driver for your system.

It is also a good idea to retension a tape after writing to it, because magnetic tapes are susceptible to stretch. The command:

```
# ftmt -f /dev/qft0 retension
```

To obtain the status of the tape device, with a formatted tape in the drive, give the command:

```
# ftmt -f /dev/qft0 status
```

2.8.4 Using floppies as file systems.

You can create a file system on a floppy as you would on a hard drive partition. For example:

```
# mke2fs /dev/fd0 1440
```

creates a file system on the floppy in /dev/fd0. The size of the file system must correspond to the size of the floppy. High-density 3.5" disks are 1.44 megabytes, or 1440 blocks, in size. High-density 5.25" disks are 1200 blocks. It is necessary to specify the size of the file system in blocks if the system cannot automatically detect the floppy's capacity.

In order to access the floppy, you must mount the file system contained on it. The command:

```
# mount /dev/fd0 /mnt
```

will mount the floppy in /dev/fd0 on the directory /mnt. Now, all of the files on the floppy will appear under /mnt on your drive.

The **mount point**, the directory where you're mounting the file system, must exist when you use the mount command. If it doesn't exist, create it with mkdir.

See earlier pages for more information on file systems, mounting, and mount points.

• Note that any I/O to the floppy is buffered the same as hard disk I/O is. If you change 3 data on the floppy, you may not see the drive light come on until the kernel flushes its I/O buffers. It's important that you not remove a floppy before you unmount it with the command:

```
# umount /dev/fd0
```

Do not simply switch floppies as you would on a MS-DOS system. Whenever you change floppies, umount the first floppy and mount the next.

2.9 Upgrading and installing new software.

Another duty of the system administrator is the upgrading and installation of new software.

Linux system development is rapid. New kernel releases appear every few weeks, and other software is updated nearly as often. Because of this, new Linux users often feel the need to upgrade their systems constantly to keep up the the rapidly changing pace. This is unnecessary and a waste of time. If you kept up with all of the changes in the Linux world, you would spend all of your time upgrading and none of your time using the system.

Some people feel that you should upgrade when a new distribution release is made; for example, when Slackware comes out with a new version. Many Linux users completely reinstall their system with the newest Slackware release every time.

The best way to upgrade your system depends on the Linux distribution you have. Debian, S.u.S.E., Caldera and Red Hat Linux all have intelligent package management software which allows easy upgrades by installing a new package. For example, the C compiler, gcc, comes in a pre-built binary package. When it is installed, all of the files of the older version are overwritten or removed.

For the most part, senselessly upgrading to "keep up with the trend" is not important at all. This isn't MS-DOS or Microsoft Windows. There is no important reason to run the. newest version of all of the software. If you find that you would like or need features that a new version offers, then upgrade. If not, don't upgrade. In other words, upgrade only what you must, when you must. Don't upgrade for the sake of upgrading. This wastes a lot of time and effort.

2.9.1 Upgrading the kernel

Upgrading the kernel is a matter of obtaining the kernel sources and compiling them. This is generally a painless procedure, but you can run into problems if you try to upgrade to a development kernel, or upgrade to a new kernel version. The version of a kernel has two parts, the kernel version and patchlevel. As of the time of this writing, the latest stable kernel is version 2.0.33.The2.0 is the kernel version and 33 is the patch level. Odd-numbered kernel versions like 2.1 are development kernels. Stay away from development kernels unless you want to live dangerously! As a general rule, you should be able to upgrade easily to another patch level, but upgrading to a new version requires the upgrade of system utilities which interact closely with the kernel.

The Linux kernel sources may be retrieved from any of the Linux FTP sites. On *sunsite.unc.edu,* for instance, the kernel sources are found in */pub/Linux/kernel,* organized into subdirectories by version number.

Kernel sources are released as a gzipped tar file. For example, the file containing the 2.0.33 kernel sources is *linux-2.0.33.tar.gz.*

Kernel sources are unpacked in the /usr/src directory, creating the directory /usr/src/linux. It is common practice for */usr/src/linux* to be a soft link to another directory which contains the version number, like */usr/src/linux-2.0.33.*

This way, you can install new kernel sources and test them out before removing the old kernel sources. The commands to create the kernel directory link are:

```
# cd /usr/src
# mkdir linux-2.0.33
# rm -r linux
# ln -s linux-2.0.33 linux
# tar xzf linux-2.0.33.tar.gz
```

When upgrading to a newer patchlevel of the same kernel version, kernel patch files can save file transfer time because the kernel source is around 7MB after being compressed by gzip. To upgrade from kernel 2.0.31 to kernel 2.0.33, you would download the patch files patch-2.0.32.gz and patch-2.0.33.gz, which can be found at the same FTP site as the kernel sources. After you have placed the patches in the /usr/src directory,. apply the patches to the kernel in sequence to update the source. One way to do this would be:

```
# cd /usr/src
# gzip -cd patch-2.0.32.gz j patch -p0
# gzip -cd patch-2.0.33.gz j patch -p0
```

After the sources are unpacked and any patches have been applied, you need to make sure that three symbolic links in /usr/include are correct for your kernel distribution. To create these links use the commands:

```
# cd /usr/include
# rm -rf asm linux scsi
# ln -s /usr/src/linux/include/asm-i386 asm
# ln -s /usr/src/linux/include/linux linux
# ln -s /usr/src/linux/include/scsi scsi
```

After you create the links, there is no reason to create them again when you install the next kernel patch or a newer kernel version. (See Section 3.11 for more about symbolic links.)

In order to compile the kernel, you must have the *gcc C* compiler installed on your system. *gcc* version 2.6.3 or a more recent version is required to compile the 2.0 kernel.

First cd to */usr/src/linux*. The command *make config* prompts you for a number of configuration options. This is the step where you select the hardware that your kernel will support. The biggest mistake to avoid is not including support for your hard disk controller. Without the correct hard disk support in the kernel, the system won't even boot. If you are unsure about what a kernel option means, a short description is available by pressing *?* and *Enter* .

Next, run the command *make dep* to update all of the source dependencies. This is an important step. *make clean* removes old binary files from the kernel source tree. The command:

```
make      zImage
```

compiles the kernel and writes it to */usr/src/linux/arch/i386/boot/zImage.*
Linux kernels on Intel systems are always compressed. Sometimes the kernel you want to compile is too large to be compressed with the compression system that *make zImage* uses. A kernel which is too large will exit the kernel compile with the error message: *Kernel Image Too Large.* If this happens, try the command *make bzImage,* which uses a compression system that supports larger kernels. The kernel is written to */usr/src/linux/arch/i386/boot/bzImage.*

Once you have the kernel compiled, you need to either copy it to a boot floppy (with a command like "cp zImage /dev/fd0") or install the image so LILO will boot from your hard drive.

2.9.2 Adding a device driver to the kernel.

Support for the Iomega Zip drive, like many other devices, is not generally compiled into stock Linux distribution kernels—the variety of devices is simply too great to support all of them in a usable kernel. However, the source code for the Zip parallel port device driver is included as part of the kernel source code distribution. This section describes how to add support for an Iomega Zip parallel port drive and have it co-exist with a printer connected to a different parallel port.

You must have installed and sucessfully built a custom Linux kernel, as described in the previous section.

Selecting the Zip drive ppa device as a kernel option requires that you answer Y to the appropriate questions during the make config step, when you determine the configuration of the custom kernel. In particular, the ppa device requires answering "Y" to three options:

```
SCSI support?        [Y/n/m]  Y
SCSI disk support?        [Y/n/m]  Y
IOMEGA Parallel Port Zip Drive SCSI support?    [Y/n/m]  Y
```

After you have sucessfully run *make config* with all of the support options you want included in the kernel, then run make *dep, make clean,*and *make zImage* to build the kernel, you must tell the kernel how to install the driver. This is done via a command line to the LILO boot loader. As described in section 4.2.1, the LILO configuration file, /etc/lilo.conf has "stanzas" for each operating system that it knows about, and also directives for presenting these options to the user at boot time.

Another directive that LILO recognizes is "append=", which allows you to add boot-time information required by various device drivers to the command line. In this case, the Iomega Zip ppa driver requires an unused interrupt and I/O port address. This is exactly analogous to specifying separate printer devices like *LPT1* : and *LPT2* : under MS-DOS.

For example, if your printer uses the hexadecimal (base 16) port address *0x378* (see the installation manual for your parallel port card if you don't know what the address is) and is polled (that is, it doesn't require an IRQ line, a common Linux configuration), you would place the following line in your system's /etc/lilo.conf file:

```
append="lp=0x378,0".
```

It is worth noting that Linux automatically recognizes one /dev/lp port at boot time, but when specifying a custom port configurations, the boot-time instructions are needed.

The "0" after the port address tells the kernel *not* to use a IRQ (interrupt request) line for the printer. This is generally acceptable because printers are much slower than CPUs, so a slower method of accessing I/O devices, known as **polling,** where the kernel periodically checks the printer status on its own, still allows the computer to keep up with the printer.

However, devices that operate at higher speeds, like serial lines and disks, each require an **IRQ,** or **interrupt request,** line. This is a hardware signal sent by the device to the processor whenever the device requires the processor's attention; for example, if the device has data waiting to be input to the processor. The processor stops whatever it is doing and handles the interrupt request of the device. The Zip drive ppa device requires a free interrupt, which must correspond to the interrupt that is set on the printer card that you connect the Zip drive to. At the time of this writing, the Linux *ppa* device driver does not support "chaining" of parallel port devices, and separate parallel ports must be used for the Zip *ppa* device and each printer.

To determine which interrupts are already in use on your system, the command:

```
# cat /proc/interrupt
```

displays a list of devices and the IRQ lines they use. However, you also need to be careful not to use any automatically configured serial port interrupts as well, which may not be listed in the /proc/interrupt file. The Linux Documentation Project's Serial HOWTO, available from the sources listed in Appendix A, describes in detail the configuration of serial ports.

• You should also check the hardware settings of various interface cards on your machine 3 by opening the machine's case and visually checking the jumper settings if necessary, to ensure that you are not co-opting an IRQ line that is already in use by another device. Multiple devices fighting for an interrupt line is perhaps the single most common cause of non-functioning Linux systems.

A typical /proc/interrupt file looks like:

```
0:  6091646 timer
1:  40691 keyboard
2:  0 cascade
4:  284686 + serial
13:  1 math error
14:  192560 + ide0
```

The first column is of interest here. These are the numbers of the IRQ lines that are in use on the system. For the ppa driver, we want to choose a line which is *not* listed. IRQ 7 is often a good choice, becuase it is seldom used in default system configurations. We also need to specify the port address which the ppa device will use. This address needs to be physically configured on the interface card. Parallel I/O ports are assigned specific addresses, so you will need to read the documentation for your parallel port card. In this example, we will use the I/O port address 0x278, which corresponds to the LPT2: printer port under MS-DOS. Adding both the IRQ line and port address to our boot-time command line, above, yields the following statement as it would appear in the appropriate stanza of the */etc/lilo.conf* file:

```
append="lp=0x378,0 ppa=0x278,7"
```

These statements are appended to the kernel's start-up parameters at boot time. They ensure that any printer attached to the system does not interfere with the Zip drive's operation. Of course, if your system does not have a printer installed, the "lp=" directive can, and should, be omitted.

After you have installed the custom kernel itself, as described in section 2.2.1, and before you reboot the system, be sure to run the command:

```
# /sbin/lilo
```

to install the new LILO configuration on the hard drive's boot sector.

2.9.3 Installing a device driver module.

Linux provides support for a variety of tape drives with IDE, SCSI, and some proprietary interfaces. Another common type of tape drive connects directly to the floppy drive controller. Linux provides the ftape device driver as a module.

At the time of this writing, the most recent version of ftape is 3.04d. You can retrieve the package from the *sunsite.unc.edu* FTP archive (see Appendix B for instructions).

The ftape archive is located in */pub/Linux/kernel/tapes.* Be sure to get the most recent version. At the time of this writing, this is *ftape-3.04d.tar.gz.*

After unpacking the ftape archive in the */usr/src* directory, typing make install in the top-level ftape directory will compile the ftape driver modules and utilities, if necessary, and install them. If you experience compatibility problems with the ftape executable distribution files and your system kernel or libraries, executing the commands. *make clean* and *make install* will ensure that the modules are compiled on your system.

• To use this version of the ftape driver, you must have module support compiled into 3 the kernel, as well as support for the kerneld kernel daemon. However, you must *not* include the kernel's built-in ftape code as a kernel option, as the more recent ftape module completely replaces this code.

make install also installs the device driver modules in the correct directories. On standard Linux systems, modules are located in the directory:

```
/lib/modules/kernel-version
```

If your kernel version is 2.0.30, the modules on your system are located in */lib/modules/2.0.30.*The *make install* step also insures that these modules are locatable by adding the appropriate statements to the modules.dep file, located in the top-level directory of the module files, in this case */lib/modules/2.0.30.*The ftape installation adds the following modules to your system (using kernel version 2.0.30 in this example):

```
/lib/modules/2.0.30/misc/ftape.o
/lib/modules/2.0.30/misc/zft-compressor.o
/lib/modules/2.0.30/misc/zftape.o
```

The instructions to load the modules also need to be added to the system-wide module configuration file. This is the file */etc/conf.modules* on many systems. To automatically load the ftape modules on demand, add the following lines to the */etc/conf.modules* file:

```
alias char-major-27 zftape
pre-install ftape /sbin/swapout 5
```

The first statement loads all of the ftape related modules if necessary when a device with the major number 27 (the ftape device) is accessed by the kernel. Because support for the zftape module (which provides automatic data compression for tape devices) requires the support of the other ftape modules, all of them are loaded on demand by the kernel. The second line specifies load-time parameters for the modules. In this case, the utility */sbin/swapout,* which is provided with the ftape package, ensures that sufficient DMA memory is available for the ftape driver to function.

To access the ftape device, you must first place a formatted tape in the drive. Instructions for formatting tapes and operation of the tape drive are given in section 2.8.3.

2.9.4 Upgrading the libraries.

As mentioned before, most of the software on the system is compiled to use shared libraries, which contain common subroutines shared among different programs.

If you see the message:

```
Incompatible library version
```

when attempting to run a program, then you need to upgrade to the version of the libraries which the program requires. Libraries are backwardly compatible. A program compiled to use an older version of the libraries should work with the new version of the libraries installed. However, the reverse is not true.

The newest version of the libraries can be found on Linux FTP sites. On sunsite.unc.edu, they are located in */pub/Linux/GCC.* The "release" files there should explain what files you need to download and how to install them. Briefly, you should get the files *image-version.tar.gz* and *inc-version*.tar.gz where *version* is the version of the libraries to install, such as 4.4.1. These are tar files compressed with gzip.The image file contains the library images to install in */lib* and */usr/lib.* The inc file contains include files to install in */usr/include.*

The *release-version.tar.gz* should explain the installation procedure in detail (the exact instructions vary with each release). In general, you need to install the library's .a and .sa files in /usr/lib. These are the libraries used at compilation time.

In addition, the shared library image files, *libc.so.version* are installed in /lib. These are the shared library images loaded at run time by programs using the libraries. Each library has a symbolic link using the major version number of the library in */lib.*

The libc library version 4.4.1 has a major version number of 4. The file containing the library is libc.so.4.4.1. A symbolic link of the name libc.so.4 is also placed in /lib pointing to the library. You must change this symbolic link when upgrading the libraries. For example, when upgrading from *libc.so.4.4* to *libc.so.4.4.1*, you need to change the symbolic link to point to the new version.

• You must change the symbolic link in one step, as described below. If you delete 3
the symbolic link *libc.so.4,* then programs which depend on the link (including basic utilities like *ls* and *cat)* will stop working. Use the following command to update the symbolic link libc.so.4 to point to the file *libc.so.4.4.1:*

```
# ln -sf /lib/libc.so.4.4.1 /lib/libc.so.4
```

You also need to change the symbolic link *libm.so.version* in the same manner. If you are upgrading to a different version of the libraries, substitute the appropriate file names, above. The library release notes should explain the details.

2.9.5 Upgrading gcc.

The *gcc* C and C++ compiler is used to compile software on your system, most importantly the kernel. The newest version of *gcc* is found on the Linux FTP sites. On sunsite.unc.edu, it is found in the directory */pub/Linux/GCC* (along with the libraries). There should be a *release* file for the *gcc* distribution detailing what files you need to download and how to install them. Most distributions have upgrade versions that work with their package management software. In general, these packages are much easier to install than "generic" distributions.

2.9.6 Upgrading other software.

Upgrading other software is often simply a matter of downloading the appropriate files and installing them. Most software for Linux is distributed as compressed tar files that include sources, binaries, or both. If binaries are not included in the release, you may need to compile them yourself. This means at least typing make in the directory where the sources are located.

Reading the Usenet newsgroup *comp.os.linux.announce* for announcements of new software releases is the easiest way to find out about new software. Whenever you are looking for software on an FTP site, downloading the *ls-lR* index file from the FTP site and using grep to find the files you want is the easiest way to locate software. If you have archie available to you, it can be of assistance as well. There are also other Internet resources which are devoted specifically to Linux. See Appendix A for more details.

2.10 Miscellaneous tasks.

Believe it or not, there are a number of housekeeping tasks for the system administrator which don't fall into any major category.

Note:

If you don't have archie, you can telnet to an archie server such as archie.rutgers.edu, login as "archie" and use the command "help".

2.10.1 System startup files.

When the system boots, a number of scripts are executed automatically by the system before any user logs in. Here is a description of what happens.

At bootup time, the kernel spawns the process */etc/init.* *Init* is a program which reads its configuration file, */etc/inittab,* and spawns other processes based on the contents of this file. One of the important processes started from inittab is the */etc/getty* process started on each virtual console. The *getty* process grabs the VC for use, and starts a login process on the VC. This allows you to login on each VC. If */etc/inittab* does not contain a getty process for a certain VC, you will not be able to login on that VC.

Another process executed from */etc/inittab* is */etc/rc,* the main system initialization file. This file is a simple shell script which executes any initialization commands needed at boot time, such as mounting the file systems and initializing swap space. On some systems, init executes the file */etc/init.d/rc.*

Your system may execute other initialization scripts as well. For example */etc/rc.local* which usually contains initialization commands specific to your own system, such as setting the host name (see the next section). *rc.local* may be started from */etc/rc* or from */etc/inittab* directly.

2.10.2 Setting the host name.

In a networked environment, the host name is used to uniquely identify a particular machine, while on a standalone machine, the host name simply gives the system personality and charm. It's like naming a pet: you can always address to your dog as "The dog," but it's much more interesting to assign the dog a name such as spot or woofie.

Setting the system's host name is a simple matter of using the *hostname* command. If you are on a network, your host name should be the full host name of your machine, such as *goober.norelco.com.* If you are not on a network of any kind, you can choose an arbitrary host and domain name, such as *loomer.vpizza.com, shoop.nowhere.edu* , or *floof.org.*

The host name must appear in the file /etc/hosts, which assigns an IP address to each host. Even if your machine is not on a network, you should include your own host name in /etc/hosts. If you are not on a TCP/IP network, and your host name is floof.org, simply include the following line in /etc/hosts:

```
127.0.0.1          floof . org   localhost
```

This assigns your host name, *floof.org,* to the loopback address 127.0.0.1. The loopback interface is present whether the machine is connected to a network or not. The *localhost* alias is always assigned to this address.

If you are on a TCP/IP network, your actual IP address and host name should appear in /etc/hosts. For example, if your host name is goober.norelco.com, and your IP address is 128.253.154.32, add the following line to /etc/hosts:

```
128.253.154.32      goober.norelco.com
```

To set your host name, simply use the hostname command. For example, the command:

```
# hostname -S goober.norelco.com
```

sets the host name to goober.norelco.com. In most cases, the hostname command is executed from one of the system startup files, like */etc/rc or /etc/rc.local.* Edit these two files and change the hostname command found there to set your own host name. Upon rebooting, the system will use the new name.

2.11 What to do in an emergency.

On some occasions, the system administrator will be faced with the problem of recovering from a complete disaster, such as forgetting the root password or trashing file systems.

The best advice is, *don't panic.* Everyone makes stupid mistakes—that's the best way to learn about system administration: the hard way.

Linux is not an unstable version of UNIX. In fact, I have had fewer problems with system hangs than with commercial versions of UNIX on many platforms. Linux also benefits from a strong complement of wizards who can help you out of a bind. (The *double entendre* is intended.)

The first step to fixing any problem youself is finding out what it is. Poke around, and see how things work. Much of the time, a system administrator posts a desperate plea for help before he or she looks into the problem at all. You'll find that fixing problems yourself is actually very easy. It is the path to enlighenment and guruhood.

There are a few times when reinstalling the system from scratch is necessary. Many new users accidentally delete some essential system file, and immediately reach for the installation disks. This is not a good idea. Before taking such drastic measures, investigate the problem and ask others for help. In many cases, you can recover your system from a maintenance diskette.

2.11.1 Recovery with a maintenance diskette.

One indispensable tool of the system administrator is the so-called "boot/root disk," a floppy that can be booted for a complete Linux system, independent of your hard drive.

Boot/root disks are actually very simple—you create a root file system on the floppy, place all of the necessary utilities on it, and install LILO and a bootable kernel on the floppy. Another technique is to use one floppy for the kernel and another for the root file system. In any case, the result is the same: you are running a Linux system completely from the floppy drive.

The canonical example of a boot/root disk is the Slackware boot disks. These diskettes contain a bootable kernel and a root file system, all on floppy. They are intended to be used to install the Slackware distribution, but come in handy when doing system maintenance.

The H.J Lu boot/root disk, available from */pub/Linux/GCC/rootdisk* on sunsite.unc.edu, is another example of a maintenance disk. If you're ambitious, you can create your own. In most cases, however, a ready-made boot/root disk is much easier to use and probably will be more complete.

Using a boot/root disk is very simple. Boot the disk on your system, and login as root (usually with no password). In order to access the files on the hard drive, you will need to mount the file systems by hand. For example, the command:

```
# mount -t ext2 /dev/hda2 /mnt
```

will mount an ext2fs file system on /dev/hda2 under /mnt. Remember that / is now on the boot/root disk itself; you need to mount your hard drive file systems under some directory in order to access the files. Therefore, /etc/passwd on your hard drive is now /mnt/etc/passwd if you mount your root file system on /mnt.

2.11.2 Fixing the root password.

If you forget your root password, this is not a problem, surprisingly. Boot the boot/root disk, mount the root file system on /mnt, and blank out the password field for root in /mnt/etc/passwd, as in this example:

```
root::0:0:root:/:/bin/sh
```

Now root has no password. When you reboot from the hard drive you should be able to login as root and reset the password using passwd.

Aren't you glad that you learned how to use vi? On your boot/root disk, editors like Emacs probably aren't available, but vi should be.

2.11.3 Trashed file systems.

If you somehow trash a file systems, you can run *e2fsck* or the appropriate form of fsck for the file system type. In most cases, it is safest to correct any damaged data on the hard drive file systems from floppy.

One common cause of file system damage is a damaged super block. The **super block** is the "header" of the file system that contains information about its status, size, free blocks, and so forth. If you damage the super block, by accidentally writing data directly to the file system's partition table for example, the system probably will not recognize the file system at all. Attempt to mount the file system will fail, and *e2fsck* won't be able to fix the problem.

Happily, an ext2fs file system type saves copies of the superblock at "block group" boundaries on the drive, usually every 8K blocks. To tell e2fsck to use a copy of the superblock, use a command like:

```
# e2fsck -b 8193 partition
```

where partition is the partition on which the file system resides. The *-b 8193* option tells *e2fsck* to use the copy of the superblock stored at block 8193 in the file system.

2.11.4 Recovering lost files.

If you accidentally delete an important file on your system, there's no way to "undelete" it. However, you can copy the relevant files from the floppy to your hard drive. If you delete /bin/login, for example, which allows you to login, simply boot the boot/root floppy, mount the root file system on /mnt, and use the command:

```
# cp -a /bin/login /mnt/bin/login
```

The -a option tells cp to preserve the permissions on the file(s) being copied.
Of course, if the files you deleted aren't essential system files that have counterparts on the boot/root floppy, you're out of luck. If you make backups however, you can always restore them.

2.11.5 Trashed libraries.

If you accidentally trash your libraries or symbolic links in /lib, more than likely the commands which depend on the libraries will no longer work. The easiest solution is to boot your boot/root floppy, mount your root file system, and fix the libraries in /mnt/lib.

Chapter 3

The X Window System

The X Window System is a graphical user interface (GUI) that was originally developed at the Massachusetts Institute of Technology. Commercial vendors have since made X the industry standard GUI for UNIX platforms. Virtually every UNIX workstation in the world now runs some form of X.

A free port of the MIT X Window System version 11, release 6 (X11R6) for 80386, 80486, and Pentium UNIX systems was developed by a team of programmers that was originally headed by David Wexelblat. This release, known as XFree86
, is available for System V/386, 386BSD, and other Intel x86 UNIX implementations, including Linux. It provides all of the binaries, support files, libraries, and tools required for installation.

Some features offered by this release are:

- complete inclusion of the X Consortium's X11R6.3 release;
- a new DPMS extension, donated by Digital Equipment Corporation;
- the Low Bandwidth X (LBX) extension in all X servers;
- Microsoft IntelliMouse support;
- support for gzip font compression.

To use the X Window System, you are encouraged to read *The X Window System: A User's Guide* (see Appendix A). Here, we describe step-by-step an XFree86 installation
1
under Linux. You still need to fill in some of the details by reading the XFree86 documentation, which is discussed below. The Linux *XFree86 HOWTO* is another good information source.

®XFree86 is a trademark of The XFree86 Project, Inc.

3.1 X Window Hardware requirements.

3.1.1 Video display.

The documentation for your video adaptor should specify the chip set. If you are in the market for a new video card, or are buying a machine that comes with a video card, ask the vendor to find out exactly what make, model, and chip set the video card comes with. The vendor may need to call the manufacturer's technical support department. Many personal computer hardware vendors state their video card is a "standard SVGA card," that "should work," with your system. Explain that your software (mention Linux and XFree86!) does not support all video chip sets, and that you must have detailed information.

You can also determine your video card chip set by running the *SuperProbe* program which is included with the XFree86 distribution. This is described below.

Video cards using these chip sets are supported on all bus types. Virtually all of the cards support 256-color graphics modes. In addition, some of the cards support color modes like monochrome, 15-bit, 16-bit, 24-bit and 32-bit. For color depths greater than 256 (8-bit), you must have the requisite amount of video dynamic RAM (DRAM) installed. The usual configuration is 16 bits per pixel (65536 colors).

The monochrome server also supports generic VGA cards, the Hercules monochrome card, the Hyundai HGC1280, Sigma LaserView, and Apollo monochrome cards.

The release notes for the current version of XFree86 should contain the complete list of supported video chip sets. The XFree86 distribution has chip set-specific README files that give detailed information on the state of support for each chip set.

One problem faced by the XFree86 developers is that some video card manufacturers use non-standard mechanisms to determine the clock frequencies that are used to drive their card. They either don't release specifications which describe how to program the card or require developers to sign non-disclosure statements to get the information. This practice restricts the free distribution of XFree86, and the XFree86 development team is unwilling to accept it. This has been a problem with older video cards manufactured by Diamond, but as of release 3.3, Diamond actively supports the XFree86 Project, Inc.

We also suggest using an accelerated card, like a S3 chip set card. You should check the XFree86 documentation and verify that your particular card is supported before you take the plunge and purchase expensive hardware. Benchmark comparisons of video cards under XFree86 are posted routinely to the Usenet news groups *comp.windows.x.i386unix* and *comp.os.linux.misc.*

It is important to note that the average accelerated video card is significantly faster than the standard graphics card of most workstations. An 80486DX2, 66-MHz Linux System with 20 megabytes of RAM, equipped with a VESA Local Bus (VLB) S3-864 chip set card with 2 megabytes of DRAM, will consistently be about 7 times as fast a Sun Sparc IPX workstation on X benchmarks with the XFree86 server version 3.1. Version 3.3 is even faster. In general, a Linux system with an accelerated SVGA card will give you much greater performance than commercial UNIX workstations, which usually employ simple frame buffers for graphics.

3.1.2 Memory, CPU, and disk space.

The suggested setup for XFree86 under Linux is a 80486 or faster machine with at least 16 megabytes of RAM. The more physical RAM installed, the less the system must swap to and from the disk when memory is low. Because swapping is inherently slow (disks are very slow compared to memory), having 16 megabytes of RAM or more is necessary to run XFree86 comfortably. A system with 4 megabytes of physical RAM could run 10 to 100 times more slowly than one with 16 megabytes or more.

A standartd, out-of-the-box XFree86 installation requires 60–80 megabytes of disk space, at a minimum. This includes space for the X server(s), fonts, libraries, and standard utilities. If you plan to add applications, you can probably run XFree86 comfortably in 200 megabytes of disk space.

3.2 XFree86 installation.

The Linux binary distribution of XFree86 is found on all CD Linux distributions and can also be found at a number of FTP sites. On sunsite.unc.edu, it is found in the directory /pub/X11/XFree86. At of the time of this writing, the current version is 3.3.1. Newer versions are released periodically. If you obtain XFree86 as part of a Linux distribution, downloading the software separately is not necessary.

These files are included in the XFree86-3.3.1 distribution.
One of the following servers is required:

File	Description
X338514.tgz	Server for 8514-based boards.
X33AGX.tgz	Server for AGX-based boards.
X33I128.tgz	Server for the Imagine I128 boards.
X33Ma64.tgz	Server for Mach64-based boards.
X33Ma32.tgz	Server for Mach32-based boards.
X33Ma8.tgz	Server for Mach8-based boards.
X33Mono.tgz	Server for monochrome video modes.
X33P9K.tgz	Server for P9000-based boards.
X33S3.tgz	Server for S3-based boards.
X33S3V.tgz	Server for S3/Virge-based boards.
X33SVGA.tgz	Server for Super VGA-based boards.
X33VGA16.tgz	Server for VGA/EGA-based boards.
X33W32.tgz	Server for ET4000/W32-based boards.

All of the following files are required:

File	Description
preinst.sh	Pre-installation script
postinst.sh	Post-installation script
X33bin.tgz	Clients, run-time libs, and app-defaults files
X33doc.tgz	Documentation
X33fnts.tgz	75dpi, misc and PEX fonts
X33lib.tgz	Data files required at run-time
X33man.tgz	Manual pages
X33set.tgz	XF86Setup utility
X33VG16.tgz	16 colour VGA server (XF86Setup needs this server)

The following is required for new installations, and optional for existing installations:

File	Description
X33cfg.tgz	sample config files for xinit, xdm

• Do not install X33cfg.tgz over an existing XFree86 installation without first backing 3 up the configuration files. Unpacking X33cfg.tgz overwrites these and other files. If you do have customized configuration files, there is no need to install this package anyway.

• The bit mapped fonts distributed with release 3.3.1 are compressed with the gzip 3 program rather than compress. You will probably want to remove the old fonts after you back them up. The X servers and font servers in previous releases cannot read fonts compressed by gzip, so keep a copy of the old fonts if you want to use older servers.

The following files are optional:

File	Description
X33f100.tgz	100dpi fonts
X33fcyr.tgz	Cyrillic fonts
X33fnon.tgz	Other fonts (Chinese, Japanese, Korean, Hebrew)
X33fscl.tgz	Scalable fonts (Speedo and Type1)
X33fsrv.tgz	Font server and config files
X33prog.tgz	X header files, config files and compile-time libs
X33nest.tgz	Nested X server
X33vfb.tgz	Virtual framebuffer X server
X33prt.tgz	X Print server
X33ps.tgz	PostScript version of the documentation
X33html.tgz	HTML version of the documentation
X33jdoc.tgz	Documentation in Japanese (for version 3.2)
X33jhtm.tgz	HTML version of the documentation in Japanese (3.2)
X33lkit.tgz	X server LinkKit

The XFree86 directory should contain README files and installation notes for the current version.

Next, as root, create the directory */usr/X11R6* if it doesn't already exist. Then run the pre-installation script, *preinst.sh.* You should copy the script, and all of the archive files for your system to the */var/tmp* directory before you run *preinst.sh.* */usr/X11R6* must be your current directory when you run the pre-installation script and unpack the archives:

cd /usr/X11R6

sh /var/tmp/preinst.sh

You should then unpack the files from /var/tmp to /usr/X11R6 with a command like:

gzip -d < /var/tmp/X33prog.tgz j tar vxf -

• These tar files are packed relative to /usr/X11R6. You must unpack the files there. 3 On some Linux distributions, the parent directory is /var/X11R6 instead.

After you have upacked the required files and any optional files you selected, run the post-installation script *postinst.sh.*

cd /usr/X11R6

sh /var/tmp/postinst.sh.

Now link the file */usr/X11R6/bin/X* to the server that supports your video card. For example, the SVGA color server, */usr/bin/X11/X* should be linked to */usr/X11R6/bin/XF86_SVGA.* To use the monochrome server instead, relink X to *XF86_ MONO* with the command:

In --sf /usr/X11R6/bin/XF86_MONO / usr / X11R6 / bin / X

The same holds true for the other servers.

You also need to ensure that the directory, */usr/X11R6/bin,* is on your path. This can be done by editing your system default */etc/profile* or */etc/csh.login* (based on the shell that you, or other users on your system, use). Or you can simply add the directory to your personal path by modifying */etc/.bashrc* or */etc/.cshrc,* based on your shell.

Finally, ensure that */usr/X11R6/lib* can be located by ld.so, the run time linker.

To do this, add the line:

```
/usr/X11R6/lib
```

to the file */etc/ld.so.conf,* and run */sbin/ldconfig,* as root.

3.3 Probing the hardware configuration.

If you aren't sure which server to use or don't know the video card's chip set, the SuperProbe program, which is found in */usr/X11R6/bin,* can attempt to determine the video chip set and other information. Write down its output for later reference.

To run SuperProbe from the command line, simply enter :

```
# SuperProbe
```

• It is possible that SuperProbe will confuse hardware that uses I/O port addresses 3 that might be used by video cards. To prevent SuperProbe from checking these addresses, use the excl argument, followed by a list of addresses that SuperProbe should not examine. For example:

```
# SuperProbe -excl 0x200-0x230,0x240
```

The addresses are given as hexadecimal numbers that are prefixed by 0x.

To display a list of video devices that SuperProbe knows about, use the command:

```
# SuperProbe -info
```

SuperProbe can print lots of information if you provide it with the *-verbose* argument. You can redirect the output to a file:

```
# SuperProbe -verbose > superprobe.out
```

• Running SuperProbe can cause the system to hang. Make certain that any non-essential 3 applications are not running, or at least have all of their data safely saved to disk, and ensure that any users are logged off. Also, a loaded system (one that is printing in the background, for example), can skew the output of software like SuperProbe or an X server that is trying to measure the video card's timing specifications.

3.4 Automatically generating the *XF86Config* file.

Creating the *XF86Config* file by hand is an arduous task, but it is not impossible. Several tools in the XFree86 version 3.3.1 can assist you. One of them, the XF86Setup program, can automatically generate an XF86Config file in the correct format. You must know the exact specifications of your video board and the Vertical and Horizontal refresh values of your monitor. Most of the information can be found in the owner's manuals.

Several other configuration programs are available as well, depending on the Linux distribution. The most common ones are *Xconfigurator* and *xf86config*. The latter program is an older version of *XF86Setup* and is included in older releases of XFree86. You should always use *XF86Setup* if both it and *xf86config* are available.

3.5 Configuring XFree86.

In this section, we describe how to create and edit the *XF86Config file,* which configures the XFree86 server. In many cases, it is best to start with an XFree86 configuration that uses a low resolution like 640x480 that is supported by nearly all video cards and monitors. Once XFree86 works at a lower, standard resolution, you can tweak the configuration to exploit the capabilities of your video hardware. This ensures that XFree86 works on your system, and that the installation is essentailly correct, before you attempt the sometimes difficult task of setting up XFree86 for high-performance use.

In addition to the information listed here, you should read the following documents:

- The XFree86 documentation in /usr/X11R6/lib/X11/doc (from the XFree86-3.1-doc package). You should especially see the file README.Config, which is an XFree86 configuration tutorial.
- Several video chip sets have separate README files in the above directory (like README.Cirrus and README.S3). Read the file that applies to your video card.
- The manual page for XFree86. The manual page for XF86Config. The manpage for the server that you are using, like XF86_SVGA or XF86_S3.

The main XFree86 configuration file is:

/usr/X11R6/lib/X11/XF86Config.

This file contains information for your mouse, video card parameters, and so on. The file XF86Config.eg is provided with the XFree86 distribution as an example. Copy this file to XF86Config and edit it as a starting point.

The XF86Config manual page explains the format of the XF86Config file. Read the manual page if you have not done so already.

We are going to describe a sample XF86Config file, a section at a time. This file may not look exactly like the sample file included in the XFree86 distribution, but the structure is the same.

• Note that the XF86Config file format may change with each version of XFree86. See 3 your distribution's release notes for errata.

• **Do not copy the configuration file listed here to your system and try to use it.** A 3 configuration file that does not correspond to your hardware can drive the monitor at a frequency which is too high. There have been reports of damage to monitors, especially fixed-frequency monitors, that has been caused by incorrectly configured XF86Config files. **Make absolutely sure that your** XF86Config **file corresponds to your hardware before you use it.**

Each section of the XF86Config file is surrounded by a pair of lines with the syntax,
Section "section-name". . .EndSection.

The first section of the XF86Config file is Files, which looks like this:

```
Section "Files"

        RgbPath         "/usr/X11R6/lib/X11/rgb"
        FontPath        "/usr/X11R6/lib/X11/fonts/misc/"
        FontPath        "/usr/X11R6/lib/X11/fonts/75dpi/"

End  Section
```

The RgbPath line sets the path to the X11R6 RGB color database, and each FontPath line sets the path to a directory containing X11 fonts. You shouldn't have to modify these lines. Simply ensure that a FontPath entry exists for each font type that you have installed; that is, for each directory in /usr/X11R6/lib/X11/fonts.

The next section is ServerFlags, which specifies several global flags for the server.
In general this section is empty:

```
Section "ServerFlags"

        # Uncomment this to cause a core dump at the spot where a signal is

        # received. This may leave the console in an unusable state, but may

        # provide a better stack trace in the core dump to aid in debugging

        # NoTrapSignals

        # Uncomment this to disable the <Crtl><Alt><BS> server abort sequence

        #       DontZap

EndSection
```

In this ServerFlags section, all of the lines are commented out.

The next section is Keyboard. This example shows a basic configuration that should work on most systems. The XF86Config file describes how to modify the configuration.

```
Section                "Keyboard"
      Protocol         "Standard"
      AutoRepeat    500 5
      ServerNumLock

End  Section
```

The next section is Pointer, which specifies parameters for the mouse device:

```
      Section            "Pointer"

      Protocol            "MouseSystems"

      Device              "/dev/mouse"

# Baudrate and SampleRate are only for some Logitech mice
# BaudRate 9600
# SampleRate 150

# Emulate3Buttons is an option for 2-button Microsoft mice
# Emulate3Buttons

# ChordMiddle is an option for some 3-button Logitech mice
# ChordMiddle

EndSection.
```

For the moment, the only options that should concern you are Protocol and Device. Protocol specifies the mouse *protocol,* which is not necessarily the same as the manufacturer. XFree86 under Linux recognizes these mouse protocols:

- BusMouse Logitech Microsoft MMSeries Mouseman
- MouseSystems PS/2 MMHitTab

BusMouse should be used for the *Logitech* bus mice. Older Logitech mice use *Logitech,* and newer *Logitech* serial mice use either *Microsoft* or *Mouseman* protocols.

Device specifies the device file by which the mouse can be accessed. On most Linux systems, this is /dev/mouse, which is usually a link to the appropriate serial port, like /dev/cua0 for serial mice and the appropriate bus mouse device for bus mice. At any rate, be sure that the device file exists.

The next section is *Monitor,* which specifies the characteristics of your monitor. As with other sections in the *XF86Config file,* there may be more than one Monitor section. This is useful if you have multiple monitors connected to a system, or use the same *XF86Config* file for multiple hardware configurations.

```
Section "Monitor"

Identifier "CTX 5468 NI"


# These values are for a CTX 5468NI only! Don't attempt to use
# them with your monitor (unless you have this model)

Bandwidth 60
HorizSync 30-38,47-50
VertRefresh 50-90

# Modes: Name dotclock horiz vert

ModeLine "640x480" 25 640 664 760 800 480 491 493 525
ModeLine "800x600" 36 800 824 896 1024 600 601 603 625
ModeLine "1024x768" 65 1024 1088 1200 1328 768 783 789 818

EndSection
```

Identifier is an arbitrary name for the *Monitor* entry. This can be any string and is used to refer to the *Monitor* entry later in the *XF86Config file.*
HorizSync specifies the valid horizontal sync frequencies for your monitor, in kHz. Multisync monitors may have a range of values, or several, comma separated ranges. Fixed-frequency monitors require a list of discrete values; for example:

```
HorizSync 31.5, 35.2, 37.9, 35.5, 48.95
```

The monitor manual should list these values in the technical specifications section. If it does not, contact the manufacturer or vendor of your monitor to obtain it.
VertRefresh specifies the valid vertical refresh rates (or vertical synchronization frequencies) for your monitor, in kHz. Like *HorizSync,* this can be a range or a list of discrete values. Your monitor manual should list them.

HorizSync and *VertRefresh* are used only to double-check that the monitor resolutions are in valid ranges. This reduces the chance that you will damage your monitor by driving it at a frequency which it was not designed for.

The *ModeLine* directive is used to specify resolution modes for your monitor. The format is:

ModeLine name clock horiz-values vert-values

name is an arbitrary string which you will use to refer to the resolution mode later in the file. dot-clock is the driving clock frequency, or "dot clock" associated with the resolution mode. A dot clock is usually specified in MHz. It is the rate at which the video card must send pixels to the monitor at this resolution. horiz-values and vert-values are four numbers each that specify when the electron gun of the monitor should fire, and when the horizontal and vertical sync pulses fire during a sweep.

The file *VideoModes.doc,* included with the XFree86 distribution, describes in detail how to determine the *ModeLine* values for each resolution mode that your monitor supports. *clock* must correspond to one of the dot clock values that your video card supports. Later in the XF86Config file, you will specify these clocks.

Two files, *modeDB.txt* and *Monitors,* may have *ModeLine* information for your monitor. They are located in */usr/X11R6/lib/X11/doc.*

Start with ModeLine values for VESA-standard monitor timings, because most monitors support them. *ModeDB.txt* includes the timing values for VESA-standard resolutions. For example, this entry:

```
# 640x480@60Hz  Non-Interlaced  mode

# Horizontal Sync =  31.5kHz

# Timing: H=  (0.95us, 3.81us, 1.59us),  V=(0.35ms, 0.064ms, 1.02ms)

#


# name       clock     horizontal timing    vertical   timing   flags

"640x480"    25.175    640   664   760  800  480  491   493  525
```

is the VESA-standard timing for a 640x480 video mode. It has a dot clock of 25.175, which your video card must support. This is described below. To include this entry in the *XF86Config file,* use the line:

```
ModeLine   "640x480"   25.175  640  664  760  800  480  491   493
525
```

The name argument to *ModeLine ("640x480")* is an arbitrary string. By convention modes are named by their resolutions, but name can, technically, be any descriptive label. For each ModeLine, the server checks the mode specifications and ensures that they fall in the range of values specified for *Bandwidth, HorizSync,* and *VertRefresh.* If they do not, the server complains when you attempt to start X. For one thing, the dot clock used by the mode should not be greater than the value used for *Bandwidth.* However, in many cases, it is safe to use a mode that has a slightly higher bandwidth than your monitor can support.

If the VESA standard timings do not work, (you'll know after you try to use them), then look in the files *modeDB.txt* and *Monitors,* which include specific mode values for many monitor types. You can create *ModeLine* entries from these values as well. Be sure only to use values for your specific monitor. Many 14 and 15-inch monitors do not support higher resolution modes, and often resolutions of 1024x768 at low dot clocks. If you can't find high-resolution modes for your monitor in these files, then your monitor probably does not support them.

If you are completely at a loss and can't find *ModeLine* values for your monitor, follow the instructions in the *VideoModes.doc* file, which is included in the XFree86. distribution, and generate values from the specifications in your monitor's manual. Your mileage will certainly vary when you attempt to generate ModeLine values by hand. But this is a good place to look if you can't find the values that you need. VideoModes.doc also describes the format of the ModeLine directive, and other aspects of the XFree86 server in gory detail.

Lastly, if you do obtain *ModeLine* values that are almost but not exactly right, you may possibly be able to modify the values a little to obtain the desired result. For example, if the XFree86 display image is shifted slightly, or the image seems to "roll," then follow

the instructions in the VideoModes.doc file and fix the values. Be sure to check the controls on the monitor itself. In many cases, you must change the horizontal or vertical size of the display after XFree86 starts, to center and size the image.

- Don't use monitor timing values or ModeLine values for monitors other than your 3 model. If you try to drive a monitor at a frequency for which it was not designed, you can damage or even destroy it.

The next section of the *XF86Config* file is *Device,* which specifies parameters for your video card. Here is an example:

```
Section "Device"

    Identifier "#9 GXE 64"

   # Nothing yet; we fill in these values later.
```

```
EndSection
```

This section defines properties for a particular video card. *Identifier* is an arbitrary, descriptive string. You will use this string to refer to the card later.

Initially, you don't need to include anything in the *Device* section except the *Identifier.* We will use the X server itself to probe for the properties of the video card and enter them into the *Device* section later. The XFree86 server is capable of probing for the video chip set, clocks, RAMDAC, and amount of video RAM on the board. This is described in Section 5.6.

Before we do this, however, we need to finish writing the *XF86Config file.* The next section is Screen, which specifies the monitor/video card combination to use for a particular server:

```
Section "Screen"
    Driver      "Accel"
    Device      "#9 GXE 64"
    Monitor     "CTX 5468 NI"

Subsection "Display"
    Depth       16
    Modes       "1024x768"   "800x600"   "640x480"
    ViewPort    0   0
    Virtual     1024    768
  EndSubsection

EndSection
```

The *Driver* line specifies the X server that you will be using. Valid *Driver* values are:

- Accel: For the XF86 S3, XF86 Mach32, XF86 Mach8, XF86 8514, XF86 P9000, XF86 AGX, and XF86 W32 servers SVGA:
- For the XF86 SVGA server; VGA16:
- For the XF86 VGA16 server; VGA2:
- For the XF86 Mono server; Mono:
- For the non-VGA monochrome drivers in the XF86 Mono and XF86 VGA16 servers.

Be sure that */usr/X11R6/bin/X* is a symbolic link to this server.
The *Device* line specifies the *Identifier* of the *Device* section that corresponds to the video card to use for this server. Above, we created a *Device* section with the line:

```
Identifier    "#9    GXE    64"
```

Therefore, we use *"#9 GXE 64"* on the *Device* line here.

Similarly, the *Monitor* line specifies the name of the *Monitor* section to be used with this server. Here, *"CTX 5468 NI"* is the *Identifier* used in the Monitor section described above.

Subsection "Display" defines several properties of the XFree86 server corresponding to your monitor/video card combination. The *XF86Config* file describes all of these options in detail. Most of them are not necessary to get the system working. The options that you should know about are:

- *Depth.* Defines the number of color planes; that is, the number of bits per pixel. Usually, *Depth* is set to 16. For the VGA16 server, you would use a depth of 4, and for the monochrome server a depth of 1. If you use an accelerated video card with enough memory to support more bits per pixel, you can set Depth to 24, or 32. If you have problems with depths higher than 16, set it back to 16 and attempt to debug the problem later.
- Modes. This is the list of mode names which have been defined using the ModeLine directive(s) in the Monitor section. In the above section, we used ModeLines named "1024x768", "800x600",and"640x48"0. Therefore, we use a Modes line of:

```
Modes    "1024x768"    "800x600"    "640x480"
```

The first mode listed on this line is the default when XFree86 starts. After XFree86 is running, you can switch between the modes listed here using the keys Ctrl - Alt -Numeric + and Ctrl - Alt - Numeric - .

It might be best, when you initially configure XFree86, to use lower resolution video modes like 640x480, which tend to work with most systems. Once you have the basic configuration working, you can modify *XF86Config* to support higher resolutions.

- *Virtual.* Set the virtual desktop size. XFree86 can use additional memory on your video card to extend the size of the desktop. When you move the mouse pointer to the edge of the display, the desktop scrolls, bringing the additional space into view. Even if you run the server at a lower video resolution like 800x600, you can set *Virtual* to the total resolution that your video card can support. A 1-megabyte video card can support 1024x768 at a depth of 8 bits per pixel; a 2-megabyte card 1280x1024 at depth 8, or 1024x768 at depth 16. Of course, the entire area will not be visible at once, but it can still be used.

The *Virtual* feature is rather limited. If you want to use a true virtual desktop, fvwm and similar window managers allow you to have large, virtual desktops by hiding windows and using other techniques, instead of storing the entire desktop in video memory. See the manual pages for fvwm for more details about this. Many Linux systems use *fvwm* by default.

- *ViewPort.* If you are using the Virtual option which is described above, *ViewPort* sets the coordinates of the upper-left-hand corner of the virtual desktop when XFree86 starts up. *Virtual 0 0* is often used. If this is unspecified, then the desktop is centered on the virtual desktop display, which may be undesirable to you.

Many other options for this section exist; see the *XF86Config* manual page for a complete description. In practice, these options are not necessary to get XFree86 working initially.

3.6 Filling in video card information.

Your *XF86Config* file is now ready, with the exception of complete information on the video card. We'll use the X server to probe for this information, and add it to *XF86Config.*

Instead of probing for this information with the X server, *XF86Config* values for many cards are listed in the files *modeDB.txt, AccelCards,* andDevices.These files are all found in */usr/X11R6/lib/X11/doc.* In addition, there are various README files for certain chip sets. You should look at these files for information on your video card and use that information (the clock values, chip set type, and any options) in the XF86Config file. If any information is missing, you can probe for it.

In most of these examples we demonstrate configuration of a #9 GXE 64 video card, which uses the *XF86 S3* chipset. First, determine the video chip set on the card. Running SuperProbe (found in */usr/X11R6/bin)* tells you this information, but you need to know the chip set name as it is known to the X server.

To do this, run the command:

```
X -showconfig
```

This gives the chip set names known to the X server. (The manual pages for each X server list these, too.) For example, with the accelerated *XF86 S3* server, we get:

```
XFree86 Version 3.1 / X Window System
(protocol Version 11, revision 0, vendor release 6000)
Operating System: Linux
Configured drivers:
S3: accelerated server for S3 graphics adaptors (Patchlevel 0)
mmio_928, s3_generic
```

The valid chip set names for this server are *mmio _928* and *s3_ generic.* The *XF86 _S3* man page describes these chip sets and video cards that use them. In the case of the #9 GXE 64 video card, *mmio _928* is appropriate.

If you don't know which chip set is in use, the X server can probe it for you. To do this, run the command:

```
X -probeonly > / tmp / x.out 2 > &1
```

if you use bash as your shell. If you use *csh,*try:

```
X -probeonly &> / tmp / x.out
```

You should run this command while the system is unloaded; that is, while no other activity occurs on the system. This command also probes for your video card dot clocks (as seen below), and system load can throw off this calculation.

The output from the above, in / tmp / x.out, should contain lines like:

```
XFree86 Version 3.1 / X Window System
(protocol Version 11, revision 0, vendor release 6000)
Operating System: Linux
Configured drivers:
S3: accelerated server for S3 graphics adaptors (Patchlevel 0)
mmio_928, s3_generic
```

Several lines deleted. . .

```
(--) S3: card type:     386/486  localbus
(--) S3: chipset:       864   rev.   0
(--) S3: chipset driver:     mmio_928
```

Here, we see that the two valid chip sets for this server (in this case, *XF86 _S3)* are *mmio _928* and *s3_ generic.* The server probed for and found a video card that has the *mmio _928* chipset.

In the Device section of the XF86Config file, add a Chipset line that has the name of the chip set as determined above. For example:

```
Section "Device"

    # We already had Identifier here...
    Identifier "#9 GXE 64"
    # Add this line:
    Chipset "mmio_928"
```

EndSection

Now, we need to determine the driving clock frequencies used by the video card. A driving clock frequency, or dot clock, is simply a rate at which the video card can send pixels to the monitor. As described above, each monitor resolution has a dot clock associated with it. We need to determine which dot clocks are made available by the video card.

First, you should look at the documentation mentioned above and see if the card's clocks are listed there. The dot clocks are usually a list of 8 or 16 values, all of which are in MHz. For example, when looking at modeDB.txt, we see an entry for the Cardinal ET4000 video card, which looks like:

```
        # chip    ram    virtual      clocks       default-mode     flags
ET4000     1024    1024    768   25 28  38  36 40 45  32  0    "1024x768"
```

The dot clocks for this card are 25, 28, 38, 36, 40, 45, 32, and 0 MHz.
In the Devices section of the *XF86Config* file, add a *Clocks* line containing the list of dot clocks for your card. For example, for the clocks above, add the line:

```
Clocks 25 28 38 36 40 45 32 0
```

to the *Devices* section of the file, after *Chipset.*

• **The order of the dot clocks is important.** Don't re-sort the list or remove duplicates. 3
If you cannot find the dot clocks associated with your card, the X server can probe for these, too. Use *X -probeonly* as described above. The output should contain lines which look like the following:

```
(--) S3: clocks: 25.18  28.32   38.02   36.15   40.33  45.32  32.00   00.00
```

We can then add a *Clocks* line which contains all of these values, as printed. You can use more than one *Clocks* line in *XF86Config* if all of the values (sometimes there are more than 8 clock values printed) do not fit onto one line. Again, be sure to keep the list of clocks in the order that they are displayed.

• Be sure that there is no *Clocks* line (or that it is commented out) in the Devices 3 section of the file when using X *-probeonly.* If there is a Clocks line present, the server does not probe for the clocks—it uses the values given in *XF86Config.*

Some video boards use a programmable clock chip. See the manual page for your X server or the XFree86 README file that describes your video card. The chip essentially allows the X server to tell the card the dot clocks to use. For video cards that have clock chips, you may not find a list of dot clocks for the card in any of the above files. Or, the list of dot clocks printed when using X *-probeonly* will only contain one or two discrete clock values, with the rest being duplicates or zero. Or, the X server may provide an explicit warning that the video card has a programmable clock chip, like:

```
(--) SVGA: cldg5434: Specifying a Clocks line makes no sense for this driver
```

This example is taken from a *XF86_SVGA* server running a Cirrus Logic PCI card. For boards which use programmable clock chips, you use a ClockChip line instead of a Clocks line in the XF86Config file. ClockChip is the name of the clock chip as used by the video card; the manual pages for each server describe them. For example, in the file README.S3, we see that several S3-864 video cards use an "ICD2061A" clock chip, and that we should use the line:

```
ClockChip    "icd2061a"
```

instead of *Clocks* in the *XF86Config* file. As with *Clocks,* this line goes in the *Devices* section, after *Chipset.*

Similarly, some video cards require that you specify the RAMDAC chip type in the XF86Config file. This is done with a *Ramdac* line. The *XF86 Accel* man page describes this option. Often the X server will correctly probe for the RAMDAC.

Some video card types require that you specify several options in the *Devices* section of XF86Config. These options are described in the manual page for your server, as well as in the various files like README.*cirrus* and README.S3. These options are enabled using an Option line. For example, the #9 GXE 64 card requires two options:

```
Option    "number_nine"

Option    "dac_8_bit"
```

An X server may work without the *Option* lines, but they are necessary to get the best performance out of the card. There are too many options to list here. They are differ-ent for each card. If you must use one, the X server manual pages and various files in */usr/X11R6/lib/X11/doc* will tell you what they are.
When you finish, you should have a Devices section that looks something like:

```
Section "Device"

   # Device section for the #9 GXE 64 only !
   Identifier "#9 GXE 64"
  Chipset "mmio_928"
  ClockChip "icd2061a"
  Option "number_nine"
  Option "dac_8_bit"

EndSection
```

There are other options which you can include in the *Devices* entry. The X server manual pages provide the gritty details.

3.7 Running XFree86.

With your XF86Config file configured, you can fire up the X server and give it a spin. Again, be sure that the */usr/X11R6/bin* directory is on your path.
The command to start XFree86 is:

```
startx
```

This is a front end to *xinit.* It starts the X server and executes the commands in the file *.xinitrc* in your home directory. *.xinitrc* is a shell script that contains the command lines of the X clients to run when the X server starts. If this file does not exist, the system default */usr/X11R6/lib/X11/xinit/xinitrc* is used.

A simple .xinitrc file looks like this:

```
#!/bin/sh

xterm -fn 7x13bold -geometry 80x32+10+50 &
xterm -fn 9x15bold -geometry 80x34+30-10 &
oclock -geometry 70x70-7+7 &
xsetroot -solid midnightblue &

exec twm
```

This script starts two xterm clients and an *oclock,* and sets the root window (background) color to *midnightblue.* Itstartstwm, the window manager. twm is executed with the shell's exec statement. This causes the *xinit* process to be replaced by twm. After the twm process exits, the X server shuts down. You can cause *twm* to exit by using the root menu. Depress mouse button 1 on the desktop background. This displays a pop-up menu that allows you to Exit *twm.*

Be sure that the last command in .xinitrc is started with exec, and that it is not placed into the background (no ampersand at the end of the line). Otherwise the X server will shut down immediately after it starts the clients in the .xinitrc file.

Alternately, you can exit X by pressing Ctrl - Alt - Backspace in combination. This kills the X server directly, exiting the window system.

The above is a only a simple desktop configuration. Again, we suggest that you read a book like *The X Window System: A User's Guide* (see Appendix A). The possible variations of X usage and configuration are too many to describe here. The xterm, oclock, and twm manual pages will provide you clues on how to begin.

3.8 When you run into trouble.

Often, something will not be quite right when you first start the X server. This is nearly always caused by something in your XF86Config file. Usually, the monitor timing values. or the video card dot clocks are set incorrectly. If the display seems to roll, or the edges are fuzzy, this indicates that the monitor timing values or dot clocks are wrong. Also, be sure that you correctly specified the video card chip set and options in the Device section of XF86Config. Be absolutely sure that you are using the correct X server and that /usr/X11R6/bin/X is a symbolic link to it.

If all else fails, try to start X "bare"; that is, with a command like:

```
X >  / tmp / x.out 2  >&1
```

You can then kill the X server (using Ctrl - Alt - Backspace) and examine the contents of /tmp/x.out. The X server reports any warnings or errors—for example, if your video card doesn't have a dot clock corresponding to a mode supported by your monitor. The file VideoModes.doc, which is included in the XFree86 distribution, contains many hints for adjusting the values in your XF86Config file.

Remember that you can use Ctrl - Alt - Numeric + and Ctrl - Alt -Numeric - to switch between the video modes listed on the Modes line of the Screen section of XF86Config. If the highest resolution mode doesn't look right, try switching to a lower resolution. This lets you know, at least, that those parts of your X configuration are working correctly.

Also, adjust the vertical and horizontal size/hold knobs on your monitor. In many cases, it is necessary to adjust these when starting up X. For example, if the display seems to be shifted slightly to one side, you can usually correct this using the monitor controls. Again, the USENET newsgroup comp.windows.x.i386unix is devoted to discussions about XFree86. It might be a good idea to read the newsgroups for postings related to video configuration. You might run across someone with the same problem.

There are also sample XF86Config files which have been contributed by users. Some of these are available on the sunsite.unc.edu archive in the /pub/Linux/X11 directory, and elsewhere. You might find a configuration file that somebody has already written for your hardware..

Chapter 4

Networking

In this chapter we discuss Networking—how to configure a connection, using TCP/IP, SLIP, PPP or UUCP, and electronic mail and news.

4.1 Networking with TCP/IP.

Linux supports a full implementation of the TCP/IP (Transport Control Protocol/ Internet Protocol) networking protocols. TCP/IP has become the most successful mechanism for networking computers worldwide. With Linux and an Ethernet card, you can network your machine to a local area network, or (with the proper network connections) to the Internet—the worldwide TCP/IP network.

Hooking up a small LAN of UNIX machines is easy. It simply requires an Ethernet controller in each machine and the appropriate Ethernet cables and other hardware. Or, if your business or university provides access to the Internet, you can easily add your Linux machine to this network.

The current implementation of TCP/IP and related protocols for Linux is called "NET-3," and before that, "NET-2." This has no relationship to the so-called NET-2 release of BSD UNIX; instead, "NET-3" in this context means the second implementation of TCP/IP for Linux.

Linux NET-3 also supports SLIP—Serial Line Internet Protocol and PPP—Point-to-Point Protocol. SLIP and PPP allow you to have dialup Internet access using a modem. If your business or university provides SLIP or PPP access, you can dial in to the SLIP or PPP server and put your machine on the Internet over the phone line. Alternately, if your Linux machine also has Ethernet access to the Internet, you can set up your Linux box as a SLIP or PPP server.

For complete information on setting up TCP/IP under Linux, we encourage you to read the Linux NET-3 HOWTO, available via anonymous FTP from sunsite.unc.edu.The NET-3 HOWTO is a complete guide to configuring TCP/IP, including Ethernet and SLIP or PPP connections, under Linux. The Linux Ethernet HOWTO is a related document that describes configuration of various Ethernet card drivers for Linux.

Also of interest is the book *TCP/IP Network Administration*, by Craig Hunt. It contains complete information on using and configuring TCP/IP on UNIX systems.

TCP/IP Hardware requirements.

You can use Linux TCP/IP without any networking hardware at all—configuring "loop-back" mode allows you to talk to yourself. This is necessary for some applications and games which use the "loopback" network device.

However, if you want to use Linux with an Ethernet TCP/IP network, you need an Ethernet card. Common cards such as the 3com 3c503, HP PCLAN (27245 and 27xxx series), Western Digital WD80x3, and Novell NE2000/NE1000 are supported, as well as many more. See the Linux Ethernet and Hardware HOWTOs for details.

There are a few common situations that you should watch out concerning supported cards: 1) Several cards are support but offer shoddy performance or have other restrictions. Examples are the 3Com 3C501 which works but gives absolutely horrible performance and the Racal-Interlan NI6510 using the am7990 lance chip which doesn't work with more than 16 megabytes of RAM. In the same vein, many cards are NE1000/NE2000 compatible clones and can have various problems. See the Linux Ethernet HOWTO for a more complete discussion of Linux Ethernet hardware compatibility.

Linux also supports SLIP and PPP, which allows you to use a modem to access the Internet over the phone line. In this case, you'll need a modem compatible with your SLIP or PPP server—most servers require a 14.4bps V.32bis modem at a minimum . Performance is greatly improved with a 33.6bps or higher modem.

4.1.1 Configuring TCP/IP on your system.

In this section we're going to discuss how to configure an Ethernet TCP/IP connection on your system. Note that this method should work for many systems, but certainly not all. This discussion should be enough to get you on the right path to configuring the network parameters of your machine, but there are numerous caveats and fine details not mentioned here. We direct you to the *Linux Network Administrators' Guide* and the NET-3-HOWTO for more information.

First, we assume that you have a Linux system that has the TCP/IP software installed. This includes basic clients such as telnet and ftp, system administration commands such as ifconfig and route (usually found in /etc), and networking configuration files (such as /etc/hosts). The other Linux-related networking documents described above explain how to go about installing the Linux networking software if you do not have it already.

We also assume that your kernel has been configured and compiled with TCP/IP support enabled. See Section 4.9 for information on compiling your kernel. To enable networking, you must answer "yes" to the appropriate questions during the make config step, and rebuild the kernel.

Once this has been done, you must modify a number of configuration files used by NET-3. For the most part this is a simple procedure. Unfortunately, however, there is wide disagreement between Linux distributions as to where the various TCP/IP configuration files and support programs should go. Much of the time, they can be found in /etc,but in other cases may be found in /usr/etc, /usr/etc/inet, or other bizarre locations. In the worst case you'll have to use the find command to locate the files on your system. Also note that not all distributions keep the NET-3 configuration files and software in the same location—they may be spread across several directories.

The following information applies primarily to Ethernet connections. If you're planning to use SLIP or PPP, read this section to understand the concepts, and follow the more specific instructions in the following sections.

Your network configuration. Before you can configure TCP/IP, you need to determine the following information about your network setup. In most cases, your local network administrator can provide you with this information.

- IP address. This is the unique machine address in dotted-decimal format. An example is 128.253.153.54. Your network admins will provide you with this number. If you're only configuring loopback mode (i.e. no SLIP, no Ethernet card, just TCP/IP connections to your own machine) then your IP address is 127.0.0.1. Some of this information is adapted from the NET-3-HOWTO by Terry Dawson and Matt Welsh..

- Your network mask ("netmask"). This is a dotted quad, similar to the IP address, which determines which portion of the IP address specifies the subnetwork number, and which portion specifies the host on that subnet. (If you're shaky on these TCP/IP networking terms, we suggest reading some introductory material on network administration.) The network mask is a pattern of bits, which when overlayed onto an address on your network, will tell you which subnet that address lives on. This is very important for routing, and if you find, for example, that you can happily talk to people outside your network, but not to some people within your network, there is a good chance that you have an incorrect mask specified.

Your network administrators will have chosen the netmask when the network was designed, and therefore they should be able to supply you with the correct mask to use. Most networks are class C subnetworks which use 255.255.255.0 as their netmask. Class B networks use 255.255.0.0. The NET-3 code will automatically select a mask that assumes no subnetting as a default if you do not specify one.

This applies as well to the loopback port. Since the loopback port's address is always 127.0.0.1, the netmask for this port is always 255.0.0.0. You can either specify this explicitly or rely on the default mask.

- Your network address. This is your IP address masked bitwise-and ed the netmask.

For example, if your netmask is 255.255.255.0, and your IP address is 128.253.154.32, your network address is 128.253.154.0. With a netmask of 255.255.0.0, this would be 128.253.0.0.

If you're only using loopback, you don't have a network address.

- Your broadcast address. The broadcast address is used to broadcast packets to every machine on your subnet. Therefore, if the host number of machines on your subnet is given by the last byte of the IP address (netmask 255.255.255.0), your broadcast address will be your network address ORed with 0.0.0.255.

For example, if your IP address is 128.253.154.32, and your netmask is 255.255.255.0, your broadcast address is 128.253.154.255.

Note that for historical reasons, some networks are setup to use the network address as the broadcast address, if you have any doubt, check with your network administrators. (In many cases, it will suffice to duplicate the network configuration of other machines on your subnet, substituting your own IP address, of course.)

If you're only using loopback, you don't have a broadcast address.

- Your gateway address. This is the address of the machine which is your "gateway" to the outside world (i.e. machines not on your subnet). In many cases the gateway machine has an IP address identical to yours but with a ".1" as its host address; e.g., if your IP address is 128.253.154.32, your gateway might be 128.253.154.1. Your network admins will provide you with the IP address of your gateway.

In fact, you may have multiple gateways. A *gateway* is simply a machine that lives on two different networks (has IP addresses on different subnets), and routes packets between them. Many networks have a single gateway to "the outside world" (the network directly adjacent to your own), but in some cases you will have multiple gateways—one for each adjacent network.

If you're only using loopback, you don't have a gateway address. The same is true if your network is isolated from all others.

- Your name server address. Most machines on the net have a name server which translates host names into IP addresses for them. Your network admins will tell you the address of your name server. You can also run a server on your own machine by running named, in which case the name server address is 127.0.0.1. Unless you absolutely *must* run your own name server, we suggest using the one provided to you on the network (if any). Configuration of named is another issue altogether; our priority at this point is to get you talking to the network. You can deal with name resolution issues later.

If you're only using loopback, you don't have a name server address.

SLIP/PPP users: You may or may not require any of the above information, except for a name server address. When using SLIP, your IP address is usually determined in one of two ways: Either (a) you have a "static" IP address, which is the same every time you connect to the network, or (b) you have a "dynamic" IP address, which is allocated from a pool available addresses when you connect to the server. In the following section on SLIP configuration this is covered in more detail.

NET-3 supports full routing, multiple routes, subnetworking (at this stage on byte boundaries only), the whole nine yards. The above describes most basic TCP/IP configurations.

Yours may be quite different: when in doubt, consult your local network gurus and check out the man pages for route and ifconfig. Configuring TCP/IP networks is very much beyond the scope of this book; the above should be enough to get most people started.

The networking rc **files.** rc files are systemwide configuration scripts executed at boot time by init, which start up all of the basic system daemons (such as sendmail, cron, etc.) and configure things such as the network parameters, system host name, and so on. rc files are usually found in the directory /etc/rc.d but on other systems may be in /etc. In general Slackware distributions use the files rc.inet1,etc.in/etc/rc.d whereas the RedHat distributions use a series of directories

Here, we're going to describe the rc files used to configure TCP/IP. There are two of them: rc.inet1 and rc.inet2. rc.inet1 is used to configure the basic network parameters (such as IP addresses and routing information) and rc.inet2 fires up the TCP/IP daemons (telnetd, ftpd, and so forth).

Many systems combine these two files into one, usually called *rc.inet* or *rc.net.* The names given to your rc files doesn't matter, as long as they perform the correct functions and are executed at boot time by init. To ensure this, you may need to edit */etc/inittab* and uncomment lines to execute the appropriate rc file(s). In the worst case you will have to create the rc.inet1 and rc.inet2 files from scratch and add entries for them to */etc/inittab.*

As we said, *rc.inet1* configures the basic network interface. This includes your IP and network address, and the routing table information for your network. The routing tables are used to route outgoing (and incoming) network datagrams to other machines. On most simple configurations, you have three routes: One for sending packets to your own machine, another for sending packets to other machines on your network, and another for sending packets to machines outside of your network (through the gateway machine). Two programs are used to configure these parameters: ifconfig and route. Both of these are usually found in */etc.*

ifconfig is used for configuring the network device interface with the parameters that it requires to function, such as the IP address, network mask, broadcast address and the like. Route is used to create and modify entries in the routing table.

For most configurations, an *rc.inet 1* file that looks like the following should work. You will, of course, have to edit this for your own system. Do *not* use the sample IP and network addresses listed here for your own system; they correspond to an actual machine on the Internet.

```
#!/bin/sh
# This is /etc/rc.d/rc.inet1 -- Configure the TCP/IP interfaces

# First, configure the loopback device.
HOSTNAME='host name'

/etc/ifconfig lo 127.0.0.1        # uses default netmask 255.0.0.0
/etc/route add 127.0.0.1          # a route to point to the loopback device

# Next,   configure the ethernet device.  If you're only using loopback or
# SLIP,   comment out the rest of these lines.

# Edit for your setup.

IPADDR="128.253.154.32" # REPLACE with YOUR IP address
NETMASK="255.255.255.0" # REPLACE with YOUR netmask
NETWORK="128.253.154.0" # REPLACE with YOUR network address
BROADCAST="128.253.154.255" # REPLACE with YOUR broadcast address, if you
# have one. If not, leave blank and edit below.

GATEWAY="128.253.154.1" # REPLACE with YOUR gateway address!

/etc/ifconfig eth0 ${IPADDR} netmask ${NETMASK} broadcast ${BROADCAST}

# If you don't have a broadcast address, change the above line to just:
# /etc/ifconfig eth0 ${IPADDR} netmask ${NETMASK}

/etc/route add ${NETWORK}

# The following is only necessary if you have a gateway; that is, your
# network is connected to the outside world.
/etc/route add default gw ${GATEWAY} metric 1

# End of Ethernet Configuration
```

Again, you may have to tweak this file somewhat to get it to work. The above should be sufficient for the majority of simple network configurations, but certainly not all.

rc.inet2 starts up various servers used by the TCP/IP suite. The most important of these is *inetd. Inetd* sits in the background and listens to various network ports. When a machine tries to make a connection to a certain port (for example, the incoming telnet port), inetd forks off a copy of the appropriate daemon for that port (in the case of the *telnet* port, *inetd* starts *in.telnetd).* This is simpler than running many separate, standalone daemons (e.g., individual copies of *telnetd, ftpd,* and so forth)—inetd starts up the daemons only when they are needed.

Syslogd is the system logging daemon—it accumulates log messages from various applications and stores them into log files based on the configuration information in */etc/syslogd.conf.* routed is a server used to maintain dynamic routing information. When your system attempts to send packets to another network, it may require additional routing table entries in order to do so. routed takes care of manipulating the routing table without the need for user intervention.

Our example *rc.inet2,* below, only starts up the bare minimum of servers. There are many other servers as well—many of which have to do with NFS configuration. When attempting to setup TCP/IP on your system, it's usually best to start with a minimal configuration and add more complex pieces (such as NFS) when you have things working.

Note that in the below file, we assume that all of the network daemons are held in */etc.* As usual, edit this for your own configuration:

```
#! /bin/sh
# Sample /etc/rc.d/rc.inet2

# Start syslogd
if [ -f /etc/syslogd ]
then
   /etc/syslogd
fi

# Start inetd
if [ -f /etc/inetd ]
then
/etc/inetd
fi

# Start routed
if [ -f /etc/routed ]
then
/etc/routed -q
fi
# Done!
```

Among the various additional servers that you may want to start in rc.inet2 is named. Named is a name server—it is responsible for translating (local) IP addresses to names, and vice versa. If you don't have a name server elsewhere on the network, or want to provide local machine names to other machines in your domain, it may be necessary to run named. (For most configurations it is not necessary, however.) Named configuration is somewhat complex and requires planning; we refer interested readers to a good book on TCP/IP network administration.

The /etc/hosts **file.** /etc/hosts contains a list of IP addresses and the host names that they correspond to. In general, /etc/hosts only contains entries for your local machine, and perhaps other "important" machines (such as your name server or gateway). Your local name server will provide address-to-name mappings for other machines on the network, transparently.

For example, if your machine is loomer.vpizza.com with the IP address 128.253.154.32, your /etc/hosts would look like:

```
127.0.0.1          localhost
128.253.154.32     loomer.vpizza.com loomer
```

If you're only using loopback, the only line in /etc/hosts should be for 127.0.0.1, with both localhost and your host name after it.

The /etc/networks **file.** The /etc/networks file lists the names and addresses of your own, and other, networks. It is used by the route command, and allows you to specify a network by name, should you so desire.

Every network you wish to add a route to using the route command (generally called from rc.inet1—see above) *must* have an entry in /etc/networks.

As an example:

```
default 0.0.0.0 # default route      - mandatory
loopnet 127.0.0.0 # loopback network   -   mandatory
mynet 128.253.154.0 #   Modify  for  your  own  network  address
```

The /etc/host.conf **file.** This file is used to specify how your system will resolve host names. It should contain the two lines:

```
order hosts,bind
multi on
```

These lines tell the resolve libraries to first check the /etc/hosts file for any names to lookup, and then to ask the name server (if one is present). The multi entry allows you to have multiple IP addresses for a given machine name in /etc/hosts.

The /etc/resolv.conf **file.** This file configures the name resolver, specifying the address of your name server (if any) and your domain name. Your domain name is your fully-qualified host name (if you're a registered machine on the Internet, for example), with the host name chopped off. That is, if your full host name is loomer.vpizza.com, your domain name is just vpizza.com.

For example, if your machine is goober.norelco.com, and has a name server at the address 128.253.154.5, your /etc/resolv.conf would look like:

```
domain          norelco.com

nameserver      127.253.154.5
```

You can specify more than one name server—each must have a *nameserver* line of its own in *resolv.conf.*

Setting your host name. You should set your system host name with the *hostname* command. This is usually called from /etc/rc or /etc/rc.local; simply search your system rc files to determine where it is invoked. For example, if your (full) host name is loomer.vpizza.com, edit the appropriate rc file to execute the command:

```
/bin/hostname     loomer.vpizza.com
```

Note that the hostname executable may not be found in /bin on your system.

Trying it out. Once you have all of these files set up, you should be able to reboot your new kernel and attempt to use the network. There are many places where things can go wrong, so it's a good idea to test individual aspects of the network configuration (e.g., it's probably not a good idea to test your network configuration by firing up Mosaic over a network-based X connection).

You can use the *netstat* command to display your routing tables; this is usually the source of the most trouble. The netstat man page describes the exact syntax of this command in detail. In order to test network connectivity, we suggest using a client such as telnet to connect to machines both on your local subnetwork and external networks. This will help to narrow down the source of the problem. (For example, if you're unable to connect to local machines, but can connect to machines on other networks, more than likely there is a problem with your netmask and routing table configuration). You can also invoke the route command directly (as root) to play with the entries in your routing table.

You should also test network connectivity by specifying IP addresses directly, instead of host names. For example, if you have problems with the command:

```
$ telnet    shoop.vpizza.com
```

the cause may be incorrect name server configuration. Try using the actual IP address of the machine in question; if that works, then you know your basic network setup is (more than likely) correct, and the problem lies in your specification of the name server address.

Debugging network configurations can be a difficult task, and we can't begin to cover it here. If you are unable to get help from a local guru we strongly suggest reading the *Linux Network Administrators' Guide* from the LDP.

4.1.2 SLIP configuration.

SLIP (Serial Line Internet Protocol) allows you to use TCP/IP over a serial line, be that a phone line, with a dialup modem, or a leased asynchronous line of some sort. Of course, to use SLIP you'll need access to a dial-in SLIP server in your area. Many universities and businesses provide SLIP access for a modest fee.

There are two major SLIP-related programs available—*dip* and *slattach*. Both of these programs are used to initiate a SLIP connection over a serial device. It is *necessary* to use one of these programs in order to enable SLIP—it will not suffice to dial up the SLIP server (with a communications program such as *kermit)* and issue *ifconfig* and *route* commands. This is because dip and slattach issue a special *ioctl()* system call to seize control of the serial device to be used as a SLIP interface.

dip can be used to dial up a SLIP server, do some handshaking to login to the server (exchanging your username and password, for example) and then initiate the SLIP connection over the open serial line. slattach, on the other hand, does very little other than grab the serial device for use by SLIP. It is useful if you have a permanent line to your SLIP server and no modem dialup or handshaking is necessary to initiate the connection. Most dialup SLIP users should use dip, on the other hand.

dip can also be used to configure your Linux system as a SLIP server, where other machines can dial into your own and connect to the network through a secondary Ethernet connection on your machine. See the documentation and man pages for dip for more information on this procedure.

SLIP is quite unlike Ethernet, in that there are only two machines on the "network"—the SLIP host (that's you) and the SLIP server. For this reason, SLIP is often referred to as a "point-to-point" connection. A generalization of this idea, known as PPP (Point to Point Protocol) has also been implemented for Linux.

When you initiate a connection to a SLIP server, the SLIP server will give you an IP address based on (usually) one of two methods. Some SLIP servers allocate "static" IP. addresses—in which case your IP address will be the same every time you connect to the server. However, many SLIP servers allocate IP addresses dynamically—in which case you receive a different IP address each time you connect. In general, the SLIP server will print the values of your IP and gateway addresses when you connect. dip is capable of reading these values from the output of the SLIP server login session and using them to configure the SLIP device.

Essentially, configuring a SLIP connection is just like configuring for loopback or ethernet. The main differences are discussed below. Read the previous section on configuring the basic TCP/IP files, and apply the changes described below.

Static IP address SLIP connections using dip. If you are using a static-allocation SLIP server, you may want to include entries for your IP address and host name in /etc/hosts. Also, configure these files listed in the above section: rc.inet2, host.conf,and resolv.conf.

Also, configure rc.inet1, as described above. However, you only want to execute ifconfig and route commands for the loopback device. If you use dip to connect to the SLIP server, it will execute the appropriate ifconfig and route commands for the SLIP device for you. (If you're using slattach, on the other hand, you *will* need to include ifconfig/route commands in rc.inet1 for the SLIP device—see below.)

dip *should* configure your routing tables appropriately for the SLIP connection when you connect. In some cases, however, dip's behavior may not be correct for your configuration, and you'll have to run ifconfig or route commands by hand after connecting to the server with dip (this is most easily done from within a shell script that runs dip and immediately executes the appropriate configuration commands). Your gateway is, in most cases, the address of the SLIP server. You may know this address before hand, or the gateway address will be printed by the SLIP server when you connect. Your dip chat script (described below) can obtain this information from the SLIP server.

ifconfig may require use of the pointopoint argument, if dip doesn't configure the interface correctly. For example, if your SLIP server address is 128.253.154.2, and your IP address is 128.253.154.32, you may need to run the command:

```
ifconfig sl0     128.253.154.32   pointopoint   128.253.154.2
```

as root, after connecting with dip. The man pages for ifconfig will come in handy. Note that SLIP device names used with the ifconfig and route commands are sl0, sl1 and so on (as opposed to eth0, eth1, etc. for Ethernet devices).

In Section 6.1.2, below, we explain how to configure dip to connect to the SLIP server.

Static IP address SLIP connections using *slattach.* If you have a leased line or cable running directly to your SLIP server, then there is no need to use dip to initiate a connection. slattach can be used to configure the SLIP device instead.

In this case, your /etc/rc.inet1 file should look something like the following:

```
#!/bin/sh
IPADDR="128.253.154.32"       # Replace with your IP address
REMADDR="128.253.154.2"
# Replace with your SLIP server address

# Modify the following for the appropriate serial device for the SLIP
# connection:
slattach -p cslip -s 19200 /dev/ttyS0
/etc/ifconfig sl0 $IPADDR pointopoint $REMADDR up
/etc/route add default gw $REMADDR
```

slattach allocates the first unallocated SLIP device (sl0, sl1, etc.) to the serial line specified.

Note that the first parameter to slattach is the SLIP protocol to use. At present the only valid values are slip and cslip. Slip is regular SLIP, as you would expect, and cslip is SLIP with datagram header compression. In most cases you should use cslip; however, if you seem to be having problems with this, try slip.

If you have more than one SLIP interface then you will have routing considerations to make. You will have to decide what routes to add, and those decisions can only be made on the basis of the actual layout of your network connections. A book on TCP/IP network configuration, as well as the man pages to route, will be of use.

Dynamic IP address SLIP connections using *dip.* If your SLIP server allocates an IP address dynamically, then you certainly don't know your address in advance—therefore, you can't include an entry for it in /etc/hosts. (You should, however, include an entry for your host with the loopback address, 127.0.0.1.)

Many SLIP servers print your IP address (as well as the server's address) when you connect. For example, one type of SLIP server prints a string such as:

Your IP address is 128.253.154.44.

Server address is 128.253.154.2.

dip can capture these numbers from the output of the server and use them to configure the SLIP device. Below, we explain how to configure dip to connect to the SLIP server.

Using *dip.*

dip can simplify the process of connecting to a SLIP server, logging in, and configuring the SLIP device. Unless you have a leased line running to your SLIP server, dip is the way to go.

To use dip, you'll need to write a "chat script" which contains a list of commands used to communicate with the SLIP server at login time. These commands can automatically send your user name/password to the server, as well as get information on your IP address from the server.

Here is an example dip chat script, for use with a dynamic IP address server. For static servers, you will need to set the variables $local and $remote to the values of your local IP address and server IP address, respectively, at the top of the script. See the dip man page for details:

```
main:

# Set Maximum Transfer Unit. This is the maximum size of packets
# transmitted on the SLIP device. Many SLIP servers use either 1500 or
# 1006; check with your network admins when in doubt.
get $mtu 1500

# Make the SLIP route the default route on your system.
default

# Set the desired serial port and speed.
port cua03
speed 38400

# Reset the modem and terminal line. If this causes trouble for you,
# comment it out.
reset

# Prepare for dialing. Replace the following with your
# modem initialization string.
send ATT&C1&D2\\N3&Q5%M3%C1N1W1L1S48=7\r
wait OK 2
if $errlvl != 0 goto error

# Dial the SLIP server
dial 2546000
if $errlvl != 0 goto error
wait CONNECT 60
if $errlvl != 0 goto error
```

```
# We are connected. Login to the system.
login:
sleep 3
send \r\n\r\n
# Wait for the login prompt
wait login: 10
if $errlvl != 0 goto error

# Send your username
send USERNAME \ n

# Wait for password prompt
wait ord: 5
if $errlvl != 0 goto error


# Send password.
send PASSWORD \ n

# Wait for SLIP server ready prompt
wait annex: 30
if $errlvl != 0 goto error

# Send commands to SLIP server to initiate connection.
send slip\n
wait Annex 30

# Get the remote IP address from the SLIP server. The 'get...remote'
# command reads text in the form xxx.xxx.xxx.xxx, and assigns it
# to the variable given as the second argument (here, $remote).
get $remote remote
if $errlvl != 0 goto error
wait Your 30

# Get local IP address from SLIP server, assign to variable $local.
get $local remote
if $errlvl != 0 goto error

# Fire up the SLIP connection
done:
print CONNECTED to $remote at $rmtip
print GATEWAY address $rmtip
print LOCAL address $local
mode SLIP
goto exit
```

error:
print SLIP to $remote failed.

exit:

dip automatically executes *ifconfig* and *route* commands based on the values of the variables *$local* and *$remote.* Here, those variables are assigned using the *get...remote* command, which obtains text from the SLIP server and assigns it to the named variable.

If the ifconfig and route commands that dip runs for you don't work, you can either run the correct commands in a shell script after executing dip, or modify the source for dip itself. Running dip with the -v option will print debugging information while the connection is being set up, which should help you to determine where things might be going awry.

Now, in order to run dip and open the SLIP connection, you can use a command such as:

```
/etc/dip/dip -v /etc/dip/mychat 2>&1
```

Where the various dip files, and the chat script *(mychat.dip),* are stored in */etc/dip.*

The above discussion should be enough to get you well on your way to talking to the network, either via Ethernet or SLIP. Again, we strongly suggest looking into a book on TCP/IP network configuration, especially if your network has any special routing considerations, other than those mentioned here.

4.2 Dial-up networking and PPP.

Linux supports a full implementation of the PPP (Point-to-Point) networking protocols. PPP is a mechanism for creating and running IP (the Internet Protocol) and other network protocols over a serial connection (using a null-modem cable), over a telnet established link or a link made using modems and telephone lines (and of course using digital lines such as ISDN). This section will only cover configuring PPP as a client connecting via an analog modem to a remote machine that provides PPP dialup service.

For complete information on setting up PPP under Linux, we encourage you to read the Linux PPP HOWTO, available via anonymous FTP from sunsite.unc.edu.The PPP HOWTO is a complete guide to configuring PPP, including modem, ISDN and null-modem cables, under Linux. Much of the information in this section was gleaned from this document. The *Linux Network Administrator's Guide*, from the Linux Documentation Project, is also available. See Appendix A for more information on these documents.

4.2.1 What you need to get started.

We assume that your kernel has been configured and compiled with TCP/IP support enabled. See Section 4.9 for information on compiling your kernel. To enable networking, you must answer "yes" to the appropriate questions during the make config step, and rebuild the kernel. We also assume that ppp has been compiled and installed on your system as well. We assume that you are using a Linux 1.2.x kernel with the PPP 2.1.2 software or Linux 1.3.X/2.0.x and PPP 2.2.0. At the time of writing, the latest official version of PPP available for Linux is ppp-2.2f. Please see the kerneld mini-HOWTO if you plan to use modules to load ppp into your kernel. *It is highly recommended that you use a version of the Linux kernel and the appropriate PPP version that are known to be stable together.*
You should also read:

- the documentation that comes with the PPP package;
- the pppd and chat man pages; (use *man chat* and *man pppd* to explore these)
- the Linux Network Administration Guide (NAG);
- the Net-2/3 HOWTO;
- Linux kernel documentation installed in /usr/src/linux/Documentation when you install the Linux source code.
- The modem setup information page—see Modem Setup Information (http://www.in.net/info/modems/index.html)
- The excellent Unix/Linux books published by O'Reilly and Associates. See (O'Reilly and Associates On-Line catalog (http://www.ora.com/). If you are new to Unix/Linux, run (don't walk) to your nearest computer book shop and invest in a number of these immediately!
- The PPP-FAQ maintained by Al Longyear, available from (ftp://sunsite.unc.edu/pub/Linux/docs/faqs; see Appendix B). This contains a great deal of useful information in question/answer format that is very useful when working out why PPP is not working (properly).

4.2.2 An overview of the steps involved.

There are several steps to setting up your system to use PPP. We recommend that you read through all of these steps thoroughly before attempting to actually bring up a PPP connection. Each of these steps will be discussed in detail later.

1. Make sure that TCP/IP support is compiled into your kernel.
2. Make sure that PPP support is compiled into your kernel either statically or as a loadable module.
3. Make sure that PPP software is compiled and installed on your systems.
4. Make sure that you have a modem configured and installed/attached to your computer and that you know which serial port the modem is assigned to.
5. Make sure you have the following information from your PPP dialup server provider (usually an ISP).

- The phone number you will dial to connect to the remote PPP dialup service provider.
- Whether or not you are using dynamic or static IP assignment. If the latter, you will need to know that static IP number.
- The IP addresss of the DNS (Domain Name Service) server that you will be using to resolve host names when connected.

Make sure that the kernel has TCP/IP support. Linux PPP operations come in two parts: 1) the PPP daemon and kernel support for PPP. Most distributions seem to provide PPP kernel support in their default installation kernels, but others do not. You should make sure that TCP/IP is compiled into your kernel. You can do this by issuing the following command:

```
grep -i "TCP/IP" / var / adm / messages
```

If you get a line similar to:

Jun 8 09:52:08 gemini kernel: Swansea University Computer Society TCP/IP for NET3.019

then you have TCP/IP support compiled in. You can also look for the above information on the console while Linux is booting. On many fast machines, this scrolls by too quickly. You can use Shift - PageUp to scroll the screen up and see this.

Make sure that the kernel has PPP support. If at boot your kernel reports messages like:

PPP Dynamic channel allocation code copyright 1995

Caldera, Inc.

PPP line discipline registered.

then your kernel has PPP support. You can also issue the command:

```
# grep -i "PPP" / var / adm / messages
```

If you get a line similar to:

Jun 8 09:52:08 gemini kernel: PPP: version 0.2.7 (4 channels) NEW_TTY_DRIVERS

that means PPP support is present.

Make sure that you have a modem configured. You should make sure that your modem is correctly set up and that you know which serial port it is connected to:

- DOS com1: = Linux /dev/cua0 (and /dev/ttyS0)
- DOS com2: = Linux /dev/cua1 (and /dev/ttyS1),
- et cetera

Historically, Linux used cua x devices for dial out and ttyS x devices for dial in. The kernel code that required this was changed in kernel version 2.0. x and you should now use ttyS x for both dial in and dial out. The cua x device names may well disappear in future kernel versions.

If you are using a high speed (external) modem (14,400 Baud or above), your serial port needs to be capable of handling the throughput that such a modem is capable of producing, particularly when the modems are compressing the data.

This requires your serial port to use a modern UART (Universal Asynchronous Receiver Transmitter) such as a 16550A. If you are using an old machine (or old serial card), it is quite possible that your serial port has only an 8250 UART, which will cause you considerable problems when used with a high speed modem.

Use the command:

```
# setserial   -a   / dev /  t t y S x
```

to get Linux to report to you the type of UART you have. If you do not have a 16550A type UART, invest in a new serial card (available for under $50).

You will need to configure your modem correctly for PPP—to do this READ YOUR MODEM MANUAL! Most modems come with a factory default setting that selects the options required for PPP. Recommended configuration specifies (in standard Hayes commands):

- Hardware flow control (RTS/CTS) (&K3 on many modems) E1
- Command/usr/src/linux-2.0.27/include/linux/serial.h Echo ON (required for chat to operate)
- Q0 Report result codes (required for chat to operate)
- S0=0 Auto Answer OFF (unless you want your modem to answer the phone)
- &C1 Carrier Detect ON only after connect
- &S0 Data Set Ready (DSR) always ON
- (depends) Data Terminal Ready

There is a site offering sample configurations for a growing variety of modem makes and models at Modem setup information (http://www.in.net/info/modems/index.html) which may assist you in this.

Use your communications software (e.g. minicom or seyon) to find out about your modem configuration and set it to what is required for PPP. Many modems report their current settings in response to AT&V, but you should consult your modem manual.

If you completely mess up the settings, you can return to sanity (usually) by issuing an AT&F—return to factory settings. (For most modem modems I have encountered, the factory settings include all you need for PPP—but you should check).

Once you have worked out the modem setup string required write it down. You now have a decision: you can store these settings in your modem non-volatile memory so they can be recalled by issuing the appropriate AT command. Alternatively you can pass the correct settings to your modem as part of the PPP dialing process.

If you only use your modem from Linux to call into your ISP or corporate server, the simplest set up will have you save your modem configuration in non-volatile RAM.

If on the other hand, your modem is used by other applications and operating systems, it is safest to pass this information to the modem as each call is made so that the modem is guaranteed to be in the correct state for the call. (This has the added advantage also of recording the modem setup string in case the modem looses the contents of its NV-RAM, which can indeed happen).

ISP information. Before you can establish your PPP connection with a remote server, you need to obtain the following information from the system administrator or technical support people of the ISP.

- The telephone number(s) to dial for the service If you are behind a PABX, you also need the PABX number that gives you an outside dial tone—this is frequently digit zero (0) or nine (9).
- Does the server use DYNAMIC or STATIC IP numbers? If the server uses STATIC IP numbers, then you may need to know what IP number to use for your end of the PPP connection. If your ISP is providing you with a subnet of valid IP numbers, you will need to know the IP numbers you can use and the network mask (netmask).

Most Internet Service Providers use DYNAMIC IP numbers. As mentioned above, this has some implications in terms of the services you can use.

However, even if you are using STATIC IP numbers, most PPP servers will never (for security reasons) allow the client to specify an IP number as this is a security risk. You do still need to know this information!.

- What are the IP numbers of the ISPs Domain Name Servers? There should be at least two although only one is needed.

There could be a problem here. The MS Windows 95 PPP setup allows the DNS address to be passed to the client as part of its connection process. So your ISP (or corporate help desk) may well tell you you don't need the IP address of the DNS server(s).

For Linux, you DO need the address of at least one DNS. The linux implementation of PPP does not allow the setting of the DNS IP number dynamically at connection time—and quite possibly will never do so.

- Does the server require the use of PAP/CHAP? If this is the case you need to know the "id" and "secret" you are to use in connecting. (These are probably your user name and password at your ISP).
- Does the server automatically start PPP or do you need to issue any commands to start PPP on the server once you are logged in? If you must issue a command to start PPP, what is it?
- Is the server a Microsoft Windows NT system and, if so, is it using the MS PAP/CHAP system? Many corporate LANs seem to use MS Windows NT this way for increased security.

Every device that connects to the Internet must have its own, unique IP number. These are assigned centrally by a designated authority for each country. Therefore to use a PPP connection must have an IP assigned to you. Due to the increased number of machines on the Internet (partly do the large number of PPP users), a dynamic scheme has been developed for PPP that provides an IP on the fly to your machine when it first establishes the PPP connection. This means that you will have a different IP address every time you connect to the remote PPP dialup service. This is the most common method for most ISPs. The other method is to use a static IP. You cannot just choose an IP to us. It must be assigned by the centralized agency in charge of issuing IP numbers. This prevents two computers from having the same IP address and causing problems on the Internet. The remote PPP dialup service provider will be able to tell you if you are using a static or dynamic IP and also provide you with the actual IP number if you are using the static method.

It is important to note that if you are using dynamic IP assignment, it will be very very difficult to provide any permanent Internet services such as World Wide Web servers, gopher services, or Internet Relay Chat servers. You can still use such services that are on. other machines but cannot offer such services on your machine without going through an extreme amount of effort. Doing this beyond the scope of this document.

PAP and CHAP are different commonly-used authentication methods. Linux supports both of them.

Testing your modem and remote service. Now that you have sorted out the serial port and modem settings it is a good idea to make sure that these setting do indeed work by dialing you ISP and seeing if you can connect.

Using you terminal communications package (such as minicom or seyon), set up the modem initialization required for PPP and dial into the PPP server you want to connect to with a PPP session.

(Note: at this stage we are NOT trying to make a PPP connection—just establishing that we have the right phone number and also to find out exactly what the server sends to us in order to get logged in and start PPP).

During this process, either capture (log to a file) the entire login process or carefully (very carefully) write down exactly what prompts the server gives to let you know it is time to enter your user name and password (and any other commands needed to establish the PPP connection).

If your server uses PAP, you should not see a login prompt, but should instead see the (text representation) of the link control protocol (which looks like garbage) starting on your screen.

A few words of warning:

- some servers are quite intelligent: you can log in using text based user name/passwords OR using PAP. So if your ISP or corporate site uses PAP but you do not see the garbage start up immediately, this may not mean you have done something wrong.
- some servers require you to enter some text initially and then start a standard PAP sequence.
- Some PPP servers are passive—that is they simply sit there sending nothing until the client that is dialing in sends them a valid lcp packet. If the PPP server you are connecting to operates in passive mode, you will never see the garbage!
- Some servers do not start PPP until you press ENTER—so it is worth trying this if you correctly log in and do not see the garbage!

It is worth dialing in at least twice—some servers change their prompts (e.g. with the time!) every time you log in. The two critical prompts your Linux box needs to be able to identify every time you dial in are:

- the prompt that requests you to enter your user name;
- the prompt that requests you to enter your password;

If you have to issue a command to start PPP on the server, you will also need to find out the prompt the server gives you once you are logged in to tell you that you can now enter the command to start PPP.

If your server automatically starts PPP, once you have logged in, you will start to see garbage on your screen—this is the PPP server sending your machine information to start up and configure the PPP connection.
This should look something like this :

```
y}#.!}!}!} }8}!}}U}"}\&} } } } }}\& ...}'}"}()"} .~y}
```

On some systems PPP must be explicitly started on the server. This is usually because the server has been set up to allow PPP logins and shell logins using the same user name/password pair. If this is the case, issue this command once you have logged in. Again, you will see the garbage as the server end of the PPP connection starts up.

If you do not see this immediately after connecting (and logging in and starting the PPP server if required), press Enter to see if this starts the PPP server.

At this point, you can hang up your modem (usually, type +++ quickly and then issue the ATH0 command once your modem responds with OK).

If you can't get your modem to work, read your modem manual, the man pages for your communications software and the Serial HOWTO. Once you have this sorted out, carry on as above.

Using Internet servers with dynamic IP numbers. If you are using dynamic IP numbers (and many service providers will only give you a dynamic IP number unless you pay significantly more for your connection), then you have to recognise the limitations this imposes.

First of all, outbound service requests will work just fine. That is, you can send email using sendmail (provided you have correctly set up sendmail), ftp files from remote sites, finger users on other machines, browse the web etc.

In particular, you can answer email that you have brought down to your machine whilst you are off line. Mail will simply sit in your mail queue until you dial back into your ISP.

However, your machine is not connected to the Internet 24 hours a day, nor does it have the same IP number every time it is connected. So it is impossible for you to receive email directed to your machine, and very difficult to set up a web or ftp server that your friends can access! As far as the Internet is concerned your machine does not exist as a unique, permanently contactable machine as it does not have a unique IP number (remember—other machines will be using the IP number when they are allocated it on dial in).

If you set up a WWW (or any other server), it is totally unknown by any user on the Internet UNLESS they know that your machine is connected AND its actual (current) IP number. There are a number of ways they can get this info, ranging from you ringing them, sending them email to tell them or cunning use of ".plan" files on a shell account at your service provider (assuming that your provider allows shell and finger access).

For most users, this is not a problem—all that most people want is to send and receive email (using your account on your service provider) and make outbound connections to WWW, ftp and other servers on the Internet. If you must have inbound connections to your server, you should really get a static IP number.

PPP connection files. You now need to be logged in as root to create the directories and edit the files needed to set up PPP. PPP uses a number of files to connect and set up a PPP connection. These differ in name and location between PPP 2.1.2 and 2.2.

For PPP 2.1.2 the files are:

/usr/sbin/pppd	# the PPP binary
/usr/sbin/ppp-on	# the dialer/connection script
/usr/sbin/ppp-off	# the disconnection script
/etc/ppp/options	# the options pppd uses for all connections
/etc/ppp/options.tty*XX*	# the options specific to a connection on this port

For PPP 2.2 the files are:

/usr/sbin/pppd	# the PPP binary
/etc/ppp/scripts/ppp-on	# the dialer/connection script
/etc/ppp/scripts/ppp-on-dialer	# part 1 of the dialer script
/etc/ppp/scripts/ppp-off	# the actual chat script itself
/etc/ppp/options	# the options pppd uses for all connections
/etc/ppp/options.tty*XX*	# the options specific to a connection on this port

Red Hat Linux users should note that the standard Red Hat 4.X installation places these scripts in /usr/doc/ppp-2.2.0f-2/scripts.

In your /etc directory there should be a ppp directory:

```
drwxrwxr-x    2  root      root     1024  Oct   9  11:01  ppp
```

If it does not exist—create it with these ownerships and permissions.
If the directory already existed, it should contain a template options file called options. tpl. This file is included below in case it does not.

Print it out as it contains an explanation of nearly all the PPP options (these are useful to read in conjunction with the pppd man pages). Whilst you can use this file as the basis of your /etc/ppp/options file, it is probably better to create your own options file that does not include all the comments in the template - it will be much shorter and easier to read/maintain.

Some distributions of PPP seem to have lost the options.tpl file. You should examine the PPP-HOWTO document for the complete version.

What options should I use? Well, as in all things that depends (sigh). The options specified here should work with most servers.

However, if it does NOT work, READ THE TEMPLATE FILE (/etc/ppp/options.tpl) and the pppd man pages and speak to the sysadmin/user support people who run the server to which you are connecting.

You should also note that the connect scripts presented here also use some command line options to pppd to make things a bit easier to change:

```
# /etc/ppp/options (no PAP/CHAP support)
#
# Prevent pppd from forking into the background -detach
#
# use the modem control lines
modem
# use uucp style locks to ensure exclusive access to the serial device
lock
# use hardware flow control
crtscts
# create a default route for this connection in the routing table
defaultroute
# do NOT set up any "escaped" control sequences
asyncmap 0
# use a maximum transmission packet size of 552 bytes
mtu 552
# use a maximum receive packet size of 552 bytes
mru 552
#
#-------END OF SAMPLE /etc/ppp/options (no PAP/CHAP support )
```

Setting up the PPP connection manually. Now that you have created your /etc/ppp/options and /etc/resolv.conf files (and, if necessary, the /etc/ppp/pap—chap-secrets file), you can test the settings by manually establishing a PPP connection. (Once we have the manual connection working, we will automate the process).

To do this, your communications software must be capable of quitting WITHOUT resetting the modem. Minicom can do this with the sequence *Control - A Q.*

- Make sure you are logged in as root.
- Fire up you communications software (such as minicom), dial into the PPP server and log in as normal. If you need to issue a command to start up PPP on the server, do so. You will now see the garbage you saw before.
- If you are using PAP or CHAP, then merely connecting to the remote system should start PPP on the remote and you will see the garbage without logging in (although this may not happen for some servers - try pressing Enter and see if the garbage starts up)
- Now quit the communications software without resetting the modem and at the Linux prompt (as root) type:

```
# pppd   -d   / dev / ttyS0   38400 &
```

Substituting the name of the device your modem is connected to, of course.

The -d option enables debugging—the PPP connection start-up conversation will be logged to your system log—which is useful for tracing problems later.

- Your modem lights should now flash as the PPP connection is established. It will take a short while for the PPP connection to be made.

At this point you can look at the PPP interface, by issuing the command:

```
# ifconfig
```

In addition to any Ethernet and loop back devices you have, you should see something like :

```
ppp0      Link encap:Point-Point Protocol
          inet addr:10.144.153.104 P-t-P:10.144.153.51 Mask:255.255.255.0
          UP POINTOPOINT RUNNING MTU:552 Metric:1
          RX packets:0 errors:0 dropped:0 overruns:0
          TX packets:0 errors:0 dropped:0 overruns:0
```

Where

- inet addr:10.144.153.10 is the IP number of your end of the link.
- P-t-P:10.144.153.5 is the SERVER's IP number.

(Ifconfig will not report these IP numbers, but the ones used by your PPP server.)

Note:

ifconfig also tells you that the link is UP and RUNNING!
You should also be able to see a route to the the remote host (and beyond). To do this, issue the command:

```
# route -n
```

You should see something like:

Kernel routing table

Destination	Gateway	Genmask	Flags	MSS	Window	Use
10.144.153.3	*	255.255.255.255	UH	1500	0	
127.0.0.0	*	255.0.0.0	U	3584	0	11
10.0.0.0	*	255.0.0.0	U	1500	0	35
default	10.144.153.3	*	UG	1500	0	

Of particular importance here, notice we have TWO entries pointing to our PPP interface.

The first is a HOST route (indicated by the H flag) and that allows us to see the host to which we are connected to—but no further.

The second is the default route (established by giving pppd the option default route. This is the route that tells our Linux PC to send any packets NOT destined for the local Ethernet(s)—to which we have specific network routes—to the PPP server itself. The PPP server then is responsible for routing our packets out onto the Internet and routing the return packets back to us.

If you do not see a routing table with two entries, something is wrong. In particular if your syslog shows a message telling you pppd is not replacing an existing default route, then you have a default route pointing at your Ethernet interface—which MUST be replaced by a specific network route: YOU CAN ONLY HAVE ONE DEFAULT ROUTE!!!

You will need to explore your system initialization files to find out where this default route is being set up (it will use a route add default... command). Change this command to something like route add net....

Now test the link by 'pinging' the server at its IP number as reported by the ifconfig output, i.e.:

```
# ping 10.144.153.51
```

You should receive output like:

```
PING 10.144.153.51 (10.144.153.51): 56 data bytes
64 bytes from 10.144.153.51: icmp_seq=0 ttl=255 time=328.3 ms


64 bytes from 10.144.153.51: icmp_seq=1 ttl=255 time=190.5 ms
64 bytes from 10.144.153.51: icmp_seq=2 ttl=255 time=187.5 ms
64 bytes from 10.144.153.51: icmp_seq=3 ttl=255 time=170.7 ms
```

This listing will go on for ever—to stop it press Control - C , at which point you will receive some more information:

```
--- 10.144.153.51 ping statistics ---
4 packets transmitted, 4 packets received, 0% packet loss
round-trip min/avg/max = 170.7/219.2/328.3 ms
```

Now try pinging a host by name (not the name of the PPP server itself) but a host at another site that you KNOW is probably going to be up and running. For example:

```
# ping sunsite.unc.edu
```

This time there will be a bit of a pause as Linux obtains the IP number for the fully qualified host name you have 'ping'ed from the DNS you specified in /etc/resolv.conf—so don't worry (but you will see your modem lights flash). Shortly you will receive output like:

```
PING sunsite.unc.edu (152.2.254.81): 56 data bytes
64 bytes from 152.2.254.81: icmp_seq=0 ttl=254 time=190.1 ms
64 bytes from 152.2.254.81: icmp_seq=1 ttl=254 time=180.6 ms
64 bytes from 152.2.254.81: icmp_seq=2 ttl=254 time=169.8 ms
64 bytes from 152.2.254.81: icmp_seq=3 ttl=254 time=170.6 ms
64 bytes from 152.2.254.81: icmp_seq=4 ttl=254 time=170.6 ms
```

Again, stop the output by pressing Control - C and get the statistics...

```
--- sunsite.unc.edu ping statistics ---
5 packets transmitted, 5 packets received, 0% packet loss
round-trip min/avg/max = 169.8/176.3/190.1 ms
```

If you don't get any response, try pinging the IP address of the DNS server at your ISP's site. If you get a result from this, then it looks like you have a problem with /etc/resolv.conf.

If this doesn't work, you have a routing problem, or your ISP has a problem routing packets back to you. Check your routing table as shown above and if that is OK, contact your ISP. A good test of the ISP is to use another operating system to connect. If you can get beyond your ISP with that, then the problem is at your end.

If everything works, shut down the connection by typing:

```
# ppp-off
```

After a short pause, the modem should hang itself up.

If that does not work, either turn off your modem or fire up your communications software and interrupt the modem with +++ and then hang up with ATH0 when you receive the modem's OK prompt.

You may also need to clean up the lock file created by pppd by typing:

rm -f /var/lock/LCK..tty*Sx*

4.2.3 Creating the connection scripts.

You can continue to log in by hand as shown above, it is much neater to set up some scripts to do this automatically for you.

A set of scripts automates the log in and PPP start up so all you have to do (as root or as a member of the PPP group) is issue a single command to fire up your connection.

If your ISP does NOT require the use of PAP/CHAP, these are the scripts for you. If the PPP package installed correctly, you should have two example files. For PPP

2.1.2 they are in /usr/sbin and for PPP 2.2 they are in /etc/ppp/scripts. They are called for PPP-2.1.2

ppp-on
ppp-off

and for PPP-2.2

ppp-off
ppp-on
ppp-on-dialer

Now, if you are using PPP 2.1.2, I strongly urge you to delete the sample files. There are potential problems with these—and don't tell me they work fine—I used them for ages too (and recommended them in the first version of this HOWTO)!

For the benefit of PPP 2.1.2 users, here are BETTER template versions, taken from the PPP 2.2 distribution. I suggest you copy and use these scripts instead of the old PPP-2.1.2 scripts.

15.2. The ppp-on script

This is the first of a PAIR of scripts that actually fire up the connection:

```
#!/bin/sh
#
# Script to initiate a PPP connection. This is the first part of the
# pair of scripts. This is not a secure pair of scripts as the codes
# are visible with the 'ps' command. However, it is simple.
#
# These are the parameters. Change as needed.
TELEPHONE=555-1212 # The telephone number for the connection
ACCOUNT=george # The account name for logon (as in 'George Burns')
PASSWORD=gracie # The password for this account (and 'Gracie Allen')
LOCAL_IP=0.0.0.0 # Local IP address if known. Dynamic = 0.0.0.0
REMOTE_IP=0.0.0.0 # Remote IP address if desired. Normally 0.0.0.0
NETMASK=255.255.255.0 # The proper netmask if needed
#
```

```
# Export them so that they will be available to 'ppp-on-dialer'
export TELEPHONE ACCOUNT PASSWORD
#
# This is the location of the script which dials the phone and logs
# in. Please use the absolute file name as the $PATH variable is not
# used on the connect option. (To do so on a 'root' account would be
# a security hole so don't ask.)
#
DIALER_SCRIPT=/etc/ppp/ppp-on-dialer
#
# Initiate the connection
#
#
exec /usr/sbin/pppd debug /dev/ttySx 38400 \
$LOCAL_IP:$REMOTE_IP \
connect $DIALER_SCRIPT
```

Here is the ppp-on-dialer script:

```
#!/bin/sh
#


# This is part 2 of the ppp-on script. It will perform the connection
# protocol for the desired connection.
#
/usr/sbin/chat -v \
TIMEOUT 3 \
ABORT '\nBUSY\r' \
ABORT '\nNO ANSWER\r' \
ABORT '\nRINGING\r\n\r\nRINGING\r' \
" \rAT \
'OK-+++\c-OK' ATH0 \
TIMEOUT 30 \
OK ATDT$TELEPHONE \
CONNECT " \
ogin:--ogin: $ACCOUNT \
assword: $PASSWORD
```

For PPP-2.2, the ppp-off script looks like:

```
#!/bin/sh
######################################################################
#
# Determine the device to be terminated.
#
```

```
if [ "$1" = "" ]; then
DEVICE=ppp0
else
DEVICE=$1
fi
######################################################################
#
# If the ppp0 pid file is present then the program is running. Stop it.
if [ -r /var/run/$DEVICE.pid ]; then
kill -INT 'cat /var/run/$DEVICE.pid'
#
# If the kill did not work then there is no process running for this
# pid. It may also mean that the lock file will be left. You may wish
# to delete the lock file at the same time.
if [ ! "$?" = "0" ]; then
rm -f /var/run/$DEVICE.pid
echo "ERROR: Removed stale pid file"
exit 1


fi
#
# Success. Let pppd clean up its own junk.
echo "PPP link to $DEVICE terminated."


exit 0
fi
#
# The ppp process is not running for ppp0
echo "ERROR: PPP link is not active on $DEVICE"
exit 1
```

4.2.4 Editing the supplied PPP startup scripts.

As the new scripts come in two parts, and we will edit them in turn.

The ppp-on script. You will need to edit the ppp-on script to reflect YOUR user name at your ISP, YOUR password at your ISP, the telephone number of your ISP.

Each of the lines like TELEPHONE= actually set up shell variables that contain the information to the right of the '=' (excluding the comments of course). So edit each of these lines so it is correct for your ISP and connection.

Also, as you are setting the IP number (if you need to) in the /etc/ppp/options file, DELETE the line that says:

```
$LOCAL_IP:$REMOTE_IP \
```

Also, make sure that the shell variable DIALER SCRIPT points at the full path and name of the dialer script that you are actually going to use. So, if you have moved this or renamed the script, make sure you edit this line correctly in the ppp-on script!

The ppp-on-dialer **script.** This is the second of the scripts that actually brings up our ppp link.

Note: a chat script is normally all on one line. the backslashes are used to allow line continuations across several physical lines (for human readability) and do not form part of the script itself.

However, it is very useful to look at it in detail so that we understand what it is actually (supposed) to be doing!

A chat script is a sequence of "expect string" "send string" pairs. In particular, note that we ALWAYS expect something before we send something.

If we are to send something WITHOUT receiving anything first, we must use an empty expect string (indicated by "") and similarly for expecting something without sending anything! Also, if a string consists of several words, (e.g. NO CARRIER), you must quote the string so that it is seen as a single entity by chat.

The chat line in our template is:

```
exec /usr/sbin/chat -v
```

Invoke chat, the -v tells chat to copy ALL its I/O into the system log (usually /var/log/messages). Once you are happy that the chat script is working reliably, edit this line to remove the -v to save unnecessary clutter in your syslog:

```
TIMEOUT        3
```

This sets the timeout for the receipt of expected input to three seconds. You may need to increase this to say 5 or 10 seconds if you are using a really slow modem!

```
ABORT          '\nBUSY\r'
```

If the string BUSY is received, abort the operation:

```
ABORT          '\nNO ANSWER\r'
```

If the string NO ANSWER is received, abort the operation;

ABORT '\nRINGING\r\n\r\nRINGING\r'
\begin{verbatim} \end{tscreen}

If the (repeated) string RINGING is received, abort the operation.
This is because someone is ringing your phone line!

\begin{tscreen} \begin{verbatim}
" \rAT

Expect nothing from the modem and send the string AT.

OK-+++\ c -OK ATH0

This one is a bit more complicated as it uses some of chat's error recovery capabilities. What is says is...Expect OK, if it is NOT received (because the modem is not in command mode) then send +++ (the standard Hayes-compatible modem string that returns the modem to command mode) and expect OK. Then send ATH0 (the modem hang up string).

This allows your script to cope with the situation of your modem being stuck on-line!

TIMEOUT 30

Set the timeout to 30 seconds for the remainder of the script. If you experience trouble with the chat script aborting due to timeouts, increase this to 45 seconds or more:

OK ATDT$TELEPHONE

Expect OK (the modem's response to the ATH0 command) and dial the number we want to call:

CONNECT "

Expect CONNECT (which our modem sends when the remote modem answers) and send nothing in reply:

ogin:--ogin: $ACCOUNT

Again, we have some error recovery built in here. Expect the login prompt (...ogin:) but if we don't receive it by the timeout, send a return and then look for the login prompt again. When the prompt is received, send the username (stored in the shell variable $ACCOUNT):

password: $PASSWORD

Expect the password prompt and send our password (again, stored in a shell variable). This chat script has reasonable error recovery capability. Chat has considerably more features than demonstrated here. For more information consult the chat manual page (man 8 chat).

4.2.5 Starting PPP at the server end.

While the ppp-on-dialer script is fine for servers that automatically start pppd at the server end once you have logged in, some servers require that you explicitly start PPP on the server.

If you need to issue a command to start up PPP on the server, you DO need to edit the ppp-on-dialer script.

At the END of the script (after the password line) add an additional expect send pair— this one would look for your login prompt (beware of characters that have a special meaning in the Bourne shell, like:

```
$[ ]
```

Once chat has found the shell prompt, chat must issue the ppp start up command required for your ISPs PPP server.

In one author's case, the PPP server uses the standard Linux Bash prompt:

```
[hartr@kepler hartr]$
```

which requires the response:

```
# ppp
```

to start up PPP on the server.

It is a good idea to allow for a bit of error recovery here, so use:

```
hartr - - hartr  ppp
```

This says, if we don't receive the prompt within the timeout, send a carriage return and looks for the prompt again.

Once the prompt is received, then send the string ppp.

Note: don't forget to add a to the end of the previous line so chat still thinks the entire chat script is on one line!

Unfortunately, some servers produce a very variable set of prompts! You may need to log in several times using minicom to understand what is going on and pick the stable "expect" strings.

4.2.6 If your PPP server uses PAP (Password Authentication Protocol).

If the server to which you are connecting requires PAP or CHAP authentication, you have a little bit more work.

To the above options file, add the following lines:

```
#
# force pppd to use your ISP user name as your 'host name' during the
# authentication process
name <your ISP user name> # you need to edit this line
#
# If you are running a PPP *server* and need to force PAP or CHAP
# uncomment the appropriate one of the following lines. Do NOT use
# these is you are a client connecting to a PPP server (even if it uses PAP
# or CHAP) as this tells the SERVER to authenticate itself to your
# machine (which almost certainly can't do---and the link will fail).
#+chap
#+pap
#
# If you are using ENCRYPTED secrets in the /etc/ppp/pap-secrets
# file, then uncomment the following line.
# Note: this is NOT the same as using MS encrypted passwords as can be
# set up in MS RAS on Windows NT.
#+papcrypt
```

4.2.7 Using MSCHAP

Microsoft Windows NT RAS can be set up to use a variation on CHAP (Chal-lenge/ Handshake Authentication Protocol). In your PPP sources you will find a file called

README.MSCHAP80 that discusses this. You can determine if the server is requesting authentication using this protocol by enabling debugging for pppd. If the server is requesting MS CHAP authentication, you will see lines like:

```
rcvd   [LCP ConfReq id = 0x2 <asyncmap 0x0>   <auth chap 80>  <magic 0x46a3>]
```

The critical information here is auth chap 80.
In order to use MS CHAP, you will need to recompile pppd to support this. Please see the instructions in the README.MSCHAP80 file in the PPP source file for instructions on how to compile and use this variation.

If you are using pap or chap authentication, then you also need to create the secrets file. These are 1)/etc/ppp/pap-secrets and 2)/etc/ppp/chap-secrets.

They must be owned by user root, group root and have file permissions 740 for security.
The first point to note about PAP and CHAP is that they are designed to authenticate computer systems not users. In other words, once your computer has made its PPP connection to the server, ANY user on your system can use that connection—not just you.

PAP can (and for CHAP DOES) require bidirectional authentication—that is a valid name and secret is required on each computer for the other computer involved. However, this is NOT the way most PPP servers offering dial up PPP PAP-authenticated connections operate.

That being said, your ISP will probably have given you a user name and password to allow you to connect to their system and thence the Internet. Your ISP is not interested in your computer's name at all, so you will probably need to use the user name at your ISP as the name for your computer. This is done using the name user name option to pppd. So, if you are to use the user name given you by your ISP, add the line:

```
name your_user name_at_your_ISP
```

to your /etc/ppp/options file.

Technically, you should really use user our user name at your ISP for PAP, but pppd is sufficiently intelligent to interpret name as user if it is required to use PAP. The advantage of using the name option is that this is also valid for CHAP.

As PAP is for authenticating computers, technically you need also to specify a remote computer name. However, as most people only have one ISP, you can use a wild card (*) for the remote host name in the secrets file.

The /etc/ppp/pap-secrets file looks like:

```
# Secrets for authentication using PAP
# client   server     secret        acceptable_local_IP_addresses
```

The four fields are white space delimited and the last one can be blank (which is what you want for a dynamic and probably static IP allocation from your ISP).

Suppose your ISP gave you a user name of fred and a password of flintstone you would set the name fred option in *letc/ppp/options* and set up your /etc/ppp/pap-secrets file as follows:

```
# Secrets for authentication using PAP
# client        server     secret         acceptable local IP addresses
fred       *         flintstone
```

This says for the local machine name fred (which we have told pppd to use even though it is not our local machine name) and for ANY server, use the password (secret) of flintstone.

Note that we do not need to specify a local IP address, unless we are required to FORCE a particular local, static IP address. Even if you try this, it is unlikely to work as most PPP servers (for security reasons) do not allow the remote system to set the IP number they are to be given.

This requires that you have mutual authentication methods—that is you must allow for both your machine to authenticate the remote server AND the remote server to authenticate your machine.

So, if your machine is fred and the remote is barney, your machine would set name fred remotename barney and the remote machine would set name barney remotename fred in their respective *\/etc/ppp/options.ttySx* files.

The /etc/chap-secrets file for fred would look like:

```
# Secrets for authentication using CHAP
# client      server     secret          acceptable local IP addresses
fred          barney     flintstone
barney        fred       wilma
```

and for barney:

```
# Secrets for authentication using CHAP
# client      server     secret          acceptable local IP addresses
barney        fred       flintstone
fred          barney     wilma
```

Note in particular that both machines must have entries for bidirectional authentication. This allows the local machine to authenticate itself to the remote AND the remote machine to authenticate itself to the local machine.

A chat script for PAP/CHAP authenticated connections. If your ISP is using PAP/CHAP, then your chat script is much simpler. All your chat script needs to do is dial the telephone, wait for a connect and then let pppd handle the logging in!

```
#!/bin/sh
#
# This is part 2 of the ppp-on script. It will perform the connection
# protocol for the desired connection.


#
exec /usr/sbin/chat -v \
        TIMEOUT         3                               \
        ABORT           '\nBUSY\r'                      \
```

```
 ABORT             '\nNO ANSWER\r'                   \
 ABORT             '\nRINGING\r\n\r\nRINGING\r'      \
''                  \rAT                                  \
'OK-+++\c-OK'     ATH0                               \
TIMEOUT            30                                     \
OK                  ATDT$TELEPHONE                   \
CONNECT           ''                                      \
```

As we have already seen, you can turn on debug information logging with the -d option to pppd. The 'debug' option is equivalent to this.

As we are establishing a new connection with a new script, leave in the debug option for now. (Warning: if your disk space is tight, logging pppd exchanges can rapidly extend your syslog file and run you into trouble—but to do this you must fail to connect and keep on trying for quite a few minutes).

Once you are happy that all is working properly, then you can remove this option.

```
exec /usr/sbin/pppd debug file options.myserver /dev/ttyS0 38400 \
```

Testing the connection script. Open a new root Xterm (if you are in X) or open a new virtual console and log in as root.

In this new session, issue the command:

```
# tail -f /var/log/messages
```

Many systems log output to /var/log/messages. If it has a different name on your system, substitute the name of your system log file in the command above.

In the first window (or virtual console) issue the command:

```
# ppp-on &
```

(or whatever name you have called your edited version of /usr/sbin/ppp-on). If you do not put the script into the background by specifying & at the end of the command, you will not get your terminal prompt back until ppp exits (when the link terminates). Now switch back to the window that is tracking your system log.

4.2.8 Shutting down the PPP link.

When you have finished with the PPP link, use the standard ppp-off command to shut it down (remember that you must be root or a member of the ppp group!).

4.2.9 Troubleshooting common problems once the link is working.

One problem you will find is that many service providers will only support the connection software package that they distribute to new accounts. This is (typically) for Microsoft Windows (—and many service provider help desks seem to know nothing about Unix (or Linux). So, be prepared for limited assistance from them!

You could of course do the individual a favour and educate then about Linux (any ISP help desk person should be reasonably 'with it' in Internet terms and that means they should have a home Linux box—of course it does)!

Address resolution problems. OK—your PPP connection is up and running and you can ping the PPP server by IP number (the second or "remote" IP number shown by ifconfig ppp0), but you can't reach anything beyond this.

First of all, try pinging the IP numbers you have specified in /etc/resolv.conf as name servers. If this works, you can see beyond your PPP server (unless this has the same IP number as the "remote" IP number of your connection). So now try pinging the full Internet name of your service provider:

```
ping   my . isp . net
```

Substituting, of course, the name of your actual ISP. If this does not work, you have a problem with name resolution. This is probably because of a typo in your /etc/resolv.conf file. Check this file carefully against the information in the sample /etc/resolve.conf file in section 6.1.1.

If it still doesn't work (and your service provider confirms that his name servers are up and running), you have a problem somewhere else—and check carefully through your Linux installation (looking particularly at file permissions).

If you still can't ping your service provider's IP name servers by IP number, either they are down (give them a voice call and check) or there is a routing problem at your service provider's end.

One possibility is that the "remote end" is a Linux PPP server where the IP forwarding option has not been specified in the kernel!

Debugging a failed attempt. There are any number of reasons that your connection does not work— chat has failed to complete correctly, you have a dirty line, etc. So check your syslog for indications.

A very common problem is that people compile PPP support into the kernel and yet when they try to run pppd, the kernel complains that it does not support ppp! There are a variety of reasons this can occur.

- You failed to boot the new kernel that you compiled with PPP support.
- You failed to install the PPP module that you compiled.
- You expected modules to be loaded automatically and they aren't.
- You are using the incorrect version of PPP for your kernel.
- You are not running pppd as root.
- You mistyped something in your startup scripts.
- You are not correctly logging into the server.
- You are not starting PPP on the server.
- The remote PPP process is slow to start.
- Default route not set.

And a host of others. Look in the PPP FAQ (which is really a series of questions and answers). This is a very comprehensive document and the answers are there! If the answer to your problems is not there, the problem is not ppp's fault!

Getting help when totally stuck. If you can't get your PPP link to work, go back through this document and check everything—in conjunction with the output created by "chat-v..." and "pppd -d" in you system log.

Also consult the PPP documentation and FAQ plus the other documents mention herein! If you are still stuck, try the comp.os.linux.misc and comp.os.linux.networking news-groups are reasonably regularly scanned by people that can help you with PPP as is: comp.protocols.ppp

If you do choose to seek help in the USENET newsgroups, please don't post a very long message consisting of debugging output. This wastes huge amounts of network bandwidth.

It is much better to describe the problem and perhaps include a few lines of debugging output (definitely no more than one screenful).

4.3 Networking with UUCP.

UUCP (UNIX-to-UNIX Copy) is an older mechanism used to transfer information between UNIX systems. Using UUCP, UNIX systems dial each other up (using a modem) and transfer mail messages, news articles, files, and so on. If you don't have TCP/IP or SLIP access, you can use UUCP to communicate with the world. Most of the mail and news software (see Sections 6.5 and 6.6) can be configured to use UUCP to transfer information to other machines. In fact, if there is an Internet site nearby, you can arrange to have Internet mail sent to your Linux machine via UUCP from that site.

The *Linux Network Administrator's Guide* contains complete information on configuring and using UUCP under Linux. Also, the Linux UUCP HOWTO, available via anonymous FTP from sunsite.unc.edu, should be of help. Another source of information on UUCP is the book *Managing UUCP and USENET*, by Tim O'Reilly and Grace Todino. See Appendix A for more information.

4.4 Networking with Microsoft Systems.

Samba is a suite of programs which work together to allow clients to access to a server's filespace and printers via the SMB (Server Message Block) protocol. Initially written for Unix, Samba now also runs on Netware, OS/2 and VMS.

In practice, this means that you can redirect disks and printers to Linux disks and printers from Lan Manager clients, Windows for Workgroups 3.11 clients, Windows NT clients, Linux clients and OS/2 clients. This gives the capability for these operating systems to behave much like a LAN Server or Windows NT Server machine, only with added functionality and flexibility designed to make life easier for administrators.

Samba: Integrating UNIX and Windows contains complete information on configuring and using Samba under Linux. The Samba home pages are located at http://samba.anu.edu.au/samba/ and the SMB HOWTO should also be of help.

4.5 Electronic mail.

Like most UNIX systems, Linux provides a number of software packages for using electronic mail. E-mail on your system can either be local (that is, you only mail other users on your system), or networked (that is, you mail, using either TCP/IP or UUCP, users on other machines on a network). E-mail software usually consists of two parts: a *mailer* and a *transport*. The mailer is the user-level software which is used to actually compose and read e-mail messages. Popular mailers include elm and mailx. The transport is the low-level software which actually takes care of delivering the mail, either locally or remotely. The user never sees the transport software; they only interact with the mailer. However, as the system administrator, it is important to understand the concepts behind the transport software and how to configure it.

The most popular transport software for Linux is sendmail. It is able to send both local and remote TCP/IP and UUCP e-mail. An alternative to sendmail is *Smail.*

The Linux Mail HOWTO gives more information on the available mail software for. Linux and how to configure it on your system. If you plan to send mail remotely, you'll need to understand either TCP/IP or UUCP, depending on how your machine is networked (see Sections 6.1 and 6.3). The UUCP and TCP/IP documents listed in Appendix A should be of help there.

Most of the Linux mail software can be retrieved via anonymous FTP from sunsite.unc.edu in the directory /pub/Linux/system/Mail.

4.6 News and Usenet.

Linux also provides a number of facilities for managing electronic news. You may choose to set up a local news server on your system, which will allow users to post "articles" to various "news groups" on the system...alivelyformofdiscussion. However, if you have access to a TCP/IP or UUCP network, then you will be able to participate in Usenet—a worldwide network news service.

There are two parts to the news software—the *server* and the *client*. The news server is the software which controls the news groups and handles delivering articles to other machines (if you are on a network). The news client, or *news reader*, is the software which connects to the server to allow users to read and post news.

There are several forms of news servers available for Linux. They all follow the same basic protocols and design. The two primary versions are "C News" and "INN". There are many types of news readers, as well, such as rn and tin. The choice of news reader is more or less a matter of taste; all news readers should work equally well with different versions of the server software. That is, the news reader is independent of the server software, and vice versa.

If you only want to run news locally (that is, not as part of Usenet), then you will need to run a server on your system, as well as install a news reader for the users. The news server will store the articles in a directory such as /var/spool/news, and the news reader will be compiled to look in this directory for news articles.

However, if you wish to run news over the network, there are several options open to you. TCP/IP network-based news uses a protocol known as NNTP (Network News Transmission Protocol). NNTP allows a news reader to read news over the network, on a remote machine. NNTP also allows news servers to send articles to each other over the network—this is the software upon which Usenet is based. Most businesses and universities have one or more NNTP servers set up to handle all of the Usenet news for that site. Every other machine at the site runs an NNTP-based news reader to read and post news over the network via the NNTP server. This means that only the NNTP server actually stores the news articles on disk.

Here are some possible scenarios for news configuration:

- You run news locally. That is, you have no network connection, or no desire to run news over the network. In this case, you need to run C News or INN on your machine, and install a news reader to read the news locally.
- You have access to a TCP/IP network and an NNTP server. If your organization has an NNTP news server set up, you can read and post news from your Linux machine by simply installing an NNTP-based news reader. (Most news readers available can be configured to run locally or use NNTP). In this case, you do not need to install a news server or store news articles on your system. The news reader will take care of

reading and posting news over the network. Of course, you will need to have TCP/IP configured and have access to the network (see Section 6.1).

- You have access to a TCP/IP network but have no NNTP server. In this case, you can run an NNTP news server on your Linux system. You can install either a local or an NNTP-based news reader, and the server will store news articles on your system. In addition, you can configure the server to communicate with other NNTP news servers to transfer news articles.
- You want to transfer news using UUCP. If you have UUCP access (see Section 6.3), you can participate in Usenet as well. You will need to install a (local) news server and a news reader. In addition, you will need to configure your UUCP software to periodically transfer news articles to another nearby UUCP machine (known as your "news feed"). UUCP does not use NNTP to transfer news; simply, UUCP provides its own mechanism for transferring news articles.

Most of the "standard" news software (available via anonymous FTP from ftp.uu.net in the directory /news) will compile out-of-the box on Linux. Necessary patches can be found on sunsite.unc.edu in /pub/Linux/system/Mail (which is, incidentally, also where mail software for Linux is found). Other news binaries for Linux may be found in this directory as well.

For more information, refer to the Linux News HOWTO from sunsite.unc.edu in /pub/Linux/docs/HOWTO. Also, the LDP's *Linux Network Administrator's Guide* contains complete information on configuring news software for Linux. The book *Managing UUCP and Usene*t, by Tim O'Reilly and Grace Todino, is an excellent guide to setting up UUCP and news software. Also of interest is the Usenet document "How to become a Usenet site," available from ftp.uu.net, in the directory /usenet/news.announce.newusers.

Command Reference

alias

```
alias [-p] [name[=value] ...]
```

Alias with no arguments or with the -p option prints the list of aliases in the form alias name=value on standard output. When arguments are supplied, an alias is defined for each name whose value is given. A trailing space in value causes the next word to be checked for alias substitution when the alias is expanded. For each name in the argument list for which no value is supplied, the name and value of the alias is printed. Alias returns true unless a name is given for which no alias has been defined.

at

ASSOCIATED COMMANDS FOR at

at, batch, atq, atrm - queue, examine or delete jobs for later execution

SYNOPSIS

```
at [-V] [-q queue] [-f file] [-mldbv] TIME
at -c job [job...]
atq [-V] [-q queue]
atrm [-V] job [job...]
batch [-V] [-q queue] [-f file] [-mv] [TIME]
```

DESCRIPTION

at and batch read commands from standard input or a specified file which are to be executed at a later time, using /bin/sh.

at executes commands at a specified time.

atq lists the user's pending jobs, unless the user is the superuser; in that case, everybody's jobs are listed. The format of the output lines (one for each job) is: Job number, date, hour, job class.

atrm deletes jobs, identified by their job number.

batch executes commands when system load levels permit; in other words, when the load average drops below 0.8, or the value specified in the invocation of atrun.

At allows fairly complex time specifications, extending the POSIX.2 standard. It accepts times of the form HH:MM to run a job at a specific time of day. (If that time is already past, the next day is assumed.) You may also specify midnight, noon, or teatime (4pm) and you can have a time-of-day suffixed with AM or PM for running in the morning or the evening. You can also say what day the job will be run, by giving a date in the form month-name day with an optional year, or giving a date of the form MMDDYY or MM/DD/YY or DD.MM.YY. The specification of a date must follow the specification of the time of day. You can also give times like now + count time-units, where the time-units can be minutes, hours, days, or weeks and you can tell at to run the job today by suffixing the time with today and to run the job tomorrow by suffixing the time with tomorrow.

For example, to run a job at 4pm three days from now, you would do at 4pm + 3 days, to run a job at 10:00am on July 31, you would do at 10am Jul 31 and to run a job at 1am tomorrow, you would do at 1am tomorrow.

The exact definition of the time specification can be input or the file specified with the -f option and executed. The working directory, the environment (except for the variables TERM, DISPLAY and _) and the umask are retained from the time of invocation. An at - or batch -

command invoked from a su(1) shell will retain the current

[at, bash]

userid. The user will be mailed standard error and standard output from his commands, if any. Mail will be sent using the command /usr/lib/sendmail. If at is executed from a su(1) shell, the owner of the login shell will receive the mail.

The superuser may use these commands in any case. For other users, permission to use at is determined by the files /etc/at.allow and /etc/at.deny.

If the file /etc/at.allow exists, only usernames mentioned in it are allowed to use at.

If /etc/at.allow does not exist, /etc/at.deny is checked, every username not mentioned in it is then allowed to use at.

If neither exists, only the superuser is allowed use of at.

An empty /etc/at.deny means that every user is allowed use these commands, this is the default configuration.

bash

bash - GNU Bourne-Again SHell

SYNOPSIS

bash [options] [file]

COPYRIGHT

Bash is Copyright (C) 1989, 1991, 1993, 1995, 1996 by the Free Software Foundation, Inc.

DESCRIPTION

Bash is an sh-compatible command language interpreter that executes commands read from the standard input or from a file. Bash also incorporates useful features from the Korn and C shells (ksh and csh).

Bash is ultimately intended to be a conformant implementation of the IEEE POSIX Shell and Tools specification (IEEE Working Group 1003.2).

[bc,cal]

bc

bc - An arbitrary precision calculator language

SYNTAX

bc [-lwsqv] [long-options] [file ...]

VERSION

This command reference documents GNU bc version 1.04.

DESCRIPTION

bc is a language that supports arbitrary precision numbers with interactive execution of statements. There are some similarities in the syntax to the C programming language. A standard math library is available by command line option. If requested, the math library is defined before processing any files. bc starts by processing code from all the files listed on the command line in the order listed. After all files have been processed, bc reads from the standard input. All code is executed as it is read. (If a file contains a command to halt the processor, bc will never read from the standard input.)

This version of bc contains several extensions beyond traditional bc implementations and the POSIX draft standard. Command line options can cause these extensions to print a warning or to be rejected. This document describes the language accepted by this processor. Extensions will be identified as such.

cal

cal [-jy] [[month] year]

DESCRIPTION

Cal displays a simple calendar. If arguments are not specified, the current month is displayed. The options are as follows:

-j Display julian dates (days one-based, numbered from January 1).

-y Display a calendar for the current year.

[cal, cat, chgrp]

A single parameter specifies the year (1 - 9999) to be displayed; notethe year must be fully specified: ``cal 89'' will not display a calendar for 1989. Two parameters denote the month (1 - 12) and year. If no parameters are specified, the current month's calendar is displayed. A year starts on Jan 1.

The Gregorian Reformation is assumed to have occurred in 1752 on the 3rd of September. By this time, most countries had recognized the reformation (although a few did not recognize it until the early 1900's.) Ten days following that date were eliminated by the reformation, so the calendar for that month is a bit unusual.

cat

cat - concatenate (combines)files and prints on the standard output.

SYNOPSIS

cat [-benstuvAET] [--number] [--number-nonblank]

[--squeeze-blank] [--show-nonprinting] [--show-ends] [--show-tabs] [--show-all] [--help] [--version] [file...]

DESCRIPTION

This documentation is no longer being maintained and may be inaccurate or incomplete. The Texinfo documentation is now the authoritative source.

This manual page documents the GNU version of cat. cat writes the contents of each given file, or the standard input if none are given or when a file named `-' is given, to the standard output.

chgrp

chgrp - change group ownership of files

SYNOPSIS

chgrp [options] group file...

POSIX options: [-R]

GNU options (shortest form): [-cfvR] [--help] [--version] [--]

[chgrp, chmod]

DESCRIPTION

chgrp changes the group ownership of each given file to group, which can be either a group name or a numeric group ID.

chmod

chmod - change access permissions of files

SYNOPSIS

chmod [options] mode file...

POSIX options: [-R]

GNU options (shortest form): [-cfvR] [--help] [--version] [--]

DESCRIPTION

chmod changes the permissions of each given file according to mode, which can be either a symbolic representation of changes to make, or an octal number representing the bit pattern for the new permissions.

The format of a symbolic mode change argument is `[ugoa...][[+-=][rwxXstugo...]...][,...]'.

Such an argument is a list of symbolic mode change commands, separated by commas. Each symbolic mode change command starts with zero or more of the letters `ugoa'; these control which users' access to the file will be changed: the user who owns it (u), other users in the file's group (g), other users not in the file's group (o), or all users (a). Thus, `a' is here equivalent to `ugo'. If none of these are given, the effect is as if `a' were given, but bits that are set in the umask are not affected.

The operator `+' causes the permissions selected to be added to the existing permissions of each file; `-' causes them to be removed; and `=' causes them to be the only permissions that the file has.

[**chmod,chown**]

The letters `rwxXstugo' select the new permissions for the affected users: read (r), write (w), execute (or access for directories) (x), execute only if the file is a directory or already has execute permission for some user (X), set user or group ID on execution (s), sticky bit (t), the permissions that the user who owns the file currently has for it (u), the permissions that other users in the file's group have for it (g), and the permissions that other users not in the file's group have for it (o). (Thus, `chmod g-s file' removes the set-group-ID (sgid) bit, `chmod ug+s file' sets both the suid and sgid bits, while `chmod o+s file' does nothing.)

The `sticky bit' is not described by POSIX. The name derives from the original meaning: keep program text on swap device. These days, when set for a directory, it means that only the owner of the file and the owner of general write permission.)

A numeric mode is from one to four octal digits (0-7), derived by adding up the bits with values 4, 2, and 1. Any omitted digits are assumed to be leading zeros. The first digit selects the set user ID (4) and set group ID (2) and save text image [`sticky'] (1) attributes. The second digit selects permissions for the user who owns the file: read (4), write (2), and execute (1); the third selects permissions for other users in the file's group, with the same values; and the fourth for other users not in the file's group, with the same values.

chmod never changes the permissions of symbolic links, since the chmod system call cannot change their permissions. This is not a problem since the permissions of symbolic links are never used. However, for each symbolic link listed on the command line, chmod changes the permissions of the pointed-to file. In contrast, chmod ignores symbolic links encountered during recursive directory traversals.

chown

chown - change file owner and group

[chown, clear]

SYNOPSIS

chown [options] user[:group] file...

POSIX options: [-R]

GNU options (shortest form): [-cfhvR] [--help] [--version] [--]

DESCRIPTION

chown changes the user and/or group ownership of each given file as specified by the first non-option argument as follows: if only a user name (or numeric user ID) is given, that user is made the owner of each given file, and the files' group is not changed. If the user name is followed by a colon and a group name (or numeric group ID), with no spaces between them, the group ownership of the files is changed as well.

GNU DETAILS

The GNU version allows a dot instead of a colon (following BSD). [This was not allowed by POSIX since a dot is a valid character in a user name.] If a colon or dot but no group name follows the user name, that user is made the owner of the files and the group of the files is changed to that user's login group. If the colon or dot and group are given, but the user name is omitted, only the group of the files is changed; in this case, chown performs the same function as chgrp.

clear

clear - clears the terminal screen

SYNOPSIS

clear

DESCRIPTION

clear clears your screen if this is possible. It looks in the environment for the terminal type and then in the terminfo database to figure out how to clear the screen.

[clear, cmp]

SEE ALSO

tput(1), terminfo(5)

cmp

cmp [-l | -s] file1 file2 [skip1 [skip2]]

DESCRIPTION

The cmp utility compares two files of any type and writes the results to the standard output. By default, cmp is silent if the files are the same; if they differ, the byte and line number at which the first difference occurred is reported.

Bytes and lines are numbered beginning with one.

The following options are available:

-l Print the byte number (decimal) and the differing byte values(octal) for each difference.
-s Print nothing for differing files; return exit status only.

The optional arguments skip1 and skip2 are the byte offsets from the beginning of file1 and file2, respectively, where the comparison will begin. The offset is decimal by default, but may be expressed as an hexadecimal or octal value by preceding it with a leading``0x'' or ``0''.

The cmp utility exits with one of the following values:

0 The files are identical.

1 The files are different; this includes the case where one file is identical to the first part of the other. In the latter case, if the -s option has not been specified, cmp writes to standard output that EOF was reached in the shorter file (before any differences were found).

>1 An error occurred.

[cmp, cp]

SEE ALSO

diff(1), diff3(1)

STANDARDS

The cmp utility is expected to be IEEE Std1003.2 (``POSIX'') compatible.

BSD Experimental June 6, 1993

cp

cp - copy files and directories

SYNOPSIS

```
cp [options] file path
cp [options] file... directory

POSIX options: [-fipRr]

GNU options (shortest form): [-abdfilprsuvxPR] [-S SUFFIX]
[-V {numbered,existing,simple}] [--sparse=WHEN] [--help]
[--version] [--]
```

DESCRIPTION

cp copies files (or, optionally, directories). You can either copy one file to a given destination, or copy arbitrarily many files to a destination directory.

If the last argument names an existing directory, cp copies each source file into that directory (retaining the same name). Otherwise, if only two files are given, it copies the first onto the second. It is an error if the last argument is not a directory and more than two non-option arguments are given.

(Thus, `cp -r /a /b' will copy /a to /b/a and /a/x to /b/a/x in case /b exists already, but it will copy /a to /b and /a/x to /b/x if there was no /b beforehand.)

The modes of the files and directories created will be the same as those of the original files, ANDed by 0777, and modified by the user's umask (unless the -p option was specified). (But during the recursive copy of directo-

ries, newly created directories will temporarily get their final mode ORed with S_IRWXU (0700), so as to allow the process to read, write and search the newly created directory.)

Nothing is done when copying a file to itself (except possibly producing an error message). When copying to a different existing file, it is opened using `open(path, O_WRONLY | O_TRUNC)'. When copying to a new file it is created using `open(path, O_WRONLY | O_CREAT, mode)'. If this fails, the file existed, and the -f option was given, cp tries to delete (unlink) the existing file, and if this succeeds proceeds as for a new file.

cpio

cpio - copy files to and from archives

SYNOPSIS

cpio {-o|--create} [-0acvABLV] [-C bytes] [-H format] [-M message] [-O [[user@]host:]archive] [-F [[user@]host:]archive] [--file=[[user@]host:]archive]

[--format=format] [--message=message] [--null] [--reset-access-time] [--verbose] [--dot] [--append] [--block-size=blocks] [--dereference] [--io-size=bytes] [--quiet] [--force-local] [--rsh-command=command] [--help] [--version] < name-list [> archive]

cpio {-i|--extract} [-bcdfmnrtsuvBSV] [-C bytes] [-E file] [-H format] [-M message] [-R [user][:.][group]] [-I [[user@]host:]archive] [-F [[user@]host:]archive] [--file=[[user@]host:]archive] [--make-directories] [--nonmatching] [--preserve-modification-time] [--numeric-uid-gid] [--rename] [--list] [--swap-bytes] [--swap] [--dot] [--unconditional] [--verbose] [--block-size=blocks] [--swap-halfwords] [--io-size=bytes] [--pattern-file=file] [--format=format] [--owner=[user][:.][group]] [--no-preserve-owner] [--message=message] [--force-local] [--no-absolute-filenames] [--sparse] [--only-verify-crc] [--quiet] [--rsh-command=command] [--help] [--version] [pattern...] [< archive]

[cpio]

cpio {-p|--pass-through} [-0adlmuvLV] [-R [user][:.][group]] [--null] [--reset-access-time] [--make-directories] [--link] [--quiet] [--preserve-modification-time] [--unconditional] [--verbose] [--dot] [--dereference] [--owner=[user][:.][group]] [--no-preserve-owner] [--sparse] [--help] [--version] destination-directory < name-list

DESCRIPTION

This manual page documents the GNU version of cpio. cpio copies files into or out of a cpio or tar archive, which is a file that contains other files plus information about them, such as their file name, owner, timestamps, and access permissions. The archive can be another file on the disk, a magnetic tape, or a pipe. cpio has three operating modes.

In copy-out mode, cpio copies files into an archive. It reads a list of filenames, one per line, on the standard input, and writes the archive onto the standard output. A typical way to generate the list of filenames is with the find command; you should give find the -depth option to minimize problems with permissions on directories that are unwritable or not searchable.

standard input. Any non-option command line arguments are shell globbing patterns; only files in the archive whose names match one or more of those patterns are copied from the archive. Unlike in the shell, an initial `.' in a filename does match a wildcard at the start of a pattern, and a `/' in a filename can match wildcards. If no patterns are given, all files are extracted.

In copy-pass mode, cpio copies files from one directory tree to another, combining the copy-out and copy-in steps without actually using an archive. It reads the list of files to copy from the standard input; the directory into which it will copy them is given as a non-option argument.

cpio supports the following archive formats: binary, old ASCII, new ASCII, crc, HPUX binary, HPUX old ASCII, old tar, and POSIX.1 tar. The binary format is obsolete because it encodes information about the files in a way

that is not portable between different machine architectures. The old ASCII format is portable between different machine architectures, but should not be used on file systems with more than 65536 i-nodes. The new ASCII format is portable between different machine architectures and can be used on any size file system, but is not supported by all versions of cpio; currently, it is only supported by GNU and Unix System V R4. The crc format is like the new ASCII format, but also contains a checksum for each file which cpio calculates when creating an archive and verifies when the file is extracted from the archive. The HPUX formats are provided for compatibility with HPUX's cpio which stores device files differently.

The tar format is provided for compatability with the tar program. It can not be used to archive files with names longer than 100 characters, and can not be used to archive "special" (block or character devices) files. The POSIX.1 tar format can not be used to archive files with names longer than 255 characters (less unless they have a "/" in just the right place).

By default, cpio creates binary format archives, for compatibility with older cpio programs. When extracting from archives, cpio automatically recognizes which kind of archive it is reading and can read archives created on machines with a different byte-order.

Some of the options to cpio apply only to certain operating modes; see the SYNOPSIS section for a list of which options are allowed in which modes.

cron

cron - daemon to execute scheduled commands (Vixie Cron)

SYNOPSIS

cron

DESCRIPTION

cron is started automatically from /etc/init.d on entering multi-user runlevels.

[cron]

cron searches its spool area (/var/spool/cron/crontabs) for crontab files (which are named after accounts in /etc/passwd); crontabs found are loaded into memory. Note that crontabs in this directory should not be accessed directly - the crontab command should be used to access and update them.

cron also reads /etc/crontab, which is in a slightly different format (see crontab(5)). Additionally, cron reads the files in /etc/cron.d; see the DEBIAN SPECIFIC section below for more details.

cron then wakes up every minute, examining all stored crontabs, checking each command to see if it should be run in the current minute. When executing commands, any output is mailed to the owner of the crontab (or to the user named in the MAILTO environment variable in the crontab, if such exists).

Additionally, cron checks each minute to see if its spool directory's modtime (or the modtime on /etc/crontab) has changed, and if it has, cron will then examine the modtime on all crontabs and reload those which have changed. Thus cron need not be restarted whenever a crontab file is modified. Note that the crontab(1) command updates the modtime of the spool directory whenever it changes a crontab.

DEBIAN SPECIFIC

cron treats the files in /etc/cron.d as extensions to the /etc/crontab file (they follow the special format of that file, i.e. they include the user field). The intended purpose of this feature is to allow packages that require finer control of their scheduling than the /etc/cron.{daily,weekly,monthly} directories allow to add a crontab file to /etc/cron.d. Such files should be named after the package that supplies them. Files must conform to the same naming convention as used by run-parts(8): they must consist solely of upper- and lower-case letters, digits, underscores, and hyphens. Like /etc/crontab, the files in the /etc/cron.d directory are monitored for changes.

[cron, crontab]

SEE ALSO

Paul Vixie <paul@vix.com>

crontab

crontab - maintain crontab files for individual users (V3)

SYNOPSIS

```
crontab [ -u user ] file
crontab [ -u user ] { -l | -r | -e }
```

DESCRIPTION

crontab is the program used to install, deinstall or list the tables used to drive the cron(8) daemon in Vixie Cron. Each user can have their own crontab, and though these are files in /var/spool/cron/crontabs, they are not intended to be edited directly.

If the /etc/cron.allow file exists, then you must be listed therein in order to be allowed to use this command. If the /etc/cron.allow file does not exist but the /etc/cron.deny file does exist, then you must not be listed in the /etc/cron.deny file in order to use this command. If neither of these files exists, then depending on site-dependent configuration parameters, only the super user will be allowed to use this command, or all users will be able to use this command. For standard Debian systems, all users may use this command.

If the -u option is given, it specifies the name of the user whose crontab is to be tweaked. If this option is not given, crontab examines "your" crontab, i.e., the crontab of the person executing the command. Note that su(8) can confuse crontab and that if you are running inside of su(8) you should always use the -u option for safety's sake.

The first form of this command is used to install a new crontab from some named file or standard input if the pseudo-filename ``-'' is given.

[crontab, crypt]

The -l option causes the current crontab to be displayed on standard output. See the note under DEBIAN SPECIFIC below.

The -r option causes the current crontab to be removed.

The -e option is used to edit the current crontab using the editor specified by the VISUAL or EDITOR environment variables. After you exit from the editor, the modified crontab will be installed automatically.

DEBIAN SPECIFIC

The "out-of-the-box" behaviour for crontab -l is to display the three line "DO NOT EDIT THIS FILE" header that is placed at the beginning of the crontab when it is installed. The problem is that it makes the sequence

non-idempotent -- you keep adding copies of the header. This causes pain to scripts that use sed to edit a crontab. Therefore, setting the environment variable CRONTAB_NOHEADER to 'Y' will cause the crontab -l command to prune the extraneous header. The reason it was not made the default is that at present, some other Debian packages have scripts that feed the output of crontab -l to a sed command that just chops the first three lines, assuming it will be the unwanted header. This special behaviour will be made the default on a future release (probably for Debian 2.1).

SEE ALSO

crontab(5), cron(8)

FILES

/etc/cron.allow
/etc/cron.deny

crypt

crypt - password and data encryption

[**crypt**]

SYNOPSIS

```
#define _XOPEN_SOURCE
#include <unistd.h>
char *crypt(const char *key, const char *salt));
```

DESCRIPTION

crypt is the password encryption function. It is based on the Data Encryption Standard algorithm with variations intended (among other things) to discourage use of hardware implementations of a key search.

key is a user's typed password.

salt is a two-character string chosen from the set [a-zA-Z0-9./]. This string is used to perturb the algorithm in one of 4096 different ways.

By taking the lowest 7 bit of each character of the key, a

56-bit key is obtained. This 56-bit key is used to encrypt repeatedly a constant string (usually a string consisting of all zeros). The returned value points to the encrypted password, a series of 13 printable ASCII characters (the first two characters represent the salt itself). The return value points to static data whose content is overwritten by each call.

Warning: The key space consists of 2**56 equal 7.2e16 possible values. Exhaustive searches of this key space are possible using massively parallel computers. Software, such as crack(1), is available which will search the portion of this key space that is generally used by humans for passwords. Hence, password selection should, at minimum, avoid common words and names. The use of a passwd(1) program that checks for crackable passwords during the selection process is recommended.

The DES algorithm itself has a few quirks which make the use of the crypt(3) interface a very poor choice for anything other than password authentication. If you are planning on using the crypt(3) interface for a cryptography project, don't do it: get a good book on encryption and one of the widely available DES libraries.

[crypt, csh, csplit]

CONFORMING TO

SVID, X/OPEN, BSD 4.3

SEE ALSO

login(1), passwd(1), encrypt(3), getpass(3), passwd(5)

csh

tcsh - C shell with file name completion and command line editing

SYNOPSIS

```
tcsh [-bcdefFimnqstvVxX] [-Dname[=value]] [arg ...]
tcsh -l
```

DESCRIPTION

tcsh is an enhanced but completely compatible version of the Berkeley UNIX C shell, csh(1). It is a command language interpreter usable both as an interactive login shell and a shell script command processor. It includes a command-line editor (see The command-line editor), programmable word completion (see Completion and listing), spelling correction (see Spelling correction), a history mechanism (see History substitution), job control (see Jobs) and a C-like syntax. The NEW FEATURES section describes major enhancements of tcsh over csh(1). Throughout this manual, features of tcsh not found in most csh(1) implementations (specifically, the 4.4BSD csh) are labeled with `(+)', and features which are present in csh(1) but not usually documented are labeled with `(u)'.

csplit

csplit - split a file into sections determined by context lines

[csplit, date]

SYNOPSIS

csplit [-sqkz] [-f prefix] [-b suffix] [-n digits] [--prefix=prefix] [--suffix-format=suffix] [--digits=digits] [--quiet] [--silent] [--keep-files] [--elide-empty-files] [--help] [--version] file pattern...

DESCRIPTION

This documentation is no longer being maintained and may be inaccurate or incomplete. The Texinfo documentation is now the authoritative source.

This manual page documents the GNU version of csplit. csplit creates zero or more output files containing sections of the given input file, or the standard input if the name `-' is given. By default, csplit prints the number of bytes written to each output file after it has been created.

The contents of the output files are determined by the pattern arguments. An error occurs if a pattern argument refers to a nonexistent line of the input file, such as if no remaining line matches a given regular expression. After all the given patterns have been matched, any remaining output is copied into one last output file.

date

date - print or set the system date and time

SYNOPSIS

date [-u] [-d datestr] [-f datefile] [-R] [-r file] [-s datestr] [--utc] [--universal] [--date=datestr] [--file=datefile] [--rfc-822] [--reference=file] [--set=datestr] [--help] [--version] [+FORMAT] [MMDDhhmm[[CC]YY][.ss]]

DESCRIPTION

This documentation is no longer being maintained and may be inaccurate or incomplete. The Texinfo documentation is now the authoritative source.

[date, dd]

This manual page documents the GNU version of date. date with no arguments prints the current time and date (as if the format string was `%a %b %e %H:%M:%S %Z %Y'; the `%' directives are described below). If given an argument that starts with a `+', it prints time and date in a format controlled by that argument, which has the same format as the format string passed to the `strftime' function. Except for directives that start with `%', characters in that string are printed unchanged.

dd

dd - convert and copy a file

SYNOPSIS

dd [--help] [--version] [if=file] [of=file] [ibs=bytes] [obs=bytes] [bs=bytes] [cbs=bytes] [skip=blocks] [seek=blocks] [count=blocks] [conv={ascii, ebcdic, ibm, block, unblock, lcase, ucase, swab, noerror, notrunc, sync}]

DESCRIPTION

dd copies a file (from standard input to standard output, by default) using specific input and output blocksizes, while optionally performing conversions on it.

It reads the input one block at a time, using the specified input block size (the default is 512 bytes). If the bs=bytes option was given, and no conversion other than sync, noerror, or notrunc was specified, it writes the amount of data read (which could be smaller than what was requested) in a separate output block. This output block has precisely the same length as was read unless the sync conversion was specified, in which case the data is padded with NULs (or spaces, see below).

Otherwise, the input, read one block at a time, is processed and the resulting output is collected and written in blocks of the specified output block size. The final output block may be shorter.

The numeric-valued options below (bytes and blocks) can be followed by a multiplier: `k'=1024, `b'=512, `w'=2, `c'=1

[date, df, diff]

(`w' and `c' are GNU extensions; `w' should never be used - it means 2 in System V and 4 in 4.2BSD). Two or more of such numeric expressions can be multiplied by putting `x' in between.

df

df - report filesystem disk space usage

SYNOPSIS

df [options] [file...]

POSIX options: [-kP]

GNU options (shortest form): [-ahikmPv] [-t fstype] [-x fstype] [--print-type] [--no-sync] [--sync] [--help] [--version] [--]

DESCRIPTION

df reports the amount of disk space used and available on filesystems.

With no arguments, df reports the space used and available on all currently mounted filesystems (of all types). Otherwise, df reports on the filesystem containing each argument file.

diff

diff - find differences between two files

SYNOPSIS

diff [options] from-file to-file

DESCRIPTION

In the simplest case, diff compares the contents of the two files from-file and to-file. A file name of - stands for text read from the standard input. As a special case, diff - - compares a copy of standard input to itself.

[diff, diff3, du]

If from-file is a directory and to-file is not, diff compares the file in from-file whose file name is that of to-file, and vice versa. The non-directory file must not be -.

If both from-file and to-file are directories, diff compares corresponding files in both directories, in alphabetical order; this comparison is not recursive unless the -r or --recursive option is given. diff never compares the actual contents of a directory as if it were a file. The file that is fully specified may not be standard input, because standard input is nameless and the notion of ``file with the same name'' does not apply.

diff options begin with -, so normally from-file and to-

file may not begin with -. However, -- as an argument by itself treats the remaining arguments as file names even if they begin with -.

diff3

diff3 - find differences between three files

SYNOPSIS

diff3 [options] mine older yours

DESCRIPTION

The diff3 command compares three files and outputs descriptions of their differences.

The files to compare are mine, older, and yours. At most one of these three file names may be -, which tells diff3 to read the standard input for that file.

du

du - estimate file space usage

[du, ed]

SYNOPSIS

du [options] [file...]

POSIX options: [-askx]

GNU options (shortest form): [-abchklmsxDLS] [--help] [--version] [--]

DESCRIPTION

du reports the amount of disk space used by the specified files, and by each directory in the hierarchies rooted at the specified files. Here `disk space used' means space used for the entire file hierarchy below the specified file.

Without arguments, du reports the disk space for the current directory.

ed

ed, red - text editor

SYNOPSIS

ed [-] [-Gs] [-p string] [file]

red [-] [-Gs] [-p string] [file]

DESCRIPTION

ed is a line-oriented text editor. It is used to create, display, modify and otherwise manipulate text files. red is a restricted ed: it can only edit files in the current directory and cannot execute shell commands.

If invoked with a file argument, then a copy of file is read into the editor's buffer. Changes are made to this copy and not directly to file itself. Upon quitting ed, any changes not explicitly saved with a `w' command are lost.

Editing is done in two distinct modes: command and input. When first invoked, ed is in command mode. In this mode

commands are read from the standard input and executed to manipulate the contents of the editor buffer.

elm

elm - an interactive mail system

SYNOPSIS

elm [-achkKmrtwz] [-f alternate-folder] [-d debug-level]
elm [-s subject] list of aliases or addresses

DESCRIPTION

Elm is an interactive screen-oriented mailer program that supersedes mail and mailx.

egrep

grep, egrep, fgrep - print lines matching a pattern

SYNOPSIS

grep [-[AB] NUM] [-CEFGVbchiLlnqsvwxyUu] [--extended-reg-exp] [--fixed-strings] [--basic-regexp] [--regexp=PATTERN] [--file=FILE] [--ignore-case] [--word-regexp] [--line-reg-exp] [--line-regexp] [--no-messages] [--revert-match] [--version] [--help] [--byte-offset] [--line-number] [--with-filename] [--no-filename] [--quiet] [--silent] [--files-without-match] [--files-with-matcces] [--count] [--before-context=NUM] [--after-context=NUM] [--context] [--binary] [--unix-byte-offsets] [-e PATTERN | -f FILE | pattern] files...

DESCRIPTION

Grep searches the named input files (or standard input if no files are named, or the file name - is given) for lines containing a match to the given pattern. By default, grep prints the matching lines.

[emacs, fgrep, file]

emacs

An up-to-date screen oriented text editor.
Check the Appendix for more details.

fgrep

grep, egrep, fgrep - print lines matching a pattern

SYNOPSIS

grep [-[AB] NUM] [-CEFGVbchiLlnqsvwxyUu] [--extended-regexp] [--fixed-strings] [--basic-regexp] [--regexp=PATTERN] [--file=FILE] [--ignore-case] [--word-regexp] [--line-regexp] [--line-regexp] [--no-messages] [--revert-match] [--version] [--help] [--byte-offset] [--line-number] [--with-filename] [--no-filename] [--quiet] [--silent] [--files-without-match] [--files-with-matcces] [--count] [--before-context=NUM] [--after-context=NUM] [--context] [--binary] [--unix-byte-offsets] [-e PATTERN | -f FILE | pattern] files...

DESCRIPTION

Grep searches the named input files (or standard input if no files are named, or the file name - is given) for lines containing a match to the given pattern. By default, grep prints the matching lines.

file

file - determines file type

SYNOPSIS

file [-vbczL] [-f namefile] [-m magicfiles] file ...

DESCRIPTION

This manual page documents version 3.26 of the file command. File tests each argument in an attempt to classify it. There are three sets of tests, performed in this order: filesystem tests, magic number tests, and language

tests. The first test that succeeds causes the file type to be printed.

find

find - search for files in a directory hierarchy

SYNOPSIS

find [path...] [expression]

DESCRIPTION

This manual page documents the GNU version of find. find searches the directory tree rooted at each given file name by evaluating the given expression from left to right, according to the rules of precedence (see section OPERATORS), until the outcome is known (the left hand side is false for and operations, true for or), at which point find moves on to the next file name.

finger

finger [-lmsp] [user ...] [user@host ...]

DESCRIPTION

The finger displays information about the system users.

ftp

ftp - file transfer protocol

ftp [-v] [-d] [-i] [-n] [-g] [host]
pftp [-v] [-d] [-i] [-n] [-g] [host]

DESCRIPTION

Ftp is the user interface to the ARPANET standard File Transfer Protocol.The program allows a user to transfer files to and from a remote network site.

[grep, gunzip]

grep

grep, egrep, fgrep - print lines matching a pattern

SYNOPSIS

grep [-[AB] NUM] [-CEFGVbchiLlnqsvwxyUu] [--extended-regexp] [--fixed-strings] [--basic-regexp] [--regexp=PATTERN] [--file=FILE] [--ignore-case] [--word-regexp] [--line-regexp] [--line-regexp] [--no-messages] [--revert-match] [--version] [--help] [--byte-offset] [--line-number] [--with-filename] [--no-filename] [--quiet] [--silent] [--files-without-match] [--files-with-matcces] [--count] [--before-context=NUM] [--after-context=NUM] [--context] [--binary] [--unix-byte-offsets] [-e PATTERN | -f FILE | pattern] files...

DESCRIPTION

Grep searches the named input files (or standard input if no files are named, or the file name - is given) for lines containing a match to the given pattern. By default, grep prints the matching lines.

gunzip

gzip, gunzip, zcat - compress or expand files

SYNOPSIS

```
gzip [ -acdfhlLnNrtvV19 ] [-S suffix] [ name ...  ]
gunzip [ -acfhlLnNrtvV ] [-S suffix] [ name ...  ]
zcat [ -fhLV ] [ name ...  ]
```

DESCRIPTION

Gzip reduces the size of the named files using Lempel-Ziv coding (LZ77). Whenever possible, each file is replaced by one with the extension .gz, while keeping the same ownership modes, access and modification times. (The default extension is -gz for VMS, z for MSDOS, OS/2 FAT, Windows NT FAT and Atari.) If no files are specified, or if a file name is "-", the standard input is compressed to the standard output. Gzip will only attempt to compress regular files. In particular, it will ignore symbolic links.

[**gunzip**]

If the compressed file name is too long for its file system, gzip truncates it. Gzip attempts to truncate only the parts of the file name longer than 3 characters. (A part is delimited by dots.) If the name consists of small parts only, the longest parts are truncated. For example, if file names are limited to 14 characters, gzip.msdos.exe is compressed to gzi.msd.exe.gz. Names are not truncated on systems which do not have a limit on file name length.

By default, gzip keeps the original file name and timestamp in the compressed file. These are used when decompressing the file with the -N option. This is useful when the compressed file name was truncated or when the time stamp was not preserved after a file transfer.

Compressed files can be restored to their original form using gzip -d or gunzip or zcat. If the original name saved in the compressed file is not suitable for its file system, a new name is constructed from the original one to make it legal.

gunzip takes a list of files on its command line and replaces each file whose name ends with .gz, -gz, .z, -z, _z or .Z and which begins with the correct magic number with an uncompressed file without the original extension. gunzip also recognizes the special extensions .tgz and .taz as shorthands for .tar.gz and .tar.Z respectively. When compressing, gzip uses the .tgz extension if necessary instead of truncating a file with a .tar extension.

gunzip can currently decompress files created by gzip, zip, compress, compress -H or pack. The detection of the input format is automatic. When using the first two formats, gunzip checks a 32 bit CRC. For pack, gunzip checks is sometimes able to detect a bad .Z file. If you get an error when uncompressing a .Z file, do not assume that the .Z file is correct simply because the standard uncompress does not complain. This generally means that the standard uncompress does not check its input, and happily generates garbage output. The SCO compress -H format (lzh compression method) does not include a CRC but also allows some consistency checks.

Files created by zip can be uncompressed by gzip only if they have a single member compressed with the 'deflation' method. This feature is only intended to help conversion of tar.zip files to the tar.gz format. To extract zip files with several members, use unzip instead of gunzip.

[gunzip, gzip]

zcat is identical to gunzip -c. (On some systems, zcat may be installed as gzcat to preserve the original link to compress.) zcat uncompresses either a list of files on the command line or its standard input and writes the uncompressed data on standard output. zcat will uncompress files that have the correct magic number whether they have a .gz suffix or not.

Gzip uses the Lempel-Ziv algorithm used in zip and PKZIP. The amount of compression obtained depends on the size of the input and the distribution of common substrings. Typically, text such as source code or English is reduced by 60-70%. Compression is generally much better than that achieved by LZW (as used in compress), Huffman coding (as used in pack), or adaptive Huffman coding (compact).

Compression is always performed, even if the compressed file is slightly larger than the original. The worst case expansion is a few bytes for the gzip file header, plus 5 bytes every 32K block, or an expansion ratio of 0.015% for large files. Note that the actual number of used disk blocks almost never increases. gzip preserves the mode, ownership and timestamps of files when compressing or decompressing.

gzip

gzip, gunzip, zcat - compress or expand files

SYNOPSIS

```
gzip [ -acdfhlLnNrtvV19 ] [-S suffix] [ name ...  ]
gunzip [ -acfhlLnNrtvV ] [-S suffix] [ name ...  ]
zcat [ -fhLV ] [ name ...  ]
```

DESCRIPTION

Gzip reduces the size of the named files using Lempel-Ziv coding (LZ77). Whenever possible, each file is replaced by one with the extension .gz, while keeping the same ownership modes, access and modification times. (The default extension is -gz for VMS, z for MSDOS, OS/2 FAT, Windows NT FAT and Atari.) If no files are specified, or if a file name is "-", the standard input is compressed to the standard output. Gzip will only attempt to compress regular files. In particular, it will ignore symbolic links.

[gzip]

If the compressed file name is too long for its file system, gzip truncates it. Gzip attempts to truncate only the parts of the file name longer than 3 characters. (A part is delimited by dots.) If the name consists of small parts only, the longest parts are truncated. For example, if file names are limited to 14 characters, gzip.msdos.exe is compressed to gzi.msd.exe.gz. Names are not truncated on systems which do not have a limit on file name length.

By default, gzip keeps the original file name and timestamp in the compressed file. These are used when decompressing the file with the -N option. This is useful when the compressed file name was truncated or when the time stamp was not preserved after a file transfer.

Compressed files can be restored to their original form using gzip -d or gunzip or zcat. If the original name saved in the compressed file is not suitable for its file system, a new name is constructed from the original one to make it legal.

gunzip takes a list of files on its command line and replaces each file whose name ends with .gz, -gz, .z, -z, _z or .Z and which begins with the correct magic number with an uncompressed file without the original extension. gunzip also recognizes the special extensions .tgz and .taz as shorthands for .tar.gz and .tar.Z respectively. When compressing, gzip uses the .tgz extension if necessary instead of truncating a file with a .tar extension.

gunzip can currently decompress files created by gzip, zip, compress, compress -H or pack. The detection of the input format is automatic. When using the first two formats, gunzip checks a 32 bit CRC. For pack, gunzip checks is sometimes able to detect a bad .Z file. If you get an error when uncompressing a .Z file, do not assume that the .Z file is correct simply because the standard uncompress does not complain. This generally means that the standard uncompress does not check its input, and happily generates garbage output. The SCO compress -H format (lzh compression method) does not include a CRC but also allows some consistency checks.

Files created by zip can be uncompressed by gzip only if they have a single member compressed with the 'deflation' method. This feature is only intended to help conversion of tar.zip files to the tar.gz format. To extract zip files with several members, use unzip instead of gunzip.

[gzip, head]

zcat is identical to gunzip -c. (On some systems, zcat may be installed as gzcat to preserve the original link to compress.) zcat uncompresses either a list of files on the command line or its standard input and writes the uncompressed data on standard output. zcat will uncompress files that have the correct magic number whether they have a .gz suffix or not.

Gzip uses the Lempel-Ziv algorithm used in zip and PKZIP. The amount of compression obtained depends on the size of the input and the distribution of common substrings. Typically, text such as source code or English is reduced by 60-70%. Compression is generally much better than that achieved by LZW (as used in compress), Huffman coding (as used in pack), or adaptive Huffman coding (compact).

Compression is always performed, even if the compressed file is slightly larger than the original. The worst case expansion is a few bytes for the gzip file header, plus 5 bytes every 32K block, or an expansion ratio of 0.015% for large files. Note that the actual number of used disk blocks almost never increases. gzip preserves the mode, ownership and timestamps of files when compressing or decompressing.

head

head - output the first part of files

SYNOPSIS

head [-c N[bkm]] [-n N] [-qv] [--bytes=N[bkm]] [--lines=N] [--quiet] [--silent] [--verbose] [--help] [--version] [file...]

head [-Nbcklmqv] [file...]

DESCRIPTION

This documentation is no longer being maintained and may be inaccurate or incomplete. The Texinfo documentation is now the authoritative source.

This manual page documents the GNU version of head. head prints the first part (10 lines by default) of each given

file; it reads from standard input if no files are given or when a filename of `-' is encountered. If more than one file is given, it prints a header consisting of the file's name enclosed in `==>' and `<==' before the output for each file.

id

id - print real and effective UIDs and GIDs

SYNOPSIS

id [-gnruG] [--group] [--name] [--real] [--user] [--groups] [--help] [--version] [username]

DESCRIPTION

This documentation is no longer being maintained and may be inaccurate or incomplete. The Texinfo documentation is now the authoritative source.

This manual page documents the GNU version of id. id prints information about the given user, or the process running it if no user is specified. By default, it prints the real user ID, real group ID, effective user ID if different from the real user ID, effective group ID if different from the real group ID, and supplemental group IDs. It prints each of these values preceded by a string identifying it and followed by the corresponding user or group name in parentheses.

The options cause id to print only part of the above information.

ksh

ksh - Public domain Korn shell

SYNOPSIS

ksh [±abCefhikmnprsuvxX] [±o option] [[-c command-string [command-name] | -s | file] [argument ...]]

[ksh, ln]

DESCRIPTION

ksh is a command interpreter that is intended for both interactive and shell script use. Its command language is a superset of the sh(1) shell language.

ln

ln - make links between files

SYNOPSIS

ln [options] source [dest]
ln [options] source... directory

POSIX options: [-f]

GNU options (shortest form): [-bdfinsvF] [-S backup-suffix] [-V {numbered,existing,simple}] [--help] [--version] [--]

DESCRIPTION

There are two concepts of `link' in Unix, usually called hard link and soft link. A hard link is just a name for a file. (And a file can have several names. It is deleted from disk only when the last name is removed. The number of names is given by ls(1). There is no such thing as an `original' name: all names have the same status. Usually, but not necessarily, all names of a file are found in the filesystem that also contains its data.)

A soft link (or symbolic link, or symlink) is an entirely different animal: it is a small special file that contains a pathname. Thus, soft links can point at files on different filesystems (possibly NFS mounted from different machines), and need not point to actually existing files. When accessed (with the open(2) or stat(2) system calls), a reference to a symlink is replaced by the operating system kernel with a reference to the file named by the path name. (However, with rm(1) and unlink(2) the link itself is removed, not the file it points to. There are special system calls lstat(2) and readlink(2) that read the status of a symlink and the filename it points to. For various other system calls there is some uncertainty and variation between operating systems as to whether the operation acts

on the symlink itself, or on the file pointed to.)

ln makes links between files. By default, it makes hard links; with the -s option, it makes symbolic (or `soft') links.

If only one file is given, it links that file into the current directory, that is, creates a link to that file in the current directory, with name equal to (the last component of) the name of that file. (This is a GNU extension.) Otherwise, if the last argument names an existing directory, ln will create links to each mentioned source file in that directory, with a name equal to (the last component of) the name of that source file. (But see the description of the --no-dereference option below.) Otherwise, if only two files are given, it creates a link named given.

By default, ln does not remove existing files or existing symbolic links. (Thus, it can be used for locking purposes: it will succeed only if dest did not exist already.) But it can be forced to do so with the option -f.

On existing implementations, if it is at all possible to make a hard link to a directory, this may be done by the superuser only. POSIX forbids the system call link(2) and the utility ln to make hard links to directories (but does not forbid hard links to cross filesystem boundaries).

lp

lp - line printer devices

SYNOPSIS

```
#include <linux/lp.h>
```

DESCRIPTION

lp[0-2] are character devices for the parallel line printers; they have major number 6 and minor number 0-2. The minor numbers correspond to the printer port base addresses 0x03bc, 0x0378 and 0x0278. Usually they have

mode 220 and are owned by root and group lp. You can use printer ports either with polling or with interrupts. Interrupts are recommended when high traffic is expected, e.g. for laser printers. For usual dot matrix printers polling will usually be enough. The default is polling.

ls

ls, dir, vdir - list directory contents

SYNOPSIS

ls [options] [file...]

POSIX options: [-CFRacdilqrtu1]

GNU options (shortest form): [-1abcdfgiklmnopqrstuxABCD-FGLNQRSUX] [-w cols] [-T cols] [-I pattern] [--full-time] [--format={long,verbose,commas,across,vertical,single-column}] [--sort={none,time,size,extension}] [--time={atime,access,use,ctime,status}] [--color[={none,auto,always}]] [--help] [--version] [--]

DESCRIPTION

The program ls lists first its non-directory file arguments, and then for each directory argument all listable files contained within that directory. If no non-option arguments are present, a default argument `.' (the current directory) is assumed.

mail

```
mail [-iInv] [-s subject] [-c cc-addr] [-b bcc-addr] to-addr...
mail [-iInNv] -f [name]
mail [-iInNv] [-u user]
```

man

man - an interface to the on-line reference manuals

[man]

man

SYNOPSIS

man [-c|-w|-tZT device] [-adhu7V] [-m system[,...]] [-L locale] [-p string] [-M path] [-P pager] [-r prompt] [-S list] [-e extension] [[section] page ...] ...
man -l [-7] [-tZT device] [-p string] [-P pager] [-r prompt] file ...
man -k [-M path] keyword ...
man -f [-M path] page ...

DESCRIPTION

man is the system's manual pager. Each page argument given to man is normally the name of a program, utility or function. The manual page associated with each of these arguments is then found and displayed. A section, if provided, will direct man to look only in that section of the manual. The default action is to search in all of the available sections, following a pre-defined order and to show only the first page found, even if page exists in several sections.

The table below shows the section numbers of the manual followed by the types of pages they contain.

1 Executable programs or shell commands
2 System calls (functions provided by the kernel)

3	Library calls (functions within system libraries)
4	Special files (usually found in /dev)
5	File formats and conventions eg /etc/passwd
6	Games
7	Macro packages and conventions eg man(7), groff(7).
8	System administration commands (usually only for root)
9	Kernel routines [Non standard]
n	new [obsolete]
l	local [obsolete]
p	public [obsolete]
o	old [obsolete]

A manual page consists of several parts.

They may be labelled NAME, SYNOPSIS, DESCRIPTION, OPTIONS, FILES, SEE ALSO, BUGS, and AUTHOR.

[man]

The following conventions apply to the SYNOPSIS section and can be used as a guide in other sections.

bold text	type exactly as shown.
italic text	replace with appropriate argument.
[-abc]	any or all arguments within [ ] are optional.
-a|-b	options delimited by | cannot be used together.
argument ...	argument is repeatable.

The command or function illustration is a pattern that should match all possible invocations. In some cases it is advisable to illustrate several exclusive invocations as is shown in the SYNOPSIS section of this manual page.

EXAMPLES

man ls
    Display the manual page for the item (program) ls.

man -a intro
    Display, in succession, all of the available intro manual pages contained within the manual. It is possible to quit between successive displays or skip any of them.

man -t alias | lpr -Pps
: Format the manual page referenced by `alias', usually a shell manual page, into the default troff or groff format and pipe it to the printer named ps. The default output for groff is usually PostScript. man --help should advise as to which processor is bound to the -t option.

man -l -Tdvi ./foo.1x.gz > ./foo.1x.dvi
: This command will decompress and format the nroff source manual page ./foo.1x.gz into a device independent (dvi) file. The redirection is necessary as the -T flag causes output to be directed to stdout with no pager. The output could be viewed with a program such as xdvi or further processed into PostScript using a program such as dvips.

[man, mawk]

man -k printf
: Search the short descriptions and manual page names for the keyword printf. Print out any matches.

man -f smail
: Lookup the manual pages referenced by smail and print out the short descriptions of any found.

mawk

mawk - pattern scanning and text processing language

SYNOPSIS

mawk [-W option] [-F value] [-v var=value] [--] 'program text' [file ...]
mawk [-W option] [-F value] [-v var=value] [-f program-file] [--] [file ...]

DESCRIPTION

mawk is an interpreter for the AWK Programming Language. The AWK language is useful for manipulation of data files, text retrieval and processing, and for prototyping and experimenting with algorithms. mawk is a new awk meaning it implements the AWK language as defined in Aho, Kernighan and Weinberger, The AWK Programming Language, Addison-Wesley Publishing, 1988. (Hereafter referred to as the AWK book.) mawk conforms to the Posix 1003.2 (draft 11.3) definition of the AWK language which contains a few features not described in the AWK book, and mawk provides a small number of extensions.

An AWK program is a sequence of pattern {action} pairs and function definitions. Short programs are entered on the command line usually enclosed in ' ' to avoid shell interpretation. Longer programs can be read in from a file with the -f option. Data input is read from the list of files on the command line or from standard input when the list is empty. The input is broken into records as determined by the record separator variable, RS. Initially, RS = "\n" and records are synonymous with lines. Each record is compared against each pattern and if it matches, the program text for {action} is executed.

[mkdir, mknod]

mkdir

mkdir - make directories

SYNOPSIS

mkdir [options] directory...

POSIX options: [-p] [-m mode]

GNU options (shortest form): [-p] [-m mode] [--verbose] [--help] [--version] [--]

DESCRIPTION

mkdir creates directories with the specified names.

By default, the mode of created directories is 0777 (`a+rwx') minus the bits set in the umask.

mknod

mknod - make block or character special files

SYNOPSIS

```
mknod [options] name {bc} major minor
mknod [options] name p
```

GNU options (shortest form): [-m mode] [--help] [--version] [--]

DESCRIPTION

mknod creates a FIFO (named pipe), character special file, or block special file with the specified name.

A special file is a triple (boolean, integer, integer) stored in the filesystem. The boolean chooses between character special file and block special file. The two integers are the major and minor device number.

Thus, a special file takes almost no place on disk, and is used only for communication with the operating system, not

for data storage. Often special files refer to hardware devices (disk, tape, tty, printer) or to operating system services (/dev/null, /dev/random).

Block special files usually are disk-like devices (where data can be accessed given a block number, and e.g. it is meaningful to have a block cache). All other devices are character special files. (Long ago the distinction was a different one: I/O to a character special file would be unbuffered, to a block special file buffered.)

The mknod command is what creates files of this type.

The argument following name specifies the type of file to make:

p	for a FIFO

b	for a block (buffered) special file

c	for a character (unbuffered) special file

The GNU version of mknod allows u (`unbuffered') as a synonym for c.

When making a block or character special file, the major and minor device numbers must be given after the file type (in decimal, or in octal with leading 0; the GNU version also allows hexadecimal with leading 0x). By default, the mode of created files is 0666 (`a+rw') minus the bits set in the umask.

-m mode, --mode=mode
Set the mode of created files to mode, which can be symbolic as in chmod(1) and then uses the default mode as the point of departure.

more

more [-dlfpcsu] [-num] [+/ pattern] [+ linenum] [file ...]

DESCRIPTION

More is a filter for paging through text one screenful at a time. This version is especially primitve. Users should realize that less(1) provides.

[more, mv]

more(1) emulation and extensive enhancements.

mv

mv - move (rename) files

SYNOPSIS

mv [option...] source target
mv [option...] source... target

POSIX options: [-fi]

GNU options (shortest form): [-bfiuv] [-S suffix] [-V {numbered,existing,simple}] [--help] [--version] [--]

DESCRIPTION

mv moves or renames files or directories.

If the last argument names an existing directory, mv moves each other given file into a file with the same name in that directory. Otherwise, if only two files are given, it renames the first as the second. It is an error if the last argument is not a directory and more than two files are given.

Thus, `mv /a/x/y /b' will rename the file /a/x/y into /b/y if /b was an existing directory, and into /b otherwise.

Let us call the file a given file is going to be moved into its destination. If destination exists, and either the -i option is given, or destination is unwritable, standard input is a terminal, and the -f option is not given, mv prompts the user for whether to replace the file, writing a question to stderr and reading an answer from stdin. If the response is not affirmative, the file is skipped.

When both source and destination are on the same filesystem, they are the same file (just the name is changed; owner, mode, timestamps remain unchanged). When they are on different filesystems, the source file is copied and

then deleted. mv will copy modification time, access time, user and group ID, and mode if possible. When copying user and/or group ID fails, the setuid and setgid bits are cleared in the copy.

nice

nice - run a program with modified scheduling priority

SYNOPSIS

nice [-n adjustment] [-adjustment] [--adjustment=adjustment] [--help] [--version] [command [arg...]]

DESCRIPTION

This documentation is no longer being maintained and may be inaccurate or incomplete. The Texinfo documentation is now the authoritative source.

This manual page documents the GNU version of nice. Note that most shells have a built-in command by the same name and with similar functionality.

If no arguments are given, nice prints the current scheduling priority, which it inherited. Otherwise, nice runs the given command with its scheduling priority adjusted. If no adjustment is given, the priority of the command is incremented by 10. The superuser can specify a negative adjustment. The priority can be adjusted by nice over the range of -20 (the highest priority) to 19 (the lowest).

passwd

passwd - change user password

SYNOPSIS

```
passwd [-f|-s] [name]
passwd [-g] [-r|R] group
passwd [-x max] [-n min] [-w warn] [-i inact] name
passwd {-l|-u|-d|-S} name
```


DESCRIPTION

passwd changes passwords for user and group accounts. A normal user may only change the password for their own account, the super user may change the password for any account. The administrator of a group may change the password for the group. passwd also changes account information, such as the full name of the user, their login shell, or password expiry dates and intervals.

pr

pr - convert text files for printing

SYNOPSIS

pr [+PAGE] [-COLUMN] [-abcdfFmrtv] [-e[in-tab-char[in-tab-width]]] [-h header] [-i[out-tab-char[out-tab-width]]] [-l page-length] [-n[number-separator[digits]]] [-o left-margin] [-s[column-separator]] [-w page-width] [--help] [--version] [file...]

DESCRIPTION

This documentation is no longer being maintained and may be inaccurate or incomplete. The Texinfo documentation is now the authoritative source.

This manual page documents the GNU version of pr. pr prints on the standard output a paginated and optionally multicolumn copy of the text files given on the command line, or of the standard input if no files are given or when the file name `-' is encountered. Form feeds in the input cause page breaks in the output.

rcp

```
rcp [-px] [-k realm] file1 file2
rcp [-px] [-r] [-k realm] file ... directory
```

DESCRIPTION

Rcp copies files between machines. Each file or directory argument is

rcp

either a remote file name of the form ``rname@rhost:path'', or a local file name (containing no `:' characters, or a `/' before any `:'s).

rm

rm - remove files or directories

SYNOPSIS

rm [options] file...

POSIX options: [-fiRr]

GNU options (shortest form): [-dfirvR] [--help] [--version] [--]

DESCRIPTION

rm removes each given file. By default, it does not remove directories. But when the -r or -R option is given, the entire directory tree below the specified directory is removed (and there are no limitations on the depth of directory trees that can be removed by `rm -r'). It is an error when the last path component of file is either . or .. (so as to avoid unpleasant surprises with `rm -r .*' or so).

If the -i option is given, or if a file is unwritable, standard input is a terminal, and the -f option is not given, rm prompts the user for whether to remove the file, writing a question to stderr and reading an answer from stdin. If the response is not affirmative, the file is skipped.

rmdir

rmdir - remove empty directories

[**rmdir, script, sdiff**]

SYNOPSIS

rmdir [options] directory...

POSIX options: [-p]

GNU options (shortest form): [-p] [--help] [--version] [--]

DESCRIPTION

rmdir removes empty directories.

If any directory argument does not refer to an existing empty directory, it is an error.

script

script [-a] [file]

DESCRIPTION

Script makes a typescript of everything printed on your terminal. It is useful for students who need a hardcopy record of an interactive session as proof of an assignment, as the typescript file can be printed out later with lpr(1).

sdiff

sdiff - find differences between two files and merge interactively

SYNOPSIS

sdiff -o outfile [options] from-file to-file

DESCRIPTION

The sdiff command merges two files and interactively outputs the results to outfile.

DESCRIPTION

If from-file is a directory and to-file is not, sdiff compares the file in from-file whose file name is that of to-file, and vice versa. from-file and to-file may not both be directories.

sdiff options begin with -, so normally from-file and to-file may not begin with -. However, -- as an argument by itself treats the remaining arguments as file names even if they begin with -. You may not use - as an input file.

sdiff without -o (or --output) produces a side-by-side difference. This usage is obsolete; use diff --side-by-side instead.

sed

sed - a Stream EDitor

SYNOPSIS

```
sed [-n] [-V] [--quiet] [--silent] [--version] [--help]
    [-e script] [--expression=script]
    [-f script-file] [--file=script-file]
    [script-if-no-other-script]
    [file...]
```

DESCRIPTION

Sed is a stream editor. A stream editor is used to perform basic text transformations on an input stream (a file or input from a pipeline). While in some ways similar to an editor which permits scripted edits (such as ed), sed works by making only one pass over the input(s), and is consequently more efficient. But it is sed's ability to filter text in a pipeline which particularly distinguishes it from other types of editors.

sh

bash - GNU Bourne-Again SHell

SYNOPSIS

bash [options] [file]

COPYRIGHT

Bash is Copyright (C) 1989, 1991, 1993, 1995, 1996 by the Free Software Foundation, Inc.

DESCRIPTION

Bash is an sh-compatible command language interpreter that executes commands read from the standard input or from a file. Bash also incorporates useful features from the Korn and C shells (ksh and csh).

Bash is ultimately intended to be a conformant implementation of the IEEE POSIX Shell and Tools specification (IEEE Working Group 1003.2).

sort

sort - sort lines of text files

SYNOPSIS

```
sort  [-cmus] [-t separator] [-o output-file] [-T tempdir]
[-bdfiMnr] [+POS1 [-POS2]] [-k POS1[,POS2]] [file...]
sort {--help,--version}
```

DESCRIPTION

This documentation is no longer being maintained and may be inaccurate or incomplete. The Texinfo documentation is now the authoritative source.

This manual page documents the GNU version of sort. sort sorts, merges, or compares all the lines from the given files, or the standard input if no files are given. A file name of `-' means standard input. By default, sort writes the results to the standard output.

[sort, stty, tail]

DESCRIPTIONS

sort has three modes of operation: sort (the default), merge, and check for sortedness.

stty

stty - changes and print terminal line settings

SYNOPSIS

stty [-F device] [--file=device] [setting...]
stty [-F device] [--file=device] {-a,--all,-g,--help,--save,--version}

DESCRIPTION

This documentation is no longer being maintained and may be inaccurate or incomplete. The Texinfo documentation is now the authoritative source.

This manual page documents the GNU version of stty. If given no arguments, stty prints the baud rate, line discipline number (on systems that support it), and line settings that have been changed from the values set by `stty sane'. Mode reading and setting are performed on the tty line connected to the standard input.

tail

tail - output the last part of files

SYNOPSIS

tail [-c [+]N[bkm]] [-n [+]N] [-fqv] [--bytes=[+]N[bkm]] [--lines=[+]N] [--follow] [--quiet] [--silent] [--verbose] [--help] [--version] [file...]

tail [{-,+}Nbcfklmqv] [file...]

[tail, tar]

DESCRIPTION

This documentation is no longer being maintained and may be inaccurate or incomplete. The Texinfo documentation is now the authoritative source.

This manual page documents the GNU version of tail. tail prints the last part (10 lines by default) of each given file; it reads from standard input if no files are given or when a filename of \`-' is encountered. If more than one file is given, it prints a header consisting of the file's name enclosed in \`==>' and \`<==' before the output for each file.

The GNU tail can output any amount of data, unlike the Unix version, which uses a fixed size buffer. It has no -r option (print in reverse). Reversing a file is really a different job from printing the end of a file; the BSD tail can only reverse files that are at most as large as its buffer, which is typically 32k. A reliable and more versatile way to reverse files is the GNU tac command.

tar

tar - The GNU version of the tar archiving utility

SYNOPSIS

tar [-] A --catenate --concatenate | c --create | d --diff --compare | r --append | t --list | u --update | x -extract --get [--atime-preserve] [-b, --block-size N] [-B, --read-full-blocks] [-C, --directory DIR] [--checkpoint] [-f, --file [HOSTNAME:]F] [--force-local] [-F, --info-script F --new-volume-script F] [-G, --incremental] [-g, --listed-incremental F] [-h, --dereference] [-i, --ignore-zeros] [--ignore-failed-read] [-I] [-k, --keep-old-files] [-K, --starting-file F] [-l, --one-file-system] [-L, --tape-length N] [-m, --modification-time] [-M, --multi-volume] [-N, --after-date DATE, --newer DATE] [-o, --old-archive, --portability] [-O, --to-stdout] [-p, --same-permissions, --preserve-permissions] [-P, --absolute-paths] [--preserve] [-R, --record-number] [--remove-files

[tar]

] [-s, --same-order, --preserve-order] [--same-owner] [--numeric-owner] [-S, --sparse] [-T, --files-from F] [--null] [--totals] [-v, --verbose] [-V, --label NAME] [--version] [-w, --interactive, --confirmation] [-W, --verify] [--exclude FILE] [-X, --exclude-from FILE] [-Z, --compress, --uncompress] [-z, --gzip, --ungzip] [--use-compress-program PROG] [--block-compress] [-[0-7][lmh]]

filename1 [filename2, ... filenameN]

directory1 [directory2, ...directoryN]

DESCRIPTION

This manual page documents the GNU version of tar , an archiving program designed to store and extract files from an archive file known as a tarfile. A tarfile may be made on a tape drive, however, it is also common to write a tarfile to a normal file. The first argument to tar must be one of the options: Acdrtux, followed by any optional functions. The final arguments to tar are the names of the files or directories which should be archived. The use of a directory name always implies that the subdirectories below should be included in the archive.

EXAMPLES

tar -xvvf foo.tar
    extract foo.tar

tar -xvvzf foo.tar.gz
    extract gzipped foo.tar.gz

tar -cvvf foo.tar foo/
    tar contents of folder foo in foo.tar

One of the following options must be used:

-A, --catenate, --concatenate
    append tar files to an archive

[tar, tee]

-c, --create
    create a new archive

-d, --diff, --compare
    find differences between archive and file system

--delete
    delete from the archive (not for use on mag tapes!)

-r, --append
    append files to the end of an archive

-t, --list
    list the contents of an archive

-u, --update
    only append files that are newer than copy in archive

-x, --extract, --get
    extract files from an archive

tee

tee - read from standard input and write to standard output and files

SYNOPSIS

tee [-ai] [--append] [--ignore-interrupts] [--help] [--version] [file...]

DESCRIPTION

This documentation is no longer being maintained and may be inaccurate or incomplete. The Texinfo documentation is now the authoritative source.

This manual page documents the GNU version of tee. The tee command copies the standard input to the standard output and any files given as arguments.

If a file being written to does not already exist, it is

DESCRIPTION

created. If a file being written to already exists, the data it previously contained is overwritten unless the -a option is used.

test

test - check file types and compare values

SYNOPSIS

test [expr]
test {--help,--version}

DESCRIPTION

This documentation is no longer being maintained and may be inaccurate or incomplete. The Texinfo documentation is now the authoritative source.

This manual page documents the GNU version of test. Note that most shells have a built-in command by the same name and with similar functionality.

test returns a status of 0 (true) or 1 (false) depending on the evaluation of the conditional expression expr. Expressions may be unary or binary. Unary expressions are often used to examine the status of a file. There are string operators and numeric comparison operators as well.

time

time - run programs and summarize system resource usage

SYNOPSIS

```
time    [ -apvV ] [ -f FORMAT ] [ -o FILE ]
        [ --append ] [ --verbose ] [ --portability ]
        [ --format=FORMAT ] [ --output=FILE ] [ --version ]
        [ --help ] COMMAND [ ARGS ]
```

[time, touch]

DESCRIPTION

time run the program COMMAND with any given arguments ARG.... When COMMAND finishes, time displays information about resources used by COMMAND (on the standard error output, by default). If COMMAND exits with non-zero status, time displays a warning message and the exit status.

time determines which information to display about the resources used by the COMMAND from the string FORMAT. If no format is specified on the command line, but the TIME environment variable is set, its value is used as the format. Otherwise, a default format built into time is used.

Options to time must appear on the command line before COMMAND. Anything on the command line after COMMAND is passed as arguments to COMMAND.

touch

touch - change file timestamps

SYNOPSIS

touch [-acm][-r ref_file|-t time] file...

Obsolescent version:
touch [-acm][ugly_time] file...

GNU version:
touch [-acfm] [-r file] [-t decimtime] [-d time] [--time={atime,access,use,mtime,modify}] [--date=time] [--reference=file] [--no-create] [--help] [--version] [--] file...

DESCRIPTION

touch changes the access and/or modification timestamps of each specified file. These timestamps are changed to the current time, unless the -r option is specified, in which case they are changed to the corresponding timestamps of the file ref_file, or the -t option is specified, in which case they are changed to the specified time. Both times are changed when neither or both of the -a and -m options

DESCRIPTION

are given. Only the access or only the modification time is changed when one of the options -a and -m is given. If the file did not exist yet, it is created (as an empty file with mode 0666, modified by the umask), unless the -c option is given.

troff

troff - format documents

SYNOPSIS

```
troff [ -abivzCERU ] [ -wname ] [ -Wname ] [ -dcs ]
      [ -ffam ] [ -mname ] [ -nnum ] [ -olist ] [ -rcn ]
      [ -Tname ] [ -Fdir ] [ -Mdir ] [ files... ]
```

DESCRIPTION

This manual page describes the GNU version of troff, which is part of the groff document formatting system. It is highly compatible with Unix troff. Usually it should be invoked using the groff command, which will also run preprocessors and postprocessors in the appropriate order and with the appropriate options.

true

true - do nothing, successfully

SYNOPSIS

true
true {--help,--version}

DESCRIPTION

This documentation is no longer being maintained and may be inaccurate or incomplete. The Texinfo documentation is now the authoritative source.

[true, tty, umount]

DESCRIPTION

This manual page documents the GNU version of true (and probably every other version, as well). true does nothing except return an exit status of 0, meaning ``success''. It can be used as a place holder in shell scripts where a successful command is needed, although the shell built-in command `:' (colon) does the same thing faster.

tty

tty - prints the file name of the terminal connected to standard input

SYNOPSIS

tty [-s] [--silent] [--quiet] [--help] [--version]

DESCRIPTION

This documentation is no longer being maintained and may be inaccurate or incomplete. The Texinfo documentation is now the authoritative source.

This manual page documents the GNU version of tty. tty prints the file name of the tty connected to its standard input. It prints `not a tty' if the standard input is not a tty. Its exit status is:
0 if the standard input is a tty
1 if the standard input is not a tty
2 if given incorrect arguments
3 if a write error occurs

umount

umount - unmount file systems

SYNOPSIS

umount [-hV]

SYNOPSIS

umount -a [-nrv] [-t vfstype]
umount [-nrv] device | dir [...]

DESCRIPTION

The umount command detaches the file system(s) mentioned from the file hierarchy. A file system is specified either by giving the directory where it has been mounted, or by giving the special device on which it lives.

Note that a file system cannot be unmounted when it is `busy' - for example, when there are open files on it, or when some process has its working directory there, or when a swap file on it is in use.

uname

uname - print system information

SYNOPSIS

uname [-snrvma] [--sysname] [--nodename] [--release] [--machine] [--all] [--help] [--version]

DESCRIPTION

This documentation is no longer being maintained and may be inaccurate or incomplete. The Texinfo documentation is now the authoritative source.

This manual page documents the GNU version of uname. uname prints information about the machine and operating system it is run on. If no options are given, uname acts as if the -s option were given. If multiple options are given or the -a option is given, the selected information is printed in the order `snrvm' with a space between items.

uncompress

gzip, gunzip, zcat - compress or expand files.

[uncompress]

SYNOPSIS

gzip [-acdfhlLnNrtvV19] [-S suffix] [name ...]
gunzip [-acfhlLnNrtvV] [-S suffix] [name ...]
zcat [-fhLV] [name ...]

DESCRIPTION

Gzip reduces the size of the named files using Lempel-Ziv coding (LZ77). Whenever possible, each file is replaced by one with the extension .gz, while keeping the same ownership modes, access and modification times. (The default extension is -gz for VMS, z for MSDOS, OS/2 FAT, Windows NT FAT and Atari.) If no files are specified, or if a file name is "-", the standard input is compressed to the standard output. Gzip will only attempt to compress regular files. In particular, it will ignore symbolic links.

If the compressed file name is too long for its file system, gzip truncates it. Gzip attempts to truncate only the parts of the file name longer than 3 characters. (A part is delimited by dots.) If the name consists of small parts only, the longest parts are truncated. For example, if file names are limited to 14 characters, gzip.msdos.exe is compressed to gzi.msd.exe.gz. Names are not truncated on systems which do not have a limit on file name length.

By default, gzip keeps the original file name and timestamp in the compressed file. These are used when decompressing the file with the -N option. This is useful when the compressed file name was truncated or when the time stamp was not preserved after a file transfer.

Compressed files can be restored to their original form using gzip -d or gunzip or zcat. If the original name saved in the compressed file is not suitable for its file system, a new name is constructed from the original one to make it legal.

gunzip takes a list of files on its command line and replaces each file whose name ends with .gz, -gz, .z, -z, _z or .Z and which begins with the correct magic number with an uncompressed file without the original extension. gunzip also recognizes the special extensions .tgz and .taz as shorthands for .tar.gz and .tar.Z respectively.

[uncompress]

DESCRIPTION

When compressing, gzip uses the .tgz extension if necessary instead of truncating a file with a .tar extension.

gunzip can currently decompress files created by gzip, zip, compress, compress -H or pack. The detection of the input format is automatic. When using the first two formats, gunzip checks a 32 bit CRC. For pack, gunzip checks is sometimes able to detect a bad .Z file. If you get an error when uncompressing a .Z file, do not assume that the .Z file is correct simply because the standard uncompress does not complain. This generally means that the standard uncompress does not check its input, and happily generates garbage output. The SCO compress -H format (lzh compression method) does not include a CRC but also allows some consistency checks.

Files created by zip can be uncompressed by gzip only if they have a single member compressed with the 'deflation' method. This feature is only intended to help conversion of tar.zip files to the tar.gz format. To extract zip files with several members, use unzip instead of gunzip.

zcat is identical to gunzip -c. (On some systems, zcat may be installed as gzcat to preserve the original link to compress.) zcat uncompresses either a list of files on the command line or its standard input and writes the uncompressed data on standard output. zcat will uncompress files that have the correct magic number whether they have a .gz suffix or not.

Gzip uses the Lempel-Ziv algorithm used in zip and PKZIP. The amount of compression obtained depends on the size of the input and the distribution of common substrings. Typically, text such as source code or English is reduced by 60-70%. Compression is generally much better than that achieved by LZW (as used in compress), Huffman coding (as used in pack), or adaptive Huffman coding (compact).

Compression is always performed, even if the compressed file is slightly larger than the original. The worst case expansion is a few bytes for the gzip file header, plus 5 bytes every 32K block, or an expansion ratio of 0.015% for large files. Note that the actual number of used disk blocks almost never increases. gzip preserves the mode, ownership and timestamps of files when compressing or decompressing.

[uniq]

uniq

uniq - remove duplicate lines from a sorted file

SYNOPSIS

uniq [-cdu] [-f skip-fields] [-s skip-chars] [-w check-chars] [-#skip-fields] [+#skip-chars] [--count] [--repeated] [--unique] [--skip-fields=skip-fields] [--skip-chars=skip-chars] [--check-chars=check-chars] [--help] [--version] [infile] [outfile]

DESCRIPTION

This documentation is no longer being maintained and may be inaccurate or incomplete. The Texinfo documentation is now the authoritative source.

This manual page documents the GNU version of uniq. uniq prints the unique lines in a sorted file, discarding all but one of a run of matching lines. It can optionally show only lines that appear exactly once, or lines that appear more than once. uniq requires sorted input because it compares only consecutive lines.

If the output file is not specified, uniq writes to the standard output. If the input file is not specified, it reads from the standard input.

Common UNIX filename Extensions

Extension	Description
.a	Archived file or assembler code.
.au	Audio file
.c	C language source file
.csh	C shell script
.enc	Encrypted file
.F	FORTRAN source code before processing
.gif	Graphics Interchange format file
.gl	Animation file
.gz	File compressed with gzip
.h	C program header file
.jpg or jpeg	Joint Photographic Experts Group format
.mm	Text file containing troff mm macros
.mpg or mpeg	Motion Picture Experts Group format video file
.ms	Text file containing troff ms macros
.o	Object file
.ps	Postscript source file
.s	Assembly language source code
.sh	Bourne shell script
.shar	Shell archive
.tar	tar archive
.tex	Text file formatted with TEX commands
.txt	ASCII text file
.uu	An uuencode file
.xx	Text file formatted with LATEX command
.z	File compressed by the pack command
.Z	File compressed by the compress command
.1 to .8	Online manual source files

Alphabetical Unix Command List:

addbib - create or extend a bibliographic database
apropos - locate commands by keyword lookup
ar - create library archives, and add or extract files
at - execute a command or script at a specified time
awk - pattern scanning and processing language
banner - display a string in large letters
basename - display portions of path names and filenames
batch - runs jobs when the system load level permits
biff - give notice of incoming mail messages
cal - display a calendar
calendar - a simple reminder service
cancel - cancel requests to a printer
cat - concatenate and display
cb - a simple C program beautifier
cc - C compiler
cd - change working directory
checknr - check nroff and troff input files; report possible errors
checkeq - checks documents formatted with memoranda macros
chgrp - change the group ownership of a file
chmod - change the permissions mode of a file
clear - clear the terminal screen
cmp - perform a byte-by-byte comparison of two files
colcrt - filter nroff output for a terminal without overstrike capability
comm - selects or rejects lines common to two sorted files
compress - compress files (see uncompress also)
cp - copy files
cpio - copy file archives in and out
cpp - the C language preprocessor
csh - a shell with a C-like syntax and advanced interactive features
ctags - create a tags file for use with ex and vi
cut - Writes selected bytes, characters, or fields from each line of a file.
date - display or set the date
dbx - source-level debugger
deroff - remove nroff, troff, tbl and eqn constructs
df - report free disk space on file systems

diff - display line-by-line differences between two text files
du - display the number of disk blocks used per directory or file
e - starts the INed editor
echo - echo arguments to the standard output
ed, red - basic line editor
edit - provides a simple line editor for the new user
eqn - formats mathematical text for the troff command
ex - edits lines interactively, with a screen display
expand - expands TAB characters to SPACE characters (see unexpand)
expr - evaluate arguments as a logical, arithmetic, or string expression
false - gives truth values (see true also)
file - determine the a type of file by examining its contents
find - locates files by name, or by other characteristics
finger - display information about users
fmt - formats mail messages before sending
fold - folds long lines for finite-width output device
ftp - file transfer program
gprof - display call-graph profile data
grep - search a file for a string or regular expression
groups - display an user's group memberships
head - display first few lines of specified files
hostname - set or print name of current host system
indent - indent and format a C program source file
install - install files
join - relational database operator
kill - send a signal to a process, or end a process
last - show last logins by a user or terminal
ld - link editor
leave - remind(s) you when you have to leave
lex - lexical analysis program generator
lint - a C program verifier
ln - generates hard or symbolic links to files

login - log in to the system
look - find words in the system dictionary or lines in a sorted list
lookbib - find references in a bibliographic database
lorder - find an ordering relation for an object library
lp - send requests to a printer
lpq - display the queue of printer jobs
lpr - send a job to the printer
lprm - removes jobs from the printer queue
ls - list the contents of a directory
mail, Mail - reads or sends mail messages
make - maintain, update, and regenerate related programs and files
man - display the manual reference pages
mesg - permit or deny terminal messages
mkdir - make a directory
mkstr - create an error message file by sending them to C source files
more - browse or page through a text file
mv - move or rename files
nice - run a command at low priority
nm - print symbol name list
neqn - formats mathematical text for the nroff command
nroff - format documents for display or line-printer
od - octal, decimal, hexadecimal, and ASCII dump
page - browse or page through a text file
passwd - change local password information
paste - joins lines from one or more files
pr - prepare files for printing, including multiple columns
prof - display profile data
ps - display the status of current processes
pwd - display the path name of the current working directory
ranlib - convert archives to random libraries
rcp - remote file copy
rev - reverse the order of characters in each line
rlogin - remote login
rm - remove files or directories

rmdir - remove directories
roffbib - format and print a bibliographic database
rsh - remote shell
rup - show host status of local machines RPC version
ruptime - show host status of local machines
rusers - who's logged in on remote machines
rwall - write to all users over a network
rwho - shows who's logged in on remote machines
sccs - front end for the Source Code Control System
script - make typescript of a terminal session
sed - stream editor
sh - shell, the standard UNIX system command interpreter and command-level language
size - display the size of an object file
sleep - suspend execution for a specified interval
sort - sort and collate lines
sortbib - sort a bibliographic database
spell - report spelling errors
split - split a file into pieces
strings - find printable strings in an object or binary file
strip - removes symbols and relocation bits from an object file
stty - sets, resets, and reports workstation operating guidelines
su - super-user;system administrator
tabs - allows you to set tab stops on a terminal
tail - display the last part of a file
talk - talk to another user
tar - create tape archives, and add or extract files
tbl - format tables for nroff or troff
tee - duplicates the standard output
telnet - user interface to a remote system using the TELNET protocol
test - evaluates conditional expressions
tftp - trivial file transfer program
time - time a command
touch - update the access and modification times of a file
troff - typeset or format documents
true - provide truth values (see false also)
tsort - topological sort

tty - display the name of the terminal
ul - do underlining
uncompress - un compress files (see compress also)
uniq - remove or report adjacent duplicate lines
units - conversion program
uptime - show hows long the system has been up
users - display a compact list of users logged in
uucp - system to system copy
unexpand - restores TAB characters from SPACE characters (see also - expand)
vacation - reply to mail automatically
vi, vedit - visual display editor
view - starts the vi editor in read-only mode
w - who is logged in, and what is they do
wait - wait for a process to finish
wall - write to all users logged in
wc - display a count of lines, words and characters
whatis - describes what function a command performs
whereis - locates source, binary, or manual for program
which - locates a program file, including aliases and pathnames
who - identifies the users currently logged in
whoami - display your user name
write - send messages to other users on the system
xargs - constructs guideline lists and runs commands
xstr - extract strings from C programs to implement shared strings
yacc - yet another compiler-compiler: parsing program generator
yes - outputs a "yes" response repetitively
zcat - display compressed files

UNIX Glossary

asynchronous terminal A device that sends data or receive data, but not both,as opposed to a synchronous terminal.An asynchronous terminal uses start and stop bits to detect whether it is ready to send or receive data.

ALUX Apple Computer's version of UNIX designed to run on Macintosh 680x0 computers.
It's based on the original UNIX System V.It is POSIX compliant.

awk A utility with a built-in programming language, used to manipulate text in files.

background job A process that is started by a parent process and started at system startup to monitor the system. Users can execute commands in the background by ending commands with an ampersand (&). Low priority jobs usually run as background jobs.

backslash The character \ is used as an escape character. A backslash before a character tells the shell to ignore anything typed after it.

backup To save a copy of a directory,file or a complete file system. If you experience a system failure, users can schedule regular backups using the cron command.

bang-style addressing A network addressing scheme that uses the exclamation point (!). "bang", separates the machine names in a path (for example, nodea!nodeb!user).

Bell Laboratories AT&T research and development adjunct,established in 1925.Bell Laboratories created and developed UNIX in 1969.

binary file A file typically stored in machine code (non-ASCII format).You can also store datum files in binary format (in contrast to text files).

bit map A graphics table that has bit settings to represent shading or color in a display. Each bit represents shading called a pixel.

block Groups of data treated as one unit during input/output (I/O) operations.Disk and tape devices are called block devices.These block devices read and write blocks of data.

boot The process of initialization that loads the kernel,initializes the memory,starts the system processes running, and prepares the user environment.

boot disk A floppy disk used to load the operating system onto the hard disk.Typically used when problems on the hard disk prevents booting properly.

Bourne shell A shell program that is named after its author Steven Bourne.

buffer A temporary storage location used to hold data before transferring it from one point to another. Buffers are used to increase the efficiency of data input/output.

bug A programming mistake that causes unpredictable results,interrupting all running processes. Programming bugs are traced and corrected using debuggers.

C language A popular, general-purpose,mid-level programming language developed by Dennis Ritchie of Bell Laboratories in the late 1960s.C is the primary programming language used to develop applications in UNIX System environments.A large percentage of the original UNIX System V Release was written in C.

C++ language An object-oriented version of the C language, developed by Bjarne Stroustrup of Bell Laboratories.

CAE (Common Applications Environment) An interface standard for the development of portable applications published by X/Open,based on the System V Interface Definition(SVID).

carriage return The ASCII character produced when the RETURN key is pressed.

cat A command used to combine files together.Mainly used to display file contents.

character special file A UNIX file that interfaces with input-output devices such as terminals that do not support file systems.

chat script A script embedded in a UUCP System file that allows you with two-way communications with a remote system.

child process A process started with the fork command to run another command. The child process is spawned from the parent process.

class A way of categorizing users,devices or processes.The shell uses these classes to verify users' access to files or programs.

client An user of network services or resources, such as file access or print services,available on a server.

client/server An architecture that divides the processes run on a network among computers that request services called the client and the computers that provide the services called the server.

command An instruction that performs an action that the shell can interpret and execute.You can combine commands with options and arguments to build a command line.

command alias An alternative assigned to a command. It reduces the typing,when building a command line.

command history A history list of command lines that analyze events or execute previous commands without retyping them.

command interpreter A program that evaluates and executes user input. The shell is a command interpreter.

command line A line consisting of one or more commands,options or arguments.The shell interprets the line,executes or rejects it, complete with error messages to the user.

command substitution back quotes (')used in shell scripts to produce a single output value from a series of related commands.

Common Desktop Environment (CDE) An industry standard graphical user interface for UNIX Systems developed for the Common Open Software Environment (COSE).

compatibility package A software package used to enable programs to run on the various versions of UNIX O/S's.

compiler A program that converts programming source code and produces machine-executable code.

compression A method of reducing file size for storage.

conditional execution Execution of a program that is dependent on the outcome of a prior program. Process status indicators are used to determine if the program completes successfully;you can check them before execution of the next program.

conditional statement A program statement that tests a condition to determine which statement should execute next.

control character Usually refers to pressing the control (CTRL) key and another keyboard key simultaneously.

CORBA (Common Object Request Broker Architecture) A specification developed by the Object Management Group detailing how object messaging are handled across different platforms.

core dump Main memory content that is produced when a program does not operate successfully.You can use this information to find out where the failure occurred.

cron An utility used to schedule processes.System file backups and machine maintenance routines are often scheduled by cron.

crontab A system utility that enters cron jobs information into a formatted file. The crontab file is checked periodically to see if a scheduled process should start.

current directory The directory that a UNIX user is in now ,also called the present working directory symbolized by the (dot) . notation and displayed by using the pwd command.

cursor An indicator used to show the current position on screen.Normally this is a blinking vertical or horizontal symbol.

daemon Pronounced "day-mon," or "de - mon." daemon is an automated process (sometimes spelled or pronounced as "demon") that performs a standard routine or service.For example,an e-mail program that sends an automated message whenever it receives an e-mail message.

Common UNIX Daemon

Daemon	Descriptions
ftpd	File transfer protocol daemon
inetd	Internet daemon
lockd	Network lock daemon
lpd	Line Printer daemon
named	Internet domain name server daemon
nfsd	NFS daemon
pppd	Point-to-point protocol daemon
uucpd	UUCP daemon

DARPA (Defense Advanced Research Projects Agency) A military agency that developed the ARPANET.You can think of this as the original Internet.

data gram A packet that contains data and addressing information.Datagrams are self-contained and carry a complete address.

debugger A program that shows the logic path and values of registers and variables during execution of a process to locate where a failure occured.Unix has a debugger named sdb that is used to locate instructions that were executed during a core dump.

default user environment The environment that is set up for new users who are added to a system by the useradd command,if installed.

default value The value used by a program for an argument or variable when the user does not specify a value.

fdev The directory that contains the filenames used to gain access hardware drivers for,printers,terminals and other devices.

device Peripheral equipment used in input or output (I/O) of data.Unix separates processes from the I/O devices to allow flexibility.Device files and names are stored in the /dev directory.

device driver Allows data to transmit among computers and their peripheral devices.

device independence The ability of a program to accept input and output with any peripheral hardware.

Idevinull A special destination file for output or input,used when output is not desired, or as an input when nothing is to be read in. A type of "throw away" trash bin file.

directory A directory is a holding area for files or other directories.You can access files by supplying all the directory names from the root down to the directory holding the file. This is called the full path name.

distributed database system A database system that appears as a single database to end users,even though the data physically resides on more than one machine.

distributed file system A file system in which user programs and data files are physically distributed over several computers on a network,but can be used by any user who has access to any of the files as if they were local files.

domain An unique name that identifies a computer on a network.Here a few of the high-level domains listed on the Internet:

.com	A commercial organization.
.edu	An educational institution.
.gov	A branch of the U.S. Government.
.int	An international organization.
.mil	A branch of the U.S. Military.
.net	A network.
.org	A nonprofit organization

DOS (Disk Operating System) An operating system for personal computers,originally developed by Microsoft for use on IBM PCs.DOS,in many ways,resembles the

UNIX O/S.

dot command A command beginning with a dot (.) and followed by a filename. A dot command tells the shell to read and execute the contents of that particular file..dot files are not usually displayed in an ordinary directory listings. (.) files are also called hidden files.
Many programs, including the Unix shells,use one or more dot files to store configuration information; you can customize your environment by creating a dot file in your current directory or in your home directory.

Filename	**Contents**
.bash_logout	Bash logout commands
.bash_profile	Bash login intialization commands
.bashrc	Bash initialization commands
.cshrc	C shell initialization commands
.elm	Directory of elm configuration files
.emacs	emacs editor initialization commands
.exrc	Vi editor initialization commands
.gopher	Gopher initialization commands
.history	History file
.login	C shell login commands
.logout	C shell logout commands
.netrc	ftp autologin information
.newsrc	A list of USENET newsgroups you can access
.mailrc	A list of mail initialization commands
.pinerc	Pine configuration information
.plan	Information displayed by finger
.project	Additional finger information
.profile	Bourne shell initialization commands
.rcrc	rc shell initialization commands
.signature	Signature file used in postings to USENET
.tcshrc	tcsh shell initialization commands
.xsession	X-Window start-up commands
.xinitrc	X-Window initialization commands
.zshenx	Zsh shell initialization commands
.zshrc	Zsh shell initialization commands
.zlogin	Zsh shell login initialization commands
.zlogout	Zsh shell logout initialization commands

.zprofile Zsh shell login initialization commands

dtox This command converts a DOS text file into a Unix text file:

```
dtox  filename  >  output-filename
```

echo A command that echoes string from the standard input (the terminal keyboard) to the standard output (the terminal screen),enabling you to see the characters as they are typed.

ed A line-oriented editor,included with the UNIX O/S that creates and modifies ASCII text files.

editor A tool for creating and managing text data within files.Popular distributed editors include line-oriented editors (such as ed) and screen-oriented editors (vi and emacs) are distributed with most UNIX O/S installations.

electronic mail (e-mail) A facility {hat lets users send messages to users on other network computers systems.

emacs A programmable, screen-oriented text editor, created by Richard Stallman at MIT.emacs uses a single mode for text editing and commands.

emulator Mimics the hardware or software of a computer causing it to act as though it were in another type of computer environment.

encryption Encodes files,via a key so that they are unreadable,to anyone without the original password.

end-of-file character (EOF) The (EOF) character marks the end of a file.The UNIX(EOF)character is CTRL-D.

environment The set of values of all shell variables. You can set these variables automatically at login and export them in your profile.

environment file A file containing guidelines that set the environment for an user under the Korn shell.

Combined with the values of variables set in users' profile files,the environment file can restrict or enhance different users' capabilities on the same system.

eqn A preprocessor for equations to be formatted by the troff text formatter.

escape A shell escape is used to escape from within a shell to perform a command. The interactive shell escape command is the exclamation point (!). The ESC key is a ASCII escape character located on the keyboard.

escape character The backslash character (\),which tells the shell to ignore the meaning of the following character and use the literal character.

exec A fundamental system call that replaces the current running process with another one.

executable file A complete application or program that is ready to run.

execute permission A permission setting (x) on a file that shows that an user can open the file. See also read permission and write permission.

external data representation (XDR) A datum format used in a network file sharing (NFS) network to provide a common representation of data on different computers running different operating systems.

fdisk A program that allows the user to change the hard disk partition table.

file descriptor A number used by programs to identify files for input and output operations.The standard input,standard output and standard error are assigned the file descriptors 0,1,2, in order.

file server A server on a local area network whose sole purpose is to provide storage and transfer of data files.

filename The name gave to a file.Filenames must be unique within a directory,although you can use the same filename in several different directories.

Here are a few characters to avoid when allocating UNIX filenames:

Character	**Descriptions**
!	Exclamation Point
#	Pound Sign
&	Ampersand
()	Parentheses
'	Single quote
"	Double quote
`	Back quote
;	Semicolon
<>	Redirection symbols
\	Backslash
@	At sign
$	Dollar sign
^	Caret
{}	Braces
~	Tilde
?	Question mark

filename extension The part of a filename that follows the period.Here are a few listed on the next page:

Common UNIX Filename Extensions

Extensions	**Descriptions**
.a	Archived file or assembler code
.au	Audio file
.c	C language source code
.csh	C shell script

.enc	Encrypted file
.f	FORTRAN source code
.F	FORTRAN source code before preprocessing.
.gif	Graphics Interchange Format File
.gl	Animation file
.gz	File compressed with the gzip command.
.h	C program header file.
.jpg or jpeg	Joint Photographic Experts Group format still image.
.mm	Text files containing troff mm macros.
.mpeg or mpg	Motion Picture Experts Group format video file.
.ms	Text file containing troff ms macros.
.o	Object file.
.ps	PostScript source file.
.s	Assembly language source code.
.sh	Bourne shell script.
.shar	Shell archive.
.tar	tar archive file.
.tex	Text file formatted with TEX commands.
.txt	ASCII text file.
.uu	An uuencode file.
.xx	Text file formatted with LATEX commands.
.z	File compressed by the pack command.
.Z	File compressed by the compress command.
.1 to .8	Online manual source files.

filling A process used by text formatters (such as troff) or word processors to put as much output on a line as the margins will allow.

filter A program that reads input and provides output based on a characteristic of the input.Filters used in a pipe is an important part of the UNIX.

Listed below are a few UNIX Filters:

Filter Names	**Descriptions**
cat	Copies standard input to standard output;combines files.
colrm	Removes the specified columns from each line.
crypt	Encrypts or decrypts data using a specified key.
cut	Extracts specified columns from each line.
fmt	Formats text.
grep	Extracts lines that contain a specified pattern.
head	Displays the first few lines of data.
less	Displays data one screen at a time.
look	Extracts lines that begin with a specified pattern.
more	Displays data one screen at a time.
nl	Creates line numbers.
paste	Combines columns of data.
pg	Displays data one screen at a time.
pr	Formats data for printing.
rev	Reverses the order of the characters in each line.
sort	Sorts data.
spell	Checks for spelling errors.
tail	Displays the last few lines of data.
tr	Translates selected characters.
uniq	Locates repeated lines.
wc	Counts characters,words or lines.

finger A command that produces detailed user information,such as login name, real name, environment information, about a local or a remote user.

foreground The processing environment in which current commands are processed before returning control to the user.

fork A system call that branches off from one process and creates another process,called a child process.

fourth-generation language (4GL) A high-level programming language used to develop customized database management applications.

freeware Software that is usually provided free of charge,asking only that the user honor the copyright laws associated with the software.

fsck An interactive UNIX tool used for diagnosing file systems and making repairs if necessary.

FSF (Free Software Foundation) A nonprofit free software distribution organization founded by Richard Stallman the late 1970's.

full path name The complete name of a file from the root directory down to the filename,including all directory names.

getty A part of the UNIX login process in which the user login and password are checked and associated with a terminal session.

global Relating to all occurrences of an object.A global change to a string in a file changes all occurrences of that particular string in the file; the global variable retains its value throughout the program.

glyph The picture of an object on a computer screen, such as a bell or a clock.

GNU (GNU's Not UNIX) Software developed by the Free Software Foundation (FSF);makes up a large part of the Linux utilities.

grap A preprocessor that produces output graphs for documents produced using the troff text formatter.

graphical user interface (GUI) An user interface that uses such objects as icons, glyphs, menus,pointers, and scroll bars to allow the user to choose different options and run programs graphically by moving, pointing and clicking.

grep Global regular expression A command that locates regular expressions in files.grep is an useful tool for finding files with references to a particular date,individual and so on.

group A class of users on a system who access data. The group ID sets file access permissions for a group of users on a system.

group ID (gid) A number assigned to an user to specify the group of the user. This class identifier can be used by the system administrator or other users to restrict or allow access to data and program files.

hard delete (of an user) Immediate delete of a user's login information and home directory.

header file A file that contains source code definitions of macros and variables.header files are usually included at the beginning of user-developed programs."include files," also have names that end with .h.These can also serve as header files.

hidden file A file that begins with a dot (.). Filenames beginning with the dot is not included in the output (unless it is an argument, such as -a,which tells it to include hidden files).An example is your .profile.

history list A list of previously issued commands. A history list is kept by the Korn shell and by the C shell.

home directory The root directory of an user's file system. You are normally placed in your home directory at login time.You can configure this directory in your .profile.

horizontal application A software application that performs functions that are not specific to a trade or industry.Word processors,contact managers, spreadsheets are examples of horizontal applications.

host a computer that is connected to a network and provides services to an user or group of users.

HP/UX A UNIX variant developed by Hewlett-Packard, based on UNIX System V Release 2.

IEEE P1003.2 The IEEE subcommittee that developed the POSIX operating system interface standard.

inode number A number assigned to a specific mode in a file system. The inode number is associated with a file and the file system uses i nodes to track information about the file.

Internet The DARPA network using the Internet protocol suite for connectivity.

interpreter A program that executes user instructions directly instead of turning them into machine language first.Shell scripts are interpreted.

interrupt A signal sent to show that an action is required by the interrupt handler.Interrupts are used to coordinate I/O devices.

IP address A 32-bit number that specifically identifies a computer on a network using TCP/IP.

job A command started process running on a system. Jobs run in the foreground or background,depending on the priority of the job.

kernel The main part of the UNIX O/S that controls process scheduling,I/O operations,hardware.The kernel is always resident in memory and is a program requiring only a small amount of system resources.This small footprint of services allows more room for other essential processes and system resources.

kill (a process) To stop the execution of a process.

Korn shell (ksh) A shell, created by David Korn.The Korn shell has enhanced features such as command line editing and a history file.

LaTeX A macro package for TeX that allows users to perform structured text formatting and typesetting.

library An archives of programming functions.Library directories usually have names that begin with /lib.

limit An useful system administration command that restricts the size of user-created files as well as core dumps.

line-oriented editor A process that acts on a line or group of lines at a time, as opposed to acting on a screen of data. The ed editor is a line-oriented editor.Screen-oriented editors are usually more proficient.

link (modules) Combines individual modules into executable programs.

Linux A freely distributed POSIX-compliant, UNIX-like operating system that runs on x86 hardware, originally developed by Linus Torvalds at the University of Helsinki.

listener A port monitor that listens for network address requests for communications across a network.

little language A term used to describe tools that perform a set of functions such as editing,shell programming,file manipulation,all within one process. perl is an example of a little language.

login To establish a session with another computer by providing a valid user ID and password to the operating system.

login ID The number that uniquely identifies a log name in the etc/passwd file;also called an user id.

login shell The shell started when an user logs in to a system.The login shell normally resides in the /etc/passwd file.

logoff To exit the system.The preferred manner to log off is to press Ctrl-D or to type exit.

macros Groups of instructions or commands combined into one instruction.

magic numbers Magic numbers are in the first bits of a file that contains coded information about the file type.Usually referenced in the /etc/magic directory.

mail (shell) A shell command used to send and receive mail from other system users.

mail surrogate A routine that controls the delivery and processing of mail sent over the UUCP System. The instructions for this mechanism is normally kept in a file called the mail surrogate file.

make A program that creates or maintains a list of all the modules necessary to form an executable program.

memorandum macros (mm macros) A set of macros used in text formatting, provided in the macro package mm.Macros contain commonly used formats for page layouts,headings and footers used in letter and memo composition.

metacharacter A special character used in a regular expression to provide specific patterns for searching. Metacharacters are used when an exact pattern is not known or wanted.

MIME (Multipurpose Internet Mail Extensions) An architecture that allows users to send non-ASCII text mail in a specified format.

modem (modulator/demodulator) A device that converts analog signals to digital,which allows computers to communicate via telephone lines.

moderated news group News groups(usually listed as .comp) on the USENET that have moderators who decide which articles get posted to a particular news group.

mount To make a file system available for use on a UNIX O/S.

mount point The directory name where a file system is mounted.

MS-DOS (Microsoft Disk Operating System) The most widely used single-task operating system for Intel and AMD-based PCs.

MUA (Mail User Agent) Software that the user uses when composing, reading or sending mail.elm,pine, mush and mailx are examples of MUAs.

Multics(Multiplexed Information and Computing Service) developed in the mid-1960s by MIT and GE. Multics is a multi-user O/S that was the predecessor to the UNIX Operating System.

multi-tasking The capability of a computer to run more than one task(process)at a time.The UNIX O/S has multi-tasking capabilities,as does Microsoft's Windows 2000 and the new Millineum O/S.

multi-user The capability of a computer to support more than one user connected to the system simultaneously and provide access to the same files or programs.Unix supports multi-users.

Xnamed pipe A special pipe that allows unrelated processes to pass data.Normally,pipes only pass data among related processes.

name server A designated machine on a TCP/IP network that provides Internet network addresses to computers communicating with one another.

network A group of computers connected either directly or over dial-up connections.Network sizes can range from local-called local area networks-to wide area networks,which can be located anywhere in the world.

Network File System (NFS) Associated programs, developed by Sun Microsystems,which allow file transfer to occur over networks.

Network Lock Manager A NFS utility that provides a locking capability for a NFS resource to allow only one client to gain access it at a time.

news Gossip,as well as,information that can be read by users by entering the news command.

news readers Programs for reading USENET news group messages.Examples of news readers are nn,rn,trn and xrn.

NNTP {Network News Transfer Protocol) A protocol that defines how USENET articles are transferred over networks,allowing a single site to store the news while multiple users access articles(messages).

noclobber A variable setting that prevents accidental overwriting of files when output is redirected to a file from the standard output.

nroff A text formatter that produces memos and letters to be output on terminal devices and line printers.

object A single entity that receives or contains information,such as a program,a printer,a page or a record.

object code Executable code produced by compiling source programs.

octal dump A display of the contents of a file in octal format.This includes printing and non-printing characters,using a program such as od. This format is helpful with viewing the contents of binary files.

owner (file) The user listed as the person who owns a file and has the owner permissions.Owners may also transfer ownership of files to other users.

pager A program that displays the contents of a file one screen at a time,such as pg or more.

parent directory The directory next highest in the UNIX file system hierarchy,also referred to and noted as the characters .. (pronounced "dot dot").

parent process A process which,forks away to generate a new process, called the child process.

parent process ID (PPID) A number given by the shell to a child process to identify the parent process.

partition A segment of disk space on a computer.The UNIX System uses separate partitions to mount the different file systems.

password aging A UNIX security feature that requires users to change their passwords at regular intervals.

pattern matching A technique to determine the occurrence of a particular character(s),using regular expressions.

pic A troff preprocessor that formats simple line drawings.

pipe A connection between the standard output of one process and the standard input of a second process.

port A connection point from a processor to an external device such as a terminal,printer or modem. Ports are reconfigureable.

portability The ability, to move easily, software code from one computer environment to another without making many modifications.The UNIX O/S is a portable operating system.

POSIX (Portable Operating System Interface for Computer Environments(x)) An IEEE standard that defines requirements for portable UNIX-like systems and the manner in which applications interact with the operating system.

PostScript A page description language,developed by Adobe Systems,that specifies high-quality output for printers.

PPP (Point-to-Point Protocol) A protocol that defines packet communications on networks such as TCP/IP, Ether net, and Novell.

preemptive multi-tasking The ability to interrupt a task to service another task,seemingly at the same time.

primary name server A Remote File Sharing domain that administers the file sharing environment for a domain. It maintains addresses of other servers on the network,tracks available resources and assigns access passwords.

primary prompt A string(the default is normally $ or #) that notifies the user that the shell is ready to accept user input.

priority The order assigned to a process(es). System processes have a higher priority than user processes.

process Processes are started by the shell and given a process ID number,used to track the process until it is finished.

.profile A description of the shell operating environment for a given user.Some of the information contained in a .profile include paths for commands, terminal descriptions and definitions of key directories used.

protocol A set of rules between two devices to allow communications to occur.

public domain software Software that can be used by anyone,because the author has given up all copyrights as well as rights to sale and distribution.The software is available without restrictions or licensing fees.

quantum (time) The maximum time allotted for a real-time process to run.

query language A language employed by database users to retrieve,modify add,or delete data.

queuing A process that occurs when a program formats and prepares output.

quota A method of limiting the amount of an user(s) disk space on a system.A soft quota warns an user that they are over the disk space limit,but a hard quota stops the user from writing new file information immediately when limits are exceeded.

quoting Use of special characters to instruct the shell that the contents contained between the quotes are to be treated as a string.

RAM (Random Access Memory) Computer memory that can read from and written to by user(s) and system programs. The contents of RAM are lost once the computer's power is turned off.

read permission A permission setting of a file that allows users to read the contents of a file.

record locking Allows only one user at a time to access records in a particular file,so that updates are executed properly.

regular expression An expression used in pattern matching in files.Regular expressions consist of letters numbers and special characters that provide specific functions while searching for and replacing text.These expressions are known as metacharacters.

Remote File Sharing (RFS) Allows computers to share file systems via a network.This eliminates the need to have a multiple copies of files stored on separate computers.

restricted shell (rsh) A shell environment that prevents user(s) from reaching all commands. System administrators use restricted shells to prevent users from accidentally getting into areas in which they could cause system or file damage.

RISC (Reduced Instruction Set Computing)A CPU architecture that reduces the number of processing instructions in the computers,utilized to increase the speed of the Central Processing Unit.RISC chips are normally installed on network servers.

root Root is the first file in the file system hierarchy.Usually root is the user ID Of the system administrator.Root has read,write,execute permissions for all users' file and processes computers running the UNIX O/S.Root is used during booting of the operating system.

root directory The base directory (identified as /) on a system.

router A device that enables communications between two computers on a network using different protocols.

RS-232C The standard protocol used between devices such as a computer and serial connection such as modems or printers.

RTFM Read the F****** Manual. A response usually given to someone asking simple questions that are answered in the manuals,help files or read me files.

sar A UNIX command that reports on system activity and resources.

scheduling Runs programs at certain designated times.A specific time of the day,week,month.You can schedule jobs with cron.

screen-oriented editor An editor that allows manipulation of a screen of data at a time.As opposed to a line-oriented editor.The vi editor is a screen-oriented editor.

secondary name server (RFS) A computer in a Remote File Sharing domain that temporarily takes over the duties of the primary name server if a failure occurs.

sed (stream editor) A text editing tool that use files for batch mode input,as opposed to the ed and vi editors ,which are interactive.

server A computer in a networked environment that provides resources,(normally files),for clients on a network.

Shadow Password File A security file that contains password information used to validate user(s) passwords.This keeps users from obtaining user passwords from the /etc/passwd file.

shared library A binary library that is loaded and then shared by different applications.This saves load time and memory resources.

Shareware Software that is evaluated on a trial basis before purchasing.Shareware is owned and copyrighted by the author.

shell A control process under which an user executes commands.

shell layers An option that allows user(s) to run multiple shell sessions at one time,under the control of the shell layer manager shi.

signal A communication sent from one process to another process to notify the two of an event taking place. The receiving process either ignores the signal,or recognize it by calling an interrupt handler.

sleep A command that stops a process for a specified time.

SMTP(Simple Mail Transfer Protocol) A protocol defining how mail is sent via TCP/IP.

sort To arrange columns within a file according to a specified order.Alphabetically or numerical.

source code File(s) that contains programming instructions written in a computing language (for example C++) which needs to be compiled or interpreted before the instructions are executed by the computer.

Source Code Control System (SCCS) A UNIX program developed by Bell Labs to document changes to source code.This enables programmers to manage and access the different versions of a source code module.

special file A type of file containing information about a device such as a disk or an user terminal(s). Special files are used by UNIX for input/output operations.

spooling Moving input or output data to a temporary memory storage device until a process is ready to receive the data. Most printer jobs are spooled to allow the processor to do other tasks.

SQL (Structured Query Language) A ANSI standard query language for database management systems.

static display A display produced by a text formatter, such as troff, which appears in the output exactly where it was in the input;contrasted to a floating display.

status monitor A system administration process that reports on the status of currently running processes.

sticky bit A permission setting that reduces the system overhead for frequently used programs.An executable image of the program is temporarily stored in swap space until the program is executed.

string A sequence of characters or symbols.

stty (set tty) A command that allows an user to set changes or view settings for a terminal device used to communicate with the processor.

subdirectory A directory contained within another directory.All directories are sub directories of the next higher level directory all the way up to the root directory.

symbolic debugger A debugger,such as sdb,that allows programmers to trace the sequence of events in a program.

system administration System maintenance of files, users and processes on a system.

system call A call made by a process to the kernel, to perform a function such as I/O or process handling.

system class A class of processes reserved for the UNIX O/S. These processes have the highest priority.

system log files Special files used by the system administrator to analyze hardware,software and other system-wide processes.

tbl A preprocessor for nroff and troff that is used to produce tables within documents.

Tcl (Tool command language) An interpreted script language (very similar to C)that enables programmers to create tools and applications that can operate with other UNIX applications.

telnet A process which enables access to remote systems on the TELNET network.

term A program that runs over a regular telephone and allows multiple connections and remote execution of X Window applications.

terminal A device used to display input/output via a computer screen.Terminals are asynchronous or synchronous;the UNIX O/S uses asynchronous terminals for display.

terminal emulator A program that allows a personal computer to emulate an asynchronous terminal.

TeX A text processing language that allows users to create typesetter-independent output files.

TLI (Transport Layer Interface) A programmable interface that allows application development independent of the networking protocols below them, while providing reliable network transmission.

TFTP (Trivial FiYe Transfer Protocol) A protocol that uses the UDP to transfer files via the Internet.TFTP does not offer any form of network security protection.

tool A program or process that makes performing a task easier.A wide variety of UNIX software offer tools for text filtering,file manipulation, programming,calculations and many more.

TSR program (Terminate-Stay Resident) A DOS program that stays in computer memory after it has finished executing.

tty A UNIX process that manages the terminal(s) data transmission to and from a host processor;also a command to display the terminal(s) device name.

UDP (User Data gram Protocol) A transmission protocol using data grams that are built on top of the Internet protocol.

UNIX The operating system developed by Ken Thompson and Dennis Ritchie at Bell Labs in 1969,which was the first (original)version of UNIX.

UNIX System VIMLS (UNIX System V/Multi-Level Security) A version of the UNIX O/S that conforms to the Bi level of security as defined by the U.S. Department of Defense.This version is for users in need of a higher degree of security than in a typical UNIX environment.

unmount To remove a mounted file system from a tape drive or other storage device.

USENET A global network, built using the UUCP System, that allows users to read and exchange messages electronically on a variety of topics.

utility A special program that performs routine system functions.

vertical application An application designed to solve problems in a specialized industry such as retail or industry.

vi A screen-oriented editor that allows full-screen text manipulation. vi is a more user friendly editor than its line-oriented counterpart,ed.

virtual File System (VFS) A file system architecture in UNIX that allows multiple types of file systems to exist on the same computer.

virtual memory A method of using hard disk space to act as additional memory for program execution.

widgets The graphical objects used by a graphical user interface (GUI).

wild card A special character (*) used in a regular expressions to match a range of patterns.

window manager A program that manages the icons, objects, macro functions, pointer, button functions and general user interface in an X Window System.

workstation A single-user high performance computer. Workstations are typically used in engineering and graphical environments.

worm A program that can copy a working version of itself onto other networks and then run itself in it's new environment.Worms are either harmless or destructive.

XWindow System Among the first of many graphical windowing systems for UNIX(also known as X Windows)and developed at MIT.

x OPEN An association of international computer and software vendors, formed in 1984,whose goal is to promote open systems (systems that may be carried out by any company or individual;the opposite of proprietary systems)

x term A X Windows terminal emulation program

The different flavas(flavours/versions) of UNIX

UNIX O/S	**Developers**
386SD	Free via the Internet
AIX	IBM
A/UX	Apple
BSD	University of California,Berkeley
BSD-Lite	University of California,Berkeley
BSD/386	Berkeley Software Design
Coherent	Mark Williams Company
DC/OS	Pyramid Technology
Dynix	Sequent Computer Systems
FreeBSD	Free via Internet
HP-UX	Hewlett-Packard
Hurd(GNU)	Free Software Foundation
Interactive UNIX	Sun Microsystems
Irix	Silicon Graphics
Linux	Linus Torvalds;Free via the Internet
Mach	Carnegie Mellon University
Minix	Andrew Tannenbaum
MKS Toolkit	Mortice Kers Systems
NetBSD	Free via the Internet
NeXTStep	NeXT
OSF/1	Digital Equipment Corporation(DEC)
SCO Open server	Santa Cruz Operation
SCO UNIX	Santa Cruz Operation
Solaris	Sun Microsystems
SunOS	Sun Microsystems
Ultrix	Digital Equipment Corporation(DEC)
Unicos	Cray Research
Unixware	Novell/Santa Cruz Operation

Linux / Unix Packages:

This appendix lists the packages that make up Red Hat Linux. In each entry, you'll find the following information:

1. The name of the package
2. The packaged software's version number
3. The size of the packaged software, in kilobytes
4. A short description of the software

Although all of the files listed here are distributed by Red Hat Linux,most popular distributions of Linux and Unix contain similar distributions of files.

In addition, some packages will have one or more of the following icons alongside the package name:

[B] This package is part of the Red Hat Linux base, meaning that it is always installed.

[W] Workstation-class installations include this package.

[S] Server-class installations include this package.

Please Note: This package list was automatically generated right before Red Hat Linux 6.0 went into production. Because of the short timeframes involved, you might find minor typesetting problems in the package lists. However, we felt that an up-to-date package list was more important than a picture-perfect package list. We hope you'll agree...

You may also notice that some packages have different versions, and that packages listed here are not mentioned in the installation program (and vice versa). Any differences in package versions are normally due to the normal bug fixing process. It's possible that ``missing'' or ``extra'' packages are the result of last-minute changes prior to pressing CDROMs. Also note that all the packages in the ``Base'' group (and subgroups) are always installed, therefore you will not see them mentioned explicitly during the installation process.

Using the Package List After Installation

This list can come in handy even after you've installed Red Hat Linux. You can use it search for documentation. Here's how:

1. Find the package in this list.

2. Note the package name (The very first thing listed in bold at

the start of each package description).

3.Enter the following command, taking care to enter the package name exactly as it is shown in the list (the package name is case-sensitive):

```
rpm -qd package-name
```

(Replacing package-name with the actual name of the package, of course.)

If you installed the package, you should get a list of filenames. Each file contains documentation relating to the package you specified. Here are some of the types of filenames you'll see:

/usr/man... something.n -- This is a man page. You can view it by using the man command (for example, man something. You might also need to include the file's ending number in the man command (as in man n something.

/usr/X11R6/man... something.nx -- This is a man page for part of the X Window System. View these files the same way as a regular man page.

/usr/doc/something... -- Files under /usr/doc can be in any number of different formats. Sometimes the end of the filename can provide a clue as to how it should be viewed:

.html -- An HTML file. View with the web browser of your choice.

.txt -- A text file. View with cat or less.

.ps -- A Postscript file. You can print it to a Postscript printer, or you can view it with gv.

.gz -- A file compressed with gzip. If you make a copy of the original file, you can use gunzip to decompress it (you'll probably want to keep the original file compressed to save space). You can then view the file as you would normally. The zless command combines gunzip and less, and makes it possible to read compressed text files without making interim copies. There are other, more elegant ways to work with compressed files, but this approach will work for those just starting to use Linux.

In general, most of the documentation files you'll find will be one of those listed above. If in doubt, it's a good bet that the file is text. You can always try the file command to see if the file's contents can be identified.

/usr/info... -- Files in /usr/info are meant to be viewed using the info (or Emacs' Info mode).
If you use Emacs,press **[Ctrl]-[I]**, followed by **[I]** to view the main **Info screen.**

D.1 Amusements

This section lists the packages that provide fun and entertainment to Red Hat Linux system owners the world over.

D.1.1 Games

This section lists packages that contain a variety of games.

cxhextris -- (Version 1.0, 39K)

CXHextris is a color version of the popular xhextris game, which is a Tetris-like game that uses hexagon shapes instead of square shapes. CXHextris runs within the X Window System.

Install cxhextris if you enjoy playing Tetris or Tetris-like games and you'd like to play one on your system. You'll need to have X installed in order to play CXHextris.

fortune-mod -- (Version 1.0, 2,342K)

Fortune-mod contains the ever-popular fortune program. Want a little bit of random wisdom revealed to you when you log in? Fortune's your program. Fun-loving system administrators can add fortune to users' .login files, so that the users get their dose of wisdom each time they log in.

Install fortune if you want a program which will bestow these random bits o' wit.

gnome-games -- (Version 1.0.2, 3,342K)

[W]

GNOME is the GNU Network Object Model Environment. That's a fancy name, but really GNOME is a nice GUI desktop environment. Its powerful, friendly and easy-to-configure interface makes using your computer easy.

This package installs some GNOME games on your system, such as gnothello, solitaire, tetris and others.

gnuchess -- (Version 4.0.pl79, 1,428K)

The gnuchess package contains the GNU chess program. By default, GNUchess uses a curses text-based interface.Alternatively, GNUchess can be used in conjunction with the xboard user interface and the X Window System for a graphical chessboard.

You should install the gnuchess package if you would like to play chess on your computer. You'll also need to install the curses package. If you'd like to use a graphical interface with GNUchess, you'll also need to install the xboard package and the X Window System.

kdegames -- (Version 1.1.1pre2, 4,962K)

Games for the K Desktop Environment. Included with this package are: kabalone, kasteroids, kblackbox,kmahjongg, kmines, konquest, kpat, kpoker, kreversi, ksame, kshisen, ksokoban, ksmiletris, ksnake, ksirtet.

trojka -- (Version 1.1, 16K)

The game of Trojka involves a set of falling blocks. The point is to move the blocks around as they fall, so that three of the same blocks end up next to each other, either horizontally or diagonally. Once the blocks fill up the entire game area, the game is over.

Install the trojka package if you want to play a non-X game of falling blocks.

xbill -- (Version 2.0, 183K)

The xbill game tests your reflexes as you seek out and destroy all forms of Bill, establish new operating systems and boldly go where no geek has gone before. Xbill has become an increasingly attractive option as the Linux Age progresses, and it is very popular at Red Hat.

xboard -- (Version 4.0.0, 601K)

Xboard is an X Window System based graphical chessboard which can be used with the GNUchess and Crafty chess programs, with Internet Chess Servers (ICSs), with chess via email, or with your own saved games.

Install the xboard package if you need a graphical chessboard.

xboing -- (Version 2.4, 1,043K)

Xboing is an X Window System based game like the Breakout arcade game. The object of the game is to keep a ball bouncing on the bricks until you've broken through all of them.

xgammon -- (Version 0.98, 3,282K)

Xgammon is an X Window System based backgammon game. Xgammon allows you to play against the computer, or you can play against another person. Xgammon also supports playing a game against another person on a remote X terminal, and will display a second board there for their use.

xjewel -- (Version 1.6, 52K)

Xjewel is an X Window System game much like Domain/Jewelbox, Sega's Columns and/or Tetris. The point of the game is to move or rotate the blocks as they fall, to get jewels in patterns of three when they come to rest.

xpat2 -- (Version 1.04, 456K)

Xpat2 is a generic patience or Solitaire game for the X Window System. Xpat2 can be used with different rules sets, so it can be used to play Spider, Klondike, and other card games.

xpilot -- (Version 3.6.2, 1,617K)

Xpilot is an X Window System based multiplayer game of aerial combat. The object of the game is to shoot each other down,or you can use the race mode to just fly around. Xpilot resembles the Commodore 64 Thrust game, which is similar to Atari's Gravitar and Asteriods (note: this is not misspelled). Unless you already have an xpilot server on your network, you'll need to set up the server on one machine, and then set up xpilot clients on all of the players' machines.

xpuzzles -- (Version 5.4.1, 469K)

A set of geometric puzzles and toys for the X Window System. Xpuzzles includes a version of Rubik's cube and various other geometric Rubik's cube style puzzles.

xtrojka -- (Version 1.2.3, 216K)

The xtrojka game is an X Window System game of falling blocks, like Xjewel or Tetris.

D.1.2 Graphics

This section lists packages that provide graphics that are fun to look at.

mxp -- (Version 1.0, 55K)

The mxp (Mandelbrot explorer) program is an X Window System application for computing and exploring Mandelbrot sets.Mxp supports zoom/un-zoom, dynamic resizing of drawing windows, setup save/load, asynchronous image generation, GIF outputs, animation, nine color schemes, color rotation, color change options, and detailed statistics.

Install the mxp package if you need a Mandelbrot set generator for the X Window System.

xbanner -- (Version 1.31, 366K)

[W] [S]

The XBanner program allows the display of text, patterns and images in the
root window, so users can customize the XDM style login screen and/or the
normal X background.

Install XBanner if you'd like to change the look of your X login screen and/or X background.

xdaliclock -- (Version 2.14, 80K)

The xdaliclock program displays a digital clock, with digits that merge into the new digits as the time changes. Xdaliclock can display the time in 12 or 24 hour modes and can will display the date if you hold your mouse button down over it. Xdaliclock has two large fonts built in, but is capable of animating other fonts.

Install the xdaliclock package if you want a fairly large clock, with a melting special effect, for your system.

xearth -- (Version 1.0, 192K)

Xearth is an X Window System based graphic that shows a globe of the Earth, including markers for major cities and Red Hat Software. The Earth is correctly shaded for the current position of the sun, and the displayed image is updated every five minutes.

xfishtank -- (Version 2.0, 388K)

The xfishtank program displays an animated aquarium background on your screen. Xfishtank works with the X Window System.

xloadimage -- (Version 4.1, 255K)

The xloadimage utility displays images in an X Window System window, loads images into the root window, or writes images into a file. Xloadimage supports many images types (GIF, TIFF, JPEG, XPM, XBM, etc.).

Install the xloadimage package if you need a utility for displaying images or loading images into the root window.

xlockmore -- (Version 4.13, 759K)

The xlockmore utility is an enhanced version of the standard xlock program, which allows you to lock an X session so that other users can't access it. Xlockmore runs a provided screensaver until you type in your password.

Install the xlockmore package if you need a locking program to secure X sessions.

xmorph -- (Version 1996.07.12, 127K)

[W]

Xmorph is a digital image warping (aka morphing) program. Xmorph provides the tools needed and comprehensible instructions for you to create morphs: changing one image into another. Xmorph runs under the X Window System.

Install the xmorph package if you need a program that will create morphed images.

xscreensaver -- (Version 3.09, 3,325K)

[W]

The xscreensaver package contains a variety of screensavers for your mind-numbing, ambition-eroding, time-wasting, hypnotized viewing pleasure.

Install the xscreensaver package if you need screensavers for use with the X Window System.

xwpick -- (Version 2.20, 50K)

The xwpick program allows you to choose an image or a rectangular piece of an image from an X Window System window and then write the image to a file in a variety of formats, incuding PostScript(TM), GIF, and PICT.

Install the xwpick program if you need to take screenshots from X Window System screens and write them to files.

D.2 Applications

This section contains packages that contain various applications for Red Hat Linux.

D.2.1 Archiving

This section contains packages that are associated with the efficient storing and/or copying of files.

cpio -- (Version 2.4.2, 70K)

[B]

GNU cpio copies files into or out of a cpio or tar archive. Archives are files which contain a collection of other files plus information about them, such as their file name, owner, timestamps, and access permissions. The archive can be another file on the disk, a magnetic tape, or a pipe. GNU cpio supports the following archive formats: binary, old ASCII, new ASCII, crc, HPUX binary, HPUX old ASCII, old tar and POSIX.1 tar. By default, cpio creates binary format archives, so that they are compatible with older cpio programs. When it is extracting files from archives, cpio automatically recognizes which kind of archive it is reading and can read archives created on machines with a different byte-order.

Install cpio if you need a program to manage file archives.

dump -- (Version 0.4b4, 153K)

The dump package contains both dump and restore. Dump examines files in a filesystem, determines which ones need to be backed up, and copies those files to a specified disk, tape or other storage medium. The restore command performs the inverse function of dump; it can restore a full backup of a filesystem. Subsequent incremental backups can then be layered on top of the full backup. Single files and directory subtrees may also be restored from full or partial backups.

Install dump if you need a system for both backing up filesystems and restoring filesystems after backups.

lha -- (Version 1.00, 56K)

[W]

LHA is an archiving and compression utility for LHarc format archives. LHA is mostly used in the DOS world, but can be used under Linux to extract DOS files from LHA archives.

Install the lha package if you need to extract DOS files from LHA archives.

ncompress -- (Version 4.2.4, 31K)

[B]

The ncompress package contains the compress and uncompress file compression and decompression utilities, which are compatible with the original UNIX compress utility (.Z file extensions). These utilities can't handle gzipped (.gz file extensions) files, but gzip can handle compressed files.

rmt -- (Version 0.4b4, 12K)

[B]

The rmt utility provides remote access to tape devices for programs like dump (a filesystem backup program), restore (a program for restoring files from a backup) and tar (an archiving program).

sharutils -- (Version 4.2, 221K)

[W] [S]

The sharutils package contains the GNU shar utilities, a set of tools for encoding and decoding packages of files (in binary or text format) in a special plain text format called shell archives (shar). This format can be sent through email (which can be problematic for regular binary files). The shar utility supports a wide range of capabilities (compressing, uuencoding, splitting long files for multi-part mailings, providing checksums), which make it very flexible at creating shar files. After the files have been sent, the unshar tool scans mail messages looking for shar files. Unshar automatically strips off mail headers and introductory text and then unpacks the shar files.

Install sharutils if you send binary files through email very often.

taper -- (Version 6.9, 847K)

Taper is a backup and restoration program with a friendly user interface. Files may be backed up to a tape drive or to a hard disk. The interface for selecting files to be backed up/restored is very similar to the Midnight Commander interface, and allows easy traversal of directories. Taper supports recursive selection of directories. Taper also supports backing up SCSI, ftape,zftape and removable drives. By default, taper is set for incremental backups and automatic most recent restore.

Install the taper package if you need a user friendly file backup and restoration program.

tar -- (Version 1.12, 474K)

[B]

The GNU tar program saves many files together into one archive and can restore individual files (or all of the files) from the archive. Tar can also be used to add supplemental files to an archive and to update or list files in the archive.

Tar includes multivolume support, automatic archive compression/ decompression, the ability to perform remote archives and the ability to perform incremental and full backups.

If you want to use Tar for remote backups, you'll also need to install the rmt package.

You should install the tar package, because you'll find its compression and decompression utilities essential for working with files.

unarj -- (Version 2.41a, 26K)

The UNARJ program is used to uncompress .arj format archives. The .arj format archive was mostly used on DOS machines.

Install the unarj package if you need to uncompress .arj format archives.

unzip -- (Version 5.31, 370K)

[W]

The unzip utility is used to list, test, or extract files from a zip archive. Zip archives are commonly found on MS-DOS systems. The zip utility, included in the zip package, creates zip archives. Zip and unzip are both compatible with archives created by PKWARE(R)'s PKZIP for MS-DOS, but the programs' options and default behaviors do differ in some respects.

Install the unzip package if you need to list, test or extract files from a zip archive.

zip -- (Version 2.1, 217K)

[W]

The zip program is a compression and file packaging utility. Zip is analogous to a combination of the UNIX tar and compress commands and is compatible with PKZIP (a compression and file packaging utility for MS-DOS systems).

Install the zip package if you need to compress files using the zip program.

D.2.2 Communications

This section contains packages that are associated with communications.

dip -- (Version 3.3.7o, 88K)

[W] [S]

Dip is a modem dialer. Dip handles the connections needed for dialup IP links like SLIP or PPP. Dip can handle both incoming and outgoing connections, using password security for incoming connections. Dip is useful for setting up PPP and SLIP connections, but isn't required for either. Netcfg uses dip for setting up SLIP connections.

Install dip if you need a utility which will handle dialup IP connections.

efax -- (Version 0.8a, 205K)

Efax is a small ANSI C/POSIX program that sends and receives faxes using any Class 1, 2 or 2.0 fax modem.

You need to install efax if you want to send faxes and you have a Class 1, 2 or 2.0 fax modem.

getty_ps -- (Version 2.0.7j, 127K)

[B]

The getty_ps package contains the getty and uugetty programs, basic programs for accomplishing the login process on a Red Hat Linux system. Getty and uugetty are used to accept logins on the console or a terminal. Getty is invoked by the init process to open tty lines and set their modes, to print the login prompt and get the user's name, and to initiate a login process for the user. Uugetty works just like getty, except that uugetty creates and uses lock files to prevent two or more processes from conflicting in their use of a tty line. Getty and uugetty can also handle answer a modem for dialup connections, but mgetty is recommended for that purpose.

kpilot -- (Version 3.1b8_pgb, 878K)

KPilot allows you to synchronize your PalmPilot with your desktop. It allows you to backup and restore the various databases (Addressbook, ToDo List, Memos, etc.) as well as install applications to the pilot. Two "conduits" for the third party application KOrganizer are included which will let you sync your ToDo list and Calendar with that program.

lrzsz -- (Version 0.12.20, 391K)

[W] [S]

Lrzsz (consisting of lrz and lsz) is a cosmetically modified zmodem/ymodem/xmodem package built from the public-domain version of the rzsz package. Lrzsz was created to provide a working GNU copyleft Zmodem solution for Linux systems.

You should install lrzsz if you're also installing a Zmodem communications program that uses lrzsz. If you're installing minicom, you need to install lrzsz.

mgetty -- (Version 1.1.14, 842K)

The mgetty package contains a "smart" getty which allows logins over a serial line (i.e., through a modem). If you're using a Class 2 or 2.0 modem, mgetty can receive faxes. If you also need to send faxes, you'll need to install the sendfax program.

If you'll be dialing in to your system using a modem, you should install the mgetty package. If you'd like to send faxes using mgetty and your modem, you'll need to install the mgetty-sendfax program. If you need a viewer for faxes, you'll also need to install the mgetty-viewfax package.

mgetty-sendfax -- (Version 1.1.14, 269K)

Sendfax is a standalone backend program for sending fax files. The mgetty program (a getty replacement for handling logins over a serial line) plus sendfax will allow you to send faxes through a Class 2 modem.

If you'd like to send faxes over a Class 2 modem, you'll need to install the mgetty-sendfax and the mgetty packages.

mgetty-viewfax -- (Version 1.1.14, 93K)

Viewfax displays the fax files received using mgetty in an X11 window. Viewfax is capable of zooming in and out on the displayed fax.

If you're installing the mgetty-viewfax package, you'll also need to install mgetty.

mgetty-voice -- (Version 1.1.14, 638K)

The mgetty-voice package contains the vgetty system, which enables mgetty and your modem to support voice capabilities. In simple terms, vgetty lets your modem act as an answering machine. How well the system will work depends upon your modem,which may or may not be able to handle this kind of implementation.

Install mgetty-voice along with mgetty if you'd like to try having your modem act as an answering machine.

minicom -- (Version 1.82, 302K)

[W] [S]

Minicom is a simple text-based modem control and terminal emulation program somewhat similar to MSDOS Telix. Minicom includes a dialing directory, full ANSI and VT100 emulation, an (external) scripting language, and other features.

Minicom should be installed if you need a simple modem control program or terminal emulator.

pilot-link -- (Version 0.9.0, 770K)

This suite of tools allows you to upload and download programs and data files between a *nix machine and the USR Pilot. It has a few extra utils that will allow for things like syncing the Pilot's calendar app with Ical. Note that you might still need to consult the sources for pilot-link if you would like the Python, Tcl, or Perl bindings.

sliplogin -- (Version 2.1.1, 54K)

The sliplogin utility turns the terminal line on standard input into a SLIP (Serial Line Internet Protocol) link to a remote host. Sliplogin is usually used to allow dial-in SLIP connections.

Install the sliplogin package if you need to support dial-in SLIP connections.

uucp -- (Version 1.06.1, 2,079K)

[W] [S]

The uucp command copies files between systems. Uucp is primarily used by remote machines downloading and uploading email and news files to local machines.

Install the uucp package if you need to use uucp to transfer files between machines.

D.2.3 Databases

This section contains packages that are associated with databases.

postgresql -- (Version 6.4.2, 6,918K)

[S]

Postgresql includes the programs needed to create and run a PostgreSQL server, which will in turn allow you to create and maintain PostgreSQL databases. PostgreSQL is an advanced Object-Relational database management system (DBMS) that supports almost all SQL constructs (including transactions, subselects and user-defined types and functions).

You should install postgresql if you want to create and maintain your own PostgreSQL databases and/or your own

PostgreSQL server. If you are installing postgresql, you should also install postgresql-data, which will help you get started with PostgreSQL.

postgresql-clients -- (Version 6.4.2, 938K)

[S]

Postgresql-clients includes the client programs and client libraries that you'll need to access a PostgreSQL database management system server. This package contains the client libraries for C, C++ and PERL, as well as command-line utilities for managing PostgreSQL databases on a remote server. If you just want to connect to an existing remote PostgreSQL server, this package is all you need.

You should install postgresql-clients if you're installing postgresql. You should also install postgresql-clients if you're not installing postgresql, but you want to access PostgreSQL databases on a remote PostgreSQL server.

D.2.4 Editors

This section contains packages that are associated with editing text files.

GXedit -- (Version 1.23, 570K)

Here is a fast, easy-to-use editor which is both network- oriented and very secure. GXedit is a graphical text editor which features a toolbar, network bar and tooltips, spell checking, inline help, the ability to send text as e-mail, macros and more. GXedit was designed to balance these and many other features without becoming too bloated.

You'll need GTK+ to use GXedit.

emacs -- (Version 20.3, 17,395K)

[W] [S]

Emacs is a powerful, customizable, self-documenting, modeless text editor. Emacs contains special code editing features, a scripting language (elisp), and the capability to read mail, news and more without leaving the editor.

This package includes the libraries you need to run the Emacs editor, so you need to install this package if you intend to use

Emacs. You also need to install the actual Emacs program package (emacs-nox or emacs-X11). Install emacs-nox if you are not going to use the X Window System; install emacs-X11 if you will be using X.

emacs-X11 -- (Version 20.3, 6,638K)

[W]

Emacs-X11 includes the Emacs text editor program for use with the X Window System (it provides support for the mouse and other GUI elements). Emacs-X11 will also run Emacs outside of X, but it has a larger memory footprint than the 'non-X' Emacs package (emacs-nox).

Install emacs-X11 if you're going to use Emacs with the X Window System. You should also install emacs-X11 if you're going to run Emacs both with and without X (it will work fine both ways). You'll also need to install the emacs package in order to run Emacs.

emacs-el -- (Version 20.3, 21,631K)

Emacs-el contains the emacs-elisp sources for many of the elisp programs included with the main Emacs text editor package.

You need to install emacs-el only if you intend to modify any of the Emacs packages or see some elisp examples.

emacs-leim -- (Version 20.3, 4,216K)

The Emacs Lisp code for input methods for various international character scripts.

emacs-nox -- (Version 20.3, 2,786K)

[W] [S]

Emacs-nox is the Emacs text editor program without support for the X Window System.

You need to install this package only if you plan on exclusively using Emacs without the X Window System (emacs-X11 will work both in X and out of X, but emacs-nox will only work outside of X). You'll also need to install the emacs package in order to run Emacs.

gedit -- (Version 0.5.1, 340K)

[W]

gEdit is a small but powerful text editor designed expressly for GNOME.

It includes such features as split-screen mode, a plugin API, which allows gEdit to be extended to support many features while remaining small at its core, multiple document editing through the use of a 'tabbed' notebook and many more functions.

GNOME is required to use gEdit (Gnome-Libs and Gtk+).

gnotepad+ -- (Version 1.1.3, 182K)

[W]

gnotepad+ is an easy-to-use, yet fairly feature-rich, simple text editor for systems running X11 and using GTK+. It is designed for as little bloat as possible, while still providing many of the common features found in a modern GUI-based text editor.

jed -- (Version 0.98.7, 140K)

Jed is a fast, compact editor based on the slang screen library. Jed features include emulation of the Emacs, EDT, WordStar and Brief editors; support for extensive customization with slang macros, colors, keybindings, etc.; and a variety of programming modes with syntax highlighting.

You should install jed if you've used it before and you like it, or if you haven't used any text editors before and you're still deciding what you'd like to use. You'll also need to have slang installed.

jed-common -- (Version 0.98.7, 1,502K)

The jed-common package contains files (such as .sl files) that are needed by any jed binary in order to run.

jed-xjed -- (Version 0.98.7, 166K)

Xjed is a version of the Jed text editor that will work with the X Window System.

You should install xjed if you like Jed and you'd like to use it with X. You'll also need to have the X Window System installed.

joe -- (Version 2.8, 276K)

Joe is an easy to use, modeless text editor which would be very appropriate for novices. Joe uses the same WordStar keybindings used in Borland's development environment.

You should install joe if you've used it before and you liked it, or if you're still deciding what text editor you'd like to use, or if you have a fondness for WordStar. If you're just starting out, you should probably install joe because it is very easy to use.

vim-X11 -- (Version 5.3, 1,395K)

VIM (VIsual editor iMproved) is an updated and improved version of the vi editor. Vi was the first real screen-based editor for UNIX, and is still very popular. VIM improves on vi by adding new features: multiple windows, multi-level undo, block highlighting and more. VIM-X11 is a version of the VIM editor which will run within the X Window System. If you install this package, you can run VIM as an X application with a full GUI interface and mouse support.

Install the vim-X11 package if you'd like to try out a version of vi with graphics and mouse capabilities. You'll also need to install the vim-common package.

vim-common -- (Version 5.3, 4,355K)

[B]

VIM (VIsual editor iMproved) is an updated and improved version of the vi editor. Vi was the first real screen-based editor for UNIX, and is still very popular. VIM improves on vi by adding new features: multiple windows, multi-level undo, block highlighting and more. The vim-common package contains files which every VIM binary will need in order to run.

If you are installing any version of the VIM editor, you'll also need to the vim-common package installed.

vim-enhanced -- (Version 5.3, 1,297K)

VIM (VIsual editor iMproved) is an updated and improved version of the vi editor. Vi was the first real screen-based editor for UNIX, and is still very popular. VIM improves on vi by adding new features: multiple windows, multi-level undo, block highlighting and more. The vim-enhanced package contains a version of VIM with extra, recently introduced features like Python and Perl interpreters.

Install the vim-enhanced package if you'd like to use a version of the VIM editor which includes recently added enhancements like interpreters for the Python and Perl scripting languages. You'll also need to install the vim-common package.

vim-minimal -- (Version 5.3, 445K)

[B]

VIM (VIsual editor iMproved) is an updated and improved version of the vi editor. Vi was the first real screen-based editor for UNIX, and is still very popular. VIM improves on vi by adding new features: multiple windows, multi-level undo, block highlighting and more. The vim-minimal package includes a minimal version of VIM, which is installed into /bin/vi for use when only the root partition is present.

D.2.5 Emulators

This section contains packages associated with the emulation of other operating systems.

dosemu -- (Version 0.99.10, 1,812K)

[W]

Dosemu is a DOS emulator. Once you've installed dosemu, start the DOS emulator by typing in the dos command.

You need to install dosemu if you use DOS programs and you want to be able to run them on your Red Hat Linux system. You may also need to install the dosemu-freedos package.

dosemu-freedos -- (Version 0.99.10, 8,194K)

Generally, the dosemu DOS emulator requires either that your system have some version of DOS available or that your system's partitions were formatted and installed with DOS. If your system does not meet either of the previous requirements, you can instead use the dosemu-freedos package, which contains an hdimage file which will be installed in teh /var/lib/dosemu directory. The hdimage file is already bootable with FreeDOS.

You will need to edit your /etc/dosemu.conf file to add the image to the list of disk 'drives' used by dosemu.

Install dosemu-freedos if you are installing the dosemu package and you don't have a version of DOS available on your system,and your system's partitions were not formatted and installed with DOS.

xdosemu -- (Version 0.99.10, 26K)

[W]

Xdosemu is a version of the dosemu DOS emulator that runs with the X Window System. Xdosemu provides VGA graphics and mouse support.

Install xdosemu if you need to run DOS programs on your system, and you'd like to do so with the convenience of graphics support and mouse capabilities.

D.2.6 Engineering

This section contains packages that are associated with the engineering arts.

bc -- (Version 1.05a, 128K)

[B]

The bc package includes bc and dc. Bc is an arbitrary precision numeric processing arithmetic language. Dc is an interactive arbitrary precision stack based calculator, which can be used as a text mode calculator.

Install the bc package if you need its number handling capabilities or if you would like to use its text mode calculator.

gnuplot -- (Version 3.7, 918K)

Gnuplot is a command-line driven, interactive function plotting program especially suited for scientific data representation. Gnuplot can be used to plot functions and data points in both two and three dimensions and in many different formats.

Install gnuplot if you need a graphics package for scientific data representation.

units -- (Version 1.0, 25K)

Units converts an amount from one unit to another, or tells you what mathematical operation you need to perform to convert from one unit to another. Units can only handle multiplicative scale changes (i.e., it can't tell you how to convert from Celsius to Fahrenheit, which requires an additive step in addition to the multiplicative conversion).

Units is a handy little program which contains a large number of conversions, from au's to parsecs and tablespoons to cups. You probably don't need to install it, but it comes in handy sometimes.

xlispstat -- (Version 3.52.9, 2,871K)

The xlispstat package contains XLISP-PLUS, an implementation of the Lisp programming language for the X Window System. XLISP-PLUS also includes extensions for performing advanced statistical computations.

Install the xlispstat package if you need a version of the Lisp programming language for X with statistics extensions.

D.2.7 File

This section contains packages that are associated with file manipulation.

bzip2 -- (Version 0.9.0c, 232K)

Bzip2 is a freely available, patent-free, high quality data compressor. Bzip2 compresses files to within 10 to 15 percent of the capabilities of the best techniques available. However, bzip2 has the added benefit of being approximately two times faster at compression and six times faster at decompression than those techniques. Bzip2 is not the fastest compression utility, but it does strike a balance between speed and compression capability.

Install bzip2 if you need a high quality compression utility.

file -- (Version 3.26, 206K)

[B]

The file command is used to identify a particular file according to the type of data contained by the file. File can identify many different file types, including ELF binaries, system libraries, RPM packages, and different graphics formats.

You should install the file package, since the file command is such a useful utility.

fileutils -- (Version 4.0, 1,283K)

[B]

The fileutils package includes a number of GNU versions of common and popular file management utilities. Fileutils includes the following tools: chgrp (changes a file's group ownership), chown (changes a file's ownership), chmod (changes a file's permissions), cp (copies files), dd (copies and converts files), df (shows a filesystem's disk usage), dir (gives a brief directory listing), dircolors (the setup program for the color version of the ls command), du (shows disk usage), install (copies files and sets permissions), ln (creates file links), ls (lists directory contents in color), mkdir (creates directories), mkfifo (creates FIFOs,which are named pipes), mknod (creates special files), mv (renames files), rm (removes/deletes files), rmdir (removes empty directories), sync (synchronizes memory and disk), touch (changes file timestamps), and vdir (provides long directory listings).

You should install the fileutils package, because it includes many file management utilities that you'll use frequently.

findutils -- (Version 4.1, 118K)

[B]

The findutils package contains programs which will help you locate files on your system. The find utility searches through a hierarchy of directories looking for files which match a certain set of criteria (such as a filename pattern). The locate utility searches a database (create by updatedb) to quickly find a file matching a given pattern. The xargs utility builds and executes command lines from standard input arguments (usually lists of file names generated by the find command).

You should install findutils because it includes tools that are very useful for finding things on your system.

git -- (Version 4.3.17, 715K)

[W]

GIT (GNU Interactive Tools) provides an extensible file system browser, an ASCII/hexadecimal file viewer, a process viewer/killer and other related utilities and shell scripts. GIT can be used to increase the speed and efficiency of copying and moving files and directories, invoking editors, compressing and uncompressing files, creating and expanding archives, compiling programs, sending mail and more. GIT uses standard ANSI color sequences, if they are available.

You should install the git package if you are interested in using its file management capabilities.

gzip -- (Version 1.2.4, 242K)

[B]

The gzip package contains the popular GNU gzip data compression program. Gzipped files have a .gz extension.

Gzip should be installed on your Red Hat Linux system, because it is a very commonly used data compression program.

slocate -- (Version 1.4, 19K)

[B]

slocate searches through a central database (updated nightly) for files which match a given glob pattern. This allows you to quickly find files anywhere on your system.

stat -- (Version 1.5, 6K)

[B]

The stat utility prints out filesystem level information about a specified file, including size, permissions, link count, inode, etc.

tree -- (Version 1.2, 19K)

The tree utility recursively displays the contents of directories in a tree-like format. Tree is basically a UNIX port of the tree DOS utility.

Install tree if you think it would be useful to view the contents of specified directories in a tree-like format.

D.2.8 Internet

This section contains packages that are associated with the Internet.

elm -- (Version 2.5.0, 616K)

[W] [S]

Elm is a popular terminal mode email user agent. Elm includes all standard mailhandling features, including MIME support via metamail.

Elm is still used by some people, but is no longer in development. If you've used Elm before and you're devoted to it, you should install the elm package. If you would like to use metamail's MIME support, you'll also need to install the metamail package.

exmh -- (Version 2.0.2, 1,814K)

[W] [S]

Exmh provides an X interface for MH/nmh mail, a feature-rich email handling system. Exmh supports almost all (but not all) of MH's features: viewing the messages in a folder, reading/deleting/refiling messages, and sorting arriving mail into different folders before the messages are read. Exmh highlights which folders have new mail, and indicates which messages have not been read (so you don't lose the sorted, unread mail).

If you like MH/nmh mail, you should install exmh, because it makes the MH/nmh mail system much more user friendly. You may also want to use exmh if you prefer a graphical user interface for your mail client. Note that you will also have to install the nmh package.

faces -- (Version 1.6.1, 141K)

Faces is a program for visually monitoring a list (typically a list of incoming mail messages, a list of jobs in a print queue or a list of system users). Faces operates in five different modes: monitoring for new mail, monitoring an entire mail file, monitoring a specified print queue, monitoring users on a machine and custom monitoring. Faces also includes a utility for including a face image (a compressed, scanned image) with mail messages. The image has to be compressed in a certain way, which can then be uncompressed and displayed on-the-fly in the mail program. This feature of faces is typically used with the exmh mail handling system.

Install faces if you'd like to use its list monitoring capability or its face image inclusion capability. If you would like to include face images in email, you'll also need to install the faces-xface package. If you would like to develop xface applications, you'll need to also install faces-devel.

faces-xface -- (Version 1.6.1, 20K)

Faces-xface includes the utilities that mail user agent programs need to handle X-Face mail headers. When an email program reads the X-face header line in an email message, it calls these utilities to display the face image included in the message.

You'll need to install faces-xface if you want your mail program to display Faces' X-face images.

fetchmail -- (Version 5.0.0, 552K)

[W] [S]

Fetchmail is a remote mail retrieval and forwarding utility intended for use over on-demand TCP/IP links, like SLIP or PPP connections. Fetchmail supports every remote-mail protocol currently in use on the Internet (POP2, POP3, RPOP, APOP,KPOP, all IMAPs, ESMTP ETRN) for retrieval. Then Fetchmail forwards the mail through SMTP, so you can read it through your normal mail client.

Install fetchmail if you need to retrieve mail over SLIP or PPP connections.

fetchmailconf -- (Version 5.0.0, 62K)

Fetchmailconf is a tcl/tk application for graphically configuring your .fetchmailrc preferences file. Fetchmail has many options which can be daunting to the new user. This utility takes some of the guesswork and hassle out of setting up fetchmail.

finger -- (Version 0.10, 32K)

[W] [S]

Finger is a utility which allows users to see information about system users (login name, home directory, name, how long they've been logged in to the system, etc.). The finger package includes a standard finger client and server. The server daemon (fingerd) runs from /etc/inetd.conf, which must be modified to disable finger requests.

You should install finger if your system is used by multiple users and you'd like finger information to be available.

ftp -- (Version 0.10, 89K)

[W] [S]

The ftp package provides the standard UNIX command-line FTP client. FTP is the file transfer protocol, which is a widely used Internet protocol for transferring files and for archiving files.

If your system is on a network, you should install ftp in order to do file transfers.

fwhois -- (Version 1.00, 8K)

[W] [S]

The fwhois program is a different style of the whois program. Both fwhois and whois query Internet whois databases to find information about system users. Fwhois is smaller and more compact than whois, and runs in a different manner.

Install fwhois if you or your system's users need a program for querying whois databases. You may also want to install whois, and then decide for yourself which program you prefer.

gftp -- (Version 1.13, 552K)

[W]

gFTP is a multithreaded FTP client for X Windows written using Gtk. It allows to have simultaneous downloads, resuming of interrupted file transfers, file transfer queues, a very nice connection manager and many more features.

ircii -- (Version 4.4, 997K)

IrcII is a popular Internet Relay Chat (IRC) client. IRC clients communicate with IRC servers, enabling users to "chat" via the Internet.

Install ircii if you want to participate in chat rooms.

kdenetwork -- (Version 1.1.1pre2, 7,466K)

Network applications for the K Desktop Environment.

Includes: karchie (ftp archive searcher); kbiff (mail delivery notification) kfinger ("finger" utility); kmail (mail client); knu (network utilities); korn (mailbox monitor tool); kppp (easy PPP connection configuration); krn (news reader); ktalkd (talkdaemon); ksirc (irc client).

kppload -- (Version 1.04, 88K)

Monitors the load on your PPP connection. Looks a lot like xload.

lynx -- (Version 2.8.1, 2,011K)

[W] [S]

Lynx is a text-based Web browser. Lynx does not display any images, but it does support frames, tables and most other HTML tags. Lynx's advantage over graphical browsers is its speed: Lynx starts and exits quickly and swiftly displays Web pages.

Install lynx if you would like to try this fast, non-graphical browser (you may come to appreciate its strengths).

mailx -- (Version 8.1.1, 89K)

[B]

The mailx package installs the /bin/mail program, which is used to send quick email messages (i.e., without opening up a full-featured mail user agent). Mail is often used in shell scripts.

You should install mailx because of its quick email sending ability, which is especially useful if you're planning on writing any shell scripts.

metamail -- (Version 2.7, 341K)

[W] [S]

Metamail is a system for handling multimedia mail, using the mailcap file. Metamail reads the mailcap file, which tells Metamail what helper program to call in order to handle a particular type of non-text mail. Note that metamail can also add multimedia support to certain non-mail programs.

Metamail should be installed if you need to add multimedia support to mail programs and some other programs, using the mailcap file.

mutt -- (Version 0.95.4us, 1,369K)

[W] [S]

Mutt is a text mode mail user agent. Mutt supports color, threading, arbitrary key remapping, and a lot of customization.

You should install mutt if you've used mutt in the past and you prefer it, or if you're new to mail programs and you haven't decided which one you're going to use.

nc -- (Version 1.10, 105K)

The nc package contains Netcat (the program is actually nc), a simple utility for reading and writing data across network connections, using the TCP or UDP protocols. Netcat is intended to be a reliable back-end tool which can be used directly or easily driven by other programs and scripts. Netcat is also a feature-rich network debugging and exploration tool, since it can create many different connections and has many built-in capabilities.

You may want to install the netcat package if you are administering a network and you'd like to use its debugging and network exploration capabilities.

ncftp -- (Version 3.0beta18, 725K)

[W] [S]

Ncftp is an improved FTP client. Ncftp's improvements include support for command line editing, command histories, recursive gets, automatic anonymous logins and more.

Install ncftp if you use FTP to transfer files and you'd like to try some of ncftp's additional features.

netscape-common -- (Version 4.51, 7,128K)

[W] [S]

This package contains the files that are shared between the Netscape Navigator Web browser and the Netscape Communicator suite of tools (the Navigator Web browser, an e-mail client, a news reader and Web page editor).

Install the netscape-common package if you're installing the netscape-navigator and/or the netscape-communicator program.

netscape-communicator -- (Version 4.51, 13,522K)

[W] [S]

Netscape Communicator is the industry-leading Web browser. It supports the latest HTML standards, Java, JavaScript and some style sheets. It also includes a full-featured Usenet news reader as well as a complete e-mail client.

Information on the Netscape Communicator license may be fund in the file /usr/doc/netscape-common-4.51/LICENSE.

netscape-navigator -- (Version 4.51, 7,242K)

Netscape Navigator is the industry-leading Web browser. It supports the latest HTML standards, Java, JavaScript and some style sheets.

Information on the Netscape Navigator license may be found in the file /usr/doc/netscape-common-4.51/LICENSE.

This will install the basic Netscape Navigator Web browser. If you want additional features, such as the Usenet news reader and HTML editor, you should install the netscape-communicator package.

nmh -- (Version 0.27, 4,646K)

[W] [S]

Nmh is an email system based on the MH email system and is intended to be a (mostly) compatible drop-in replacement for MH. Nmh isn't a single comprehensive program. Instead, it consists of a number of fairly simple single-purpose programs for sending, receiving, saving, retrieving and otherwise manipulating email messages. You can freely intersperse nmh commands with other shell commands or write custom scripts which utilize nmh commands. If you want to use nmh as a true email user agent, you'll want to also install exmh to provide a user interface for it--nmh only has a command line interface.

If you'd like to use nmh commands in shell scripts, or if you'd like to use nmh and exmh together as your email user agent, you should install nmh.

pine -- (Version 4.10, 3,427K)

[W] [S]

Pine is a very popular, easy to use, full-featured email user agent which includes a simple text editor called pico. Pine supports MIME extensions and can also be used to read news. Pine also supports IMAP, mail and MH style folders.

Pine should be installed because Pine is a very commonly used email user agent and it is currently in development.

rsh -- (Version 0.10, 116K)

[W] [S]

The rsh package contains a set of programs which allow users to run commmands on remote machines, login to other machines and copy files between machines (rsh, rlogin and rcp). All three of these commands use rhosts style authentication. This package contains the clients and servers needed for all of these services. It also contains a server for rexec, an alternate method of executing remote commands. All of these servers are run by inetd and configured using /etc/inetd.conf and PAM. The rexecd server is disabled by default, but the other servers are enabled.

The rsh package should be installed to enable remote access to other machines.

rsync -- (Version 2.3.1, 218K)

Rsync uses a quick and reliable algorithm to very quickly bring remote and host files into sync. Rsync is fast because it just sends the differences in the files over the network (instead of sending the complete files). Rsync is often used as a very powerful mirroring process or just as a more capable replacement for the rcp command. A technical report which describes the rsync algorithm is included in this package.

Install rsync if you need a powerful mirroring program.

slrn -- (Version 0.9.5.4, 413K)

[W] [S]

SLRN is a powerful, easy to use, threaded Internet news reader. SLRN is highly customizable and allows you to design complex filters to sort or kill news articles. SLRN works well over slow network connections, and includes a utility for reading news off-line.

Install slrn if you need a full-featured news reader, if you have a slow network connection, or if you'd like to save on-line time by reading your news off-line.

slrn-pull -- (Version 0.9.5.4, 64K)

This package provides slrnpull, which allows set up of a small news spool for offline news reading.

talk -- (Version 0.11, 36K)

[W] [S]

The ntalk package provides client and daemon programs for the Internet talk protocol, which allows you to chat with other users on different systems. Talk is a communication program which copies lines from one terminal to the terminal of another user.

Install ntalk if you'd like to use talk for chatting with users on different systems.

tcpdump -- (Version 3.4, 214K)

[W] [S]

Tcpdump is a command-line tool for monitoring network traffic. Tcpdump can capture and display the packet headers on a particular network interface or on all interfaces. Tcpdump can display all of the packet headers, or just the ones that match particular criteria.

Install tcpdump if you need a program to monitor network traffic.

telnet -- (Version 0.10, 137K)

[W] [S]

Telnet is a popular protocol for logging into remote systems over the Internet. The telnet package provides a command line telnet client as well as a telnet daemon, which will support remote logins into the host machine. The telnet daemon is enabled by default. You may disable the telnet daemon by editing /etc/inetd.conf.

Install the telnet package if you want to telnet to remote machines and/or support remote logins to your own machine.

tin -- (Version 1.4_990216, 1,193K)

[W] [S]

Tin is a basic, easy to use Internet news reader. Tin can read news locally or remotely via an NNTP (Network News Transport Protocol) server.

Install tin if you need a basic news reader.

traceroute -- (Version 1.4a5, 27K)

[W] [S]

The traceroute utility displays the route used by IP packets on their way to a specified network (or Internet) host. Traceroute displays the IP number and host name (if possible) of the machines along the route taken by the packets. Traceroute is used as a network debugging tool. If you're having network connectivity problems, traceroute will show you where the trouble is coming from along the route.

Install traceroute if you need a tool for diagnosing network connectivity problems.

trn -- (Version 3.6, 446K)

[W] [S]

Trn is a basic news reader that supports threading. This version is configured to read news from an NNTP news server.

Install trn if you need a basic news reader that shows you newsgroup postings in threaded format.

urlview -- (Version 0.7, 37K)

urlview extracts URLs from a given text file, and presents a menu of URLs to view using a user specified command.

w3c-libwww-apps -- (Version 5.2.8, 49K)

Web applications built using Libwww: Robot, Command line tool, line mode browser. The Robot can crawl web sites faster,and with lower load, than any other web walker that we know of, due to its extensive pipelining and use of HTTP/1.1.

The command line tool (w3c) is very useful for manipulation of Web sites that implement more than just HTTP GET (e.g. PUT,POST, etc.).

The line mode browser is a minimal line mode web browser; often useful to convert to ascii text. Currently unavailable until someone updates it to some new interfaces. (hint, hint...)

wget -- (Version 1.5.3, 335K)

GNU Wget is a file retrieval utility which can use either the HTTP or FTP protocols. Wget features include the ability to work in the background while you're logged out, recursive retrieval of directories, file name wildcard matching, remote file timestamp storage and comparison, use of Rest with FTP servers and Range with HTTP servers to retrieve files over slow or unstable connections, support for Proxy servers, and configurability.

Install wget if you need to retrieve large numbers of files with HTTP or FTP, or if you need a utility for mirroring web sites or FTP directories.

xchat -- (Version 0.9.4, 196K)

[W]

X-Chat is yet another IRC client for the X Window System, using the Gtk+ toolkit. It is pretty easy to use compared to the other Gtk+ IRC clients and the interface is quite nicely designed.

xmailbox -- (Version 2.5, 33K)

[W] [S]

The xmailbox program is an X Window System program which notifies you when mail arrives. Xmailbox is similar to the xbiff program, but it offers more features and notification options.

Install the xmailbox package if you'd like a graphical program for X which will notify you when new mail arrives.

xrn -- (Version 9.01, 253K)

[W] [S]

A simple Usenet News reader for the X Window System. Xrn allows you to point and click your way through reading, replying and posting news messages.

Install the xrn package if you need a simple news reader for X.

ytalk -- (Version 3.1, 68K)

The YTalk program is essentially a chat program for multiple users. YTalk works just like the UNIX talk program and even communicates with the same talk daemon(s), but YTalk allows for multiple connections (unlike UNIX talk). YTalk also supports redirection of program output to other users as well as an easy-to-use menu of commands.

Install the ytalk package if you need a chat program for multiple users.

D.2.9 Multimedia

This section contains packages that are associated with multimedia.

ImageMagick -- (Version 4.2.2, 3,025K)

[W] [S]

ImageMagick is a powerful image display, coversion and manipulation tool. It runs in an X session. With this tool, you can view, edit and display a variety of image formats.

This package installs the necessary files to run ImageMagick.

aktion -- (Version 0.3.3, 314K)

Movie player for the K Desktop Environment. Requires 'xanim' to function.

aumix -- (Version 1.18.2, 65K)

[W]

Aumix is a tty based, interactive method of controlling a sound card mixer. It lets you adjust the input levels from the CD,microphone, and on board synthesizers, as well as the output volume. Aumix can adjust audio mixers from the command line,from a script, or interactively at the console or terminal with a full-screen ncurses-based interface.

Install aumix if you need to control an audio mixer. If you install aumix, you will also need to install ncurses (since aumix's interface is based on ncurses) and gpm (for mouse support).

awesfx -- (Version 0.4.3a, 299K)

[W]

The awesfx package contains necessary utilities for the AWE32 sound driver.

If you must use an AWE32 sound driver, you should install this package.

cdp -- (Version 0.33, 39K)

[W]

The cdp program plays audio CDs in your computer's CD-ROM drive. Cdp includes a full-screen interface version and a command line version.

Install cdp to play audio CDs on your system.

desktop-backgrounds -- (Version 1.0.0, 10,198K)

[W]

If you use a desktop environment like GNOME you can use these images to spruce up your background.

ee -- (Version 0.3.8, 450K)

[W]

The ee package contains the Electric Eyes image viewer for the GNOME desktop environment. Electric Eyes is primary an image viewer, but it also allows many types of image manipulations. Electric Eyes can handle almost any type of image.

Install the ee package if you need an image viewer.

giftrans -- (Version 1.12.2, 22K)

Giftrans will convert an existing GIF87 file to GIF89 format. In other words, Giftrans can make one color in a .gif image (normally the background) transparent.

Install the giftrans package if you need a quick, small, one-purpose graphics program to make transparent .gifs out of existing .gifs.

gimp -- (Version 1.0.4, 6,508K)

[W]

The GIMP is an image manipulation program suitable for photo retouching, image composition and image authoring. Many people find it extremely useful in creating logos and other graphics for web pages. The GIMP has many of the tools and filters you would expect to find in similar commercial offerings, and some interesting extras as well.

The GIMP provides a large image manipulation toolbox, including channel operations and layers, effects, sub-pixel imaging and anti-aliasing, and conversions, all with multi-level undo.

This version of The GIMP includes a scripting facility, but many of the included scripts rely on fonts that we cannot distribute. The GIMP ftp site has a package of fonts that you can install by yourself, which includes all the fonts needed to run the included scripts. Some of the fonts have unusual licensing requirements; all the licenses are documented in the package. Get ftp://ftp.gimp.org/pub/gimp/fonts/freefonts-0.10.tar.gz and ftp://ftp.gimp.org/pub/gimp/fonts/sharefonts-0.10.tar.gz if you are so inclined. Alternatively, choose fonts which exist on your system before running the scripts.

gimp-data-extras -- (Version 1.0.0, 7,825K)

Patterns, gradients etc. for gimp. This package isn't required, but contains lots of goodies for gimp.

gnome-audio -- (Version 1.0.0, 828K)

[W] [S]

If you use the GNOME desktop environment, you may want to install this package of complementary sounds.

gnome-media -- (Version 1.0.1, 291K)

[W]

GNOME (GNU Network Object Model Environment) is a user-friendly set of applications and desktop tools to be used in conjunction with a window manager for the X Window System. GNOME is similar in purpose and scope to CDE and KDE, but GNOME is based completely on Open Source software.

GNOME's powerful environment is pleasing on the eye, easy to configure and use.

This package will install such media features as the GNOME CD player.

kdegraphics -- (Version 1.1.1pre2, 2,784K)

Graphics applications for the K Desktop Environment.

Includes: kdvi (displays TeX .dvi files); kfax (displays fax files); kfract (a fractal generator); kghostview (displays postscript files); kiconedit (icon editor); kpaint (a simple drawing program); ksnapshot (screen capture utility); kview (image viewer for GIF, JPEG, TIFF, etc.).

kdemultimedia -- (Version 1.1.1pre2, 2,366K)

Multimedia applications for the K Desktop Environment. Included: kmedia (media player); kmid (midi/karaoke player); kmidi (midi-to-wav player/converter); kmix (mixer); kscd (CD audio player)

libgr-progs -- (Version 2.0.13, 1,580K)

[W] [S]

The libgr-progs package contains a group of scripts for manipulating the graphics files in formats which are supported by the libgr library. For example, libgr-progs includes the rasttopnm script, which will convert a Sun rasterfile into a portable anymap. Libgr-progs contains many other scripts for converting from one graphics file format to another.

If you need to use these conversion scripts, you should install libgr-progs. You'll also need to install the libgr package.

libungif-progs -- (Version 4.1.0, 336K)

The libungif-progs package contains various programs for manipulating GIF format image files.

Install this package if you need to manipulate GIF format image files. You'll also need to install the libungif package.

mikmod -- (Version 3.1.5, 784K)

[W]

MikMod is one of the best and most well known MOD music file players for UNIX-like systems. This particular distribution is intended to compile fairly painlessly in a Linux environment. MikMod uses the OSS /dev/dsp driver including all recent kernels for output, and will also write .wav files. Supported file formats include MOD, STM, S3M, MTM, XM, ULT, and IT. The player uses ncurses for console output and supports transparent loading from gzip/pkzip/zoo archives and the loading/saving of playlists.

Install the mikmod package if you need a MOD music file player.

mpg123 -- (Version 0.59q, 206K)

[W]

Mpg123 is a fast, free and portable MPEG audio player for Unix. It supports MPEG 1.0/2.0 layers 1, 2 and 3 ("mp3" files).For full CD quality playback (44 kHz, 16 bit, stereo) a Pentium CPU is required. Mono and/or reduced quality playback (22kHz or 11 kHz) is possible on 486 CPUs.

For information on the MP3 License, please visit:
http://www.mpeg.org/

multimedia -- (Version 2.1, 344K)

[W]

The multimedia package contains several X Window System utilities for handling multimedia files: xplaycd, xmixer and xgetfile. Xplaycd is a CD player for playing audio CDs on your machine's CD-ROM drive. Xmixer controls the volume settings on your machine's sound card. Xgetfile is a versatile file browser, intended for use in shell scripts.

Install the multimedia package if you need an audio CD player, a sound card volume controller, or a file browser for use in shell scripts.

playmidi -- (Version 2.4, 133K)

[W]

Playmidi plays MIDI (Musicial Instrument Digital Interface) sound files through a sound card synthesizer. This package includes basic drum samples for use with simple FM synthesizers.

Install playmidi if you want to play MIDI files using your computer's sound card.

playmidi-X11 -- (Version 2.4, 39K)

[W]

Playmidi-X11 provides an X Window System interface for playing MIDI (Musical Instrument Digital Interface) sound files through a sound card synthesizer. This package includes basic drum samples for use with simple FM synthesizers.

Install playmidi-X11 if you want to use an X interface to play MIDI sound files using your computer's sound card.

rhsound -- (Version 1.8, 11K)

[W]

The rhsound package provides a script which can save and restore the mixer settings and volume level of the standard kernel sound drivers. These mixer settings are preserved through shutdowns and restarts.

Install the rhsound package if you need to preserve the kernel sound driver module's mixer settings through shutdowns and reboots.

sndconfig -- (Version 0.33, 306K)

[W]

Sndconfig is a text based tool which sets up the configuration files you'll need to use a sound card with a Red Hat Linux system. Sndconfig can be used to set the proper sound type for programs which use the /dev/dsp, /dev/audio and /dev/mixer devices. The sound settings are saved by the aumix and sysV runlevel scripts.

Install sndconfig if you need to configure your sound card.

sox -- (Version 12.15, 233K)

[W]

SoX (Sound eXchange) is a sound file format converter for Linux, UNIX and DOS PCs. The self-described 'Swiss Army knife of sound tools,' SoX can convert between many different digitized sound formats and perform simple sound manipulation functions, including sound effects.

Install the sox package if you'd like to convert sound file formats or manipulate some sounds.

transfig -- (Version 3.2.1, 292K)

The transfig utility creates a makefile which translates FIG (created by xfig) or PIC figures into a specified LaTeX graphics language (for example, PostScript(TM)). Transfig is used to create TeX documents which are portable (i.e., they can print in a wide variety of environments).

x11amp -- (Version 0.9_alpha3, 1,342K)

[W]

X11amp is a X Windows based mp3 player with a nice interface borrowed from WinAMP.

For information on the MP3 License, please visit: http://www.mpeg.org/

xanim -- (Version 27070, 847K)

[W]

The XAnim program is an animation/video/audio viewer for the X Window System. XAnim can display a large variety of animation, audio and video formats.

Install the xanim package if you need a viewer for an animation, video or audio file.

xfig -- (Version 3.2.2, 2,545K)

Xfig is an X Window System tool for creating basic vector graphics, including bezier curves, lines, rulers and more. The resulting graphics can be saved, printed on PostScript printers or converted to a variety of other formats (e.g., X11 bitmaps,Encapsulated PostScript, LaTeX).

You should install xfig if you need a simple program to create vector graphics.

xpaint -- (Version 2.4.9, 448K)

[W]

XPaint is an X Window System color image editing program which supports most standard paint program options. XPaint also supports advanced features like image processing algorithms. XPaint allows you to edit multiple images simultaneously and supports a variety of image formats, including PPM, XBM, TIFF, JPEG, etc.

Install the xpaint package if you need a paint program for X.

zgv -- (Version 3.0, 175K)

Zgv is an image viewer which can display graphics in GIF, JPEG/JFIF, PNG, PBM/PGM/PPM, BMP, TGA, PCX and MRF formats on VGA and SVGA displays. Zgv can also display thumbnails of the images. Zgv is based on svgalib, which you will need to have on your system in order to use zgv.

Install zgv if you need an image viewer.

D.2.10 Productivity

This section contains packages that are associated with increasing productivity.

gnome-pim -- (Version 1.0.7, 666K)

[W]

The GNOME Personal Information Manager consists of applications to make keeping up with your busy life easier.

Currently these apps are present:

- gnomecal : personal calendar and todo list - gnomecard: contact list of friends and business associates

gnumeric -- (Version 0.23, 5,036K)

[W]

GNOME is the GNU Network Object Model Environment. This powerful environment is both easy to use and easy to configure.

This package will install Gnumeric the GNOME spreadsheet program. This program is intended to be a replacement for a commercial spreadsheet, so quite a bit of work has gone into the program.

Install this package if you want to use the GNOME spreadsheet Gnumeric.

ical -- (Version 2.2, 790K)

[W] [S]

Ical is an X Window System based calendar program. Ical will easily create/edit/delete entries, create repeating entries, remind you about upcoming appointments, print and list item occurrences, and allow shared calendars between different users.

Install ical if you need a calendar program to track your schedule. You'll need to have the X Window System installed in order to use ical.

korganizer -- (Version 1.1.1pre2, 1,477K)

KOrganizer is a complete calendar and scheduling program for KDE. It allows interchange with other calendar applications through the industry standard vCalendar file format.

D.2.11 Publishing

This section contains packages that are associated with publishing.

enscript -- (Version 1.6.1, 1,515K)

Enscript is a print filter. It can take ASCII input and format it into PostScript output. At the same time, it can also do nice transformations like putting two ASCII pages on one physical page (side by side) or changing fonts.

ghostscript -- (Version 5.10, 3,330K)

[W] [S]

Ghostscript is a set of software that provides a PostScript(TM) interpreter, a set of C procedures (the Ghostscript library, which implements the graphics capabilities in the PostScript language) and an interpreter for Portable Document Format (PDF)files. Ghostscript translates PostScript code into many common, bitmapped formats, like those understood by your printer or screen. Ghostscript is normally used to display PostScript files and to print PostScript files to non-PostScript printers.

If you need to display PostScript files or print them to non-PostScript printers, you should install ghostscript. If you install ghostscript, you also need to install the ghostscript-fonts package.

ghostscript-fonts -- (Version 5.10, 1,490K)

[W] [S]

These fonts can be used by the GhostScript interpreter during text rendering. They are in addition to the shared fonts between GhostScript and X11.

groff -- (Version 1.11a, 2,842K)

[B]

Groff is a document formatting system. Groff takes standard text and formatting commands as input and produces formatted output. The created documents can be shown on a display or printed on a printer. Groff's formatting commands allow you to specify font type and size, bold type, italic type, the number and size of columns on a page, and more.

You should install groff if you want to use it as a document formatting system. Groff can also be used to format man pages. If you are going to use groff with the X Window System, you'll also need to install the groff-gxditview package.

groff-gxditview -- (Version 1.11a, 73K)

Gxditview displays the groff text processor's output on an X Window System display.

If you are going to use groff as a text processor, you should install gxditview so that you preview your processed text files in X.You'll also need to install the groff package and the X Window System.

gv -- (Version 3.5.8, 424K)

[W] [S]

Gv provides a user interface for the ghostscript PostScript(TM) interpreter. Derived from the ghostview program, gv can display PostScript and PDF documents using the X Window System.

Install the gv package if you'd like to view PostScript and PDF documents on your system. You'll also need to have the ghostscript package installed, as well as the X Window System.

lout -- (Version 3.08, 3,452K)

Lout is a high-level language for document formatting. Lout reads a high-level description of a document (similar in style to LaTeX) and can produce a PostScript(TM) file for printing or produce plain text. Lout supports the typesetting of documents which contain floating figures, table, diagrams, rotated and scaled text or graphics, footnotes, running headers, footers, an index, a table of contents and bibliography, cross-references, mathematical equations and statistical graphs. Lout can be extended with definitions that should be easier to write than other languages, since Lout is a high-level language. Lout supports (with hyphenation) a variety of languages: Czech, Danish, Dutch, English, Finnish, French, German, Norwegian, Russian,Slovenian, Spanish and Swedish.

Install the lout package if you'd like to try the Lout document formatting system. Unless you're already a Lout expert, you'll probably want to also install the lout-doc package, which contains the documentation for Lout.

lout-doc -- (Version 3.08, 2,069K)

The lout-doc package includes all of the documentation for the Lout document formatting language. The documentation includes manuals for regular users and for experts, written in Lout and available as PostScript(TM) files. The documentation provides good examples for how to write large documents with Lout.

If you're installing the lout package, you should install the lout-doc package.

mpage -- (Version 2.4, 90K)

[W] [S]

The mpage utility takes plain text files or PostScript(TM) documents as input, reduces the size of the text, and prints the files on a PostScript printer with several pages on each sheet of paper. Mpage is very useful for viewing large printouts without using up tons of paper. Mpage supports many different layout options for the printed pages.

Mpage should be installed if you need a useful utility for viewing long text documents without wasting paper.

printtool -- (Version 3.40, 113K)

[W] [S]

The printtool is a printer configuration tool with a graphical user interface. Printtool can manage both local and remote printers, including Windows (SMB) and NetWare (NCP) printers.

Printtool should be installed so that you can manage local and remote printers.

rhs-printfilters -- (Version 1.51, 92K)

[W] [S]

The rhs-printfilters package contains a set of print filters which are primarily meant to be used with the Red Hat printtool. These print filters provide an easy way for users to handle printing numerous file formats.

sgml-tools -- (Version 1.0.9, 1,877K)

SGMLtools is a text formatting package based on SGML (Standard Generalized Markup Language). SGMLtools allows you to produce LaTeX, HTML, GNU info, LyX, RTF, plain text (via groff), and other format outputs from a single source.SGMLtools is intended for writing technical software documentation.

Install SGMLTools if you need a text formatting program that can produce a variety of different formats from a single source file. You should probably also install and try SGMLTtools if you're going to write technical software documentation.

tetex -- (Version 0.9, 40,085K)

[W]

TeTeX is an implementation of TeX for Linux or UNIX systems. TeX takes a text file and a set of formatting commands as input and creates a typesetter independent .dvi (DeVice Independent) file as output. Usually, TeX is used in conjunction with a higher level formatting package like LaTeX or PlainTeX, since TeX by itself is not very user-friendly.

Install tetex if you want to use the TeX text formatting system. If you are installing tetex, you will also need to install tetex-afm (a PostScript(TM) font converter for TeX), tetex-dvilj (for converting .dvi files to HP PCL format for printing on HP and HP compatible printers), tetex-dvips (for converting .dvi files to PostScript format for printing on PostScript printers), tetex-latex (a higher level formatting package which provides an easier-to-use interface for TeX) and tetex-xdvi (for previewing .dvi files in X). Unless you're an expert at using TeX, you'll also want to install the tetex-doc package, which includes the documentation for TeX.

tetex-afm -- (Version 0.9, 2,029K)

[W]

Tetex-afm provides afm2tfm, a converter for PostScript font metric files. PostScript fonts are accompanied by .afm font metric files which describe the characteristics of each font. To use PostScript fonts with TeX, TeX needs .tfm files that contain similar information. Afm2tfm will convert .afm files to .tfm files.

If you are installing tetex in order to use the TeX text formatting system, you will need to install tetex-afm. You will also need to install tetex-dvilj (for converting .dvi files to HP PCL format for printing on HP and HP compatible printers), tetex-dvips (for converting .dvi files to PostScript format for printing on PostScript printers), tetex-latex (a higher level formatting package which provides an easier-to-use interface for TeX) and tetex-xdvi (for previewing .dvi files in X). Unless you're an expert at using TeX, you'll probably also want to install the tetex-doc package, which includes documentation for TeX.

tetex-doc -- (Version 0.9, 34,933K)

The tetex-doc package contains documentation for the TeX text formatting system.

If you want to use TeX and you're not an expert at it, you should install the tetex-doc package. You'll also need to install the tetex package, tetex-afm (a PostScript font converter for TeX), tetex-dvilj (for converting .dvi files to HP PCL format for printing on HP and HP compatible printers), tetex-dvips (for converting .dvi files to PostScript format for printing on PostScript printers), tetex-latex (a higher level formatting package which provides an easier-to-use interface for TeX) and tetex-xdvi (for previewing .dvi files).

tetex-dvilj -- (Version 0.9, 336K)

[W]

Dvilj and dvilj's siblings (included in this package) will convert TeX text formatting system output .dvi files to HP PCL (HP Printer Control Language) commands. Using dvilj, you can print TeX files to HP LaserJet+ and fully compatible printers. With dvilj2p, you can print to HP LaserJet IIP and fully compatible printers. And with dvilj4, you can print to HP LaserJet4 and fully compatible printers.

If you are installing tetex, so that you can use the TeX text formatting system, you will also need to install tetex-dvilj. In addition,you will need to install tetex-afm (for converting PostScript font description files), tetex-dvips (for converting .dvi files to PostScript format for printing on PostScript printers), tetex-latex (a higher level formatting package which provides an easier-to-use interface for TeX) and tetex-xdvi (for previewing .dvi files in X). If you're installing TeX and you're not a TeX expert, you'll also want to install the tetex-doc package, which contains documentation for TeX.

tetex-dvips -- (Version 0.9, 839K)

[W]

Dvips converts .dvi files produced by the TeX text formatting system (or by another processor like GFtoDVI) to PostScript(TM) format. Normally the PostScript file is sent directly to your printer.

If you are installing tetex, so that you can use the TeX text formatting system, you will also need to install tetex-dvips. In addition, you will need to install tetex-afm (for converting PostScript font description files), tetex-dvilj (for converting .dvi files to HP PCL format for printing on HP and HP compatible printers), tetex-latex (a higher level formatting package which provides an easier-to-use interface for TeX) and tetex-xdvi (for previewing .dvi files in X). If you're installing TeX and you're not an expert at it, you'll also want to install the tetex-doc package, which contains documentation for the TeX system.

tetex-latex -- (Version 0.9, 8,332K)

[W]

LaTeX is a front end for the TeX text formatting system. Easier to use than TeX, LaTeX is essentially a set of TeX macros which provide convenient, predefined document formats for users.

If you are installing tetex, so that you can use the TeX text formatting system, you will also need to install tetex-latex. In addition, you will need to install tetex-afm (for converting PostScript font description files), tetex-dvilj (for converting .dvi files to HP PCL format for printing on HP and HP compatible printers), tetex-dvips (for converting .dvi files to PostScript format for printing on PostScript printers) and tetex-xdvi (for previewing .dvi files in X). If you're not an expert at TeX, you'll probably also want to install the tetex-doc package, which contains documentation for TeX.

tetex-xdvi -- (Version 0.9, 964K)

[W] [S]

Xdvi allows you to preview the TeX text formatting system's output .dvi files on an X Window System.

If you are installing tetex, so that you can use the TeX text formatting system, you will also need to install tetex-xdvi. In addition, you will need to install tetex-afm (a PostScript font converter for TeX), tetex-dvilj (for converting .dvi files to HP PCL format for printing on HP and HP compatible printers), tetex-dvips (for converting .dvi files to PostScript format for printing on PostScript printers), and tetex-latex (a higher level formatting package which provides an easier-to-use interface for TeX). If you're not a TeX expert, you'll probably also want to install the tetex-doc package, which contains documentation for the TeX text formatting system.

texinfo -- (Version 3.12f, 799K)

[W] [S]

Texinfo is a documentation system that can produce both online information and printed output from a single source file. Normally, you'd have to write two separate documents: one for online help or other online information and the other for a typeset manual or other printed work. Using Texinfo, you only need to write one source document. Then when the work needs revision, you only have to revise one source document. The GNU Project uses the Texinfo file format for most of its documentation.

Install texinfo if you want a documentation system for producing both online and print documentation from the same source file and/or if you are going to write documentation for the GNU Project.

xpdf -- (Version 0.80, 1,351K)

Xpdf is an X Window System based viewer for Portable Document Format (PDF) files. PDF files are sometimes called Acrobat files, after Adobe Acrobat (Adobe's PDF viewer). Xpdf is a small and efficient program which uses standard X fonts.

Install the xpdf package if you need a viewer for PDF files.

D.2.12 System

This section contains packages that are associated with system-level operations.

SVGATextMode -- (Version 1.8, 852K)

SVGATextMode is a utility for reprogramming (S)VGA hardware, which can improve the appearance of text consoles. You should install SVGATextMode if you want to alter the appearance of your text consoles. The utility uses a configuration file (Xconfig or XF86Config) to set up textmodes with higher resolution, larger fonts, higher display refresh rates, etc.

Although SVGATextMode can be used to program any text mode size, your results will depend on your VGA card.

arpwatch -- (Version 2.1a4, 104K)

The arpwatch package contains arpwatch and arpsnmp. Arpwatch and arpsnmp are both network monitoring tools. Both utilities monitor Ethernet or FDDI network traffic and build databases of Ethernet/IP address pairs, and can report certain changes via email.

Install the arpwatch package if you need networking monitoring devices which will automatically keep traffic of the IP addresses on your network.

bind-utils -- (Version 8.2, 1,320K)

[W] [S]

Bind-utils contains a collection of utilities for querying DNS (Domain Name Service) name servers to find out information about Internet hosts. These tools will provide you with the IP addresses for given host names, as well as other information about registered domains and network addresses.

You should install bind-utils if you need to get information from DNS name servers.

comanche -- (Version 990405, 375K)

Comanche (COnfiguration MANager for apaCHE) is a front-end for the Apache Web server, the most popular Web server used on the Internet. Comanche aims to to make it easier to manage and configure Apache.

Install the commanche package if you need a configuration manager for the Apache Web server. You'll also need to install the apache package.

console-tools -- (Version 19990302, 1,460K)

[B]

This package contains utilities to load console fonts and keyboard maps. It also includes a number of different fonts and keyboard maps.

dialog -- (Version 0.6, 88K)

[W]

Dialog is a utility that allows you to show dialog boxes (containing questions or messages) in TTY (text mode) interfaces. Dialog is called from within a shell script. The following dialog boxes are implemented: yes/no, menu, input, message, text, info,checklist, radiolist, and gauge.

Install dialog if you would like to create TTY dialog boxes.

ext2ed -- (Version 0.1, 288K)

Ext2ed is a program which provides a text and window interface for examining and editing an ext2 filesystem. Ext2ed is supposed to be easier to use than debugfs, but debugfs is more powerful. Note that this program should only be used by someone who is very experienced at hacking filesystems.

Install ext2ed if you want to examine and/or edit your ext2 filesystem, and you know what you're doing.

fbset -- (Version 2.0.19990118, 34K)

fbset is a utility for querying and changing video modes of fbcon consoles.

gnome-linuxconf -- (Version 0.22, 320K)

[W] [S]

GNOME (GNU Network Object Model Environment) is a user-friendly set of applications and desktop tools to be used in conjunction with a window manager for the X Window System. The gnome-linuxconf package includes GNOME's front end for the linuxconf system configuration utility.

gnome-utils -- (Version 1.0.1, 767K)

[W]

GNOME is the GNU Network Object Model Environment. This powerful environment is both easy to use and easy to configure.

This package will install some GNOME utilities, such as the calendar and calculator.

gnorpm -- (Version 0.8, 394K)

[W] [S]

Gnome RPM is a graphical front end to RPM, similar to Glint, but written with the GTK widget set and the GNOME libraries.It is currently under development, so there are some features missing, but you can currently query packages in the filesystem and database, install upgrade, uninstall and verify packages.

gtop -- (Version 1.0.1, 267K)

[W]

GNOME is the GNU Network Object Model Environment. This powerful environment is both easy to use and easy to configure.

This package will install the GNOME system monitor gtop, which shows memory graphs and processes.

hdparm -- (Version 3.3, 37K)

[B]

Hdparm is a useful system utility for setting (E)IDE hard drive parameters. For example, hdparm can be used to tweak hard drive performance and to spin down hard drives for power conservation.

ipxutils -- (Version 2.2.0.12, 53K)

[S]

The ipxutils package includes utilities (ipx_configure, ipx_internal_net, ipx_interface, ipx_route) necessary for configuring and debugging IPX interfaces and networks under Linux. IPX is the low-level protocol used by Novell's NetWare file server system to transfer data.

Install ipxutils if you need to configure IPX networking on your network.

isicom -- (Version 1.0, 38K)

Binary images and loader for Multitech IntelligentSerialInternal (ISI) data files.

kdeadmin -- (Version 1.1.1pre2, 1,465K)

System Administration tools for the K Desktop Environment.

Included with this package are: kdat (tape backup); ksysv (sysV init editor); kuser (user administration tool)

kdeutils -- (Version 1.1.1pre2, 3,375K)

Utilities for the K Desktop Environment. Includes: ark (tar/gzip archive manager); kab (address book); karm (personal time tracker); kcalc (scientific calculator); kedit (simple text editor); kfloppy (floppy formatting tool); khexedit (hex editor); kjots (note taker); klipper (clipboard tool); kljettool(HP printer configuration tool); klpq (print queue manager) knotes (post-it notes for the desktop); kpm (process manager similar to 'top', but more advanced);kwrite (improved text editor).

kernelcfg -- (Version 0.5, 58K)

[W] [S]

The kernelcfg package contains an X Window System based graphical user interface tool for configuring the kernel daemon(kerneld). Kerneld automatically loads some hardware and software support into memory as needed and unloads the support when it is no longer being used. The kernel configurator tool can be used to tell kerneld what hardware support to load when it is presented with a generic hardware request.

Kernelcfg should be installed because it is a useful utility for managing the kernel daemon.

knfsd-clients -- (Version 1.2.2, 10K)

The nfs-server-clients package contains the showmount program. Showmount queries the mount daemon on a remote host for information about the NFS (Network File System) server on the remote host. For example, showmount can display the clients which are mounted on that host. This package is not needed to mount NFS volumes.

Install nfs-server-clients if you'd like to use the showmount tool for querying NFS servers.

linuxconf -- (Version 1.14r4, 11,306K)

[B]

Linuxconf is an extremely capable system configuration tool. Linuxconf provides four different interfaces for you to choose from: command line, character-cell (like the installation program), an X Window System based GUI and a web-based interface. Linuxconf can manage a large proportion of your system's operations, including networking, user accounts, filesystems, boot parameters, and more.

Linuxconf will simplify the process of configuring your system. Unless you are completely happy with configuring your system manually, you should install the linuxconf package and use linuxconf instead.

macutils -- (Version 2.0b3, 218K)

The macutils package includes a set of utilities for manipulating files that are commonly used by Macintosh machines. Macutils includes utilities like binhex, hexbin, macunpack, etc.

Install macutils if you need to manipulate files that are commonly used by Macintosh machines.

mkdosfs-ygg -- (Version 0.3b, 17K)

[W]

The mkdosfs program is used to create an MS-DOS FAT file system on a Linux system device, usually a disk partition.

The mkdosfs package should be installed if your machine needs to support MS-DOS style file systems.

mkisofs -- (Version 1.12b5, 153K)

The mkisofs program is used as a pre-mastering program; i.e., it generates the ISO9660 filesystem. Mkisofs takes a snapshot of a given directory tree and generates a binary image of the tree which will correspond to an ISO9660 filesystem when written to a block device. Mkisofs is used for writing CD-ROMs, and includes support for creating bootable El Torito CD-ROMs.

Install the mkisofs package if you need a program for writing CD-ROMs.

mkxauth -- (Version 1.7, 15K)

[W] [S]

The mkxauth utility helps create and maintain X authentication databases (.Xauthority files). Mkxauth is used to create an .Xauthority file or to merge keys from another local or remote .Xauthority file. .Xauthority files are used by the xauth user-oriented access control program, which grants or denies access to X servers based on the contents of the .Xauthority file.

The mkxauth package should be installed if you're going to use user-oriented access control to provide security for your X Window System (a good idea).

modemtool -- (Version 1.21, 15K)

[W] [S]

The modemtool is a simple graphical configuration tool for selecting the serial port to which your modem is connected.

Install modemtool if you use a modem.

mt-st -- (Version 0.5b, 67K)

[B]

The mt-st package contains the mt and st tape drive management programs. Mt (for magnetic tape drives) and st (for SCSI tape devices) can control rewinding, ejecting, skipping files and blocks and more.

This package can help you manage tape drives.

mtools -- (Version 3.9.1, 486K)

[W]

Mtools is a collection of utilities for accessing MS-DOS files. Mtools allow you to read, write and move around MS-DOS filesystem files (normally on MS-DOS floppy disks). Mtools supports Windows 95 style long file names, OS/2 Xdf disks, and 2m disks.

Mtools should be installed if you need to use MS-DOS disks.

ncpfs -- (Version 2.2.0.12, 553K)

[S]

Ncpfs is a filesystem which understands the Novell NetWare(TM) NCP protocol. Functionally, NCP is used for NetWare the way NFS is used in the TCP/IP world. For a Linux system to mount a NetWare filesystem, it needs a special mount program.The ncpfs package contains such a mount program plus other tools for configuring and using the ncpfs filesystem.

Install the ncpfs package if you need to use the ncpfs filesystem to use Novell NetWare files or services.

netcfg -- (Version 2.20, 165K)

[W] [S]

A Red Hat Linux tool which provides a graphical user interface for setting up and configuring networking for your machine.

open -- (Version 1.4, 13K)

The open command starts a specified command with the first available virtual console, or on a virtual console that you specify.

Install the open package if you regularly use virtual consoles to run programs.

pciutils -- (Version 1.99.5, 121K)

This package contains various utilities for inspecting and setting devices connected to the PCI bus.

It requires kernel version 2.1.82 or newer (supporting the /proc/bus/pci interface).

procinfo -- (Version 16, 54K)

The procinfo command gets system data from the /proc directory (the kernel filesystem), formats it and displays it on standard output. You can use procinfo to acquire information about your system from the kernel as it is running.

Install procinfo if you'd like to use it to gather and display system data.

procps -- (Version 2.0.2, 298K)

[B]

The procps package contains a set of system utilities which provide system information. Procps includes ps, free, skill, snice,tload, top, uptime, vmstat, w, and watch. The ps command displays a snapshot of running processes. The top command provides a repetitive update of the statuses of running processes. The free command displays the amounts of free and used memory on your system. The skill command sends a terminate command (or another specified signal) to a specified set of processes. The snice command is used to change the scheduling priority of specified processes. The tload command prints a graph of the current system load average to a specified tty. The uptime command displays the current time, how long the system has been running, how many users are logged on and system load averages for the past one, five and fifteen minutes. The w command displays a list of the users who are currently logged on and what they're running. The watch program watches a running program.

The vmstat command displays virtual memory statistics about processes, memory, paging, block I/O, traps and CPU activity.

procps-X11 -- (Version 2.0.2, 0K)

The procps-X11 package contains the XConsole shell script, a backwards compatibility wrapper for the xconsole program.

psacct -- (Version 6.3, 87K)

The psacct package contains several utilities for monitoring process activities, including ac, lastcomm, accton and sa. The ac command displays statistics about how long users have been logged on. The lastcomm command displays information about previous executed commands. The accton command turns process accounting on or off. The sa command summarizes information about previously executed commmands.

Install the psacct package if you'd like to use its utilities for monitoring process activities on your system.

psmisc -- (Version 18, 46K)

[B]

The psmisc package contains utilities for managing processes on your system: pstree, killall and fuser. The pstree command displays a tree structure of all of the running processes on your system. The killall command sends a specified signal(SIGTERM if nothing is specified) to processes identified by name. The fuser command identifies the PIDs of processes that are using specified files or filesystems.

rdate -- (Version 0.960923, 5K)

[W] [S]

The rdate utility retrieves the date and time from another machine on your network, using the protocol described in RFC 868. If you run rdate as root, it will set your machine's local time to the time of the machine that you queried. Note that rdate isn't scrupulously accurate. If you are worried about milliseconds, get the xntpd program instead.

rdist -- (Version 6.1.5, 141K)

[W] [S]

The rdist program maintains identical copies of files on multiple hosts. If possible, rdist will preserve the owner, group, mode and mtime of files and it can update programs that are executing.

rhmask -- (Version 1.0, 8K)

The rhmask utility creates mask files from original and updated files. The mask files, which may be the latest new versions of software, can then be freely distributed on public Internet servers. The mask files are only useful for people who who already have a copy of the original package. The rhmask utility uses a simple XOR scheme for creating the file mask and uses file size and md5 sums to ensure the integrity of the result.

Install the rhmask package if you need a utility for creating file masks.

rhs-hwdiag -- (Version 0.36, 75K)

[B]

The rhs-hwdiag package contains the Red Hat Hardware Discovery Tools. These tools probe the serial and parallel ports on your system, and are useful for finding and reporting hardware errors to Red Hat support if you're having problems. These tools could cause adverse side-effects in some situations, so you should use them carefully.

screen -- (Version 3.7.6, 360K)

The screen utility allows you to have multiple logins on just one terminal. Screen is useful for users who telnet into a machine or are connected via a dumb terminal, but want to use more than just one login.

Install the screen package if you need a screen manager that can support multiple logins on one terminal.

setconsole -- (Version 1.0, 3K)

[B]

Setconsole is a basic system utility for setting up the /etc/inittab, /dev/systty and /dev/console files to handle a new console. The console can be either the local terminal (i.e., directly attached to the system via a video card) or a serial console.

setserial -- (Version 2.15, 37K)

[B]

Setserial is a basic system utility for displaying or setting serial port information. Setserial can reveal and allow you to alter the I/O port and IRQ that a particular serial device is using, and more.

You should install setserial because you may find it useful for detecting and/or altering device information.

setuptool -- (Version 1.2, 7K)

[B]

Setuptool is a user-friendly text mode menu utility which allows you to access all of the text mode configuration programs included in the Red Hat Linx operating system.

You should install the setuptool package because you will find yourself using its features for essential system administration.

statserial -- (Version 1.1, 289K)

[W] [S]

The statserial utility displays a table of the signals on a standard 9-pin or 25-pin serial port and indicates the status of the handshaking lines. Statserial is useful for debugging serial port and/or modem problems.

Install the statserial package if you need a tool to help debug serial port or modem problems.

swatch -- (Version 2.2, 129K)

The Swatch utility monitors system log files, filters out unwanted data and takes specified actions (i.e., sending email, executing a script, etc.) based upon what it finds in the log files.

Install the swatch package if you need a program that will monitor log files and alert you in certain situations.

symlinks -- (Version 1.2, 212K)

The symlinks utility performs maintenance on symbolic links. Symlinks checks for symlink problems, including dangling symlinks which point to nonexistent files. Symlinks can also automatically convert absolute symlinks to relative symlinks.

Install the symlinks package if you need a program for maintaining symlinks on your system.

time -- (Version 1.7, 18K)

[B]

The GNU time utility runs another program, collects information about the resources used by that program while it is running and displays the results.

Time can help developers optimize their programs.

timetool -- (Version 2.5, 22K)

[W] [S]

The timetool utility provides a graphical user interface for setting the current date and time on your system.

tksysv -- (Version 1.0, 35K)

[W] [S]

Tksysv is an X Window System based graphical interface for editing the services provided by different runlevels. Tksysv is used to set which services are stopped and which services are started in the different runlevels on your system.

Install the tksysv package if you'd like to use a graphical tool for editing runlevel services.

tunelp -- (Version 1.3, 9K)

The tunelp utility sets various parameters for lp devices (/dev/lp0, /dev/lp1, /dev/lp2). Tunelp can set parameters like the lp device's interrupt usage, polling rate, etc.

Install the tunelp package if you need a utility for setting lp device parameters.

ucd-snmp-utils -- (Version 3.6.1, 252K)

[W] [S]

The ucd-snmp package contains various utilities for use with the UCD-SNMP network management project.

Install this package if you need utilities for managing your network using the SNMP protocol. You'll also need to install the ucd-snmp package.

usermode -- (Version 1.9, 98K)

[W] [S]

The usermode package contains several graphical tools for users: userinfo, usermount and userpasswd. Userinfo allows users to change their finger information. Usermount lets users mount, unmount, and format filesystems. Userpasswd allows users to change their passwords.

Install the usermode package if you would like to provide users with graphical tools for certain account management tasks.

usernet -- (Version 1.0.9, 24K)

[W] [S]

The usernet utility provides a graphical interface for manipulating network interfaces (bringing them up or down and viewing their status). Users can only manipulate interfaces that are user-controllable. The superuser can control all interfaces.

Install the usernet package if you'd like to provide a graphical utility for manipulating network interfaces.

vlock -- (Version 1.3, 9K)

The vlock program locks one or more sessions on the console. Vlock can lock the current terminal (local or remote) or the entire virtual console system, which completely disables all console access. The vlock program unlocks when either the password of the user who started vlock or the root password is typed.

Install vlock if you need to disable access to one console or to all virtual consoles.

which -- (Version 1.0, 7K)

[B]

The which command shows the full pathname of a specified program, if the specified program is in your PATH.

xcpustate -- (Version 2.5, 33K)

The xcpustate utility is an X Window System based monitor which shows the amount of time that the CPU is spending in different states. On a Linux system, xcpustate displays a bar that indicates the amounts of idle, user, nice and system time (from left to right) used by the CPU.

Install the xcpustate package if you'd like to use a horizontal bar style CPU state monitor.

xosview -- (Version 1.7.1, 109K)

The xosview utility displays a set of bar graphs which show the current system state, including memory usage, CPU usage,system load, etc. Xosview runs under the X Window System.

Install the xosview package if you need a graphical tool for monitoring your system's performance.

xsysinfo -- (Version 1.6, 22K)

Xsysinfo is a graphic kernel monitoring tool for the X Window System. Xsysinfo displays vertical bars for certain kernel parameters: CPU load average, CPU load, memory and swap sizes.

Install the xsysinfo package if you'd like to use a graphical kernel monitoring tool.

xtoolwait -- (Version 1.2, 10K)

Xtoolwait is a utility which starts an X client in the background, waits for a window to be mapped on the root window, and then exits. Xtoolwait can improve performance for users who start a bunch of X clients automatically (for example, xterm,xlock, xconsole, whatever) when the X session starts.

Install xtoolwait if you'd like to try to speed up the startup time for X sessions.

D.2.13 Text

This section contains packages that are associated with the manipulation of text.

diffutils -- (Version 2.7, 161K)

[B]

Diffutils includes four utilities: diff, cmp, diff3 and sdiff. Diff compares two files and shows the differences, line by line. The cmp command shows the offset and line numbers where two files differ, or cmp can show the characters that differ between the two files. The diff3 command shows the differences between three files. Diff3 can be used when two people have made independent changes to a common original; diff3 can produce a merged file that contains both persons' changes and warnings about conflicts. The sdiff command can be used to merge two files interactively.

Install diffutils if you need to compare text files.

ed -- (Version 0.2, 102K)

[B]

Ed is a line-oriented text editor, used to create, display, and modify text files (both interactively and via shell scripts). For most purposes, ed has been replaced in normal usage by full-screen editors (emacs and vi, for example).

Ed was the original UNIX editor, and may be used by some programs. In general, however, you probably don't need to install it and you probably won't use it much.

gawk -- (Version 3.0.3, 2,280K)

[B]

The gawk packages contains the GNU version of awk, a text processing utility. Awk interprets a special-purpose programming language to do quick and easy text pattern matching and reformatting jobs. Gawk should be upwardly compatible with the Bell Labs research version of awk and is almost completely compliant with the 1993 POSIX 1003.2 standard for awk.

Install the gawk package if you need a text processing utility. Gawk is considered to be a standard Linux tool for processing text.

grep -- (Version 2.3, 287K)

[B]

The GNU versions of commonly used grep utilities. Grep searches one or more input files for lines which contain a match to a specified pattern and then prints the matching lines. GNU's grep utilities include grep, egrep and fgrep.

You should install grep on your system, because it is a very useful utility for searching through text files, for system administration tasks, etc.

indent -- (Version 1.9.1, 81K)

Indent is a GNU program for beautifying C code, so that it is easier to read. Indent can also convert from one C writing style to a different one. Indent understands correct C syntax and tries to handle incorrect C syntax.

Install the indent package if you are developing applications in C and you'd like to format your code automatically.

ispell -- (Version 3.1.20, 4,049K)

[W] [S]

Ispell is the GNU interactive spelling checker. Ispell will check a text file for spelling and typographical errors. When it finds a word that is not in the dictionary, it will suggest correctly spelled words for the misspelled word.

You should install ispell if you need a program for spell checking (and who doesn't...).

less -- (Version 332, 142K)

[B]

The less utility is a text file browser that resembles more, but has more capabilities. Less allows you to move backwards in the file as well as forwards. Since less doesn't have to read the entire input file before it starts, less starts up more quickly than text editors (for example, vi).

You should install less because it is a basic utility for viewing text files, and you'll use it frequently.

m4 -- (Version 1.4, 120K)

[W] [S]

A GNU implementation of the traditional UNIX macro processor. M4 is useful for writing text files which can be logically parsed, and is used by many programs as part of their build process. M4 has built-in functions for including files, running shell commands, doing arithmetic, etc. The autoconf program needs m4 for generating configure scripts, but not for running configure scripts.

Install m4 if you need a macro processor.

mawk -- (Version 1.2.2, 131K)

Mawk is a version of the awk programming language. Awk interprets a special-purpose programming language to do quick text pattern matching and reformatting. Mawk improves on awk in certain ways and can sometimes outperform gawk, the standard awk program for Linux. Mawk conforms to the POSIX 1003.2 (draft 11.3) definition of awk.

You should install mawk if you use awk.

rgrep -- (Version 0.98.7, 17K)

The rgrep utility can recursively descend through directories as it greps for the specified pattern. Note that this ability does take a toll on rgrep's performance, which is somewhat slow. Rgrep will also highlight the matching expression.

Install the rgrep package if you need a recursive grep which can highlight the matching expression.

sed -- (Version 3.02, 68K)

[B]

The sed (Stream EDitor) editor is a stream or batch (non-interactive) editor. Sed takes text as input, performs an operation or set of operations on the text and outputs the modified text. The operations that sed performs (substitutions, deletions, insertions,etc.) can be specified in a script file or from the command line.

textutils -- (Version 1.22, 694K)

[B]

A set of GNU utilities for modifying the contents of files, including programs for splitting, joining, comparing and modifying files.

D.3 Development

This section contains packages that are associated with the development of software under Red Hat Linux.

D.3.1 Debuggers

This section contains packages that are associated with debugging programs under Red Hat Linux.

gdb -- (Version 4.17.0.11, 1,136K)

[W] [S]

Gdb is a full featured, command driven debugger. Gdb allows you to trace the execution of programs and examine their internal state at any time. Gdb works for C and C++ compiled with the GNU C compiler gcc.

If you are going to develop C and/or C++ programs and use the GNU gcc compiler, you may want to install gdb to help you debug your programs.

lslk -- (Version 1.19, 35K)

Lslk is a lock file lister. Lslk attempts to list all of the locks on the executing system's local files (i.e., on the active inodes).

Install lslk if you need a utility for listing file locks.

lsof -- (Version 4.42, 549K)

Lsof's name stands for LiSt Open Files, and it does just that. It lists information about files that are open by the processes running on a UNIX system.

ltrace -- (Version 0.3.6, 75K)

Ltrace is a debugging program which runs a specified command until the command exits. While the command is executing,ltrace intercepts and records both the dynamic library calls called by the executed process and the signals received by the executed process. Ltrace can also intercept and print system calls executed by the process.

You should install ltrace if you need a sysadmin tool for tracking the execution of processes.

strace -- (Version 3.1, 100K)

[W] [S]

The strace program intercepts and records the system calls called and received by a running process. Strace can print a record of each system call, its arguments and its return value. Strace is useful for diagnosing problems and debugging, as well as for instructional purposes.

Install strace if you need a tool to track the system calls made and received by a process.

xxgdb -- (Version 1.12, 103K)

[W]

Xxgdb is an X Window System graphical interface to the GNU gdb debugger. Xxgdb provides visual feedback and supports a mouse interface for the user who wants to perform debugging tasks like the following: controlling program execution through breakpoints, examining and traversing the function call stack, displaying values of variables and data structures, and browsing source files and functions.

Install the xxgdb package if you'd like to use a graphical interface with the GNU gdb debugger. You'll also need to have thegdb package installed.

D.3.2 Languages

This section contains packages that are associated with the programming languages available under Red Hat Linux.

compat-egcs -- (Version 5.2, 2,096K)

This package includes a compiler that can be used to generated binaries that will run on older Red Hat Linux systems (namely Red Hat Linux 5.2, or glibc 2.0.X based systems). This package includes the C compiler and required compiler libraries for those systems.

compat-egcs-c++ -- (Version 5.2, 3,219K)

This package includes a compiler that can be used to generated binaries that will run on older Red Hat Linux systems (namely Red Hat Linux 5.2, or glibc 2.0.X based systems). This packge includes the C++ compiler and libraries for those older systems.

compat-egcs-g77 -- (Version 5.2, 2,104K)

This package includes a compiler that can be used to generated binaries that will run on older Red Hat Linux systems (namely Red Hat Linux 5.2, or glibc 2.0.X based systems). This packge includes the Fortran 77 compiler and libraries for those older systems.

compat-egcs-objc -- (Version 5.2, 1,490K)

This package includes a compiler that can be used to generated binaries that will run on older Red Hat Linux systems (namely Red Hat Linux 5.2, or glibc 2.0.X based systems). This packge includes the Objective C compiler and libraries for those older systems.

cpp -- (Version 1.1.2, 135K)

[W] [S]

The C preprocessor is a 'macro processor' which is used automatically by the C compiler to transform your program before actual compilation. It is called a macro processor because it allows you to define 'macros,' which are abbreviations for longer constructs.

The C preprocessor provides four separate facilities that you can use as you see fit:

* Inclusion of header files. These are files of declarations that can be substituted into your program. * Macro expansion. You can define 'macros,' which are abbreviations for arbitrary fragments of C code, and then the C preprocessor will replace the macros with their definitions throughout the program. * Conditional compilation. Using special preprocessing directives, you can include or exclude parts of the program according to various conditions. * Line control. If you use a program to combine or rearrange source files into an intermediate file which is then compiled, you can use line control to inform the compiler about where each source line originated.

You should install this package if you are a programmer who is searching for such a macro processor.

egcs -- (Version 1.1.2, 3,525K)

[W] [S]

EGCS is a free software project that intends to further the development of GNU compilers using an open development environment. The egcs package contains the egcs compiler, a compiler aimed at integrating all the optimizations and features necessary for a high-performance and stable development environment.

Install egcs if you'd like to use an experimental GNU compiler.

egcs-c++ -- (Version 1.1.2, 5,912K)

[W]

This package adds C++ support to the GNU C compiler. It includes support for most of the current C++ specification,including templates and exception handling. It does include the static standard C++ library and C++ header files; the library for dynamically linking programs is available separately.

egcs-g77 -- (Version 1.1.2, 4,631K)

The egcs-g77 package provides support for compiling Fortran 77 programs with the GNU gcc compiler.

You should install egcs-g77 if you are going to do Fortran development and you would like to use the gcc compiler. You will also need to install the gcc package.

egcs-objc -- (Version 1.1.2, 1,969K)

Egcs-objc provides Objective C support for the GNU C compiler (gcc). Mainly used on systems running NeXTSTEP,Objective C is an object-oriented derivative of the C language.

Install egcs-objc if you are going to do Objective C development and you would like to use the gcc compiler. You will also need to install the gcc package.

expect -- (Version 5.28, 739K)

[W] [S]

Expect is a tcl extension for automating interactive applications such as telnet, ftp, passwd, fsck, rlogin, tip, etc. Expect is also useful for testing the named applications. Expect makes it easy for a script to control another program and interact with it.

Install the expect package if you'd like to develop scripts which interact with interactive applications. You'll also need to install the tcl package.

gnome-objc -- (Version 1.0.2, 653K)

This package installs basic libraries you must have to use GNOME programs that are built with Objective C.

GNOME is the GNU Network Object Model Environment. It's a powerful, pleasing, easy to use and configure environment for your computer.

guavac -- (Version 1.2, 2,157K)

The guavac package includes guavac and guavad. Guavac is a stand-alone compiler for the Java programming language.Guavac was written entirely in C++ and it should be portable to any platform supporting GNU's C++ (gcc) or a similar compiler. Guavad is guavac's disassembler.

Install guavac if you need a Java compiler on your system.

guile -- (Version 1.3, 1,029K)

[W]

GUILE (GNU's Ubiquitous Intelligent Language for Extension) is a library implementation of the Scheme programming language, written in C. GUILE provides a machine-independent execution platform that can be linked in as a library during the building of extensible programs.

Install the guile package if you'd like to add extensibility to programs that you are developing. You'll also need to install the guile-devel package.

itcl -- (Version 3.0.1, 4,251K)

[incr Tcl] is an object-oriented extension of the Tcl language. It was created to support more structured programming in Tcl.Tcl scripts that grow beyond a few thousand lines become extremely difficult to maintain. This is because the building blocks of vanilla Tcl are procedures and global variables, and all of these building blocks must reside in a single global namespace. There is no support for protection or encapsulation.

[incr Tcl] introduces the notion of objects. Each object is a bag of data with a set of procedures or "methods" that are used to manipulate it. Objects are organized into "classes" with identical characteristics, and classes can inherit functionality from one another. This object-oriented paradigm adds another level of organization on top of the basic variable/procedure elements, and the resulting code is easier to understand and maintain.

kaffe -- (Version 1.0.b4, 1,977K)

Kaffe is a free virtual machine designed to execute Java(TM) bytecode. Kaffe can be configured in two modes. In the first mode, it operates as a pure bytecode interpreter (not unlike Javasoft's machine). In the second mode, it performs "just-in-time"code conversion from the abstract code to the host machine's native code. The second mode will ultimately allow execution of Java code at the same speed as standard compiled code, while also maintaining the advantages and flexibility of code independence.

Install the kaffe package if you need a Java virtual machine.

p2c -- (Version 1.22, 697K)

P2c is a system for translating Pascal programs into the C language. P2c accepts input source files in certain Pascal dialects:HP Pascal, Turbo/UCSD Pascal, DEC VAX Pascal, Oregon Software Pascal/2, Macintosh Programmer's Workshop Pascal and Sun/Berkeley Pascal. P2c outputs a set of .c and .h files which make up a C program equivalent to the original Pascal program. The C program can then be compiled using a standard C compiler, such as gcc.

Install the p2c package if you need a program for translating Pascal code into C code.

p2c-devel -- (Version 1.22, 25K)

The p2c-devel package contains the files necessary for development of the p2c Pascal to C translation system.

Install the p2c-devel package if you want to do p2c development.

perl -- (Version 5.00503, 15,777K)

[B]

Perl is a high-level programming language with roots in C, sed, awk and shell scripting. Perl is good at handling processes and files, and is especially good at handling text. Perl's hallmarks are practicality and efficiency. While it is used to do a lot of different things, Perl's most common applications (and what it excels at) are probably system administration utilities and web programming. A large proportion of the CGI scripts on the web are written in Perl. You need the perl package installed on your system so that your system can handle Perl scripts.

perl-MD5 -- (Version 1.7, 30K)

[S]

The perl-MD5 package provides the MD5 module for the Perl programming language. MD5 is a Perl interface to the RSA Data Security Inc. Message Digest Algorithm, which allows Perl programs to use the algorithm.

The perl-MD5 package should be installed if any Perl programs on your system are going to use RSA's Message Digest Algorithm.

pygnome -- (Version 1.0.1, 1,650K)

PyGNOME is an extension module for python that gives you access to the base GNOME libraries. This means you have access to more widgets, simple configuration interface, metadata support and many other features.

pygtk -- (Version 0.5.12, 2,259K)

PyGTK is an extension module for python that gives you access to the GTK+ widget set. Just about anything you can write in C with GTK+ you can write in python with PyGTK (within reason), but with all of python's benefits.

python -- (Version 1.5.1, 5,829K)

[W] [S]

Python is an interpreted, interactive, object-oriented programming language often compared to Tcl, Perl, Scheme or Java.Python includes modules, classes, exceptions, very high level dynamic data types and dynamic typing. Python supports interfaces to many system calls and libraries, as well as to various windowing systems (X11, Motif, Tk, Mac and MFC).

Programmers can write new built-in modules for Python in C or C++. Python can be used as an extension language for applications that need a programmable interface. This package contains most of the standard Python modules, as well as modules for interfacing to the Tix widget set for Tk and RPM.

Note that documentation for Python is provided in the python-docs package.

tcl -- (Version 8.0.4, 5,516K)

[W] [S]

Tcl is a simple scripting language designed to be embedded into other applications. Tcl is designed to be used with Tk, a widget set, which is provided in the tk package. This package also includes tclsh, a simple example of a Tcl application.

If you're installing the tcl package and you want to use Tcl for development, you should also install the tk and tclx packages.

tclx -- (Version 8.0.4, 1,954K)

[W] [S]

TclX is a set of extensions which make it easier to use the Tcl scripting language for common UNIX/Linux programming tasks.TclX enhances Tcl support for files, network access, debugging, math, lists, and message catalogs. TclX can be used with both Tcl and Tcl/Tk applications.

Install TclX if you are developing applications with Tcl/Tk. You'll also need to install the tcl and tk packages.

tix -- (Version 4.1.0.6, 2,732K)

[W] [S]

Tix (Tk Interface Extension), an add-on for the Tk widget set, is an extensive set of over 40 widgets. In general, Tix widgets are more complex and more capable than the widgets provided in Tk. Tix widgets include a ComboBox, a Motif-style FileSelectBox, an MS Windows-style FileSelectBox, a PanedWindow, a NoteBook, a hierarchical list, a directory tree and a file manager.

Install the tix package if you want to try out more complicated widgets for Tk. You'll also need to have the tcl and tk packages installed.

tk -- (Version 8.0.4, 5,289K)

[W] [S]

Tk is a X Windows widget set designed to work closely with the tcl scripting language. It allows you to write simple programs with full featured GUI's in only a little more time then it takes to write a text based interface. Tcl/Tk applications can also run on Windows and Macintosh platforms.

tkinter -- (Version 1.5.1, 643K)

[W] [S]

The Tkinter (Tk interface) program is an graphical user interface for the Python scripting language.

You should install the tkinter package if you'd like to use a graphical user interface for Python programming.

umb-scheme -- (Version 3.2, 1,211K)

[W]

UMB Scheme is a public domain implementation of the Scheme programming language. Scheme is a statically scoped and properly tail-recursive dialect of the Lisp programming language, designed with clear and simple semantics and a minimal number of ways to form expressions.

Install the umb-scheme package if you need an implementation of the Scheme programming language.

D.3.3 Libraries

This section contains packages that are associated with the libraries used during the development of software under Red Hat Linux.

ImageMagick-devel -- (Version 4.2.2, 1,584K)

If you want to create applications that will use ImageMagick code or APIs, you'll need to install these packages as well as ImageMagick. These additional packages aren't necessary if you simply want to use ImageMagick, however.

ImageMagick-devel is an addition to ImageMagick which includes static libraries and header files necessary to develop applications.

ORBit-devel -- (Version 0.4.3, 1,219K)

ORBit is a high-performance CORBA ORB (object request broker) with support for the C language. It allows programs to send requests and receive replies from other programs, regardless of the locations of the two programs.

This package contains the header files, libraries and utilities necessary to write programs that use CORBA technology.

XFree86-devel -- (Version 3.3.3.1, 7,796K)

[W]

XFree86-devel includes the libraries, header files and documentation you'll need to develop programs which run in X clients.XFree86 includes the base Xlib library as well as the Xt and Xaw widget sets.

For guidance on programming with these libraries, O'Reilly & Associates produces a series on X programming which you might find useful.

Install XFree86-devel if you are going to develop programs which will run as X clients.

Xaw3d-devel -- (Version 1.3, 657K)

[W]

Xaw3d is an enhanced version of the MIT Athena widget set for the X Window System. Xaw3d adds a three-dimensional look to those applications with minimal or no source code changes. Xaw3d-devel includes the header files and static libraries for developing programs that take full advantage of Xaw3d's features.

You should install Xaw3d-devel if you are going to develop applications using the Xaw3d widget set. You'll also need to install the Xaw3d package.

apache-devel -- (Version 1.3.6, 269K)

The apache-devel package contains the source code for the Apache 1.3.1 Web server and the APXS binary you'll need to build Dynamic Shared Objects (DSOs) for Apache.

If you are installing the Apache Web server version 1.3.1, and you want to be able to compile or develop additional modules for Apache, you'll need to install this package.

audiofile-devel -- (Version 0.1.6, 99K)

Libraries, include files and other resources you can use to develop audiofile applications.

bind-devel -- (Version 8.2, 1,294K)

The bind-devel package contains all the include files and the library required for DNS (Domain Name Service) development for bind versions 8.x.x.

You should install bind-devel if you want to develop bind DNS applications. If you install bind-devel, you'll need to install bind, as well.

compat-glibc -- (Version 5.2, 4,331K)

This package contains the version 2.0.7 of the GNU C library for compiling binaries that will run on Red Hat Linux 2.0 and other glibc 2.0.x Linux based systems. This package includes the runtime libraries.

compat-libs -- (Version 5.2, 2,282K)

This package includes a number of run-time libraries that are compiled on Red Hat Linux 5.2. This package is required if you want to do development for Red Hat Linux 5.2 and other glibc 2.0 based systems.

control-center-devel -- (Version 1.0.5, 38K)

If you're interested in developing panels for the GNOME control center, you'll want to install this package.

Control-center-devel helps you create the 'capplets' which are used in the control center.

e2fsprogs-devel -- (Version 1.14, 260K)

E2fsprogs-devel contains the libraries and header files needed to develop second extended (ext2) filesystem-specific programs.

You should install e2fsprogs-devel if you want to develop ext2 filesystem-specific programs. If you install e2fsprogs-devel, you'll also want to install e2fsprogs.

esound-devel -- (Version 0.2.12, 48K)

Libraries, include files and other resources you can use to develop EsounD applications.

faces-devel -- (Version 1.6.1, 22K)

[W]

Faces-devel contains the faces program development environment, (i.e., the static libraries and header files).

If you want to develop Faces applications, you'll need to install faces-devel. You'll also need to install the faces package.

fnlib-devel -- (Version 0.4, 34K)

Headers, static libraries and documentation for Fnlib.

freetype-devel -- (Version 1.2, 511K)

This package is only needed if you intend to develop or compile applications which rely on the FreeType library. If you simply want to run existing applications, you won't need this package.

gd-devel -- (Version 1.3, 7K)

[W]

These are the development libraries and header files for gd, the .gif graphics library.

If you're installing the gd graphics library, you must install gd-devel.

gdbm-devel -- (Version 1.7.3, 72K)

[W]

Gdbm-devel contains the development libraries and header files for gdbm, the GNU database system. These libraries and header files are necessary if you plan to do development using the gdbm database.

Install gdbm-devel if you are developing C programs which will use the gdbm database library. You'll also need to install the gdbm package.

gedit-devel -- (Version 0.5.1, 8K)

gEdit is a small but powerful text editor for GTK+ and/or GNOME. This package allows you to develop plugins that work within gEdit. Plugins can create new documents and manipulate documents in arbitrary ways.

gimp-devel -- (Version 1.0.4, 253K)

Static libraries and header files for writing GIMP plugins and extensions.

glib-devel -- (Version 1.2.1, 303K)

[W]

Static libraries and header files for the support library for the GIMP's X libraries, which are available as public libraries. GLIB includes generally useful data structures.

glibc-devel -- (Version 2.1.1, 32,869K)

[W] [S]

To develop programs which use the standard C libraries (which nearly all programs do), the system needs to have these standard header files and object files available for creating the executables.

glibc-profile -- (Version 2.1.1, 30,464K)

When programs are being profiled used gprof, they must use these libraries instrad of the standard C libraries for gprof to be able to profile them correctly.

gmp-devel -- (Version 2.0.2, 319K)

The static libraries, header files and documentation for using the GNU MP arbitrary precision library in applications.

If you want to develop applications which will use the GNU MP library, you'll need to install the gmp-devel package. You'll also need to install the gmp package.

gnome-core-devel -- (Version 1.0.4, 127K)

Panel libraries and header files for creating GNOME panels.

gnome-games-devel -- (Version 1.0.2, 42K)

This packages installs the libraries and files needed to develop some GNOME games.

gnome-libs-devel -- (Version 1.0.8, 7,449K)

GNOME (GNU Network Object Model Environment) is a user-friendly set of applications and desktop tools to be used in conjunction with a window manager for the X Window System. GNOME is similar in purpose and scope to CDE and KDE, but GNOME is based completely on Open Source software. The gnome-libs-devel package includes the libraries and include files that you will need to develop GNOME applications.

You should install the gnome-libs-devel package if you would like to develop GNOME applications. You don't need to install gnome-libs-devel if you just want to use the GNOME desktop environment. If you are going to develop GNOME applications and/or you're going to use the GNOME desktop environment, you'll also need to install the gnome-core and gnome-libs packages. If you want to use linuxconf with a GNOME front end, you'll also need to install the gnome-linuxconf package.

gnome-objc-devel -- (Version 1.0.2, 886K)

Libraries, include files and other files you can use to develop Objective C GNOME applications.

If you're interested in developing GNOME applications, you should install this package.

gnome-pim-devel -- (Version 1.0.7, 36K)

Files needed to develop apps which interact with gnome-pim applications via CORBA.

gpm-devel -- (Version 1.17.5, 27K)

[W]

The gpm-devel program contains the libraries and header files needed for development of mouse driven programs. This package allows you to develop text-mode programs which use the mouse.

Install gpm-devel if you need to develop text-mode programs which will use the mouse. You'll also need to install the gpm package.

gtk+-devel -- (Version 1.2.1, 2,422K)

[W]

The gtk+-devel package contains the static libraries and header files needed for developing GTK+ (GIMP ToolKit)applications. The gtk+-devel package contains glib (a collection of routines for simplifying the development of GTK+applications), GDK (the General Drawing Kit, which simplifies the interface for writing GTK+ widgets and using GTK+widgets in applications), and GTK+ (the widget set).

Install gtk+-devel if you need to develop GTK+ applications. You'll also need to install the gtk+ package.

guile-devel -- (Version 1.3, 963K)

The guile-devel package includes the libraries, header files, etc., that you'll need to develop applications that are linked with the GUILE extensibility library.

You need to install the guile-devel package if you want to develop applications that will be linked to GUILE. You'll also need to install the guile package.

imlib-devel -- (Version 1.9.5, 544K)

The header files, static libraries and documentation needed for developing Imlib applications. Imlib is an image loading and rendering library for X11R6.

Install the imlib-devel package if you want to develop Imlib applications. You'll also need to install the imlib and imlib_cfgeditor packages.

inn-devel -- (Version 2.2, 1,737K)

The inn-devel package contains the INN (InterNetNews) library, which several programs that interface with INN need in order to work (for example, newsgate and tin).

If you are installing a program which must interface with the INN news system, you should install inn-devel.

libghttp-devel -- (Version 1.0.2, 42K)

Libraries and includes files you can use for libghttp development.

libgr-devel -- (Version 2.0.13, 320K)

[W]

The libgr-devel package contains the header files and static libraries, etc., for developing programs which can handle the various graphics file formats supported by the libgr library.

Install libgr-devel if you want to develop programs for handling the graphics file formats supported by the libgr library. You'll also need to have the libgr package installed.

libgtop-devel -- (Version 1.0.1, 326K)

GNOME (GNU Network Object Model Environment) is a user-friendly set of applications and desktop tools to be used in conjunction with a window manager for the X Window System. GNOME is similar in purpose and scope to CDE and KDE, but GNOME is based completely on Open Source software. The gnome-libs-devel package includes the libraries and include files that you will need to develop GNOME applications.

You should install the gnome-libs-devel package if you would like to develop GNOME applications. You don't need to install gnome-libs-devel if you just want to use the GNOME desktop environment. If you are going to develop GNOME applications and/or you're going to use the GNOME desktop environment, you'll also need to install the gnome-core and gnome-libs packages. If you want to use linuxconf with a GNOME front end, you'll also need to install the gnome-linuxconf package.

libjpeg-devel -- (Version 6b, 233K)

[W]

The libjpeg-devel package includes the header files and static libraries necessary for developing programs which will manipulate JPEG files using the libjpeg library.

If you are going to develop programs which will manipulate JPEG images, you should install libjpeg-devel. You'll also need to have the libjpeg package installed.

libpcap -- (Version 0.4, 121K)

Libpcap provides a portable framework for low-level network monitoring. Libpcap can provide network statistics collection, security monitoring and network debugging. Since almost every system vendor provides a different interface for packet capture, the libpcap authors created this system-independent API to ease in porting and to alleviate the need for several system-dependent packet capture modules in each application.

Install libpcap if you need to do low-level network traffic monitoring on your network.

libpng-devel -- (Version 1.0.3, 485K)

[W]

The libpng-devel package contains the header files and static libraries necessary for developing programs using the PNG (Portable Network Graphics) library.

If you want to develop programs which will manipulate PNG image format files, you should install libpng-devel. You'll also need to install the libpng package.

libtermcap-devel -- (Version 2.0.8, 12K)

[W]

This package includes the libraries and header files necessary for developing programs which will access the termcap database.

If you need to develop programs which will access the termcap database, you'll need to install this package. You'll also need to install the libtermcap package.

libtiff-devel -- (Version 3.4, 1,614K)

[W]

This package contains the header files and static libraries for developing programs which will manipulate TIFF format image files using the libtiff library.

If you need to develop programs which will manipulate TIFF format image files, you should install this package. You'll also need to install the libtiff package.

libungif-devel -- (Version 4.1.0, 271K)

[W]

This package contains the static libraries, header files and documentation necessary for development of programs that will use the libungif library to load and save GIF format image files.

You should install this package if you need to develop programs which will use the libungif library functions for loading and saving GIF format image files. You'll also need to install the libungif package.

libxml-devel -- (Version 1.0.0, 127K)

This packages contains the libraries, include and other files you can use to develop libxml applications.

linuxconf-devel -- (Version 1.14r4, 3,742K)

[W]

Linuxconf is an extremely capable system configuration tool. It provides a variety of interfaces through which you can configure your Linux system and manage a large proportion of the system's operations.

This package provides the components necessary for developing Linuxconf modules outside of the linuxconf source tree and/or developing stand-alone utilities using the linuxconf interface toolkit.

Install linuxconf-devel if you want to develop Linuxconf modules. You must also have linuxconf installed.

ncurses-devel -- (Version 4.2, 7,108K)

[W]

The header files and libraries for developing applications that use the ncurses CRT screen handling and optimization package.

Install the ncurses-devel package if you want to develop applications which will use ncurses.

newt-devel -- (Version 0.40, 118K)

[W]

The newt-devel package contains the header files and libraries necessary for developing applications which use newt. Newt is a development library for text mode user interfaces. Newt is based on the slang library.

Install newt-devel if you want to develop applications which will use newt.

pilot-link-devel -- (Version 0.9.0, 1,635K)

This package contains the development headers that are used to build the pilot-link package. It also includes the static libraries necessary to build static pilot apps.

postgresql-devel -- (Version 6.4.2, 662K)

[S]

This package contains the header files and libraries needed to compile applications which will directly interact with a Postgre SQL server.

Install this package if you want to develop applications which will interact with a PostgreSQL server.

python-devel -- (Version 1.5.1, 3,499K)

The Python programming language's interpreter can be extended with dynamically loaded extensions and can be embedded in other programs. This package contains the header files and libraries needed to do these types of tasks.

Install python-devel if you want to develop Python extensions. The python package will also need to be installed. You'll probably also want to install the python-docs package, which contains Python documentation.

qt-devel -- (Version 1.44, 12,155K)

Contains the files necessary to develop applications using Qt: header files, the Qt meta object compiler, man pages, HTML documentation and example programs. See http://www.troll.no for more information about Qt, or file:/usr/lib/qt/html/index.html for Qt documentation in HTML.

readline-devel -- (Version 2.2.1, 250K)

[W]

The readline library will read a line from the terminal and return it. Use of the readline library allows programmers to provide an easy to use and more intuitive interface for users.

If you want to develop programs which will use the readline library, you'll need to have the readline-devel package installed. You'll also need to have the readline package installed.

rpm-devel -- (Version 3.0, 330K)

[W]

This package contains the RPM C library and header files. These development files will simplify the process of writing programs which manipulate RPM packages and databases and are intended to make it easier to create graphical package managers or any other tools that need an intimate knowledge of RPM packages in order to function.

This package should be installed if you want to develop programs that will manipulate RPM packages and databases.

slang-devel -- (Version 1.2.2, 1,192K)

[W]

This package contains the S-Lang extension language static libraries and header files which you'll need if you want to develop S-Lang based applications. Documentation which may help you write S-Lang based applications is also included.

Install the slang-devel package if you want to develop applications based on the S-Lang extension language.

sox-devel -- (Version 12.15, 855K)

This package contains the library needed for compiling applications which will use the SoX sound file format converter.

Install sox-devel if you want to develop applications which will use SoX.

svgalib-devel -- (Version 1.3.1, 785K)

[W]

The svgalib-devel package contains the libraries and header files needed to build programs which will use the SVGAlib low-level graphics library.

Install the svgalib-devel package if you want to develop applications which will use the SVGAlib library.

ucd-snmp-devel -- (Version 3.6.1, 269K)

The ucd-snmp-devel package contains the development libraries and header files for use with the UCD-SNMP project's network management tools.

Install the ucd-snmp-devel package if you would like to develop applications for use with the UCD-SNMP project's network management tools. You'll also need to have the ucd-snmp and ucd-snmp-utils packages installed.

w3c-libwww-devel -- (Version 5.2.8, 1,620K)

Static libraries and header files for libwww, which are available as public libraries.

x11amp-devel -- (Version 0.9_alpha3, 13K)

Static libraries and header files for building x11amp plugins.

xpm-devel -- (Version 3.4j, 221K)

[W]

The xpm-devel package contains the development libraries and header files necessary for developing applications which will use the XPM library. The XPM library is used by many programs for displaying pixmaps in the X Window System.

Install the xpm-devel package if you want to develop applications using the XPM pixmap library. You'll also need to install the xpm package.

zlib-devel -- (Version 1.1.3, 165K)

[W]

The zlib-devel package contains the header files and libraries needed to develop programs that use the zlib compression and decompression library.

Install the zlib-devel package if you want to develop applications that will use the zlib library.

D.3.4 System

This section contains packages that are associated with building system-level software under Red Hat Linux.

kernel-headers -- (Version 2.2.5, 2,700K)

[W] [S]

Kernel-headers includes the C header files for the Linux kernel. The header files define structures and constants that are needed for building most standard programs. The header files are also needed for rebuilding the kernel.

kernel-source -- (Version 2.2.5, 46,352K)

The kernel-source package contains the source code files for the Linux kernel. These source files are needed to build most C programs, since they depend on the constants defined in the source code. The source files can also be used to build a custom kernel that is better tuned to your particular hardware, if you are so inclined (and you know what you're doing).

D.3.5 Tools

This section contains packages that are associated with the various tools needed to develop software under Red Hat Linux.

ElectricFence -- (Version 2.1, 44K)

[W] [S]

If you know what malloc() violations are, you'll be interested in ElectricFence. ElectricFence is a tool which can be used for C programming and debugging. It uses the virtual memory hardware of your system to detect when software overruns malloc()buffer boundaries, and/or to detect any accesses of memory released by free(). ElectricFence will then stop the program on the first instruction that caused a bounds violation and you can use your favorite debugger to display the offending statement.

This package will install ElectricFence, which you can use if you're searching for a debugger to find malloc() violations.

autoconf -- (Version 2.13, 580K)

[W] [S]

GNU's Autoconf is a tool for configuring source code and Makefiles. Using Autoconf, programmers can create portable and configurable packages, since the person building the package is allowed to specify various configuration options.

You should install Autoconf if you are developing software and you'd like to use it to create shell scripts which will configure your source code packages. If you are installing Autoconf, you will also need to install the GNU m4 package.

Note that the Autoconf package is not required for the end user who may be configuring software with an Autoconf-generated script; Autoconf is only required for the generation of the scripts, not their use.

automake -- (Version 1.4, 867K)

[W] [S]

Automake is an experimental Makefile generator. Automake was inspired by the 4.4BSD make and include files, but aims to be portable and to conform to the GNU standards for Makefile variables and targets.

You should install Automake if you are developing software and would like to use its capabilities of automatically generating GNU standard Makefiles. if you install Automake, you will also need to install GNU's Autoconf package.

bin86 -- (Version 0.4, 73K)

[W] [S]

The bin86 package provides an assembler and linker for real mode 80x86 instructions. You'll need to have this package installed in order to build programs that run in real mode, including LILO and the kernel's bootstrapping code, from theirsources.

You should install bin86 if you intend to build programs that run in real mode from their source code.

binutils -- (Version 2.9.1.0.23, 5,168K)

[B] [W] [S]

Binutils is a collection of binary utilities, including ar (for creating, modifying and extracting from archives), nm (for listing symbols from object files), objcopy (for copying and translating object files), objdump (for displaying information from object files), ranlib (for generating an index for the contents of an archive), size (for listing the section sizes of an object or archive file), strings (for listing printable strings from files), strip (for discarding symbols), c++filt (a filter for demangling encoded C++ symbols), addr2line (for converting addresses to file and line), and nbnconv (for converting object code into an NLM).

Install binutils if you need to perform any of these types of actions on binary files. Most programmers will want to install binutils.

bison -- (Version 1.27, 153K)

[W] [S]

Bison is a general purpose parser generator which converts a grammar description for an LALR context-free grammar into a C program to parse that grammar. Bison can be used to develop a wide range of language parsers, from ones used in simple desk calculators to complex programming languages. Bison is upwardly compatible with Yacc, so any correctly written Yacc grammar should work with Bison without any changes. If you know Yacc, you shouldn't have any trouble using Bison (but you do need to be very proficient in C programming to be able to use Bison). Many programs use Bison as part of their build process. Bison is only needed on systems that are used for development.

If your system will be used for C development, you should install Bison since it is used to build many C programs.

blt -- (Version 2.4g, 3,966K)

BLT is an extension to the Tk toolkit. BLT's most useful feature is the provision of more widgets for Tk, but it also provides more geometry managers and miscellaneous other commands. Note that you won't need to do any patching of the Tcl or Tk source files to use BLT, but you will need to have Tcl/Tk installed in order to use BLT.

If you are programming with the Tk toolkit, you should install BLT. You will need to have Tcl/Tk installed.

byacc -- (Version 1.9, 54K)

[W] [S]

Byacc (Berkeley Yacc) is a public domain LALR parser generator which is used by many programs during their build process.

If you are going to do development on your system, you will want to install this package.

cdecl -- (Version 2.5, 80K)

[W] [S]

The cdecl package includes the cdecl and c++decl utilities, which are used to translate English to C or C++ function declarations and vice versa.

You should install the cdecl package if you intend to do C and/or C++ programming.

compat-binutils -- (Version 5.2, 3,566K)

This package includes the binutils required by the Red HAt Linux 5.2 backwards compatibility kit. Binutils is a collection of binary utilities, including ar (for creating, modifying and extracting from archives), nm (for listing symbols from object files),objcopy (for copying and translating object files), objdump (for displaying information from object files), ranlib (for generating an index for the contents of an archive), size (for listing the section sizes of an object or archive file), strings (for listing printable strings from files), strip (for discarding symbols), c++filt (a filter for demangling encoded C++ symbols), addr2line (for converting addresses to file and line), and nbnconv (for converting object code into an NLM).

Install this package if you will be developing programs that need to run on Red Hat Linux 5.2 or other glibc 2.0.x based systems.

cproto -- (Version 4.6, 85K)

[W] [S]

Cproto generates function prototypes and variable declarations from C source code. Cproto can also convert function definitions between the old style and the ANSI C style. This conversion will overwrite the original files, however, so be sure to make a backup copy of your original files in case something goes wrong. Since cproto uses a Yacc generated parser, it shouldn't be confused by complex function definitions as much as other prototype generators) because it uses a Yacc generated parser.

Cproto will be useful for C programmers, so install cproto if you are going to do any C programming.

ctags -- (Version 3.2, 146K)

[W] [S]

Ctags generates an index (or tag) file of C language objects found in C source and header files. The index makes it easy for text editors or other utilities to locate the indexed items. Ctags can also generate a cross reference file which lists information about the various objects found in a set of C language files in human readable form. Exuberant Ctags improves on ctags because it can find all types of C language tags, including macro definitions, enumerated values (values inside enum...), function and method definitions, enum/struct/union tags, external function prototypes, typedef names and variable declarations. Exuberant Ctags is far less likely to be fooled by code containing #if preprocessor conditional constructs than ctags. Exuberant ctags supports output of emacs style TAGS files and can be used to print out a list of selected objects found in source files.

Install ctags if you are going to use your system for C programming.

cvs -- (Version 1.10.5, 3,088K)

[W] [S]

CVS means Concurrent Version System; it is a version control system which can record the history of your files (usually, but not always, source code). CVS only stores the differences between versions, instead of every version of every file you've ever created. CVS also keeps a log of who, when and why changes occurred, among other aspects.

CVS is very helpful for managing releases and controlling the concurrent editing of source files among multiple authors. Instead of providing version control for a collection of files in a single directory, CVS provides version control for a hierarchical collection of directories consisting of revision controlled files.

These directories and files can then be combined together to form a software release.

Install the cvs package if you need to use a version control system.

diffstat -- (Version 1.25, 11K)

The diff command compares files line by line. Diffstat reads the output of the diff command and displays a histogram of the insertions, deletions and modifications in each file. Diffstat is commonly used to provide a summary of the changes in large, complex patch files.

Install diffstat if you need a program which provides a summary of the diff command's output. You'll need to also install diffutils.

flex -- (Version 2.5.4a, 302K)

[W] [S]

The flex program generates scanners. Scanners are programs which can recognize lexical patterns in text. Flex takes pairs of regular expressions and C code as input and generates a C source file as output. The output file is compiled and linked with a library to produce an executable. The executable searches through its input for occurrences of the regular expressions. When a match is found, it executes the corresponding C code. Flex was designed to work with both Yacc and Bison, and is used by many programs as part of their build process.

You should install flex if you are going to use your system for application development.

gettext -- (Version 0.10.35, 889K)

[W] [S]

The GNU gettext package provides a set of tools and documentation for producing multi-lingual messages in programs. Tools include a set of conventions about how programs should be written to support message catalogs, a directory and file naming organization for the message catalogs, a runtime library which supports the retrieval of translated messages, and stand-alone programs for handling the translatable and the already translated strings. Gettext provides an easy to use library and tools for creating, using, and modifying natural language catalogs and is a powerful and simple method for internationalizing programs.

If you would like to internationalize or incorporate multi-lingual messages into programs that you're developing, you should install gettext.

gperf -- (Version 2.7, 122K)

Gperf is a perfect hash function generator written in C++. Simply stated, a perfect hash function is a hash function and a data structure that allows recognition of a key word in a set of words using exactly one probe into the data structure.

Install gperf if you need a program that generates perfect hash functions.

libtool -- (Version 1.2f, 973K)

The libtool package contains the GNU libtool, a set of shell scripts which automatically configure UNIX and UNIX-like architectures to generically build shared libraries. Libtool provides a consistent, portable interface which simplifies the process of using shared libraries.

If you are developing programs which will use shared libraries, you should install libtool.

make -- (Version 3.77, 259K)

[W] [S]

A GNU tool for controlling the generation of executables and other non-source files of a program from the program's source files. Make allows users to build and install packages without any significant knowledge about the details of the build process.The details about how the program should be built are provided for make in the program's makefile.

The GNU make tool should be installed on your system because it is commonly used to simplify the process of installing programs.

patch -- (Version 2.5, 99K)

[W] [S]

The patch program applies diff files to originals. The diff command is used to compare an original to a changed file. Diff lists the changes made to the file. A person who has the original file can then use the patch command with the diff file to add the changes to their original file (patching the file).

Patch should be installed because it is a common way of upgrading applications.

pmake -- (Version 2.1.33, 1,031K)

[W] [S]

Make is a GNU tool which allows users to build and install programs without any significant knowledge of the build process. Details about how the program should be built are included in the program's Makefile. Pmake is a particular version (BSD 4.4)of make. Pmake supports some additional syntax which is not in the standard make program. Some Berkeley programs have Makefiles written for pmake.

Pmake should be installed on your system so that you will be able to build programs which require using pmake instead of make.

pmake-customs -- (Version 2.1.33, 982K)

Customs is a remote execution facility for PMake. Customs is designed to run on a network of machines with a consistent,shared filesystem. Customs requires Sun RPC in order to use XDR (eXternal Data Representation) routines for logging functions.

A single server is designated as the master agent and is additionally responsible for noting when a machine goes down, from which machines any given machine will accept jobs and parcelling out available machines to requesting clients. The job of master is not given to any one machine but, rather, is decided among the active agents whenever the previous master dies.

Clients are provided to: - alter the availability criteria for the local machine (importquota) - find the status of all registered hosts on the net (reginfo). - abort, restart or ping any customs agent on the network (cctrl). - export a command from the shell(export).
- accept log information from all hosts on the net (logd).

rcs -- (Version 5.7, 536K)

[W] [S]

The Revision Control System (RCS) is a system for managing multiple versions of files. RCS automates the storage, retrieval,logging, identification and merging of file revisions. RCS is useful for text files that are revised frequently (for example,programs,documentation, graphics, papers and form letters).

The rcs package should be installed if you need a system for managing different versions of files.

D.4 Documentation

This section contains packages that are associated with documentation for Linux in general and Red Hat Linux in particular.

XFree86-doc -- (Version 3.3.3.1, 9,678K)

XFree86-doc provides a great deal of extensive PostScript documentation on the various X APIs, libraries, and other interfaces. If you need low level X documentation, you will find it here.

Topics include the X protocol, the ICCCM window manager standard, ICE session management, the font server API, etc.

bash2-doc -- (Version 2.03, 2,275K)

This is a separate documentation package for the GNU Bourne Again shell.

faq -- (Version 6.0, 1,164K)

The faq package includes the text of the Frequently Asked Questions (FAQ)about Linux from the SunSITE website: (http://sunsite.unc.edu/pub/Linux/docs/faqs/linux-faq/Linux-FAQ). The Linux FAQ is a great source of information about Linux.

Install faq if you'd like to read the Linux FAQ off your own machine.

gimp-manual -- (Version 1.0.0, 17,979K)

The gimp-manual package contains the GIMP (GNU Image Manipulation Program) User Manual (GUM) in HTML format.

Please note that the HTML version of the GUM is not as good a quality as the other versions, which can be obtained from the GUM website at http://manual.gimp.org/pub/manual. On the GUM website, The manual is provided in HTML (for viewing the GUM online), in PostScript(TM) and PDF formats (for printing) as well as in FM (FrameMaker) source code. TheFrameMaker source code is provided for people who would like to contribute to the Graphic Documentation Project.Submissions to the GUM are covered by the manual's license agreement and terms, included in the file COPYING.

The GUM is a complete guide for using the GIMP. This version of the GUM includes improvements over previous versions. Be sure to check out the new Gallery chapter, which provides a good overview of what the GIMP can do. The Gallery displays cool images and give you hints on how to create them with the GIMP.

For more information about the GUM, check the GUM website at http://manual.gimp.org/.

gnome-users-guide -- (Version 1.0.5, 7,135K)

[W]

This package will install the users' guide for the GNOME Desktop Environment on your computer.

You should install this package if you are going to use GNOME and you want a quick, handy reference.

helptool -- (Version 2.4, 23K)

[W] [S]

The helptool provides a unified graphical user interface for searching through many of the help sources available (including man pages and GNU texinfo documents).

Install helptool if you'd like to use it to search for help files. You'll need to have the X Window System installed to use the helptool.

howto -- (Version 6.0, 11,103K)

Linux HOWTOs are detailed documents which describe a specific aspect of configuring or using Linux. Linux HOWTOs are a great source of practical information about your system. The latest versions of these documents are located at http://sunsite.unc.edu/linux.

Install the howto package if you'd like to be able to access the Linux HOWTO documentation from your own system.

howto-chinese -- (Version 6.0, 13,445K)

The howto-chinese package contains the Linux HOWTO documents that have been translated into Chinese. Linux HOWTOs are detailed documents describing a specific aspect of configuring or using Linux.

Install the howto-chinese package if you'd like to use the Linux HOWTO documentation in Chinese. Please note that not all of the HOWTOs have been translated. If you need to have a complete set of HOWTOs, you'll need to install the English version(the howto package).

howto-croatian -- (Version 6.0, 1,897K)

The howto-chinese package contains the Linux HOWTO documents that have been translated into Croatian. Linux HOWTOs are detailed documents which describe a specific aspect of configuring or using Linux.

Install the howto-croatian package if you'd like to use the Linux HOWTO documentation in Croatian. Please note that not all of the HOWTOs have been translated. If you need to have a complete set of HOWTOs, you'll need to install the English version(the how to package).

howto-french -- (Version 6.0, 29,195K)

This package contains the Linux HOWTO documents that have been translated into French. Linux HOWTOs are detailed documents which describe a specific aspect of configuring or using Linux.

Install the howto-french package if you'd like to use the Linux HOWTOs in French. Please note that not all of the HOWTOs have been translated. If you need to have a complete set of HOWTOs, you'll need to install the English version (the howto package).

howto-german -- (Version 6.0, 22,361K)

This package contains the Linux HOWTO documents that have been translated into German. Linux HOWTOs are detailed documents which describe a specific aspect of configuring or using Linux.

Install the howto-german package if you'd like to use the Linux HOWTOs in German. Please note that not all of the HOWTOs have been translated. If you need to have a complete set of HOWTOs, you'll need to install the English version (the howto package).

howto-greek -- (Version 6.0, 7,712K)

This package contains the Linux HOWTO documents that have been translated into Greek. Linux HOWTOs are detailed documents which describe a specific aspect of configuring or using Linux.

Install the howto-greek package if you'd like to use the Linux HOWTOs in Greek. Please note that not all of the HOWTOs have been translated. If you need to have a complete set of HOWTOs, you'll need to install the English version (the howto package).

howto-html -- (Version 6.0, 12,824K)

This package contains the Linux HOWTO documents in HTML format, so they can be viewed with a web browser. Linux HOWTOs are detailed documents which describe a specific aspect of configuring or using Linux.

Install the howto-html package if you'd like to view the Linux HOWTOs with your web browser off your own machine, or if you'd like to provide the HTML HOWTOs from your web server.

howto-indonesian -- (Version 6.0, 8,491K)

This package contains the Linux HOWTO documents that have been translated into Indonesian. Linux HOWTOs are detailed documents which describe a specific aspect of configuring or using Linux.

Install the howto-indonesian package if you'd like to use the Linux HOWTOs in Indonesian. Please note that not all of the HOWTOs have been translated. If you need to have a complete set of HOWTOs, you'll need to install the English version (the howto package).

howto-italian -- (Version 6.0, 21,596K)

This package contains the Linux HOWTO documents that have been translated into Italian. Linux HOWTOs are detailed documents which describe a specific aspect of configuring or using Linux.

Install the howto-italian package if you'd like to use the Linux HOWTOs in Italian. Please note that not all of the HOWTOs have been translated. If you need to have a complete set of HOWTOs, you'll need to install the English version (the howto package).

howto-japanese -- (Version 6.0, 11,888K)

This package contains the Linux HOWTO documents that have been translated into Japanese. Linux HOWTOs are detailed documents which describe a specific aspect of configuring or using Linux.

Install the howto-japanese package if you'd like to use the Linux HOWTOs in Japanese. Please note that not all of the HOWTOs have been translated. If you need to have a complete set of HOWTOs, you'll need to install the English version (the howto package).

howto-korean -- (Version 6.0, 19,242K)

This package contains the Linux HOWTO documents that have been translated into Korean. Linux HOWTOs are detailed documents which describe a specific aspect of configuring or using Linux.

Install the howto-korean package if you'd like to use the Linux HOWTOs in Korean. Please note that not all of the HOWTOs are translated. If you need to have a complete set of HOWTOs, you'll need to install the English version (the howto package).

howto-polish -- (Version 6.0, 9,474K)

This package contains the Linux HOWTO documents that have been translated into Polish. Linux HOWTOs are detailed documents which describe a specific aspect of configuring or using Linux.

Install the howto-polish package if you'd like to use the Linux HOWTOs in Polish. Please note that not all of the HOWTOs have been translated. If you need to have a complete set of HOWTOs, you'll need to install the English version (the howto package).

howto-serbian -- (Version 6.0, 37K)

This package contains the Linux HOWTO documents that have been translated into Serbian. Linux HOWTOs are detailed documents which describe a specific aspect of configuring or using Linux.

Install the howto-serbian package if you'd like to use the Linux HOWTOs in Serbian. Please note that not all of the HOWTOs are translated. If you need to have a complete set of HOWTOs, you'll need to install the English version (the howto package).

howto-sgml -- (Version 6.0, 9,767K)

The howto-sgml package contains the Linux HOWTO documents in SGML format. The SGML format documents are the ``source'' files. Other file formats (text, PostScript(TM), DVI, HTML) are translated from the SGML documents. Linux HOWTOs are detailed documents which describe a specific aspect of configuring or using Linux.

Install the howto-sgml package if you'd like to use the Linux HOWTO documents in SGML format.

howto-slovenian -- (Version 6.0, 3,791K)

This package contains the Linux HOWTO documents that have been translated into Slovenian. Linux HOWTOs are detailed documents which describe a specific aspect of configuring or using Linux.

Install the howto-slovenian package if you'd like to use the Linux HOWTOs in Slovenian. Please note that not all of the HOWTOs have been translated. If you need to have a complete set of HOWTOs, you'll need to install the English version (the howto package).

howto-spanish -- (Version 6.0, 7,739K)

This package contains the Linux HOWTO documents that have been translated into Spanish. Linux HOWTOs are detailed documents which describe a specific aspect of configuring or using Linux.

Install the howto-spanish package if you'd like to use the Linux HOWTOs in Spanish. Please note that not all of the HOWTOs have been translated. If you need to have a complete set of HOWTOs, you'll need to install the English version (the howto package).

howto-swedish -- (Version 6.0, 4,009K)

This package contains the Linux HOWTO documents that have been translated into Swedish. Linux HOWTOs are detailed documents which describe a specific aspect of configuring or using Linux.

Install the howto-swedish package if you'd like to use the Linux HOWTOs in Swedish. Please note that not all of the HOWTOs have been translated. If you need to have a complete set of HOWTOs, you'll need to install the English version (the howto package).

howto-turkish -- (Version 6.0, 816K)

This package contains the Linux HOWTO documents that have been translated into Turkish. Linux HOWTOs are detailed documents which describe a specific aspect of configuring or using Linux.

Install the howto-turkish package if you'd like to use the Linux HOWTOs in Turkish. Please note that not all of the HOWTOs have been translated. If you need to have a complete set of HOWTOs, you'll need to install the English version (the howto package).

indexhtml -- (Version 6.0, 17K)

[W] [S]

The indexhtml package contains the HTML page and graphics for a welcome page shown by your Web browser, which you'll see after you've successfully installed Red Hat Linux.

The Web page provided by indexhtml tells you how to register your Red Hat software and how to get any support that you might need.

install-guide -- (Version 3.2, 1,373K)

The install-guide contains the Linux Documentation Project (LDP) Getting Started Guide in HTML format. The LDP Getting Started Guide is intended to be an installation manual and an entry-level guide to Linux. If you're installing the Red Hat Linux operating system, you should ignore the installation instructions included here and instead use Red Hat's Installation.

You should install the install-guide package if you'd like to use the LDP's Getting Started Guide in HTML format using your web browser off your own machine, or if you'd like to provide the LDP's Getting Started Guide on your web server.

kernel-doc -- (Version 2.2.5, 2,307K)

This package contains documentation files form the kernel source. Various bits of information about the Linux kernel and the device drivers shipped with it are documented in these files. You also might want install this package if you need a reference to the options that can be passed to Linux kernel modules at load time.

lpg -- (Version 0.4, 1,739K)

The lpg package includes a generic guide for programming on Linux systems, in HTML format. You may want to check the Linux Documentation Project's website at http://sunsite.unc.edu/LDP/ for more information and possible updates to the programming guide.

If you'd like to view the Linux programming guide using your web browser from files on your own machine, or if you'd like to provide it from your web server, you should install the lpg package.

man-pages -- (Version 1.23, 1,795K)

[W] [S]

A large collection of man pages (reference material) from the Linux Documentation Project (LDP). The man pages are organized into the following sections:

Section 1: User commands (intro only) **Section 2:** System calls **Section 3:** Libc calls Section 4: Devices (e.g., hd, sd) **Section 5:** File formats and protocols (e.g., wtmp, /etc/passwd, nfs) **Section 6:** Games (intro only) **Section 7:** Conventions, macro packages, etc. (e.g., nroff, ascii) **Section 8:** System administration (intro only).

nag -- (Version 1.0, 1,217K)

The nag package contains the Linux Documentation Project's Network Administrators' Guide. The NAG covers the wide world of Linux networking, including TCP/IP, UUCP, SLIP, DNS, mail systems, NNTP and news systems, and NFS. Be sure to check the LDP's website at http://sunsite.unc.edu/linux/ldp.html for possible updates to the NAG.

Install the nag package if you'd like to use the LDP's Network Administrators' Guide off your own machine.

python-docs -- (Version 1.5.1, 2,611K)

The python-docs package contains documentation on the Python programming language and interpreter. The documentation is provided in ASCII text files and in LaTeX source files.

Install the python-docs package if you'd like to use the documentation for the Python language.

rhl-alpha-install-addend-en -- (Version 6.0, 200K)

The rhl-alpha-install-addend-en package contains the Red Hat Linux 6.0 Alpha Installation Addendum document in HTML format.

Install the rhl-alpha-install-addend-en package if you'd like to use an HTML version of the Alpha Installation Addendum loaded on your own machine.

rhl-getting-started-guide-en -- (Version 6.0, 709K)

The rhl-getting-started-guide-en contains the Red Hat Linux 6.0 Getting Started Guide document in HTML format.

Install the rhl-getting-started-guide-en package if you'd like to use an HTML version of the Getting Started Guide loaded on your own machine.

rhl-install-guide-en -- (Version 6.0, 2,428K)

The rhl-install-guide-en package contains the Red Hat Linux 6.0 Installation Guide in HTML format. An online copy of the Red Hat **Linux 6.0 Installation Guide** is available from the Red Hat, Inc. web page at **http://www.redhat.com.**

Install the rhl-install-guide-en package if you would like to use an HTML version of the Installation Guide from your own machine.

sag -- (Version 0.6, 644K)

The Linux Documentation Project's System Administrators' Guide, provided in HTML format. This document provides a generic guide to Linux system administration. Check the Linux Documentation Project's website at http://sunsite.unc.edu/LDP/ldp.html for other formats of this document or for any updates.

Install the sag package if you'd like to use the HTML version of the LDP's System Administrators' Guide on your own machine.

sendmail-doc -- (Version 8.9.3, 1,360K)

The sendmail-doc package contains documentation about the Sendmail Mail Transport Agent (MTA) program, including release notes, the Sendmail FAQ and a few papers written about Sendmail. The papers are provided in PostScript(TM) and troff formats.

Install the sendmail-doc package if you need documentation about Sendmail.

specspo -- (Version 6.0, 859K)

The specspo package contains the portable object catalogues used to internationalize Red Hat packages.

D.5 System Environment

This section contains packages that are required to provide the Red Hat Linux system environment.

D.5.1 Base

This section contains packages that are required for the basic system environment.

MAKEDEV -- (Version 2.5, 34K)

[B]

The /dev directory contains important files which correspond to the hardware on your system, such as sound cards, serial or printer ports, tape and CD-ROM drives and more. MAKEDEV is a script which helps you create and maintain the files in your /dev directory.

These are the files needed to install MAKEDEV.

SysVinit -- (Version 2.74, 151K)

[B]

The SysVinit package contains a group of processes that control the very basic functions of your system. SysVinit is the first program started by the Linux kernel when the system boots, controlling the startup, running and shutdown of all other programs.

adjtimex -- (Version 1.3, 23K)

Adjtimex is a kernel clock management program, which the superuser may use to correct any drift in the system's clock. Users can use adjtimex to view the time variables.

authconfig -- (Version 1.8, 27K)

[B]

Authconfig is a terminal mode program for setting up Network Information Service (NIS) and shadow (more secure)passwords on your system. Authconfig also configures the system to automatically turn on NIS at system startup.

basesystem -- (Version 6.0, 0K)

[B]

Basesystem defines the components of a basic Red Hat Linux system (for example, the package installation orderto use during bootstrapping).Basesystem should be the first package installed on a system, and it should never be removed.

chkconfig -- (Version 1.0.6, 82K)

[B]

Chkconfig is a basic system utility. It updates and queries runlevel information for system services. Chkconfig manipulates the numerous symbolic links in /etc/rc.d, so system administrators don't have to manually edit the symbolic links as often.

chkfontpath -- (Version 1.4.1, 18K)

[W] [S]

This is a simple terminal mode program for adding, removing and listing the directories contained in the X font server's path. It is mostly intended to be used 'internally' by RPM when packages with fonts are added or removed, but it may be useful as a stand-alone utility in some instances.

control-panel -- (Version 3.11, 175K)

[W] [S]

The Red Hat control panel is an X program launcher for the X Window System. Both convenient and pleasing, the Red Hat control panel allows you easy access to numerous X-based system administration tools included in your Red Hat Linux system.

Eventually, you'll want to work with many of your system administration tools; this package helps you locate and launch many of them.

crontabs -- (Version 1.7, 4K)

[B]

The crontabs package contains root crontab files. Crontab is the program used to install, uninstall or list the tables used to drive the cron daemon. The cron daemon checks the crontab files to see when particular commands are scheduled to be executed. If commands are scheduled, it executes them.

Crontabs handles a basic system function, so it should be installed on your system.

dev -- (Version 2.7.7, 45K)

[B]

The Red Hat Linux operating system uses file system entries to represent devices (CD-ROMs, floppy drives, etc.) attached to the machine. All of these entries are in the /dev tree (although they don't have to be). This package contains the most commonly used /dev entries.

The dev package is a basic part of your Red Hat Linux system and it needs to be installed.

e2fsprogs -- (Version 1.14, 1,134K)

[B]

The e2fsprogs package contains a number of utilities for creating, checking, modifying and correcting any inconsistencies in second extended (ext2) filesystems. E2fsprogs contains e2fsck (used to repair filesystem inconsistencies after an unclean shutdown), mke2fs (used to initialize a partition to contain an empty ext2 filesystem), debugfs (used to examine the internal structure of a filesystem, to manually repair a corrupted filesystem or to create test cases for e2fsck), tune2fs (used to modify filesystem parameters) and most of the other core ext2fs filesystem utilities.

You should install the e2fsprogs package if you need to manage the performance of an ext2 filesystem.

eject -- (Version 2.0.2, 46K)

[B]

The eject program allows the user to eject removable media (typically CD-ROMs, floppy disks or Iomega Jaz or Zip disks) using software control. Eject can also control some multi- disk CD changers and even some devices' auto-eject features.

Install eject if you'd like to eject removable media using software control.

etcskel -- (Version 2.0, 2K)

[B]

The etcskel package is part of the basic Red Hat system. Etcskel provides the /etc/skel directory's files. These files (.Xdefaults, .bash_logout, .bash_profile, .bashrc) are then placed in every new user's home directory when new accounts are created.

filesystem -- (Version 1.3.4, 80K)

[B]

The filesystem package is one of the basic packages that is installed on a Red Hat Linux system. Filesystem contains the basic directory layout for a Linux operating system, including the correct permissions for the directories.

genromfs -- (Version 0.3, 12K)

Genromfs is a tool for creating romfs filesystems, which are lightweight, read-only filesystems supported by the Linux kernel.

info -- (Version 3.12f, 245K)

[B]

The GNU project uses the texinfo file format for much of its documentation. The info package provides a standalone TTY-based browser program for viewing texinfo files.

You should install info, because GNU's texinfo documentation is a valuable source of information about the software on your system.

initscripts -- (Version 4.16, 152K)

[B]

The initscripts package contains the basic system scripts used to boot your Red Hat system, change run levels, and shut the system down cleanly. Initscripts also contains the scripts that activate and deactivate most network interfaces.

ipchains -- (Version 1.3.8, 316K)

[W] [S]

Linux IP Firewalling Chains is an update to (and hopefully an improvement upon) the normal Linux Firewalling code, for 2.0 and 2.1 kernels. It lets you do things like firewalls, IP masquerading, etc.

isapnptools -- (Version 1.18, 237K)

[B]

The isapnptools package contains utilities for configuring ISA Plug-and-Play (PnP) cards/boards which are in compliance with the PnP ISA Specification Version 1.0a. ISA PnP cards use registers instead of jumpers for setting the board address and interrupt assignments. The cards also contain descriptions of the resources which need to be allocated. The BIOS on your system, or isapnptools, uses a protocol described in the specification to find all of the PnP boards and allocate the resources so that none of them conflict.

Note that the BIOS doesn't do a very good job of allocating resources. So isapnptools is suitable for all systems, whether or not they include a PnP BIOS. In fact, a PnP BIOS adds some complications. A PnP BIOS may already activate some cards so that the drivers can find them. Then these tools can unconfigure them or change their settings, causing all sorts of nasty effects. If you have PnP network cards that already work, you should read through the documentation files very carefully before you use isapnptools.

Install isapnptools if you need utilities for configuring ISA PnP cards.

kbdconfig -- (Version 1.9.2, 58K)

[B]

The kbdconfig utility is a terminal mode program for setting the keyboard map for your system. Keyboard maps are necessary for using any keyboard besides the US default keyboard. Kbdconfig will load the selected keymap before exiting and configure your machine to use that keymap automatically after rebooting.

You should install kbdconfig if you need a utility for changing your keyboard map.

ld.so -- (Version 1.9.5, 247K)

[B]

This package contains the shared library configuration tool, ldconfig, which is required by many packages. It also includes the shared library loader and dynamic loader for Linux libc 5.

ldconfig -- (Version 1.9.5, 223K)

[B]

Ldconfig is a basic system program which determines run-time link bindings between ld.so and shared libraries. Ldconfig scans a running system and sets up the symbolic links that are used to load shared libraries properly. It also creates a cache (/etc/ld.so.cache) which speeds the loading of programs which use shared libraries.

lilo -- (Version 0.21, 1,095K)

[B]

LILO (LInux LOader) is a basic system program which boots your Linux system. LILO loads the Linux kernel from a floppy or a hard drive, boots the kernel and passes control of the system to the kernel. LILO can also boot other operating systems.

logrotate -- (Version 3.2, 50K)

[B]

The logrotate utility is designed to simplify the administration of log files on a system which generates a lot of log files. Logrotate allows for the automatic rotation compression, removal and mailing of log files. Logrotate can be set to handle a log file daily,weekly, monthly or when the log file gets to a certain size. Normally, logrotate runs as a daily cron job.

Install the logrotate package if you need a utility to deal with the log files on your system.

losetup -- (Version 2.9o, 9K)

[B]

Linux supports a special block device called the loop device, which maps a normal file onto a virtual block device. This allows for the file to be used as a "virtual file system" inside another file.

Losetup is used to associate loop devices with regular files or block devices, to detach loop devices and to query the status of a loop device.

mailcap -- (Version 2.0.1, 34K)

[B]

The mailcap file is used by the metamail program. Metamail reads the mailcap file to determine how it should display non-text or multimedia material. Basically, mailcap associates a particular type of file with a particular program that a mail agent or other program can call in order to handle the file.

Mailcap should be installed to allow certain programs to be able to handle non-text files.

man -- (Version 1.5g, 215K)

[B]

The man package includes three tools for finding information and/or documentation about your Linux system: man, apropos and whatis. The man system formats and displays on-line manual pages about commands or functions on your system. Apropos searches the whatis database (containing short descriptions of system commands) for a string. Whatis searches its own database for a complete word.

The man package should be installed on your system because it is the primary way for finding documentation.

mingetty -- (Version 0.9.4, 32K)

[B]

The mingetty program is a lightweight, minimalist getty program for use only on virtual consoles. Mingetty is not suitable for serial lines (you should use the mgetty program instead for that purpose).

mkbootdisk -- (Version 1.2, 5K)

[B]

The mkbootdisk program creates a standalone boot floppy disk for booting the running system. The created boot disk will look for the root filesystem on the device mentioned in /etc/fstab and includes an initial ramdisk image which will load any necessary SCSI modules for the system.

mkinitrd -- (Version 2.0, 7K)

[B]

Mkinitrd creates filesystem images for use as initial ramdisk (initrd) images. These ramdisk images are often used to preload the block device modules (SCSI or RAID) needed to access the root filesystem.

In other words, generic kernels can be built without drivers for any SCSI adapters which load the SCSI driver as a module.Since the kernel needs to read those modules, but in this case it isn't able to address the SCSI adapter, an initial ramdisk is used. The initial ramdisk is loaded by the operating system loader (normally LILO) and is available to the kernel as soon as the ramdisk is loaded. The ramdisk image loads the proper SCSI adapter and allows the kernel to mount the root filesystem. The mkinitrd program creates such a ramdisk using information found in the /etc/conf.modules file.

mkkickstart -- (Version 1.2, 5K)

The mkkickstart program writes a kickstart description from the host machine. The kickstart description can then be used, during a CD-ROM or NFS installation, to automatically build that machine's configuration of Red Hat Linux on one or more other machines.

Install mkkickstart if you want to use the kickstart method to automatically install Red Hat Linux.

mktemp -- (Version 1.5, 8K)

[B]

The mktemp utility takes a given file name template and overwrites a portion of it to create a unique file name. This allows shell scripts and other programs to safely create and use /tmp files.

Install the mktemp package if you need to use shell scripts or other programs which will create and use unique /tmp files.

mount -- (Version 2.9o, 132K)

[B]

The mount package contains the mount, umount, swapon and swapoff programs. Accessible files on your system are arranged in one big tree or hierarchy. These files can be spread out over several devices. The mount command attaches a filesystem on some device to your system's file tree. The umount command detaches a filesystem from the tree. Swapon and swapoff,respectively, specify and disable devices and files for paging and swapping.

mouseconfig -- (Version 3.9, 184K)

[B]

Mouseconfig is a text-based mouse configuration tool. Mouseconfig sets up the files and links needed for configuring and using a mouse on a Red Hat Linux system. The mouseconfig tool can be used to set the correct mouse type for programs like gpm,and can be used with Xconfigurator to set up the mouse for the X Window System.

net-tools -- (Version 1.51, 395K)

[B]

The net-tools package contains the basic tools needed for setting up networking: arp, rarp, ifconfig, netstat, ethers and route.

ntsysv -- (Version 1.0.6, 23K)

[B]

ntsysv updates and queries runlevel information for system services. ntsysv relieves system administrators of having to directly manipulate the numerous symbolic links in /etc/rc.d.

pam -- (Version 0.66, 1,898K)

[B]

PAM (Pluggable Authentication Modules) is a system security tool which allows system administrators to set authentication policy without having to recompile programs which do authentication.

passwd -- (Version 0.58, 15K)

[B]

The passwd package contains a system utility (passwd) which sets and/or changes passwords, using PAM (Pluggable Authentication Modules).

To use passwd, you should have PAM installed on your system.

pwdb -- (Version 0.58, 424K)

[B]

The pwdb package contains libpwdb, the password database library. Libpwdb is a library which implements a generic user information database. Libpwdb was specifically designed to work with Linux's PAM (Pluggable Authentication Modules). Libpwdb allows configurable access to and management of security tools like /etc/passwd, /etc/shadow and network authentication systems including NIS and Radius.

quota -- (Version 1.66, 77K)

[B]

The quota package contains system administration tools for monitoring and limiting users' and or groups' disk usage, per filesystem.

raidtools -- (Version 0.90, 135K)

This package includes the tools you need to set up and maintain a software RAID device under Linux. It only works with Linux 2.2 kernels and later, or 2.0 kernel specifically patched with newer raid support.

redhat-logos -- (Version 1.0.5, 512K)

[B]

redhat-logos (the "Package") contains files of the Red Hat "Shadow Man" logo and the RPM logo (the "Logos"). Red Hat, the Red Hat "Shadow Man" logo, RPM, and the RPM logo are trademarks or registered trademarks of Red Hat, Inc. in the United States and other countries.

Red Hat, Inc. grants you the right to use the Package during the normal operation of other software programs that call upon the Package. Red Hat, Inc. grants to you the right and license to copy and redistribute the Package, but only in conjunction with copying or redistributing additional software packages that call upon the Package during the normal course of operation. Such rights are granted to you without fee, provided that:

1. The above copyright notice and this license are included with each copy you make, and they remain intact and are not altered, deleted, or modified in any way; 2. You do not modify the Package, or the appearance of any or all of the Logos in any manner; and 3.

You do not use any or all of the Logos as, or as part of, a trademark, trade name, or trade identifier; or in any other fashion except as set forth in this license.

NO WARRANTY. THIS PACKAGE IS PROVIDED "AS IS" AND ANY EXPRESS OR IMPLIED WARRANTIES,INCLUDING, BUT NOT LIMITED TO, THE IMPLIED WARRANTIES OF MERCHANTABILITY AND FITNESS FOR A PARTICULAR PURPOSE ARE DISCLAIMED. IN NO EVENT SHALL RED HAT SOFTWARE, INC. BE LIABLE FOR ANY DIRECT, INDIRECT, INCIDENTAL, SPECIAL, EXEMPLARY, OR CONSEQUENTIAL DAMAGES (INCLUDING, BUT NOT LIMITED TO, PROCUREMENT OF SUBSTITUTE GOODS OR SERVICES;LOSS OF USE, DATA OR PROFITS; OR BUSINESS INTERRUPTION) HOWEVER CAUSED AND ON ANY THEORY OF LIABILITY, WHETHER IN CONTRACT, STRICT LIABILITY, OR TORT (INCLUDING NEGLIGENCE OR OTHERWISE) ARISING IN ANY WAY OUT OF THE USE OF THIS PACKAGE, EVEN IF ADVISED OF THE POSSIBILITY OF SUCH DAMAGE.

redhat-release -- (Version 6.0, 0K)

[B]

Red Hat Linux release file

rootfiles -- (Version 5.2, 1K)

[B]

The rootfiles package contains basic required files that are placed in the root user's account. These files are basically the same as the files found in the etcskel package, which are placed in regular users' home directories.

rpm -- (Version 3.0, 1,659K)

[B]

The Red Hat Package Manager (RPM) is a powerful command line driven package management system capable of installing, uninstalling, verifying, querying, and updating software packages. Each software package consists of an archive of files along with information about the package like its version, a description, etc.

setup -- (Version 2.0.2, 15K)

[B]

The setup package contains a set of very important system configuration and setup files, such as passwd, group, profile and more.

You should install the setup package because you will find yourself using its many features for system administration.

shadow-utils -- (Version 980403, 584K)

[B]

The shadow-utils package includes the necessary programs for converting UNIX password files to the shadow password format, plus programs for managing user and group accounts. The pwconv command converts passwords to the shadow password format. The pwunconv command unconverts shadow passwords and generates an npasswd file (a standard UNIX password file). The pwck command checks the integrity of password and shadow files. The lastlog command prints out the last login times for all users. The useradd, userdel and usermod commands are used for managing user accounts. The groupadd,groupdel and groupmod commands are used for managing group accounts.

shapecfg -- (Version 2.0.36, 6K)

The Shapecfg program configures and adjusts traffic shaper bandwidth limiters. Traffic shaping means setting parameters to which traffic should conform - setting the standards for bandwidth consumption.

To use Shapecfg, you must have also installed the kernel which supports the shaper module (kernel versions 2.0.36 or later and late 2.1.x kernels).

Install the shapecfg package if you want to set traffic bandwidth parameters, and if you have the appropriate kernel.

termcap -- (Version 9.12.6, 424K)

[B]

The termcap package provides the /etc/termcap file. /etc/termcap is a database which defines the capabilities of various terminals and terminal emulators. Certain programs use the /etc/termcap file to access various features of terminals (the bell, colors, and graphics, etc.).

timeconfig -- (Version 2.7, 388K)

[B]

The timeconfig package contains two utilities: timeconfig and setclock. Timeconfig provides a simple text mode tool for configuring the time parameters in /etc/sysconfig/clock and /etc/localtime. The setclock tool sets the hardware clock on the system to the current time stored in the system clock.

tmpwatch -- (Version 1.7, 9K)

[B]

The tmpwatch utility recursively searches through specified directories and removes files which have not been accessed in a specified period of time. Tmpwatch is normally used to clean up directories which are used for temporarily holding files (for example, /tmp). Tmpwatch ignores symlinks, won't switch filesystems and only removes empty directories and regular files.

utempter -- (Version 0.5, 21K)

[B]

Utempter is a utility which allows programs to log information to a privledged file (/var/run/utmp), without compromising system security. It accomplishes this task by acting as a buffer between root and the programs.

util-linux -- (Version 2.9o, 960K)

[B]

The util-linux package contains a large variety of low-level system utilities that are necessary for a Linux system to function. Among many features, Util-linux contains the fdisk configuration tool and login program.

You should install util-linux for its essential system tools.

vixie-cron -- (Version 3.0.1, 57K)

[B]

The vixie-cron package contains the Vixie version of cron. Cron is a standard UNIX daemon that runs specified programs at scheduled times. Vixie cron adds better security and more powerful configuration options to the standard version of cron.

yp-tools -- (Version 2.2, 160K)

[W] [S]

The Network Information Service (NIS) is a system which provides network information (login names, passwords, home directories, group information) to all of the machines on a network. NIS can enable users to login on any machine on the network, as long as the machine has the NIS client programs running and the user's password is recorded in the NIS passwd database. NIS was formerly known as Sun Yellow Pages (YP).

This package's NIS implementation is based on FreeBSD's YP and is a special port for glibc 2.x and libc versions 5.4.21 and later. This package only provides the NIS client programs. In order to use the clients, you'll need to already have an NIS server running on your network. An NIS server is provided in the ypserv package.

Install the yp-tools package if you need NIS client programs for machines on your network. You will also need to install the ypbind package on every machine running NIS client programs. If you need an NIS server, you'll need to install the ypserv package on one machine on the network.

D.5.2 Daemons

This section contains packages associated with the daemon processes that run under Red Hat Linux.

ORBit -- (Version 0.4.3, 871K)

[W] [S]

ORBit is a high-performance CORBA ORB (object request broker). It allows programs to send requests and receive replies from other programs, regardless of the locations of the two programs.

You will need to install this package and the related header files, libraries and utilities if you want to write programs that use CORBA technology.

XFree86-xfs -- (Version 3.3.3.1, 485K)

[W] [S]

This is a font server for XFree86. You can serve fonts to other X servers remotely with this package, and the remote system will be able to use all fonts installed on the font server, even if they are not installed on the remote computer.

am-utils -- (Version 6.0, 1,945K)

Am-utils includes an updated version of Amd, the popular BSD automounter. An automounter is a program which maintains a cache of mounted filesystems. Filesystems are mounted when they are first referenced by the user and unmounted after a certain period of inactivity. Amd supports a variety of filesystems, including NFS, UFS, CD-ROMS and local drives.

You should install am-utils if you need a program for automatically mounting and unmounting filesystems.

anonftp -- (Version 2.8, 1,540K)

[S]

The anonftp package contains the files you need in order to allow anonymous FTP access to your machine. Anonymous FTP access allows anyone to download files from your machine without having a user account. Anonymous FTP is a popular way of making programs available via the Internet.

You should install anonftp if you would like to enable anonymous FTP downloads from your machine.

apache -- (Version 1.3.6, 2,056K)

[S]

Apache is a powerful, full-featured, efficient and freely-available Web server. Apache is also the most popular Web server on the Internet.

This package will install the Apache Web server on your machine.

apmd -- (Version 3.0beta5, 54K)

[B]

This is a Advanced Power Management daemon and utilities. It can watch your notebook's battery and warn all users when the battery is low.

Patches to Rik Faith's original version have been added for shutting down the PCMCIA sockets before a suspend.

at -- (Version 3.1.7, 64K)

[B]

At and batch read commands from standard input or from a specified file. At allows you to specify that a command will be run at a particular time (now or a specified time in the future). Batch will execute commands when the system load levels drop to a particular level. Both commands use /bin/sh to run the commands.

You should install the at package if you need a utility that will do time-oriented job control. Note: you should use crontab instead, if it is a recurring job that will need to be repeated at the same time every day/week/etc.

autofs -- (Version 3.1.3, 127K)

Autofs controls the operation of the automount daemons. The automount daemons automatically mount filesystems when you use them and unmount them after a period of inactivity. Filesystems can include network filesystems, CD-ROMs, floppies and others.

Install this package if you want a program for automatically mounting and unmounting filesystems. If your Red Hat Linux machine is on a network, you should install autofs.

bdflush -- (Version 1.5, 10K)

[B]

The bdflush process starts the kernel daemon which flushes dirty buffers back to disk (i.e., writes all unwritten data to disk). This helps to prevent the buffers from growing too stale.

Bdflush is a basic system process that must run for your system to operate properly.

bind -- (Version 8.2, 4,370K)

[S]

Bind includes the named name server, which resolves host names to IP addresses (and vice versa), and a resolver library (a set of routines in a system library that provide the interface for programs to use when accessing domain name services). A name server is a network service which enables clients to name resources or objects and share this information with other network machines. The named name server can be used on workstations as a caching name server, but is generally only needed on one machine for an entire network. Note that the configuration files for making bind act as a simple caching nameserver are included in the caching-nameserver package.

Install the bind package if you need a name server for your network. If you want bind to act a caching name server, you will also need to install the caching-nameserver package.

bootparamd -- (Version 0.10, 18K)

The bootparamd process provides bootparamd, a server process which provides the information needed by diskless clients in order for them to successfully boot. Bootparamd looks first in /etc/bootparams for an entry for that particular client; if a local bootparams file doesn't exist, it looks at the appropriate Network Information Service (NIS) map. Some network boot loaders (notably Sun's) rely on special boot server code on the server, in addition to the rarp and tftp servers. This bootparamd server process is compatible with SunOS bootparam clients and servers which need that boot server code.

You should install bootparamd if you need to provide boot information to diskless clients on your network.

caching-nameserver -- (Version 6.0, 3K)

[S]

The caching-nameserver package includes the configuration files which will make bind, the DNS name server, act as a simple caching nameserver. Many users on dialup connections use this package along with bind for such a purpose.

If you would like to set up a caching name server, you'll need to install the caching-nameserver package; you'll also need to install bind.

cleanfeed -- (Version 0.95.7b, 107K)

[S]

Cleanfeed is an automatic spam filter for Usenet news servers and routers (INN, Cyclone, Typhoon, Breeze and NNTPRelay). Cleanfeed is highly configurable, easily modified and very fast. It can be configured to block binary posts to non-binary newsgroups, to cancel already-rejected articles, and to reject some spamming from local users.

Install the cleanfeed package if you need a spam filter for a Usenet news server.

comsat -- (Version 0.10, 17K)

The biff client and comsat server are an antiquated method of asynchronous mail notification. Although they are still supported, most users use their shell's MAIL variable (or csh shell's mail variable) to check for mail, or a dedicated application like xbiff or xmailbox. If the comsat service is not enabled, biff won't work and you'll need to use either the MAIL or mail variable.

You may want to install biff if you'd like to be notified when mail arrives. However, you should probably check out the more modern methodologies of mail notification (xbiff or xmailbox) instead.

dhcp -- (Version 2.0b1pl6, 217K)

DHCP (Dynamic Host Configuration Protocol) is a protocol which allows individual devices on an IP network to get their own network configuration information (IP address, subnetmask, broadcast address, etc.) from a DHCP server. The overall purpose of DHCP is to make it easier to administer a large network. The dhcp package includes the DHCP server and a DHCP relay agent.

You should install dhcp if you want to set up a DHCP server on your network. You will also need to install the dhcpcd package, which provides the DHCP client daemon, on client machines.

dhcpcd -- (Version 1.3.17pl2, 332K)

dhcpcd is an implementation of the DHCP client specified in draft-ietf-dhc-dhcp-09 (when -r option is not speci- fied) and RFC1541 (when -r option is specified).

It gets the host information (IP address, netmask, broad- cast address, etc.) from a DHCP server and configures the network interface of the machine on which it is running. It also tries to renew the lease time according to RFC1541 or draft-ietf-dhc-dhcp-09.

esound -- (Version 0.2.12, 183K)

[W] [S]

EsounD -- the Enlightened Sound Daemon -- is a server process that allows multiple applications to share a single sound card. For example, when you're listening to music from your CD and you receive a sound-related event from ICQ, your applications won't have to jockey for the attention of your sound card.

EsounD mixes several audio streams for playback by a single audio device.

Install esound if you'd like to allow for such event sharing by your audio device.

gated -- (Version 3.5.10, 2,434K)

GateD is a modular software program consisting of core services, a routing database, and protocol modules which support multiple routing protocols (RIP versions 1 and 2, DCN HELLO, OSPF version 2, EGP version 2, BGP versions 2 through 4). GateD is designed to handle dynamic routing with a routing database built from the information exchanged by routing protocols.

Install gated if you need a routing daemon.

gpm -- (Version 1.17.5, 258K)

[B]

Gpm provides mouse support to text-based Linux applications like the emacs editor, the Midnight Commander file management system, and other programs. Gpm also provides console cut-and-paste operations using the mouse and includes a program to allow pop-up menus to appear at the click of a mouse button.

Gpm should be installed if you intend to use a mouse with your Red Hat Linux system.

imap -- (Version 4.5, 1,447K)

The imap package provides server daemons for both the IMAP (Internet Message Access Protocol) and POP (Post Office Protocol) mail access protocols. The POP protocol uses a "post office" machine to collect mail for users and allows users to download their mail to their local machine for reading. The IMAP protocol provides the functionality of POP, but allows a user to read mail on a remote machine without downloading it to their local machine.

Install the imap package if you need a server to support the IMAP or the POP mail access protocols.

inews -- (Version 2.2, 74K)

The inews program is used by some news programs (for example, inn and trn) to post Usenet news articles to local news servers. Inews reads an article from a file or standard input, adds headers, performs some consistency checks and then sends the article to the local news server specified in the inn.conf file.

Install inews if you need a program for posting Usenet articles to local news servers.

inn -- (Version 2.2, 6,262K)

[S]

INN (InterNetNews) is a complete system for serving Usenet news and/or private newsfeeds. INN includes innd, an NNTP (NetNews Transport Protocol) server, and nnrpd, a newsreader that is spawned for each client. Both innd and nnrpd vary slightly from the NNTP protocol, but not in ways that are easily noticed.

Install the inn package if you need a complete system for serving and reading Usenet news. You may also need to install inn-devel, if you are going to use a separate program which interfaces to INN, like newsgate or tin.

intimed -- (Version 1.10, 210K)

The intimed package contains a server (in.timed), which keeps networked machines' clocks correctly synchronized to the server's time.

Install intimed if you need a network time server.

knfsd -- (Version 1.2.2, 158K)

[W] [S]

This is the *new* kernel NFS server and related tools. It provides a much higher level of performance than the traditional Linux user-land NFS server.

lpr -- (Version 0.35, 180K)

[W] [S]

The lpr package provides the basic system utility for managing printing services. Lpr manages print queues, sends print jobs to local and remote printers and accepts print jobs from remote clients.

If you will be printing from your system, you'll need to install the lpr package.

mars-nwe -- (Version 0.99pl15, 657K)

[S]

The mars_nwe (MARtin Stover's NetWare Emulator) package enables Linux to provide both file and print services for NetWare clients (i.e., providing the services of a Novell NetWare file server). Mars_nwe allows the sharing of files between Linux machines and Novell NetWare clients, using NetWare's native IPX protocol suite.

Install the mars_nwe package if you need a Novell NetWare file server on your Red Hat Linux system.

mcserv -- (Version 4.5.30, 19K)

The Midnight Commander file management system will allow you to manipulate the files on a remote machine as if they were local. This is only possible if the remote machine is running the mcserv server program. Mcserv provides clients running Midnight Commander with access to the host's file systems.

Install mcserv on machines if you want to access their file systems remotely using the Midnight Commander file management system.

mod_perl -- (Version 1.19, 1,557K)

Mod_perl incorporates a Perl interpreter into the Apache web server, so that the Apache web server can directly execute Perl code. Mod_perl links the Perl runtime library into the Apache web server and provides an object-oriented Perl interface for Apache's C language API. The end result is a quicker CGI script turnaround process, since no external Perl interpreter has to be started.

Install mod_perl if you're installing the Apache web server and you'd like for it to directly incorporate a Perl interpreter.

mod_php -- (Version 2.0.1, 676K)

PHP is an HTML-embedded scripting language. PHP attempts to make it easy for developers to write dynamically generated web pages. PHP also offers built-in database integration for several commercial and non-commercial database management systems, so writing a database-enabled web page with PHP is fairly simple. The most common use of PHP coding is probably as a replacement for CGI scripts. The mod_php module enables the Apache web server to understand and process the embedded PHP language in web pages.

This package contains PHP/FI, or PHP version 2.01. Unless you use applications which specifically rely on PHP/FI, you should instead install the mod_php3 package, which contains PHP3. PHP3 is an improved and more capable update to PHP/FI.

mod_php3 -- (Version 3.0.7, 3,903K)

PHP is an HTML-embedded scripting language. PHP attempts to make it easy for developers to write dynamically generated web pages. PHP also offers built-in database integration for several commercial and non-commercial database management systems, so writing a database-enabled web page with PHP is fairly simple. The most common use of PHP coding is probably as a replacement for CGI scripts. The mod_php module enables the Apache web server to understand and process the embedded PHP language in web pages.

This package contains PHP3, or PHP version 3.05. If you use applications which specifically rely on PHP/FI, you should instead install the PHP/FI module contained in the mod_php package. If you're just starting with PHP, you should install this package. You'll also need to install the Apache web server.

netkit-base -- (Version 0.10, 60K)

[W] [S]

The netkit-base package contains the basic networking tools ping and inetd. The ping command sends a series of ICMP protocol ECHO_REQUEST packets to a specified network host and can tell you if that machine is alive and receiving network traffic. Inetd listens on certain Internet sockets for connection requests, decides what program should receive each request, and starts up that program.

The netkit-base package should be installed on any machine that is on a network.

nscd -- (Version 2.1.1, 33K)

nscd caches name service lookups; it can dramatically improve performance with NIS+, and may help with DNS as well.

You cannot use nscd with 2.0 kernels, due to bugs in the kernel-side thread support. nscd happens to hit these bugs particularly hard.

pidentd -- (Version 2.8.5, 129K)

[W] [S]

The pidentd package contains identd, which implements the RFC1413 identification server. Identd looks up specific TCP/IP connections and returns either the user name or other information about the process that owns the connection.

portmap -- (Version 4.0, 49K)

[W] [S]

The portmapper program is a security tool which prevents theft of NIS (YP), NFS and other sensitive information via the portmapper. A portmapper manages RPC connections, which are used by protocols like NFS and NIS.

The portmap package should be installed on any machine which acts as a server for protocols using RPC.

ppp -- (Version 2.3.7, 300K)

[W] [S]

The ppp package contains the PPP (Point-to-Point Protocol) daemon and documentation for PPP support. The PPP protocol provides a method for transmitting datagrams over serial point-to-point links.

The ppp package should be installed if your machine need to support the PPP protocol.

procmail -- (Version 3.13.1, 201K)

[B]

The procmail program is used by Red Hat Linux for all local mail delivery. In addition to just delivering mail, procmail can be used for automatic filtering, presorting and other mail handling jobs. Procmail is also the basis for the SmartList mailing list processor.

pump -- (Version 0.6.4, 30K)

[B]

DHCP (Dynamic Host Configuration Protocol) and BOOTP (Boot Protocol) are protocols which allow individual devices on an IP network to get their own network configuration information (IP address, subnetmask, broadcast address, etc.) from network servers. The overall purpose of DHCP and BOOTP is to make it easier to administer a large network.

Pump is a combined BOOTP and DHCP client daemon, which allows your machine to retrieve configuration information from a server. You should install this package if you are on a network which uses BOOTP or DHCP.

routed -- (Version 0.10, 39K)

[W] [S]

The routed routing daemon handles incoming RIP traffic and broadcasts outgoing RIP traffic about network traffic routes, in order to maintain current routing tables. These routing tables are essential for a networked computer, so that it knows where packets need to be sent.

The routed package should be installed on any networked machine.

rusers -- (Version 0.10, 54K)

[W] [S]

The rusers program allows users to find out who is logged into various machines on the local network. The rusers command produces output similar to who, but for the specified list of hosts or for all machines on the local network.

Install rusers if you need to keep track of who is logged into your local network.

rwall -- (Version 0.10, 18K)

The rwall command sends a message to all of the users logged into a specified host. Actually, your machine's rwall client sends the message to the rwall daemon running on the specified host, and the rwall daemon relays the message to all of the users logged in to that host. The rwall daemon is run from /etc/inetd.conf and is disabled by default on Red Hat Linux systems (it can be very annoying to keep getting all those messages when you're trying to play Quake--I mean trying to get some work done).

Install rwall if you'd like the ability to send messages to users logged in to a specified host machine.

rwho -- (Version 0.10, 33K)

[W] [S]

The rwho command displays output similar to the output of the who command (it shows who is logged in) for all machines on the local network running the rwho daemon.

Install the rwho command if you need to keep track of the users who are logged in to your local network.

samba -- (Version 2.0.3, 6,339K)

[S]

Samba provides an SMB server which can be used to provide network services to SMB (sometimes called "Lan Manager")clients, including various versions of MS Windows, OS/2, and other Linux machines. Samba also provides some SMB clients,which complement the built-in SMB filesystem in Linux. Samba uses NetBIOS over TCP/IP (NetBT) protocols and does NOT need NetBEUI (Microsoft Raw NetBIOS frame) protocol.

Samba-2 features an almost working NT Domain Control capability and includes the new SWAT (Samba Web Administration Tool) that allows samba's smb.conf file to be remotely managed using your favourite web browser. For the time being this is being enabled on TCP port 901 via inetd.

Please refer to the WHATSNEW.txt document for fixup information. This binary release includes encrypted password support. Please read the smb.conf file and ENCRYPTION.txt in the docs directory for implementation details.

NOTE: Red Hat Linux 5.X Uses PAM which has integrated support for Shadow passwords. Do NOT recompile with the SHADOW_PWD option enabled. Red Hat Linux has built in support for quotas in PAM.

sendmail -- (Version 8.9.3, 506K)

[B]

The Sendmail program is a very widely used Mail Transport Agent (MTA). MTAs send mail from one machine to another.Sendmail is not a client program, which you use to read your email. Sendmail is a behind-the-scenes program which actually moves your email over networks or the Internet to where you want it to go.

If you ever need to reconfigure Sendmail, you'll also need to have the sendmail.cf package installed. If you need documentation on Sendmail, you can install the sendmail-doc package.

sendmail-cf -- (Version 8.9.3, 502K)

This package includes the configuration files which you'd need to generate the sendmail.cf file distributed with the sendmail package. You'll need the sendmail-cf package if you ever need to reconfigure and rebuild your sendmail.cf file. For example, the default sendmail.cf file is not configured for UUCP. If someday you needed to send and receive mail over UUCP, you'd need to install the sendmail-cf package to help you reconfigure Sendmail.

Install the sendmail-cf package if you need to reconfigure your sendmail.cf file.

squid -- (Version 2.2.STABLE1, 1,825K)

Squid is a high-performance proxy caching server for web clients, supporting FTP, gopher, and HTTP data objects. Unlike traditional caching software, Squid handles all requests in a single, non-blocking, I/O-driven process.

Squid keeps meta data and especially hot objects cached in RAM, caches DNS lookups, supports non-blocking DNS lookups, and implements negative caching of failed requests.

Squid supports SSL, extensive access controls, and full request logging. By using the lightweight Internet Cache Protocol,Squid caches can be arranged in a hierarchy or mesh for additional bandwidth savings.

Squid consists of a main server program squid, a Domain Name System lookup program dnsserver, a program for retrieving FTP data ftpget, and some management and client tools. When squid starts up, it spawns a configurable number of dnsserver processes, each of which can perform a single, blocking Domain Name System (DNS) lookup. This reduces the amount of time the cache waits for DNS lookups.

Squid is derived from the ARPA-funded Harvest project.

sysklogd -- (Version 1.3.31, 111K)

[B]

The sysklogd package contains two system utilities (syslogd and klogd) which provide support for system logging. Syslogd and klogd run as daemons (background processes) and log system messages to different places, like sendmail logs, security logs,error logs, etc.

tcp_wrappers -- (Version 7.6, 270K)

[W] [S]

The tcp_wrappers package provides small daemon programs which can monitor and filter incoming requests for systat, finger,ftp, telnet, rlogin, rsh, exec, tftp, talk and other network services.

Install the tcp_wrappers program if you need a security tool for filtering incoming network services requests.

tftp -- (Version 0.10, 33K)

[W] [S]

The Trivial File Transfer Protocol (TFTP) is normally used only for booting diskless workstations. The tftp package provides the user interface for TFTP, which allows users to transfer files to and from a remote machine. This program, and TFTP, provide very little security, and should not be enabled unless it is expressly needed.
The TFTP server is run from /etc/inetd.conf, and is disabled by default on Red Hat Linux systems.

timed -- (Version 0.10, 71K)

[W] [S]

The timed package contains the timed daemon and the timedc program for controlling the timed program. Timed synchronizes its host machine's time with the time on other local network machines. The timedc program is used to control and configure the operation of timed.

Install the timed package if you need a system for keeping networked machines' times in synchronization.

ucd-snmp -- (Version 3.6.1, 1,491K)

[W] [S]

SNMP (Simple Network Management Protocol) is a protocol used for network management (hence the name). The UCD-SNMP project includes various SNMP tools: an extensible agent, an SNMP library, tools for requesting or setting information from SNMP agents, tools for generating and handling SNMP traps, a version of the netstat command which uses SNMP, and a Tk/Perl mib browser. This package contains the snmpd and snmptrapd daemons, documentation, etc.

Install the ucd-snmp package if you need network management tools. You will probably also want to install the ucd-snmp-utils package, which contains UCD-SNMP utilities.

wu-ftpd -- (Version 2.4.2vr17, 394K)

[S]

The wu-ftpd package contains the wu-ftpd FTP (File Transfer Protocol) server daemon. The FTP protocol is a method of transferring files between machines on a network and/or over the Internet. Wu-ftpd's features include logging of transfers,logging of commands, on the fly compression and archiving, classification of users' type and location, per class limits, per directory upload permissions, restricted guest accounts, system wide and per directory messages, directory alias, cdpath,filename filter and virtual host support.

Install the wu-ftpd package if you need to provide FTP service to remote users.

xntp3 -- (Version 5.93, 963K)

The Network Time Protocol (NTP) is used to synchronize a computer's time with another reference time source. The xntp3 package contains utilities and daemons which will synchronize your computer's time to Coordinated Universal Time (UTC) via the NTP protocol and NTP servers. Xntp3 includes ntpdate (a program for retrieving the date and time from remote machines via a network) and xntpd (a daemon which continuously adjusts system time).

Install the xntp3 package if you need tools for keeping your system's time synchronized via the NTP protocol.

ypbind -- (Version 3.3, 33K)

[W] [S]

The Network Information Service (NIS) is a system which provides network information (login names, passwords, home directories, group information) to all of the machines on a network. NIS can enable users to login on any machine on the network, as long as the machine has the NIS client programs running and the user's password is recorded in the NIS passwd database. NIS was formerly known as Sun Yellow Pages (YP).

This package provides the ypbind daemon. The ypbind daemon binds NIS clients to an NIS domain. Ypbind must be running on any machines which are running NIS client programs.

Install the ypbind package on any machines which are running NIS client programs (included in the yp-tools package). If you need an NIS server, you'll also need to install the ypserv package to a machine on your network.

ypserv -- (Version 1.3.6.91, 289K)

The Network Information Service (NIS) is a system which provides network information (login names, passwords, home directories, group information) to all of the machines on a network. NIS can enable users to login on any machine on the network, as long as the machine has the NIS client programs running and the user's password is recorded in the NIS passwd database. NIS was formerly known as Sun Yellow Pages (YP).

This package provides the NIS server, which will need to be running on your network. NIS clients do not need to be running the server.

Install ypserv if you need an NIS server for your network. You'll also need to install the yp-tools and ypbind packages onto any NIS client machines.

D.5.3 Kernel

This section contains packages that are related to the Linux kernel on which Red Hat Linux is based.

kernel -- (Version 2.2.5, 9,913K)

[B]

The kernel package contains the Linux kernel (vmlinuz), the core of your Red Hat Linux operating system. The kernel handles the basic functions of the operating system: memory allocation, process allocation, device input and output, etc.

kernel-BOOT -- (Version 2.2.5, 5,908K)

This package includes a trimmed down version of the Linux 2.2.5 kernel. This kernel is used on the installation boot disks only and should not be used for an installed system, as many features in this kernel are turned off because of the size constraints.

kernel-ibcs -- (Version 2.2.5, 61K)

This package allows you to run programs in the iBCS2 (Intel Binary Compatibility Standard, version 2) and related executable formats. iBCS is a standard for binary portability between UNIX and UNIX-like systems.

kernel-pcmcia-cs -- (Version 2.2.5, 561K)

[B]

Many laptop machines (and some non-laptops) support PCMCIA cards for expansion. Also known as "credit card adapters," PCMCIA cards are small cards for everything from SCSI support to modems. PCMCIA cards are hot swappable (i.e., they can be exchanged without rebooting the system) and quite convenient to use. The kernel-pcmcia-cs package contains a set of loadable kernel modules that implement an applications program interface, a set of client drivers for specific cards and a card manager daemon that can respond to card insertion and removal events by loading and unloading drivers on demand. The daemon also supports hot swapping, so that the cards can be safely inserted and ejected at any time.

Install the kernel-pcmcia-cs package if your system uses PCMCIA cards.

kernel-smp -- (Version 2.2.5, 9,586K)

This package includes a SMP version of the Linux 2.2.5 kernel. It is required only on machines with two or more CPUs, although it should work fine on single-CPU boxes.

modutils -- (Version 2.1.121, 835K)

[B]

The modutils packages includes the kerneld program for automatic loading of modules under 2.0 kernels and unloading of modules under 2.0 and 2.2 kernels, as well as other module management programs.

Loaded and unloaded modules are device drivers and filesystems, as well as other things.

D.5.4 Libraries

This section contains the packages associated with the libraries that are required to run programs under Red Hat Linux.

XFree86-libs -- (Version 3.3.3.1, 1,991K)

[W] [S]

XFree86-libs contains the shared libraries that most X programs need to run properly. These shared libraries are in a separate package in order to reduce the disk space needed to run X applications on a machine without an X server (i.e, over a network).

If you are installing the X Window System on your machine, you will need to install XFree86-libs. You will also need to install the XFree86 package, the XFree86-75dpi-fonts package or the XFree86-100dpi-fonts package (depending upon your monitor's resolution), the Xconfigurator package and the X11R6-contrib package. And, finally, if you are going to be developing applications that run as X clients, you will also need to install XFree86-devel.

Xaw3d -- (Version 1.3, 292K)

[W] [S]

Xaw3d is an enhanced version of the MIT Athena Widget set for the X Window System. Xaw3d adds a three-dimensional look to applications with minimal or no source code changes.

You should install Xaw3d if you are using applications which incorporate the MIT Athena widget set and you'd like to incorporate a 3D look into those applications.

audiofile -- (Version 0.1.6, 180K)

[W] [S]

Library to handle various audio file formats. Used by the esound daemon.

cracklib -- (Version 2.7, 74K)

[B]

CrackLib tests passwords to determine whether they match certain security-oriented characteristics. You can use CrackLib to stop users from choosing passwords which would be easy to guess. CrackLib performs certain tests:

* It tries to generate words from a username and gecos entry and checks those words against the password; * It checks for simplistic patterns in passwords; * It checks for the password in a dictionary.

CrackLib is actually a library containing a particular C function which is used to check the password, as well as other C functions. CrackLib is not a replacement for a passwd program; it must be used in conjunction with an existing passwd program.

Install the cracklib package if you need a program to check users' passwords to see if they are at least minimally secure. If you install CrackLib, you'll also want to install the cracklib-dicts package.

cracklib-dicts -- (Version 2.7, 226K)

[B]

The cracklib-dicts package includes the CrackLib dictionaries. CrackLib will need to use the dictionary appropriate to your system, which is normally put in /usr/dict/words. Cracklib-dicts also contains the utilities necessary for the creation of new dictionaries.

If you are installing CrackLib, you should also install cracklib-dicts.

fnlib -- (Version 0.4, 352K)

[W]

Fnlib is a library that provides full, scalable 24-bit color font rendering abilities for X.

freetype -- (Version 1.2, 937K)

[W] [S]

The FreeType engine is a free and portable TrueType font rendering engine. It has been developed to provide TT support to a great variety of platforms and environments. Note that FreeType is a library, not a stand-alone application, though some utility applications are included.

gd -- (Version 1.3, 314K)

[B]

Gd is a graphics library for drawing .gif files. Gd allows your code to quickly draw images (lines, arcs, text, multiple colors, cutting and pasting from other images, flood fills) and write out the result as a .gif file. Gd is particularly useful in web applications, where .gifs are commonly used as inline images. Note, however, that gd is not a paint program.

Install gd if you are developing applications which need to draw .gif files. If you install gd, you'll also need to install the gd-devel package.

gdbm -- (Version 1.7.3, 28K)

[B]

Gdbm is a GNU database indexing library, including routines which use extensible hashing. Gdbm works in a similar way to standard UNIX dbm routines. Gdbm is useful for developers who write C applications and need access to a simple and efficient database or who are building C applications which will use such a database.

If you're a C developer and your programs need access to simple database routines, you should install gdbm. You'll also need to install gdbm-devel.

gimp-libgimp -- (Version 1.0.4, 168K)

[W]

Libraries used to communicate between The GIMP and other programs which may function as "GIMP plugins".

glib -- (Version 1.2.1, 310K)

[B] [W]

Glib is a handy library of utility functions. This C library is designed to solve some portability problems and provide other useful functionality which most programs require.

Glib is used by GDK, GTK+ and many applications. You should install Glib because many of your applications will depend on this library.

glib10 -- (Version 1.0.6, 54K)

[W] [S]

The glib package contains a useful library of utility functions, which are necessary for the successful operation of many different programs on your Red Hat Linux system.

glibc -- (Version 2.1.1, 26,192K)

[B]

Contains the standard libraries that are used by multiple programs on the system. In order to save disk space and memory, as well as to ease upgrades, common system code is kept in one place and shared between programs. This package contains the most important sets of shared libraries, the standard C library and the standard math library. Without these, a Linux system will not function. It also contains national language (locale) support and timezone databases.

gmp -- (Version 2.0.2, 117K)

[B]

The gmp package contains GNU MP, a library for arbitrary precision arithmetic, signed integers operations, rational numbers and floating point numbers. GNU MP is designed for speed, for both small and very large operands. GNU MP is fast for several reasons: It uses fullwords as the basic arithmetic type, it uses fast algorithms, it carefully optimizes assembly code for many CPUs' most common inner loops and it generally emphasizes speed over simplicity/elegance in its operations.

Install the gmp package if you need a fast arbitrary precision library.

gnome-audio-extra -- (Version 1.0.0, 2,659K)

[W]

This package contains extra sound files useful for customizing the sounds that the GNOME desktop environment makes.

gnome-libs -- (Version 1.0.8, 2,205K)

[W] [S]

GNOME (GNU Network Object Model Environment) is a user-friendly set of applications and desktop tools to be used in conjunction with a window manager for the X Window System. GNOME is similar in purpose and scope to CDE and KDE,but GNOME is based completely on Open Source software. The gnome-libs package includes libraries that are needed by GNOME.

You should install the gnome-libs package if you would like to use the GNOME desktop environment. You'll also need to install the gnome-core package. If you would like to develop GNOME applications, you'll also need to install gnome-libs-devel. If you want to use linuxconf with a GNOME front end, you'll also need to install the gnome-linuxconf package.

gsl -- (Version 0.3f, 868K)

The gsl package includes the GNU Scientific Library (GSL). The GSL is a collection of routines for numerical analysis, written in C. The GSL is in alpha development. It now includes a random number suite, an FFT package, simulated annealing and root finding. In the future, it will include numerical and Monte Carlo integration and special functions. Linking against the GSL allows programs to access functions which can handle many of the problems encountered in scientific computing.

Install the gsl package if you need a library for high-level scientific numerical analysis.

gtk+ -- (Version 1.2.1, 1,942K)

[W] [S]

The gtk+ package contains the GIMP ToolKit (GTK+), a library for creating graphical user interfaces for the X Window System. GTK+ was originally written for the GIMP (GNU Image Manipulation Program) image processing program, but is now used by several other programs as well.

If you are planning on using the GIMP or another program that uses GTK+, you'll need to have the gtk+ package installed.

gtk+10 -- (Version 1.0.6, 1,140K)

[W] [S]

The X libraries originally written for the GIMP, which are now used by several other programs as well.

This RPM is a set of compatibility libraries needed to run applications linked against the 1.0 series of gtk+ and glib.

gtk-engines -- (Version 0.5, 2,234K)

[W]

These are the graphical engines for the various GTK+ toolkit themes. Included themes are:

- Notif - Redmond95 - Pixmap - Metal (swing-like)

imlib -- (Version 1.9.5, 423K)

[W] [S]

Imlib is a display depth independent image loading and rendering library. Imlib is designed to simplify and speed up the process of loading images and obtaining X Window System drawables. Imlib provides many simple manipulation routines which can be used for common operations.

Install imlib if you need an image loading and rendering library for X11R6. You may also want to install the imlib-cfgeditor package, which will help you configure Imlib.

imlib-cfgeditor -- (Version 1.9.5, 333K)

[W]

The imlib-cfgeditor package contains the imlib_config program, which you can use to configure the Imlib image loading and rendering library. Imlib_config can be used to control how Imlib uses color and handles gamma corrections, etc.

If you're installing the imlib package, you should also install imlib_cfgeditor.

kdelibs -- (Version 1.1.1pre2, 5,680K)

Libraries for the K Desktop Environment: KDE Libraries included: kdecore (KDE core library), kdeui (user interface), kfm (file manager), khtmlw (HTML widget), kfile (file access), kspell (spelling checker), jscript (javascript), kab (addressbook), kimgio (image manipulation), mediatool (sound, mixing and animation).

kdesupport -- (Version 1.1.1pre2, 2,134K)

Support Libraries for the K Desktop Environment, but not part of it.

Libraries included: QwSpriteField, js (javascript), uulib, mimelib, rdb; depending on the Red Hat release, libraries gdbm jpeg and gif are either also included, or the versions supplied by Red Hat are required.

This package also provides extra KDE support for Red Hat Linux: a script "usekde" that users can run to set up KDE as their default desktop (which is also done automatically when a new user is created), and scripts for activating the KDE X Display Manager "kdm" to replace "xdm".

libPropList -- (Version 0.8.3, 111K)

The purpose of PL is to closely mimic the behavior of the property lists used in the GNUstep/OPENSTEP (they're formed with the NSString, NSData, NSArray and NSDictionary classes) and to be duly compatible.

PL enables programs that use configuration or preference3 files to make these compatible with GNUstep/OPENSTEP's user defaults handling mechanism, without needing to use Objective-C or GNUstep/ OPENSTEP themselves.

libc -- (Version 5.3.12, 5,365K)

[B]

Older Linux systems (including all Red Hat Linux releases between 2.0 and 4.2, inclusive) were based on libc version 5. The libc package includes the libc5 libraries and other libraries based on libc5. With these libraries installed, old applications which need them will be able to run on your glibc (libc version 6) based system.

The libc package should be installed so that you can run older applications which need libc version 5.

libelf -- (Version 0.6.4, 76K)

The libelf package contains a library for accessing ELF object files. Libelf allows you to access the internals of the ELF object file format, so you can see the different sections of an ELF file.

Libelf should be installed if you need access to ELF object file internals.

libghttp -- (Version 1.0.2, 85K)

[W] [S]

Library for making HTTP 1.1 requests.

libgr -- (Version 2.0.13, 235K)

[W] [S]

The libgr package contains a library of functions which support programs for handling various graphics file formats, including .pbm (portable pitmaps), .pgm (portable graymaps), .pnm (portable anymaps), .ppm (portable pixmaps) and others.

libgtop -- (Version 1.0.1, 431K)

[W]

A library that fetches information about the running system such as CPU and memory useage, active processes and more.

On Linux systems, this information is taken directly from the /proc filesystem while on other systems a server is used to read that information from other /dev/kmem, among others.

libgtop-examples -- (Version 1.0.1, 937K)

These are examples for LibGTop, a library which retrieves information about your system, such as CPU and memory usage.

libjpeg -- (Version 6b, 239K)

[W] [S]

The libjpeg package contains a library of functions for manipulating JPEG images, as well as simple client programs for accessing the libjpeg functions. Libjpeg client programs include cjpeg, djpeg, jpegtran, rdjpgcom and wrjpgcom. Cjpeg compresses an image file into JPEG format. Djpeg decompresses a JPEG file into a regular image file. Jpegtran can perform various useful transformations on JPEG files. Rdjpgcom displays any text comments included in a JPEG file. Wrjpgcom inserts text comments into a JPEG file.

libjpeg6a -- (Version 6a, 137K)

This package is a library of functions that manipulate jpeg images, along with simple clients for manipulating jpeg images.

This version of the package includes only a library that is needed for preserving the backwards compatibility with previous releases of Red Hat Linux.

libpng -- (Version 1.0.3, 270K)

[W] [S]

The libpng package contains a library of functions for creating and manipulating PNG (Portable Network Graphics) image format files. PNG is a bit-mapped graphics format similar to the GIF format. PNG was created to replace the GIF format, since GIF uses a patented data compression algorithm.

Libpng should be installed if you need to manipulate PNG format image files.

libstdc++ -- (Version 2.9.0, 3,421K)

[B]

EGCS is a free software project that intends to further the development of GNU compilers using an open development environment. The egcs package contains the egcs compiler, a compiler aimed at integrating all the optimizations and features necessary for a high-performance and stable development environment. EGCS includes the shared libraries necessary for running C++ appplications, along with additional GNU tools.

Install egcs if you'd like to use an experimental GNU compiler.

libtermcap -- (Version 2.0.8, 58K)

[B]

The libtermcap package contains a basic system library needed to access the termcap database. The termcap library supports easy access to the termcap database, so that programs can output character-based displays in a terminal-independent manner.

libtiff -- (Version 3.4, 568K)

[W] [S]

The libtiff package contains a library of functions for manipulating TIFF (Tagged Image File Format) image format files. TIFF is a widely used file format for bitmapped images. TIFF files usually end in the .tif extension and they are often quite large.

The libtiff package should be installed if you need to manipulate TIFF format image files.

libungif -- (Version 4.1.0, 80K)

[W] [S]

The libungif package contains a shared library of functions for loading and saving GIF format image files. The libungif library can load any GIF file, but it will save GIFs only in uncompressed format (i.e., it won't use the patented LZW compression used to save "normal" compressed GIF files).

Install the libungif package if you need to manipulate GIF files. You should also install the libungif-progs package.

libxml -- (Version 1.0.0, 154K)

[W] [S]

This library allows you to manipulate XML files.

ncurses -- (Version 4.2, 2,616K)

[B]

The curses library routines are a terminal-independent method of updating character screens with reasonable optimization. The ncurses (new curses) library is a freely distributable replacement for the discontinued 4.4BSD classic curses library.

ncurses3 -- (Version 1.9.9e, 330K)

The curses library routines are a terminal-independent method of updating character screens with reasonable optimization. The ncurses (new curses) library is a freely distributable replacement for the discontinued 4.4BSD classic curses library.

newt -- (Version 0.40, 125K)

[B]

Newt is a programming library for color text mode, widget based user interfaces. Newt can be used to add stacked windows,entry widgets, checkboxes, radio buttons, labels, plain text fields, scrollbars, etc., to text mode user interfaces. This package also contains the shared library needed by programs built with newt, as well as a /usr/bin/dialog replacement called whiptail. Newt is based on the slang library.

popt -- (Version 1.3, 53K)

Popt is a C library for parsing command line parameters. Popt was heavily influenced by the getopt() and getopt_long() functions, but it improves on them by allowing more powerful argument expansion. Popt can parse arbitrary argv[] style arrays and automatically set variables based on command line arguments. Popt allows command line arguments to be aliased via configuration files and includes utility functions for parsing arbitrary strings into argv[] arrays using shell-like rules.

Install popt if you're a C programmer and you'd like to use its capabilities.

pythonlib -- (Version 1.22, 236K)

[W] [S]

The pythonlib package contains Python code used by a variety of Red Hat Linux programs. Pythonlib includes code needed for multifield listboxes and entry widgets with non-standard keybindings, among other things.

qt -- (Version 1.44, 2,103K)

Qt is a GUI software toolkit. Qt simplifies the task of writing and maintaining GUI (graphical user interface) applications for X Windows.

Qt is written in C++ and is fully object-oriented. It has everything you need to create professional GUI applications. And it enables you to create them quickly.

Qt is a multi-platform toolkit. When developing software with Qt, you can run it on the X Window System (Unix/X11) or Microsoft Windows NT and Windows 95/98. Simply recompile your source code on the platform you want.

This package contains the shared library needed to run Qt applications, as well as the README files for Qt.

readline -- (Version 2.2.1, 251K)

[B]

The readline library reads a line from the terminal and returns it, allowing the user to edit the line with standard emacs editing keys. The readline library allows programmers to provide an easy to use and more intuitive interface for users.

If you want to develop programs that will use the readline library, you'll also need to install the readline-devel package.

slang -- (Version 1.2.2, 250K)

[B]

S-Lang is an interpreted language and a programming library. The S-Lang language was designed so that it can be easily embedded into a program to provide the program with a powerful extension language. The S-Lang library, provided in this package, provides the S-Lang extension language. S-Lang's syntax resembles C, which makes it easy to recode S-Lang procedures in C if you need to.

svgalib -- (Version 1.3.1, 753K)

[W]

The svgalib package provides the SVGAlib low-level graphics library for Linux. SVGAlib is a library which allows applications to use full screen graphics on a variety of hardware platforms. Many games and utilities use SVGAlib for their graphics.

You'll need to have the svgalib package installed if you use any of the programs which rely on SVGAlib for their graphics support.

w3c-libwww -- (Version 5.2.8, 2,155K)

Libwww is a general-purpose Web API written in C for Unix and Windows (Win32). With a highly extensible and layered API, it can accommodate many different types of applications including clients, robots, etc. The purpose of libwww is to provide a highly optimized HTTP sample implementation as well as other Internet protocols and to serve as a testbed for protocol experiments.

words -- (Version 2, 411K)

[B]

The words file is a dictionary of English words for the /usr/dict directory. Programs like ispell use this database of words to check spelling.

xpm -- (Version 3.4j, 60K)

[W] [S]

The xpm package contains the XPM pixmap library for the X Window System. The XPM library allows applications to display color, pixmapped images, and is used by many popular X programs.

zlib -- (Version 1.1.3, 61K)

[B]

The zlib compression library provides in-memory compression and decompression functions, including integrity checks of the uncompressed data. This version of the library supports only one compression method (deflation), but other algorithms may be added later, which will have the same stream interface. The zlib library is used by many different system programs.

D.5.5 Shells

This section contains packages that are associated with the shells that provide the command-line user interface on Red Hat Linux.

ash -- (Version 0.2, 361K)

[B]

The ash shell is a clone of Berkeley's Bourne shell. Ash supports all of the standard sh shell commands, but is considerably smaller than bash. The ash shell lacks some features (for example, command-line histories), but needs a lot less memory.

You should install ash if you need a lightweight shell with many of the same capabilities as the bash shell.

bash -- (Version 1.14.7, 545K)

[B]

Bash is a GNU project sh-compatible shell or command language interpreter. Bash (Bourne Again shell) incorporates useful features from the Korn shell (ksh) and the C shell (csh). Most sh scripts can be run by bash without modification.

Bash offers several improvements over sh, including command line editing, unlimited size command history, job control, shell functions and aliases, indexed arrays of unlimited size and integer arithmetic in any base from two to 64. Bash is ultimately intended to conform to the IEEE POSIX P1003.2/ISO 9945.2 Shell and Tools standard.

Bash is the default shell for Red Hat Linux. You should install bash because of its popularity and power. You'll probably end up using it.

bash2 -- (Version 2.03, 1,168K)

Bash is a GNU project sh-compatible shell or command language interpreter. Bash (Bourne Again shell) incorporates useful features from the Korn shell (ksh) and the C shell (csh). Most sh scripts can be run by bash without modification.

Bash offers several improvements over sh, including command line editing, unlimited size command history, job control, shell functions and aliases, indexed arrays of unlimited size and integer arithmetic in any base from two to 64. Bash is ultimately intended to conform to the IEEE POSIX P1003.2/ISO 9945.2 Shell and Tools standard.

mc -- (Version 4.5.30, 903K)

[W]

Midnight Commander is a visual shell much like a file manager, only with way more features. It is text mode, but also includes mouse support if you are running GPM. Its coolest feature is the ability to ftp, view tar, zip files, and poke into RPMs for specific files. :-)

pdksh -- (Version 5.2.13, 402K)

The pdksh package contains PD-ksh, a clone of the Korn shell (ksh). The ksh shell is a command interpreter intended for both interactive and shell script use. Ksh's command language is a superset of the sh shell language.

Install the pdksh package if you want to use a version of the ksh shell.

sash -- (Version 2.1, 402K)

[B]

Sash is a simple, standalone, statically linked shell which includes simplified versions of built-in commands like ls, dd and gzip. Sash is statically linked so that it can work without shared libraries, so it is particularly useful for recovering from certain types of system failures. Sash can also be used to safely upgrade to new versions of shared libraries.

sh-utils -- (Version 1.16, 351K)

[B]

The GNU shell utilities are a set of useful system utilities which are often used in shell scripts. The sh-utils package includes basename (to remove the path prefix from a specified pathname), chroot (to change the root directory), date (to print/set the system time and date), dirname (to remove the last level or the filename from a given path), echo (to print a line of text), env (to display/modify the environment), expr (to evaluate expressions), factor (to print prime factors), false (to return an unsuccessful exit status), groups (to print the groups a specified user is a member of), id (to print the real/effective uid/gid), logname (to print the current login name), nice (to modify a scheduling priority), nohup (to allow a command to continue running after logging out), pathchk (to check a file name's portability), printenv (to print environment variables), printf (to format and print data), pwd (to print the current directory), seq (to print numeric sequences), sleep (to suspend execution for a specified time), stty (to print/change terminal settings), su (to become another user or the superuser), tee (to send output to multipleles), test (to evaluate an expression), true (to return a successful exit status), tty (to print the terminal name), uname (to print system information), users (to print current users' names), who (to print a list of the users who are currently logged in), whoami (to print the effective user id), and yes (to print a string indefinitely).

tcsh -- (Version 6.08.00, 488K)

[B]

Tcsh is an enhanced but completely compatible version of csh, the C shell. Tcsh is a command language interpreter which can be used both as an interactive login shell and as a shell script command processor. Tcsh includes a command line editor, programmable word completion, spelling correction, a history mechanism, job control and a C language like syntax.

zsh -- (Version 3.0.5, 956K)

The zsh shell is a command interpreter usable as an interactive login shell and as a shell script command processor. Zsh resembles the ksh shell (the Korn shell), but includes many enhancements. Zsh supports command line editing, built-in spelling correction, programmable command completion, shell functions (with autoloading), a history mechanism and more.

Install the zsh package if you'd like to try out a different shell.

D.6 User Interface

This section contains packages that are associated with providing a user interface on Red Hat Linux.

D.6.1 Desktops

This section contains packages that are associated with the desktop environments available on Red Hat Linux.

AfterStep -- (Version 1.7.90, 4,148K)

[W] [S]

AfterStep is a continuation of the BowMan window manager which was originally put together by Bo Yang. BowMan was based on the fvwm window manager, written by Robert Nation. Fvwm was based on code from twm. And so on... It was originally designed to emulate some of the look and feel of the NEXTSTEP user interface, but has since taken steps towards adding more useful, requested, and neat features especially in 1.4 version ! The changes which comprise AfterStep's personality were originally part of bowman development, but due to a desire to move past simple emulation and into a niche as its own valuable window manager, AfterStep designers decided to change the project name and move on.

Important features of AfterStep include:

1. Wharf: a free-floating application loader which can "Swallow" running programs and also can contain "Folders" of more applications. 2. Gradient filled TitleBars with 5 button : help/zap, action/tasks, iconize/maximise, shade/stick & close/destroy buttons 3. Gradient filled root window PopUp menus which can be configured to accommodate different tastes and styles of management 4. NEXTSTEP style icons which give a consistent look to the entire desktop 5. Pixmapped Pager with desktop pixmmaping 6. Easy to use look files, to share you desktop appearance with your friends 7. Start menu entries in a hierarchy of directories 8. WinList : a tasklist which can be horizontal or vertical 9. Many modules & asapps to give a good look to your Xwindow station.

AfterStep-APPS -- (Version 990329, 1,078K)

[W] [S]

What's a cool window manager without some cool applets? Well... it's still cool, but these applets which can be used in the Wharf module for AfterStep or Window Maker can add both spice and productivity to your preferred window manager, such as a handy clock and information about system resources.

If you've installed the AfterStep packages, you should also install these packages. Enjoy!

AnotherLevel -- (Version 0.9, 288K)

[W] [S]

AnotherLevel is a custom configuration of the popular fvwm2 window manager. Fvwm stands for (?) virtual window manager. You can fill in the blank for the 'f': fast, flexible, friendly and fabulous all could apply. This window manager is based on TheNextLevel desktop configuration, created by Greg J. Badros, which won the 1996 Red Hat Desktop Contest.

AnotherLevel is designed to be easily configured by the user.

WindowMaker -- (Version 0.52.0, 3,654K)

Window Maker is an X11 window manager which emulates the look and feel of the NeXTSTEP (TM) graphical user interface. It is relatively fast, feature rich and easy to configure and use. Window Maker is part of the official GNU project, which means that Window Maker can interoperate with other GNU projects, such as GNOME.

Window Maker allows users to switch themes 'on the fly,' to place favorite applications on either an application dock, similar to AfterStep's Wharf or on a workspace dock, a 'clip' which extends the application dock's usefulness.

You should install the WindowMaker package if you use Window Maker as your window manager or if you'd like to try using it. If you do install the WindowMaker package, you may also want to install the AfterStep-APPS package, which includes applets that will work with both AfterStep and Window Maker window managers.

control-center -- (Version 1.0.5, 985K)

[W]

Control-center is a configuration tool for easily setting up your GNOME environment.

GNOME is the GNU Network Object Model Environment. That's a fancy name, but really GNOME is a nice GUI desktop environment.

It's a powerful, easy to configure environment which helps to make your computer easy to use.

enlightenment -- (Version 0.15.5, 3,835K)

[W]

Enlightenment is a window manager for the X Window System that is designed to be powerful, extensible, configurable and pretty darned good looking! It is one of the more graphically intense window managers.

Enlightenment goes beyond managing windows by providing a useful and appealing graphical shell from which to work. It is open in design and instead of dictating a policy, allows the user to define their own policy, down to every last detail.

This package will install the Enlightenment window manager.

enlightenment-conf -- (Version 0.15, 384K)

[W]

A Configuration tool for easily setting up Enlightenment

fvwm -- (Version 1.24r, 573K)

[W] [S]

FVWM (the F stands for whatever you want, but the VWM stands for Virtual Window Manager) is a window manager for the X Window System. FVWM was derived from the twm window manager. FVWM is designed to minimize memory consumption, to provide window frames with a 3D look, and to provide a simple virtual desktop. FVWM can be configured to look like Motif.

Install the fvwm package if you'd like to use the FVWM window manager. If you install fvwm, you'll also need to install fvwm2-icons.

fvwm2 -- (Version 2.2, 1,730K)

[W] [S]

FVWM2 (the F stands for whatever you want, but the VWM stands for Virtual Window Manager) is an improved version of the FVWM window manager for the X Window System and shares the same characteristics as FVWM.

Install the fvwm2 package if you'd like to use the FVWM2 window manager. If you install fvwm2, you'll also need to install fvwm2-icons.

fvwm2-icons -- (Version 2.2, 445K)

[W] [S]

The fvwm2-icons package contains icons, bitmaps and pixmaps used by the FVWM and FVWM2 X Window System window managers.

You'll need to install fvwm2-icons if you are installing fvwm and/or fvwm2.

gmc -- (Version 4.5.30, 2,257K)

[W]

Midnight Commander is a visual shell much like a file manager, only with way more features. This is the GNOME version. It's coolest feature is the ability to ftp, view tar, zip files and poke into RPMs for specific files. The GNOME version of Midnight Commander is not yet finished though. :-(

gnome-core -- (Version 1.0.4, 2,889K)

[W]

GNOME (GNU Network Object Model Environment) is a user-friendly set of applications and desktop tools to be used in conjunction with a window manager for the X Window System. GNOME is similar in purpose and scope to CDE and KDE, but GNOME is based completely on Open Source software. The gnome-core package includes the basic programs and libraries that are needed to install GNOME.

You should install the gnome-core package if you would like to use the GNOME desktop environment. You'll also need to install the gnome-libs package. If you want to use linuxconf with a GNOME front end, you'll also need to install the gnome-linuxconf package.

kdebase -- (Version 1.1.1pre2, 12,022K)

Core applications for the K Desktop Environment. Included are: kdm (replacement for xdm), kwm (window manager), kfm (filemanager, web browser, ftp client, ...), konsole (xterm replacement), kpanel (application starter and desktop pager), kaudio (audio server), kdehelp (viewer for kde help files, info and man pages), plus other KDE components (kcheckpass, kikbd, kvt, kscreensaver, kcontrol, kfind, kfontmanager, kmenuedit, kappfinder).

PAM password authentication is supported via PAM service: kde.

switchdesk -- (Version 1.7.0, 90K)

[W]

The Desktop Switcher is a tool which enables users to easily switch between various desktop environments that they have installed. The tool includes support for GNOME, KDE, and AnotherLevel. Support for different environments on different computers is available, as well as setting a "global default."

switchdesk-gnome -- (Version 1.7.0, 11K)

[W]

Provides the desktop switching tool with a GNOME look and feel.

switchdesk-kde -- (Version 1.7.0, 22K)

Provides the desktop switching Tool with a KDE look and feel.

wmakerconf -- (Version 1.99.1, 1,012K)

Wmakerconf is a GTK+ based graphical user interface configuration tool for the Window Maker window manager.Wmakerconf supports all Window Maker attributes. Wmakerconf provides a font selection browser, a pixmap preview browser, a color selection dialog, a shortcut dialog, and a file selection dialog. Wmakerconf also provides tooltips in multiple languages.

If you use the Window Maker window manager, you should probably install the wmakerconf package, because it will make configuration a little easier.

wmconfig -- (Version 0.9.5, 52K)

[W] [S]

The wmconfig program is a helper program which provides output for use in configuring window managers. Wmconfig will produce a list of menu definitions for a specified X window manager (currently, FVWM2, FVWM95, AfterStep, MWM, IceWM and KDE are supported). Wmconfig's output can be placed into your .rc file or you can use the output for other configuration purposes.

xfm -- (Version 1.3.2, 706K)

[W]

Xfm is a file manager for the X Window System. Xfm supports moving around the directory tree, multiple windows,moving/copying/deleting files, and launching programs.

Install xfm if you would like to use a graphical file manager program.

D.6.2 X Hardware Support

This section contains packages that are associated with providing hardware support for specific video cards under Red Hat Linux.

XFree86-3DLabs -- (Version 3.3.3.1, 2,169K)

X server for cards built around 3D Labs GLINT and Permedia chipsets, including GLINT 500TX with IBM RGB526 RAMDAC, GLINT MX with IBM RGB526 and IBM RGB640 RAMDAC, Permedia with IBM RGB526 RAMDAC and the Permedia 2 (classic, 2a, 2v).

XFree86-8514 -- (Version 3.3.3.1, 1,702K)

If you are installing the X Window System and the video card in your system is an older IBM 8514 or a compatible from a company such as ATI, you should install XFree86-8514.

To install the X Window System, you will need to install the XFree86 package, one or more of the XFree86 fonts packages, the X11R6-contrib package, the Xconfigurator package and the XFree86-libs package.

If you are going to develop applications that run as X clients, you will also need to install the XFree86-devel package.

XFree86-AGX -- (Version 3.3.3.1, 1,883K)

This is the X server for AGX-based cards, such as the Boca Vortex, Orchid Celsius, Spider Black Widow and Hercules Graphite.

If you are installing the X Window System and the video card in your system is an AGX, you'll need to install XFree86-AGX. To install the X Window System, you will need to install the XFree86 package, one or more of the XFree86 fonts packages, the X11R6-contrib package, the Xconfigurator package and the XFree86-libs package.

Finally, if you are going to develop applications that run as X clients, you will also need to install the XFree86-devel package.

XFree86-FBDev -- (Version 3.3.3.1, 1,960K)

This is the X server for the generic frame buffer device used on Amiga, Atari and Macintosh/m68k machines.

Support for Intel and Alpha architectures is included in the Linux 2.2 kernel, as well.

XFree86-I128 -- (Version 3.3.3.1, 2,141K)

This is the X server for the #9 Imagine 128 and similar video boards.

XFree86-Mach32 -- (Version 3.3.3.1, 1,845K)

XFree86-Mach32 is the X server package for video cards built around ATI's Mach32 chip, including the ATI Graphics Ultra Pro and Ultra Plus.

If you are installing the X Window System and the video card in your system is based on the Mach32 chip, you need to install XFree86-Mach32. You will also need to install the XFree86 package, one or more of the XFree86 fonts packages, the X11R6-contrib package, the Xconfigurator package and the XFree86-libs package. And, finally, if you are going to develop applications that run as X clients, you will also need to install XFree86-devel.

XFree86-Mach64 -- (Version 3.3.3.1, 1,966K)

XFree86-Mach64 is the server package for cards based on ATI's Mach64 chip, such as the Graphics Xpression, GUP Turbo, and WinTurbo cards. Note that this server is known to have problems with some Mach64 cards. Check http://www.xfree86.org for current information on updating this server.

If you are installing the X Window System and the video card in your system is based on the Mach64 chip, you need to install XFree86-Mach64. You will also need to install the XFree86 package, one or more of the XFree86 fonts packages, the X11R6-contrib package, the Xconfigurator package and the XFree86-libs package. And, finally, if you are going to be developing applications that run as X clients, you will also need to install XFree86-devel.

XFree86-Mach8 -- (Version 3.3.3.1, 1,713K)

XFree86-Mach 8 is the X server for video cards built around ATI's Mach8 chip, including the ATI 8514 Ultra and Graphics Ultra.

If you are installing the X Window System and the video card in your system is based on the Mach8 chip, you need to install XFree86-Mach8. You will also need to install the XFree86 package, one or more of the XFree86 fonts packages, the X11R6-contrib package, the Xconfigurator package and the XFree86-libs package. And, finally, if you are going to be developing applications that run as X clients, you will also need to install XFree86-devel.

XFree86-Mono -- (Version 3.3.3.1, 2,006K)

XFree86-Mono is a generic monochrome (2 color) server for VGA cards. XFree86-Mono will work for nearly all VGA compatible cards, but will only support a monochrome display.

If you are installing the X Window System and your VGA card is not currently supported, you should install and try either XFree86-Mono or XFree86-VGA16, depending upon the capabilities of your display. You will also need to install the XFree86 package, one or more of the XFree86 fonts packages, the X11R6-contrib package, the Xconfigurator package and the XFree86-libs package. And, finally, if you are going to develop applications that run as X clients, you will also need to install XFree86-devel.

XFree86-P9000 -- (Version 3.3.3.1, 1,904K)

XFree86-P9000 is the X server for video cards built around the Weitek P9000 chip, such as most Diamond Viper cards and the Orchid P9000 card.

If you are installing the X Window System and you have a Weitek P9000 based video card, you should install XFree86-P9000. You will also need to install the XFree86 package, one or more of the XFree86 fonts packages, the X11R6-contrib package, the Xconfigurator package and the XFree86-libs package. And, finally, if you are going to develop applications that run as X clients, you will also need to install XFree86-devel.

XFree86-S3 -- (Version 3.3.3.1, 2,388K)

XFree86-S3 is the X server for video cards based on S3 chips, including most #9 cards, many Diamond Stealth cards, Orchid Farenheits, Mirco Crystal 8S, most STB cards, and some motherboards with built-in graphics accelerators (such as the IBM ValuePoint line). Note that if you have an S3 ViRGE based video card, you'll need XFree86-S3V instead of XFree86-S3.

If you are installing the X Window System and you have a video card based on an S3 chip, you should install XFree86-S3. You will also need to install the XFree86 package, one or more XFree86 fonts packages, the X11R6-contrib package, the Xconfigurator package and the XFree86-libs package. And, finally, if you are going to develop applications that run as X clients, you will also need to install XFree86-devel.

XFree86-S3V -- (Version 3.3.3.1, 2,118K)

XFree86-S3V is the X server for video cards based on the S3 ViRGE chipset.

If you are installing the X Window System and you have a video card based on an S3 ViRGE chip, you should install XFree86-S3V. You will also need to install the XFree86 package, one or more of the XFree86 fonts packages, the X11R6-contrib package, the Xconfigurator package and the XFree86-libs package. And, finally, if you are going to develop applications that run as X clients, you will also need to install XFree86-devel.

XFree86-SVGA -- (Version 3.3.3.1, 3,044K)

X server for most simple framebuffer SVGA devices, including cards built from ET4000 chips, Cirrus Logic chips, Chips and Technologies laptop chips, Trident 8900 and 9000 chips, and Matrox chips. It works for Diamond Speedstar, Orchid Kelvins, STB Nitros and Horizons, Genoa 8500VL, most Actix boards, the Spider VLB Plus, etc. It also works for many other chips and cards, so try this server if you are having problems.

XFree86-VGA16 -- (Version 3.3.3.1, 1,898K)

XFree86-VGA16 is a generic 16 color server for VGA boards. XFree86-VGA16 will work on nearly all VGA style graphics boards, but will only support a low resolution, 16 color display.

If you are installing the X Window System and your VGA video card is not specifically supported by another X server package, you should install either XFree86-Mono or XFree86-VGA16, depending upon the capabilities of your display. You will also need to install the XFree86 package, one or more of the XFree86 fonts packages, the X11R6-contrib package, the Xconfigurator package and the XFree86-libs package. And, finally, if you are going to be develop applications that run as X clients, you will also need to install XFree86-devel.

XFree86-W32 -- (Version 3.3.3.1, 1,750K)

XFree86-W32 is the X server for cards built around ET4000/W32 chips, including the Genoa 8900 Phantom 32i, the Hercules Dynamite, the LeadTek WinFast S200, the Sigma Concorde, the STB LightSpeed, the TechWorks Thunderbolt, and the ViewTop PCI.

If you are installing the X Window System and your VGA video card is based on the ET4000/W32 chipset, you should install XFree86-W32. You will also need to install the XFree86 package, one or more of the XFree86 fonts packages, the X11R6-contrib package, the Xconfigurator package and the XFree86-libs package. And, finally, if you are going to develop applications that run as X clients, you will also need to install XFree86-devel.

XFree86-XF86Setup -- (Version 3.3.3.1, 588K)

XF86Setup is a graphical user interface configuration tool for setting up and configuring XFree86 servers. XF86Setup can configure video settings, keyboard layouts, mouse types, etc. XF86Setup can't be used with non-VGA compatible video cards, with fixed-frequency monitors, or with OS/2.

Install XF86Setup if you have used it before and prefer to keep using it to configure your X server. If you do not have a preference for XF86Setup, you should instead install and use Xconfigurator, Red Hat's graphical user interface configuration tool for the X Window System.

XFree86-Xnest -- (Version 3.3.3.1, 2,181K)

Xnest is an X Window System server which runs in an X window. Xnest is a 'nested' window server, actually a client of the real X server, which manages windows and graphics requests for Xnest, while Xnest manages the windows and graphics requests for its own clients.

You will need to install Xnest if you require an X server which will run as a client of your real X server (perhaps for testing purposes).

XFree86-Xvfb -- (Version 3.3.3.1, 2,648K)

Xvfb (X Virtual Frame Buffer) is an X Windows System server that is capable of running on machines with no display hardware and no physical input devices. Xvfb emulates a dumb framebuffer using virtual memory. Xvfb doesn't open any devices, but behaves otherwise as an X display. Xvfb is normally used for testing servers. Using Xvfb, the mfb or cfb code for any depth can be exercised without using real hardware that supports the desired depths. Xvfb has also been used to test X clients against unusual depths and screen configurations, to do batch processing with Xvfb as a background rendering engine, to do load testing, to help with porting an X server to a new platform, and to provide an unobtrusive way of running applications which really don't need an X server but insist on having one.

If you need to test your X server or your X clients, you may want to install Xvfb for that purpose.

Xconfigurator -- (Version 4.2.3, 561K)

[W] [S]

Xconfigurator is a full-screen, menu-driven program which walks you through setting up your X server. Xconfigurator is based on the sources for xf86config, a utility from XFree86.

You should install Xconfigurator if you are installing the X Window

System.

D.6.3 X

This section contains packages associated with the X Window System graphical user interface.

X11R6-contrib -- (Version 3.3.2, 474K)

[W] [S]

If you want to use the X Window System, you should install X11R6-contrib.
This package holds many useful programs from the X Window System, version 11, release 6 contrib tape. The programs, contributed by various users, include listres, xbiff, xedit, xeyes, xcalc, xload and xman, among others.

You will also need to install the XFree86 package, the XFree86 package which corresponds to your video card, one or more of the XFree86 fonts packages, the Xconfigurator package and the XFree86-libs package.

Finally, if you are going to develop applications that run as X clients, you will also need to install XFree86-devel.

XFree86-100dpi-fonts -- (Version 3.3.3.1, 1,228K)

If you're going to use the X Window System and you have a high resolution monitor capable of 100 dpi, you should install XFree86-100dpi-fonts. This package contains a set of 100 dpi fonts used on most Linux systems.

If you are installing the X Window System, you will also need to install the XFree86 package, the XFree86 package corresponding to your video card, the X11R6- contrib package, the Xconfigurator package and the XFree86-libs package. If you need to display certain fonts, you may also need to install other XFree86 fonts packages.

And finally, if you are going to develop applications that run as X clients, you will also need to install the XFree86-devel package.

XFree86 -- (Version 3.3.3.1, 14,268K)

[W] [S]

If you want to install the X Window System (TM) on your machine, you'll need to install XFree86.

The X Window System provides the base technology for developing graphical user interfaces. Simply stated, X draws the elements of the GUI on the user's screen and builds methods for sending user interactions back to the application. X also supports remote application deployment--running an application on another computer while viewing the input/output on your machine. X is a powerful environment which supports many different applications, such as games, programming tools, graphics programs, text editors, etc. XFree86 is the version of X which runs on Linux, as well as other platforms.

This package contains the basic fonts, programs and documentation for an X workstation. However, this package doesn't provide the program which you will need to drive your video hardware. To control your video card, you'll need the particular X server package which corresponds to your computer's video card.

In addition to installing this package, you will need to install the XFree86 package which corresponds to your video card, the X11R6-contrib package, the Xconfigurator package and the XFree86-libs package. You may also need to install one of the XFree86 fonts packages.

And finally, if you are going to develop applications that run as X clients, you will also need to install XFree86-devel.

XFree86-75dpi-fonts -- (Version 3.3.3.1, 1,060K)

[W] [S]

XFree86-75dpi-fonts contains the 75 dpi fonts used on most X Window Systems. If you're going to use the X Window System, you should install this package, unless you have a monitor which can support 100 dpi resolution. In that case, you may prefer the 100dpi fonts available in the XFree86-100dpi-fonts package.

You may also need to install other XFree86 font packages.

To install the X Window System, you will need to install the XFree86 package, the XFree86 package corresponding to your video card, the X11R6-contrib package, the Xconfigurator package and the XFree86-libs package.

Finally, if you are going to develop applications that run as X clients, you will also need to install the XFree86-devel package.

XFree86-ISO8859-2 -- (Version 1.0, 77K)

If you use the X Window System and you want to display Central European fonts, you should install the XFree86-ISO8859-2 package.

This package contains a full set of Central European fonts, in compliance with the ISO 8859-2 standard. The fonts included in this package are distributed free of charge and can be used freely, subject to the accompanying copyright:

Copyright (c) 1996, 1997 BIZNET Poland, Inc. All Rights Reserved. BIZNET is a registered trademark of BIZNET Poland, Inc.

You may also need to install one or more other XFree86 fonts packages.

To install the X Window System, you will need to install the XFree86 package, the XFree86 package which corresponds to your video card, the X11R6-contrib package, the Xconfigurator package and the XFree86-libs package.

Finally, if you are going to develop applications that run as X clients, you will also need to install XFree86-devel.

XFree86-ISO8859-2-100dpi-fonts -- (Version 1.0, 1,003K)

The XFree86-ISO8859-2-100dpi-fonts package includes Central European (ISO 8859-2) fonts, in 100 dpi resolution, for the X Window System.

If you need to display the special characters used by Central European languages on your X Window System, and your monitor can support 100 dpi resolution, you should install the XFree86-ISO8859-2-100dpi-fonts package. You may need to install one or more of the other XFree86 fonts packages, as well. To install the X Window System, you will need to install the XFree86 package, the XFree86 video card package which corresponds to your video card, the X11R6-contrib package, the Xconfigurator package and the XFree86-libs package. If you're going to develop applications which run as X clients, you'll also need to install XFree86-devel.

XFree86-ISO8859-2-75dpi-fonts -- (Version 1.0, 877K)

The XFree86-ISO8859-2-75dpi-fonts package contains a set of Central European language fonts in 75 dpi resolution for the X Window System. If you have a high resolution monitor capable of supporting 100 dpi, you should install the 100 dpi version of this package instead.

If you are installing the X Window System and you need to display Central European language characters in 75 dpi resolution, you should install this package. You may also need to install one or more of the other XFree86 fonts packages as well. To install the

X Window System, you will need to install the XFree86 package, the XFree86 video card package that corresponds to your video card, the X11R6-contrib package, the Xconfigurator package and the XFree86-libs package. If you are going to develop applications that will run as X clients, you will also need to install XFree86-devel.

XFree86-ISO8859-2-Type1-fonts -- (Version 1.0, 1,905K)

The XFree86-ISO8859-2-Type1-fonts package contains Central European Type 1 fonts for the X Window System. This set of fonts is known as the ulT1mo (or ultimo) collection. All of the included fonts are copyrighted to their authors and freeware. Original fonts were taken from the Internet or CDs.

If you need to display Central European language fonts on your X Window System, you should install the XFree86-ISO8859-2-Type1-fonts package. You may need to also install one or more of the other XFree86 fonts packages. To install the X Window System, you will need to install the XFree86 package, the XFree86 video card package which corresponds to your video card, the X11R6-contrib package, the Xconfigurator package and the XFree86-libs package. Finally, if you are going to develop applications that will run as X clients, you'll need to install XFree86-devel.

XFree86-ISO8859-9-100dpi-fonts -- (Version 2.1.2, 1,142K)

The XFree86-ISO8859-9-100dpi-fonts package contains a set of Turkish language fonts in 100 dpi resolution and in accordance with the ISO8859-9 standard for the X Window System.

If you need to display Turkish language fonts for the X Window System, and your monitor is capable of supporting 100 dpi resolution, you should install this package. You may also need to install one or more of the other XFree86 fonts packages. To install the X Window System, you will need to install the XFree86 package, the XFree86 video card package which corresponds to your video card, the X11R6-contrib package, the Xconfigurator package and the XFree86-libs package.

If you are going to develop applications that will run as X clients, you will also need to install XFree86-devel.

XFree86-ISO8859-9 -- (Version 2.1.2, 85K)

The XFree86-ISO8859-9 package contains Turkish language (ISO8859-9) terminal fonts, modmaps for the Q and F style of Turkish keyboard mappings and a simple utility for changing the modmap.

If you need to display Turkish language fonts on your X Window

System, or if you need a to use the Q and F style keyboard mappings, you should install the XFree86-ISO8859-9 package. You may also need to install other XFree86 font packages. If you're installing the X Window System, you'll need to install the XFree86 package, the XFree86 video card package which corresponds to your video card, the X11R6-contrib package, the Xconfigurator package and the XFree86-libs package. If you're going to develop applications that run as X clients, you will also need to install XFree86-devel.

XFree86-ISO8859-9-75dpi-fonts -- (Version 2.1.2, 1,032K)

The XFree86-ISO8859-9-75dpi-fonts package contains a set of Turkish language (ISO8859-9) fonts in 75 dpi resolution for the X Window System.

If you need to display Turkish language fonts on your X Window System, you should install this package. If your monitor is capable of supporting 100 dpi resolution, you should instead install the 100 dpi font package. You may also need to install one or more of the other XFree86 fonts packages. If you're installing the X Window System, you need to install the XFree86 package, the XFree86 video card package which corresponds to your video card, the X11R6-contrib package, the Xconfigurator package and the XFree86-libs package. Finally, if you are going to develop applications that will run as X clients, you will also need to install XFree86-devel.

XFree86-cyrillic-fonts -- (Version 3.3.3.1, 301K)

The Cyrillic fonts included with XFree86 3.3.2 and higher. Those who use a language requiring the Cyrillic character set should install this package.

gdm -- (Version 1.0.0, 244K)

[W]

GNOME Display Manager allows you to log into your system with the X Window System running. It is highly configurable, allowing you to run several different X sessions at once on your local machine, and can manage login connections from remote machines as well.

gqview -- (Version 0.6.0, 186K)

[W]

GQview is a browser for graphics files. Offering single click viewing of your graphics files. Includes thumbnail view, zoom and filtering features. And external editor support.

kterm -- (Version 6.2.0, 154K)

The kterm package provides a terminal emulator for the Kanji Japanese character set.

Install kterm if you need a Kanji character set terminal emulator. You'll also need to have the X Window System installed.

rxvt -- (Version 2.6.PRE2, 490K)

[W] [S]

Rxvt is a color VT102 terminal emulator for the X Window System. Rxvt is intended to be an xterm replacement for users who don't need the more esoteric features of xterm, like Tektronix 4014 emulation, session logging and toolkit style configurability. Since it doesn't support those features, rxvt uses much less swap space than xterm uses. This is a significant advantage on a machine which is serving a large number of X sessions.

The rxvt package should be installed on any machine which serves a large number of X sessions, if you'd like to improve that machine's performance.

urw-fonts -- (Version 1.1, 2,160K)

[W] [S]

Free versions of the 35 standard PostScript fonts. With newer releases of ghostscript quality versions of the standard 35 Type 1 PostScript fonts are shipped. They were donated and licenced under the GPL by URW. The fonts.dir was specially made to match the original Adobe names of the fonts, e.g. Times, Helvetica etc. With X, LaTeX, or Ghostscript, these fonts are a must to have!

x3270 -- (Version 3.1.1.6, 561K)

The x3270 program opens a window in the X Window System which emulates the actual look of an IBM 3278/3279 terminal, commonly used with mainframe applications. x3270 also allows you to telnet to an IBM host from the x3270 window.

Install the x3270 package if you need to access IBM hosts using an IBM 3278/3279 terminal emulator.

xinitrc -- (Version 2.3, 9K)

[W] [S]

The xinitrc package contains the xinitrc file, a script which is used to configure your X Window System session or to start a window manager.

The xinitrc package should be installed if you use the X Window System.

Unix Quick Command Reference
by Patrick Sadler
KnowledgeWorks; ISBN: 0970308337
Retail: $21.99
Book Description
Fantastic book for introducing anyone to the Unix Operating System.It covers all of the necessary basic commands needed to navigate within the Unix environment. An easy read and a quick and easy way to find important Unix commands.
Unix Quick Command Reference is the perfect introduction to the Unix O/S. This book actually shows you how to navigate within Unix, without a lot of confusing examples or terminology.
Using Unix is very similar to using microsoft's MSDOS. In this book the author has attemped to explain the many different commands within Unix in a simple manner,easy enough for anyone to comprehend and master.
Unix Quick Command Reference is a complete introduction to Unix. Inside this book, you'll discover:
*Step-By-Step Unix command instructions.
*Dictionary of Unix and Network terms.
*Covers all popular Unix commands.
*Learn how to create and delete files,directories among networked computers.
*Locate Unix commands the quick and easy way.
*Learn about the World-Wide computer network of Usenet Newsgroups and how to navigate and communicate within them.
*Have all of your introductory questions answered in plain english.
*Find the commands you need the quick and easy way.
*Find out why and how Unix is the chief O/S that controls the Internet.
Unix Quick Command Reference is one of the best books for learning this fantastic Unix Operating System.
Linux Quick Command Reference
by Patrick Sadler
KnowledgeWorks; ISBN: 0970308329
Retail: $21.99
Book Description
Fantastic book for introducing anyone to the Linux Operating System.It covers all of the necessary basic commands needed to navigate within the Linux environment.
An easy read and a quick and easy way to find important Linux commands.

Linux Quick Command Reference is the perfect introduction to the Linux O/S. This book actually shows you how to navigate within Linux, without a lot of confusing examples or terminology.

Using Linux is very similar to using microsoft's MSDOS. In this book the author has attemped to explain the many different commands within Linux in a simple manner,easy enough for anyone to comprehend and master.

Linux Quick Command Reference is a complete introduction to Linux. Inside this book, you'll discover:

*Step-By-Step Linux command instructions.

*Dictionary of Linux and Network terms.

*Covers all popular Linux commands.

*Learn how to create and delete files,directories among networked computers.

*Locate Linux commands the quick and easy way.

*Learn about the World-Wide computer network of Usenet Newsgroups and how to navigate and communicate within them.

*Have all of your introductory questions answered in plain english.

*Find the commands you need the quick and easy way.

Linux Quick Command Reference is one of the best books for learning the fantastic Linux Operating System.

Unix Crash Course
by Patrick Sadler
KnowledgeWorks; ISBN: 0970308310
Retail: $29.99

Book Description

This book is meant for UNIX novices and gurus alike. It contains information, software installation, a tutorial for new UNIX users(outlining general commands and procedures), and an introduction to system administration. It is meant to be general enough to be applicable to any distribution of UNIX.It serves as a definitive introductory guide into the world of computer networking.

Send payment for books or software to:

KnowledgeWorks Inc.
364 Green Street N.E.
P.O. Box 2701
Gainesville Georgia 30503

Name______________________Street Address______________City______________

State______________Zip__________Country__________________________

Email Address__________________

Borland C++ Builder Professional 5 **$ 799.99** + Shipping & Handling

---